Exploring Literature

AGS

by Ann Chatterton Klimas

American Guidance Service, Inc.
Circle Pines, Minnesota 55014-1796
800-328-2560

About the Author

Ann Chatterton Klimas has spent more than twenty years developing educational materials for both traditional and electronic media. She received her Bachelor of Arts from Mary Washington College of the University of Virginia and Master of Arts from The Johns Hopkins University. As a teacher, Ms. Klimas has worked with students of all levels, teaching language arts and history, broadcast journalism, and screenwriting. She has written textbooks and instructional materials for a variety of media, including public and commercial broadcast television. In her current position with Maryland Public Television, Ms. Klimas has contributed to the design and production of several award-winning educational television series, as well as a series of regional interactive electronic field trips.

Literature Consultant

Jack Cassidy, Ph.D.
Texas A&M University
Corpus Christi, Texas

Original cover art: Connie Hayes

Printed in the United States of America

ISBN 0-7854-1813-X

Product Number 92050

A 0 9 8 7

Contents

How to Use This Book

Exploring Literature

This book is an anthology of literature. A literature anthology is a collection of literary selections written by different authors. The selections can be poems, plays, short stories, essays, parts of novels, folktales, legends, or myths. Sometimes, an anthology is organized around selections from a certain country or continent. For example, you might have an anthology with great literature from America. The first section of an American literature anthology could include a section with early American Indian poetry or Puritan diaries. Sometimes, anthologies are organized around different types of literature (genres). Then, you might have sections on poems, short stories, plays, essays, or folktales.

Why is a literature anthology important?

This anthology contains many enjoyable literary selections. An anthology helps you understand yourself and other people. Sometimes, you will read about people from other countries. You will sometimes read about people who lived in the past. Try to relate what the author is saying to your own life. Have I ever felt this way? Have I known anyone like this person? Have I seen anything like this?

A literature anthology can also help you appreciate the beauty of language. As you read, find phrases or sentences that you particularly like. You may want to start a notebook of these. You could also include words that are difficult.

This anthology is also important because it introduces you to great works of literature. Many times, you will find references to these works in everyday life. Sometimes, you will hear a quotation on TV or read it in the newspaper. Reading great literature helps you to become more literate. Generally, literate people are more likely to get better paying jobs.

What is in this book?

This book is filled with interesting works of literature. Great literature can come in many forms. On the next page are definitions of some kinds of literature genres in an anthology.

Genre Definitions

autobiography The story of a person's life written by that person.

biography The story of a person's life written by someone else. You will find many biographies of famous authors in this book.

diary A record of personal events, thoughts, or private feelings. Usually people write in a diary every day or weekly. Mostly, people write diaries for themselves. Sometimes authors will create a fictional diary.

drama A play that often involves intense emotional conflict. Usually, a drama is serious.

essay A written work that shows a writer's opinions on some basic or current issue.

fable A short story or poem with a moral, often with animals who act like humans. Aesop was a famous author of fables.

fiction Writing that is made up and usually intended to entertain. Fiction is usually in prose form. Short stories, novels, folktales, myths, legends, and most plays are works of fiction.

folktale A story that has been handed down from one generation to another. The characters are usually either good or bad. Folktales make use of rhyme and repetitive phrases. Sometimes, they are called tall tales, particularly if they are humorous and exaggerated. They are also called folklore.

journal Writing that expresses an author's feelings or first impressions about a subject. A journal is like a diary, but it expresses more of the author's feelings. Sometimes, students keep journals that give their feelings about what they have read.

legend A traditional story that at one time was told orally and was handed down from one generation to another. Legends are like myths, but they do not have as many supernatural forces. Usually, they have some historical base.

myth A story designed to explain the mysteries of life. A myth explains natural events, such as the change of seasons. Like fables and folktales, myths were first oral stories. Most early cultures have myths.

nonfiction Writing about real people and events. Nonfiction is usually designed to explain, argue, or describe. Essays, speeches, diaries, journals, autobiographies, and biographies are all usually nonfiction.

novel Fiction that is book-length and has more plot and character details than a short story.

poem A short piece of literature that usually has rhythm and paints powerful or beautiful impressions with words. Often, poems have sound patterns such as rhyme. Songs are poetry set to music. Prose is the opposite of poetry.

prose Written language that is not verse. Short stories, novels, autobiographies, biographies, diaries, journals, and essays are examples of prose.

science fiction A type of literature that deals with people, places, and events that could not happen in our reality. However, science fiction is sometimes based on projected scientific developments. Most stories are set in the future. Stories about space are examples of science fiction. Jules Verne was one of the first science fiction authors.

short story A brief prose narrative. Short stories are designed to create unified impressions forcefully. Edgar Allan Poe was a great writer of short stories.

What is a literary term?

Literary terms are words or phrases that we use to study and discuss works of literature. These terms describe the devices that an author uses to make us enjoy and understand what we are reading. Some of the terms also describe a genre. In this anthology, you will see shaded boxes on the side of the Introducing the Selection pages that define some literary terms. These terms are important in understanding and discussing the selection being read. By understanding these literary terms, we can appreciate the author's craft.

Below are literary terms that apply to all works of literature. You should be familiar with these terms as you read this anthology. All of the literary terms used in this book can be found on page 470 in the Handbook of Literary Terms.

Literary Terms

autobiography the story of a person's life, written by that person

setting a story's time and place

Glossary of Key Literary Terms

characterization The devices authors use to reveal characters. Characters are revealed by their actions, speech, appearance, others' comments, or the author's comments.

conflict The struggle the main character of a story faces. Conflict is an important part of the plot of a short story or novel. Main characters can struggle against themselves, other people, society, or nature. Three types of conflict are person-against-person, person-against-self, and person-against-environment.

plot The series of events in a story. The plot shows what happens to the characters. Plots have conflict and resolutions to that conflict. Plots are very important in stories. Plots should have rising action, foreshadowing, a climax, and falling action.

setting The time and place in a story. Sometimes authors describe the setting in detail. Sometimes, the setting is left unclear so the reader can imagine it. A setting can even be a person's mind.

theme The idea that holds the whole piece of literature together. A theme is a generalization about humankind that the author wants to make. Themes are underlying statements about a topic. A theme is the topic of a piece of literature and the author's opinion about that topic.

How do I read this book?

Different works of literature should be read in different ways. However, you can use some strategies with all works of literature.

Before beginning a unit:
- Read the unit title and selection titles.
- Read any introductory paragraphs about the unit.
- Look at the pictures and other graphics in the unit.
- Think about the unit's main topic.
- Think about what you want to learn about this topic.
- Think about what you already know about the unit.
- Develop questions in your mind that you think will be answered in this unit.

Before beginning the reading of a selection:
- Read the selection's title.
- Look at the pictures and other visuals.
- Read the background material included in About the Author and About the Selection.
- Predict what you think the selection is going to be about.
- Ask yourself questions about the material.

As you read the selections:
- Think about the predictions that you made before reading. Were they right?
- Make new predictions as you read.
- Read the notes in the side columns. These will help you understand and think about the main concepts.
- Think of people or events in your own life that are similar to those described.
- Reread sentences or paragraphs that you do not understand.
- Refer to the definitions at the bottom of the page for words that you do not know.
- In a notebook or on note cards, record words that you do not know. Also, record words defined in the text that you find interesting or unusual.

INTRODUCING the SELECTION | **Thank You, M'am**
Langston Hughes

Langston Hughes
1902–1967

About the Author
In the 1920s, a section of New York City called Harlem became the center of a great explosion of African-American art. Today, we call this movement the Harlem Renaissance. Langston Hughes became one of the best-known writers of the Harlem Renaissance.

Hughes was born in Joplin, Missouri. He always knew he loved to write. He enrolled at Columbia University, on the edge of Harlem, in 1921. While Hughes was working in a Washington hotel, the well-known poet Vachel Lindsay took an interest in his writing. Lindsay helped bring attention to Hughes's work. By age twenty-seven, Hughes was making a living with his writing.

Langston Hughes wrote short stories, plays, and novels, but is perhaps best known for his poetry.

Literary Terms
antagonist the person or force opposing the protagonist

conflict the struggle of the protagonist against himself or herself, another person, or nature

protagonist the main character; also called the hero

rising action the events of the plot that add to the conflict

sudden fiction brief short stories

About the Selection
"Thank You, M'am" is brief, even for a short story. This kind of story is sometimes called **sudden fiction**. Sudden fiction has all the features of short stories—plot, character, setting, point of view, and theme. However, sudden fiction stories are shorter than other short stories.

Like most stories, this one is about **conflict**. Conflict is a struggle between two forces. In fiction, the main character struggles against himself or herself, another person, or nature. In this story, the **protagonist**, or main character, struggles against an **antagonist**, a person who tries to keep the protagonist from reaching his goal.

Readers learn about the main character's problem at the very beginning of the story: Roger tries and fails to steal a purse. The story moves in unexpected ways from that point on. The plot's twists and turns are part of the **rising action** of the story.

The Short Story Unit 4 **183**

| **affirm** to state positively | **miseries** things that cause one to suffer | **tedious** tiresome; boring |

Thank You, M'am
Langston Hughes

Directions Write the answers to these questions using complete sentences.

Comprehension: Identifying Facts

1. What happens when Roger tries to grab Mrs. Jones's purse?

2. What does Roger want to buy with the money from Mrs. Jones's purse?

3. What does Mrs. Jones give Roger after they eat?

Comprehension: Understanding Main Ideas

4. What do we find out about Roger's home life from this story?

5. What do we find out about Mrs. Jones's life?

6. When Mrs. Jones goes behind the screen to prepare supper, why does Roger sit away from the purse, where Mrs. Jones can easily see him?

Understanding Literature: Rising Action

Short stories usually explore a conflict that the main character faces. For example, in "American History," Elena, the protagonist, wants to be friends with Eugene. However, the conflict is that she and Eugene live in two very different worlds. The way the plot of the story moves toward Elena's realizing she can't be friends with Eugene is the rising action of the story. The rising action adds to the conflict.

7. In your own words, what is rising action in a short story?

8. What are some events in the rising action of "Thank You, M'am" that add to Roger's conflict?

Critical Thinking

9. What might Mrs. Jones have done after she caught Roger trying to steal her purse? Why do you think she decides to take him home?

10. In the beginning of the story, Roger thinks it was all right for him to steal money to buy shoes. How do you think he feels at the end of the story? Why do you think so?

 Writing on Your Own Imagine that you are Roger. Write a letter to Mrs. Jones. Tell her what you think or how you feel about what she did.

The Short Story Unit 4 **189**

After reading the selections:

- Think about the questions that you asked yourself before you read. Were your answers to these questions right?
- Reread interesting or difficult parts of the selection.
- Reflect on what you have learned.
- Write the answers to the review questions in the Reviewing the Selection.
- Use graphic organizers to help you organize and remember information. (See "What is a graphic organizer?" on page 13 to get some ideas.)

How do I read specific types of literature?

The strategies already described will work for all kinds of literature, but some types of literature need specific strategies.

When reading poetry:

- Read the poem aloud.
- Listen to the sounds of the words.
- Picture the images the author is describing.
- Reread poems over and over again to appreciate the author's use of language.

When reading essays:

- Review the questions in the Reviewing the Selection before you begin reading.
- Use the questions to help you make your own predictions before reading.
- Remember that essays usually express an author's opinions. Try to understand how the author arrived at these opinions.

When reading plays:

- Picture the setting of the play. Usually, you do not have much description. Try to relate it to what you have seen before.
- Pay attention to the dialogue. How does the dialogue reveal the character's personality? Have you ever known anyone like this? Are you like this?

What is a graphic organizer?

A graphic organizer is visual representation of information. It can help you see how ideas are related to each other. A graphic organizer can help you study for a test or organize information before writing an essay. Following are some examples.

Character Analysis Guide

The graphic organizer below can help you better understand characters in a story or real people in a biography or autobiography. Fill in the character trait on the ray and then list events in the story or in the person's life that demonstrate that character trait.

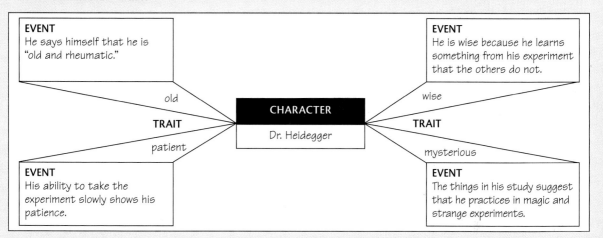

EVENT
He says himself that he is "old and rheumatic."

EVENT
He is wise because he learns something from his experiment that the others do not.

old

wise

CHARACTER
Dr. Heidegger

TRAIT

TRAIT

patient

mysterious

EVENT
His ability to take the experiment slowly shows his patience.

EVENT
The things in his study suggest that he practices in magic and strange experiments.

Venn Diagram

A Venn Diagram can help you compare and contrast two characters, two authors, or two pieces of literature. List the similarities on the overlap between the circles. List the differences on the parts of the circles that do not overlap.

Remember that all graphic organizers can be used in various ways. They can be used to help you organize your writing. They can be used to help you analyze your thoughts, and they can be used to help you study for a test. You can even create your own graphic organizer.

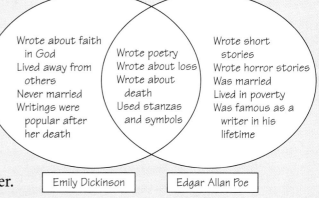

Wrote about faith in God
Lived away from others
Never married
Writings were popular after her death

Wrote poetry
Wrote about loss
Wrote about death
Used stanzas and symbols

Wrote short stories
Wrote horror stories
Was married
Lived in poverty
Was famous as a writer in his lifetime

Emily Dickinson

Edgar Allan Poe

What strategies should I use when I encounter a word that I don't know?

■ If the word is boldface, look for the definition of the word at the bottom of the page.

■ If the word is not boldface, read to the end of the sentence and maybe the next sentence. Can you determine the unknown word now?

■ If your teacher has given you a Selection Glossary, use it to look up additional terms that are not boldface.

■ Look at the beginning sound of the unknown word.

■ Ask yourself, "What word would make sense here that begins with this sound"?

■ Sound out the syllables of the word.

■ If you still cannot determine the unknown word, see if you know any parts of the word: prefixes, suffixes, or roots.

■ If this does not work, write the word on a note card or in a vocabulary notebook and look it up in the dictionary after you have finished reading the selection.

■ If the word is necessary to understand the passage, look it up in a dictionary or glossary immediately.

Word Study Tip

■ Start a vocabulary file with note cards to use for review.

■ Write one word on the front of each card. Write the unit number, selection title, and the definition on the back.

■ You can use these cards as flash cards by yourself or with a study partner to test your knowledge.

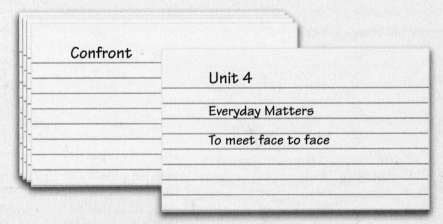

Confront

Unit 4

Everyday Matters

To meet face to face

What should I know about taking a literature test?

Before the test day:
- Read all the works assigned.
- Review your class notes, the Unit Summary, and the Unit Review.
- Ask your teacher what kinds of questions will be on the test.
- Review any notes that you have taken or graphic organizers developed.
- Try to predict what questions will be asked and develop answers to those questions.
- Review the Test-Taking Tips at the bottom of the Unit Review pages in this book.

UNIT 4 SUMMARY

Short stories are among the most popular forms of fiction. Like all fiction, short stories have plot, setting, characters, point of view, and theme. Unlike longer forms, however, short stories tend to feature a brief time period and only one main setting. Writers tend to include only the most important descriptive details. Everything in a short story works to set a mood and to develop one or more themes.

Short stories are part of the kind of literature called prose. Prose—all writing that is not poetry—also includes the fables, myths, tall tales, and legends you have studied in other units.

This unit has presented five short stories with very different styles, moods, and effects. From the set, you get a sense of the wide range offered by this literary form.

Selections
- "The Celebrated Jumping Frog of Calaveras County," by Mark Twain, describes the funny adventures of a gambling man.
- "Everyday Use," by Alice Walker, is about an African-American mother and her two daughters, one of whom has come home for a visit.
- "American History," by Judith Ortiz-Cofer, tells of an important day in American history that becomes important in another way for a Puerto Rican girl living in New Jersey.
- "Thank You, M'am," by Langston Hughes, is the story of an attempted purse-snatching that does not go at all the way a young man intended.
- "Unfinished Message," by Toshio Mori, concerns a Japanese-American mother, her two sons, and a strange event that happens after her death.

The Short Story Unit 4 **197**

UNIT 4 REVIEW

Directions Write the answers to these questions using complete sentences.

Comprehension: Identifying Facts

1. What are some ways short stories are different from other kinds of fiction?
2. What kind of conflict is most important in "Unfinished Message"?
3. What is a symbol? In which story do we find symbols?
4. What is the difference between the *mood* of "The Celebrated Jumping Frog of Calaveras County" and its *tone*?
5. Why do humorists like Mark Twain often use caricature in their writing?

Comprehension: Understanding Main Ideas

6. What events are part of the rising action in "Everyday Use"?
7. What is the point of view in each of the stories in this unit?
8. What makes "The Celebrated Jumping Frog of Calaveras County" funny? What are some ways Twain adds humor to the story?
9. How are short stories different from myths and fables? In what ways are they the same?

10. Describe two conflicts in "American History": one between the main character and the conditions of her life, the other inside the main character herself.

Understanding Literature: Fiction and Nonfiction

Prose is usually divided into fiction and nonfiction. In fiction, the author creates the events and characters. Plots and characters come from the writer's imagination. Although fictional stories may be based on real events and real people, writers change information to serve the needs of the story. Fables, myths, tall tales, legends, short stories, plays, and novels are all forms of fiction.

Nonfiction is literature that describes something that actually happened. In nonfiction, readers expect that the author hasn't added anything that isn't true. Nonfiction includes reports, biographies, autobiographies, and essays.

11. In your own words, what is the difference between fiction and nonfiction?
12. What are some responsibilities that a nonfiction writer has that a fiction writer does not have?
13. What are some of the nonfiction elements in "Unfinished Message"?

14. Judith Ortiz-Cofer says that she is not the main character in "American History" because she was only eleven when President Kennedy died. Why might readers think that the story is true, or nonfiction?
15. Which story in this unit do you think comes closest to nonfiction? Why?

Critical Thinking

16. In your opinion, what is the main theme of "Thank You, M'am"?
17. Which protagonist, or main character, in these short stories do you like the best? Why? How does the author make the character come alive for you?
18. With which author do you identify the most? Does this help you understand that author's short story? Explain.
19. How would the effect of "Unfinished Message" be different if it had been told more like a ghost story? Why do you think the author chose to use a matter-of-fact tone?
20. "The Celebrated Jumping Frog of Calaveras County," "Everyday Use," and "Thank You, M'am" all include humor. Compare each narrator's use of amusing details and dialogue.

Speak and Listen

Mark Twain is one of America's finest storytellers. Create your own version of the story he tells in "The Celebrated Jumping Frog of Calaveras County" and tell it to your class.

Beyond Words

Create a series of sketches that might be used to illustrate one of the short stories in this unit.

> **Writing on Your Own** Choose a moral from a fable in Unit 1. Write a short story with that moral as its theme, or main idea.

> **Test-Taking Tip** Before you begin an exam, skim through the whole test to find out what is expected of you. Try to set aside enough time to complete each section.

198 *Unit 4 The Short Story*

The Short Story Unit 4 **199**

During the test:
- Come to the test with a positive attitude.
- Preview the test and read the directions carefully.
- Plan your time.
- Answer the essay questions and the questions that you know first.
- Go back and answer the more difficult questions.
- Allow time to reread all of the questions and your answers.
- Put your name on the paper.

"If a nation loses its storytellers, it loses its childhood."

—Peter Handke, in *The Independent*, 9 June 1988

"Storytelling is the oldest form of education."

—Terry Tempest Williams, *Pieces of White Shell*, 1984

The Tortoise and the Hare, Ted Pearsall

UNIT 1 *Fables*

Fables are one of the oldest forms of stories. Since the time of Aesop, who probably lived between 600 and 500 B.C., people have told, written, and passed along fables. One reason fables have remained popular is that they teach truths about human life that never go out of style. They teach these truths using colorful characters and amusing events that people have always enjoyed.

In this unit, you will read fables from several cultures and from different periods in history.

UNIT 1 ■ ABOUT FABLES

As long as there have been people, there have been stories. People create stories to entertain themselves, to pass the time, or to help them remember. They tell stories to explain the world around them.

Some stories, called fables, try to teach people something about life. Fables are one of the oldest kinds of stories. Some of the fables we still read and tell each other today are more than 2,000 years old. Many of these come from the ancient Greek storyteller Aesop.

Fables are fictional stories. This means they are made up, or invented. However, fables usually tell truths that all people can recognize. This is one reason that people today still enjoy fables created centuries ago.

Fables share some other characteristics:

■ Many fables were not written down at first. They were told out loud. Long ago, most people did not know how to read and write. Instead, they handed stories down to their children and others by telling the stories over and over again.

■ Fables are usually short and simple. They tell an entire story in a few paragraphs. Fables have characters and plots, just as other, longer stories do. In fables, though, the characters are not fully described. The plot—or what happens in the story—does not take long to unfold.

■ The characters in fables are often animals who act like people. They speak to each other as people would. They care about the things people value. For example, in the fable "The Fox and the Grapes," the fox decides that some grapes that are growing too high for him to reach are probably sour anyway. Even if he could reach them, he would not want to eat them. We know that a fox would not think this way. But we probably have heard people say, "Well, I didn't want it anyway," about something they really wanted very much. Giving animals or objects the characteristics of humans is called personification.

■ Fables do not spend much time describing what characters look like or how they behave. Instead, they depend on what we already know about such characters. For example, we know what an owl looks like. We usually think of owls as wise creatures. When we read about an owl in a fable, we expect the owl to behave wisely.

The characters in fables are called flat characters. We don't find out much about them. They do not change or develop the way characters do in other kinds of stories.

■ Fables usually teach a lesson about life. This lesson is called a moral. For example, in the fable "The Mouse and the Lion," the lion spares the mouse's life when the mouse pleads with him. She tells him that she will surely repay his kindness some day. Even though the lion doubts what the mouse says, he decides to let her go. Later, the mouse saves the lion by chewing away the nets in which he has become tangled. The moral of the story, or its message about life, is that both strong and weak creatures need each other.

Each fable in this unit has a moral. The first four are from Aesop: "The Dog and His Reflection," "The Dog in the Manger," "The Milkmaid and Her Pail," and "The North Wind and the Sun." The next three fables come from different cultures. "How the Fly Saved the River" is an Ojibwa fable. "The Singing Turtle" is a fable from Haiti. "The King and the Shirt" is adapted from a fable written by the great Russian author Leo Tolstoy.

The Wolf Disguised as a Shepherd Betrays Himself When He Speaks, Gustave Paul Doré

Aesop's Fables

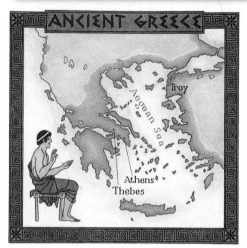

About the Author

We all know the **fable** about the famous race between the tortoise and the hare. When the slower tortoise crosses the finish line first, we all cheer for him. He was slow but steady. He shows us that, no matter what, we all have a chance to win the race.

This story is one of the fables introduced to the world by the Greek slave Aesop. We know very little about this man, except that he was born between 600 and 500 B.C. Aesop himself never wrote down his fables, but he told them to many people. Hundreds of years after Aesop died, his fables were collected in books and translated into many languages. The first collection of Aesop's fables, called *Assemblies of Aesophic Tales,* is one of the best sources we have of the actual fables Aesop told.

Some people think that Aesop did not actually create these fables, but simply retold old stories he had heard. We may never know whether this is true. We do know that many writers have used Aesop's work as a starting point for their own writing. Some of these writers include Jean de la Fontaine, James Thurber, and James Joyce.

About the Selections

"The Dog and His Reflection" and "The Dog in the Manger" are two of Aesop's fables. The main **character** in each story is a dog that thinks, speaks, and behaves like a human being. In literature, giving animals or objects the characteristics of humans is called **personification**. In both fables, the **moral**—the lesson about life—focuses on the actions of two very selfish dogs. Aesop probably created these fables to show people what can happen if they act selfishly.

Literary Terms

character a person or animal in a story, poem, or play

fable a story that teaches a lesson about life, called a moral, often with animals who act like humans

moral a lesson or message about life told in a story

personification giving characters such as animals or objects the characteristics of humans

The Dog and His Reflection

The Dog took his daily stroll through the town. As he passed the shops, the butcher threw him a bone. The Dog hurried off, holding his tasty prize firmly in his jaw.

As he crossed a narrow bridge over the river, he happened to look down. To his surprise, he saw another dog looking up at him from beneath the water. The dog in the water had an even bigger bone than he did. The Dog thought, "That dog down there is really not so big. Surely I can take that bone away from him. Then I will have two fine bones to enjoy tonight."

The Dog quickly dropped his bone into the water and jumped off the bridge. But suddenly, things seemed to go all wrong. The water was much deeper than it looked. There was no dog in the water. Worse than that, there was no bone.

The Dog was dismayed. He swam slowly to the shore and dragged himself out of the river. He never saw his bone again.

Being greedy is very foolish.

As you read, look for the characteristics that make this story a fable.

Here the Dog is thinking as a human being would. This is an example of personification.

Hound Dog (II), Christian Pierre

Birddog II, **Diana Ong**

As you read, look for the characters in this fable.

A *manger* is a trough or open box that holds feed for farm animals.

The Dog in the Manger

The Farmer had just finished filling the manger with soft, dry hay when the Dog came by. The Dog sniffed the fresh-smelling hay. It was delightful. "Might as well curl up here for a nap," he thought. He circled in the manger to make a fine bed. Then he settled down, tucking his nose under his tail. Before long, he was asleep.

The Cattle came into the barn after working all day in the field. They were tired and hungry. When they smelled the new hay, they moved quickly toward the manger.

Their noise woke up the Dog. He sprang up and began to bark loudly. "How dare you lowly creatures try to eat my bed," he snarled. He would not let them come anywhere near the manger.

The Cattle looked at the Dog with disgust. "How selfish he is," said the oldest Cow. "Everyone knows that Cattle—not dogs—eat hay. A bone or some juicy meat is much more to his liking. But will he let us near the manger? Not him! How could such a thing happen?" The other Cattle lowed hungrily in agreement.

The Farmer heard the Cattle. He hurried into the barn. When he saw what the Dog was doing, he took a stick and chased him out. The Cattle then enjoyed their dinner of fresh hay for which they had worked so hard.

Do not keep others from enjoying something you cannot enjoy yourself.

What is another way to state the moral of this fable, in your own words?

Aesop's Fables

Directions Write the answers to these questions using complete sentences.

Comprehension: Identifying Facts

1. Who is the main character in both of these fables?

2. In "The Dog and His Reflection," why does the Dog jump into the water?

3. In "The Dog in the Manger," why does the Farmer chase the Dog out of the barn?

Comprehension: Understanding Main Ideas

4. In "The Dog and His Reflection," what words besides *selfish* could you use to describe the Dog?

5. In "The Dog and His Reflection," how does the Dog feel when he realizes he has lost one bone and has not found a second bone?

6. In "The Dog in the Manger," why does the Dog try to keep the Cattle away from the manger?

Understanding Literature: Personification

The characters in fables are often animals that think, speak, and behave like humans. Giving animals or objects the characteristics of humans is called personification. The term personification means "to make human."

Authors use this technique to make ideas come alive for the reader. We sometimes do this in our own lives. For example, at New Year's Eve celebrations, someone may dress as a baby to represent the new year. This suggests that the new year is like a baby, just starting out in life. We personify the new year.

7. In "The Dog and His Reflection," what does the Dog do that a real dog would do? In what ways is he more like a human being?

8. What does it mean if you tell someone they are behaving "like a dog in a manger"?

Critical Thinking

9. Do you think the moral of "The Dog and His Reflection" is good advice? Why or why not?

10. Do you think the moral of "The Dog in the Manger" is good advice? Explain your answer.

Writing on Your Own Write a character sketch about an animal as if the animal were a person. What would the animal think about or say? How would it behave?

More Aesop's Fables

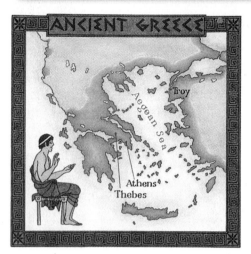

About the Author

Although we do not know much about Aesop's life, many people think of him as wise. There are fables about Aesop himself that show this. One of them tells about Aesop and his master, Xanthus.

Xanthus ordered his slaves to prepare for a long trip. Before they left, Aesop asked his master if he could pick the basket he would carry during the trip. Xanthus agreed. Aesop picked the heaviest basket, the one that held all the food for the journey. All the others laughed at him.

Literary Terms

flat character a character that is based on a single trait or quality and is not well developed

plot the series of events in a story

At dawn, the group set out on their trip. By noon, Aesop was exhausted. When they stopped for lunch, he was very happy to set his basket down. He even helped give out food to the others. When the group started out again, Aesop was pleased to see that his basket was much lighter, just as he expected.

The same thing happened at dinner. The slaves were very hungry. By the time they finished eating, there was hardly anything left in the food basket.

For the rest of the night and into the next day, the group trudged on. Each slave felt his basket grow heavier with each step—each slave except Aesop.

About the Selections

"The Milkmaid and Her Pail" and "The North Wind and the Sun" are two more of Aesop's fables. In the **plots** of these fables, some of the characters are people. However, we do not learn very much about them. In fact, we don't even know their names. We do not know much more about them at the end of the fable than we did at the beginning. They are **flat characters**. The English novelist E. M. Forster first gave this kind of character that name.

The Milkmaid and Her Pail

Woman with Pitcher,
Rufino Tamayo

The Milkmaid had just finished milking her cows. Her pail was full of fresh milk. She placed the heavy container carefully on her head, and began to walk back to her home. As she walked, she began to think to herself.

"This is fine, rich milk," she thought. "The cows must have been eating well. Their milk has plenty of cream in it. It will be easy to churn it into golden butter. People at the market will surely buy it all. With the money I get, I will buy many eggs to hatch. Won't the yard look pretty with all the little yellow chicks pecking at the ground? When the spring comes, the chicks will be big enough to sell. With the money I get from that, I will buy a lovely dress to wear to the fair. Everyone will see how beautiful I am. Every man there will want me to be his wife. But that is not how I want to live my life. I will just turn my head and tell them to go away."

When she thought this, she turned her head quickly—to show those men what she thought of them. The pail of milk toppled down. The rich milk quickly disappeared into the soil. With the spilt milk went her dreams of the butter and the chicks and the dress and the men—and the Milkmaid's pride.

Do not count your chickens before they hatch.

As you read, decide why the Milkmaid is a flat character.

In this paragraph, the Milkmaid dreams of her bright future. What is the first thing that must happen if her dreams are to come true?

Why does the Milkmaid's pride disappear with the milk?

The North Wind and the Sun

As you read, note the plot, or series of events, in the story.

The North Wind and the Sun were quarreling. Each one thought she was stronger than the other. The Sun said her warm rays were much more powerful than the North Wind's icy blasts. The North Wind said this was nonsense.

As the two argued, a Traveler came along, wearing a heavy, long, gray overcoat. As he passed, the North Wind and the Sun stopped for a moment.

"Our arguing is senseless. There is only one way to settle this—a contest," said the Sun.

"Fine with me," the North Wind blasted back. "What do you have in mind?"

"Do you see the Traveler over there, the one with the huge coat? The first one that can make him take it off is surely the strongest."

Hawthorn Dusk,
Diane Griffiths

"Agreed," said the North Wind. "It will be simple." At once, she drew in her breath and aimed an icy blast of wind at the Traveler. The wind pushed at the edges of his coat and they fluttered wildly. The Traveler immediately buttoned up his coat and turned up the collar. The North Wind tried even harder. Her gusts became even colder and stronger. But, the colder the wind, the tighter the Traveler held onto the coat.

Then it was the Sun's turn. At first, her beams were very gentle. The Traveler looked up with relief. It was a pleasure to feel the Sun's warmth after the freezing gales of the North Wind. He turned down his collar. The Sun's rays grew warmer. The Traveler unbuttoned the coat. He was beginning to feel uncomfortably warm. Finally, he could not stand it any longer. He shed his coat and sat under a shady tree to cool off.

You can accomplish more with kindness than you can with force.

Sol, Felix Lazo

Who wins the argument?

More Aesop's Fables

Directions Write the answers to these questions using complete sentences.

Comprehension: Identifying Facts

1. In "The Milkmaid and Her Pail," what has the Milkmaid just finished doing and where is she going?

2. In "The North Wind and the Sun," why are the characters arguing?

3. What happens when the North Wind blows hard at the Traveler? What happens when the Sun shines on him?

Comprehension: Understanding Main Ideas

4. Why does the Milkmaid spill the milk?

5. Why do the Milkmaid's dreams and her pride disappear with the milk?

6. Who wins the argument: the North Wind or the Sun? How do you know?

Understanding Literature: Flat Characters

In creating stories, authors often have to decide whether they will focus more on the story or on the characters. In fables, the story is more important than the characters. So the characters in fables often are flat. Readers do not find out much about them. Flat characters stay about the same throughout the fable. They do not change the way characters in other kinds of stories do.

7. What do we learn about the Milkmaid in "The Milkmaid and Her Pail"? What don't we know? Why do we call her a flat character?

8. What do we learn about the characters in "The North Wind and the Sun"? What don't we know? Why do we call these flat characters?

Critical Thinking

9. Does the moral *It is foolish to cry over spilt milk* also fit "The Milkmaid and Her Pail"? Why or why not?

10. Why are the North Wind and the Sun good character choices for a fable whose moral is: *You can accomplish more with kindness than you can with force?* What other two characters might Aesop have used to show this moral?

Writing on Your Own Many schools, sports teams, and even countries, have an animal as their mascot, or symbol. Write a short essay explaining why, in your opinion, the eagle is the right or wrong mascot, or symbol, for the United States.

How the Fly Saved the River

Retold by Ril Gaiashk

Ril Gaiashk

1951–

About the Author

The writer and artist Ril Gaiashk was born in 1951 in Toronto, Ontario. He is an Odawa Indian and a member of the Wikwemikong band on Manitoulin Island in eastern Canada. His telling of this Ojibwa tale can be found in the front hall of a school in Toronto, along with an enormous painting of the animal characters. Gaiashk created the mural in 1977 as part of a program in Toronto called Artists in the Schools.

About the Selection

Aesop's **fables** are stories about the animals and people from his world of ancient Greece. In "How the Fly Saved the River," Ril Gaiashk tells a story about the animals in the northeastern part of North America. This fable, about an unusual **hero**, comes from the culture of the Ojibwa people.

The Ojibwa people belong to the Algonquian language group. Both *Ojibwa* and *Chippewa* come from the Algonquian word for the wrinkled seam of the moccasins the people wore. In earlier times, the Ojibwa lived in the forests of eastern Canada in birchbark-covered wigwams. They were one of the most powerful native groups in North America.

Most Ojibwa people today live in Canada, Michigan, Minnesota, Montana, North Dakota, and Wisconsin. Many have been very interested in helping their people improve their lives. For example, in 1968, three Chippewas founded AIM, the American Indian Movement. This powerful organization fights for civil rights and improved social conditions for all American Indians.

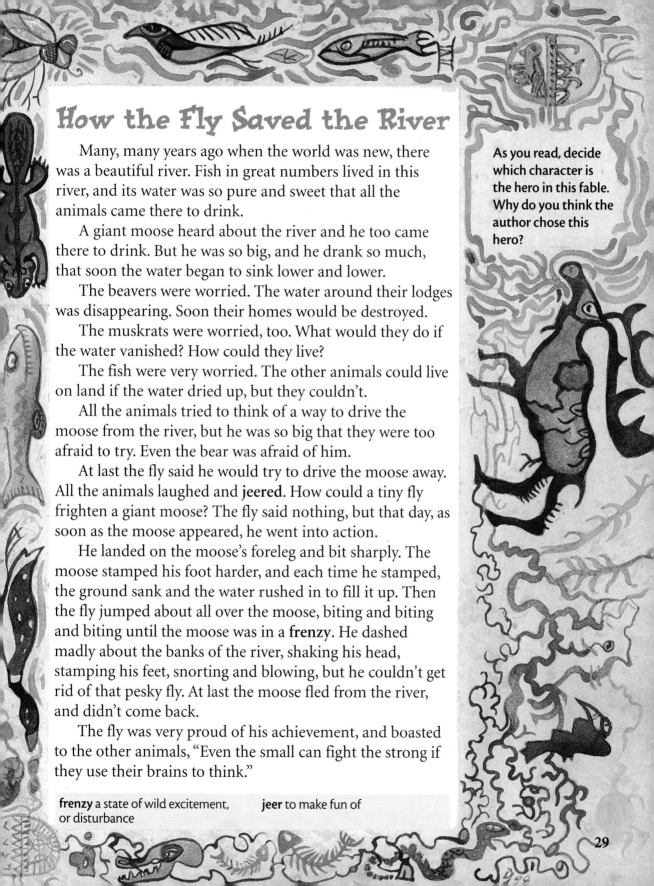

How the Fly Saved the River

Many, many years ago when the world was new, there was a beautiful river. Fish in great numbers lived in this river, and its water was so pure and sweet that all the animals came there to drink.

A giant moose heard about the river and he too came there to drink. But he was so big, and he drank so much, that soon the water began to sink lower and lower.

The beavers were worried. The water around their lodges was disappearing. Soon their homes would be destroyed.

The muskrats were worried, too. What would they do if the water vanished? How could they live?

The fish were very worried. The other animals could live on land if the water dried up, but they couldn't.

All the animals tried to think of a way to drive the moose from the river, but he was so big that they were too afraid to try. Even the bear was afraid of him.

At last the fly said he would try to drive the moose away. All the animals laughed and **jeered**. How could a tiny fly frighten a giant moose? The fly said nothing, but that day, as soon as the moose appeared, he went into action.

He landed on the moose's foreleg and bit sharply. The moose stamped his foot harder, and each time he stamped, the ground sank and the water rushed in to fill it up. Then the fly jumped about all over the moose, biting and biting and biting until the moose was in a **frenzy**. He dashed madly about the banks of the river, shaking his head, stamping his feet, snorting and blowing, but he couldn't get rid of that pesky fly. At last the moose fled from the river, and didn't come back.

The fly was very proud of his achievement, and boasted to the other animals, "Even the small can fight the strong if they use their brains to think."

frenzy a state of wild excitement, or disturbance

jeer to make fun of

As you read, decide which character is the hero in this fable. Why do you think the author chose this hero?

How the Fly Saved the River

Retold by Ril Gaiashk

Directions Write the answers to these questions using complete sentences.

Comprehension: Identifying Facts

1. What is the moose doing to the water in the river?

2. What do the beavers, muskrats, and fish think about the moose's actions?

3. What does the fly do to drive away the moose?

Comprehension: Understanding Main Ideas

4. Would you say the moose is selfish? Explain your reasoning.

5. Why don't the other animals believe the fly can help them?

6. Why do you think the moose never comes back to the river?

Understanding Literature: The Hero

You have probably heard the word *hero* used to describe someone who saves another person's life. In literature, though, hero has a different meaning. When people talk about the hero of a story or novel, they are talking about the main character. The main character is the one most important to the story. However, the hero of a story may or may not do anything brave. The hero can be a person or, as in this fable, an animal.

7. What are some reasons for thinking that the fly is the hero of this fable?

8. What would happen to the fable if we removed the character of the fly?

Critical Thinking

9. How would the fable be different if the fly failed to chase the moose away?

10. Many cultures have stories with plots that are like the plot of "How the Fly Saved the River." Small or weak characters defeat large or strong characters by doing what they do best. Why do you think many writers have used this plot?

Writing on Your Own Write a short description of a time you saw or heard about a smaller person winning by using brainpower rather than physical strength, just as the fly does in this fable.

The Singing Turtle
Philippe Thoby-Marcelin and Pierre Marcelin

Philippe Thoby-Marcelin
1904–1975

Pierre Marcelin
1908–

Literary Terms

dialect the speech of a particular region of a country, or of a certain group of people

setting a story's time and place

About the Authors

Philippe Thoby-Marcelin and his younger brother Pierre Marcelin were born in Port-au-Prince, the capital of Haiti, a country in the West Indies. The brothers grew up in a home where writers and politicians often came to visit.

Together, the brothers wrote many stories and novels, including the first book by a writer from Haiti ever translated into English. This book was called *Canape-Vert,* or *The Green Sofa.* Like all the books the brothers wrote together, *Canape-Vert* was first written in French.

In their novels and stories, the Marcelin brothers told about the lives of the poorer people of their country. They described ancient customs many people of Haiti shared, including the *vodun* (voodoo) rituals they brought with them from Africa. In doing this, the two writers helped preserve the native culture of their Caribbean nation. They also introduced Haitian literature to the world.

About the Selection

"The Singing Turtle" is part of a collection of Haitian folktales called *Contes et Legendes d'Haiti* (*Tales and Legends of Haiti*), first published in 1967. Although much of the fable has been translated into English, you will still see some French phrases or **dialect**. For example, one of the main characters is a person called Tonton Jean. *Tonton* is a familiar form of the French word for *uncle*. People use this word to talk to someone they know very well.

As in all fables, the **setting**—meaning the time and place of the story—is never completely described. As you read, try to gather clues that will tell you more about the setting for this fable.

The Singing Turtle

As you read, look for clues about the setting for this fable.

Millet is a grass grown for its grain, which is used for food

On the bank of the river where he lived, a turtle was quietly warming himself in the sun, when a flock of birds flew overhead.

"Where are you going?" asked the turtle.

"Over to Tonton Jean's garden to harvest the millet," the birds boldly replied.

And they invited the turtle to go along on the expedition.

"I would very much like to join you," he said, sighing, "but, alas, I have no wings! If Tonton Jean should catch us in his garden, you'll get away without any trouble, but I . . ."

"We'll give you wings," said the birds.

They all pulled a few of their feathers and gave them to the turtle, who fastened them to his shoulders with mud and took flight along with them. Finally they reached Tonton Jean's garden and began to fill their bags with millet. The turtle, who was a good musician, made up a very entertaining song to encourage his comrades in their work:

"Tonton Jean planted millet,
So the birds could eat it,
Waya, waya!
Tonton Jean planted millet,
So the birds could eat it,
Waya, waya . . ."

Waya, waya is an example of dialect. What other uses of dialect can you find in this fable?

After a while the turtle took off his wings because they hindered his movements and he lay them on a stone so that, in case of danger, he could easily get them again. Then, picking up two iron rods, he began striking them against each other:

"Ting ti-ting ting,
Ting ti-ting ting,
Ting ti-ting ting . . ."

And the birds joined in the song with him:

"Tonton Jean planted millet
So the birds could eat it,
Waya, waya . . ."

The harvesting was going along very well and their bags were three-quarters full when one of the robbers who was on the look-out sounded the alarm: "Here comes Tonton Jean: let's fly away, quick, my friends!"

All the birds flew away with their bags, while the turtle, who went to get his wings to fasten them on his shoulders again, was horrified to see that the sun had dried the mud. He tried to get away on foot. Alas! he had gone only a little way when Tonton Jean caught up with him. But, being clever, he began singing a very sad **ballad**:

Why do you think the "clever" turtle sings this song when he is caught by Tonton Jean?

> "Colico, Tonton Jean, oh!
> If I still had wings,
> I would have flown away.
> It is really a shame,
> I no longer have them!
> The pigeon gave me feathers,
> The guinea hen gave me feathers,
> The duck gave me feathers,
> And the hen gave me some, too!

ballad a simple song

Colico, Tonton Jean, oh!
If I still had wings,
I would have flown away.
It is really a shame,
I no longer have them!"

Tonton Jean could not believe his ears. To make sure he had not been tricked, he asked the turtle to sing his song once more. You may be sure the turtle was glad to oblige. And when he finished singing, Tonton Jean took him home and carefully put him in a big earthenware jar. Then he went to the marketplace of the nearby town, where he publicly boasted about his great discovery. Everyone took Tonton Jean for a liar, but that was exactly what he expected.

"Who wants to bet that I don't have a singing turtle?" he asked in a **provocative** way.

Tonton Jean is eager to take bets on whether or not he has a singing turtle. He expects to make lots of money from the townspeople.

At that very moment the king happened to pass by. He ordered his carriage stopped and asked the crowd what was going on. They explained that Tonton Jean claimed he had a turtle that could sing and was challenging all who did not believe him to bet he was not telling the truth.

"This man is an **impostor**," said the king to the **dignitaries** accompanying him.

Then, addressing Tonton Jean, "I bet two hundred dollars that you are lying."

"I am only a poor peasant," said Tonton Jean. "How can I bet such a big sum of money?"

"It doesn't matter," replied the king. "If you lose, I'll have you thrown in the river with a stone around your neck."

Meantime, Sor Mise—that was the name of Tonton Jean's wife—hearing that her husband had found a singing turtle, ran home as fast as she could. She uncovered the jar and asked the turtle to sing something for her.

How did the turtle trick Sor Mise into letting him go?

"I can sing only on the riverbank," replied the turtle.

"Very well!" said Sor Mise.

And she took him to the riverbank.

dignitary someone who holds a high rank or position	impostor one who pretends to be someone else	provocative intended to stir up, anger, or excite

"You'll have to wet my feet," said the turtle.

"Very well!" said Sor Mise.

And she leaned over the water to wet the turtle's feet. But the animal slipped out of her hands and plunged into the river, where he disappeared like lightning.

At that very moment, paf! a silly toad fell to the ground a few feet away from Sor Mise, who, in her **disarray**, asked him: "Can you sing?"

"Yes," answered the toad, puffing out his chest.

"Then sing something for me," said Sor Mise sweetly. And our toad started in with his lips all puckered up:

"Ah! . . . Oh! . . . Oh! . . . Of! . . .
Ah! . . . Oh! . . . Oh! . . . Of! . . . "

"Sing something else for me," begged Sor Mise. "A real song, a very, very pretty one!"

But the toad, **imperturbable**, started up again:

"Ah! . . . Oh! . . . Oh! . . . Of! . . .
Ah! . . . Oh! . . . Oh! . . . Of! . . ."

"Brother," said Sor Mise, despairing, "your song is absolutely worthless!"

However, since she just had to have an animal that could sing, she caught hold of the toad, took it home, and simply put it in the jar, hoping that when her husband got back she would come out all right by pretending she did not know anything.

But when the king arrived, followed by Tonton Jean, the dignitaries, and the whole crowd of the curious, Sor Mise, imagining the fatal **consequences** of her foolish action, fell face down in a faint. No one paid attention to her, not even her husband, who walked over to the jar in smiles.

"Brother turtle, my little treasure," he said gently, "sing something for our king."

And the little treasure self-confidently started right up:

"Ah! . . . Oh! . . . Oh! . . . Of! . . .
Ah! . . . Oh! . . . Oh! . . . Of! . . ."

> What do you think will happen when Tonton Jean gets back?

---

consequence a result or effect

disarray confusion

imperturbable calm, steady, impossible to upset

"Get hold of that impostor!" said the king coldly, pointing to Tonton Jean, "and throw him into the river with a stone around his neck!"

It so happened that the turtle had a kind heart. When he realized he would be to blame if they drowned Tonton Jean, he came up out of the water and spoke to the crowd of people gathered around.

"Don't kill my poor master!" he said. "He did not tell a lie."

And since the king was wide-eyed with astonishment, he added: "The proof is, ladies and gentlemen, that I am going to sing you a little song of my own."

Striking the little rods against each other,

"Ting ti-ting ting,
Ting ti-ting ting,
Ting ti-ting ting"
he sang:
"Colico, Tonton Jean, oh!
If I still had wings,
I would have flown away.
It is really a shame,
I no longer have them!
The pigeon gave me feathers,
The guinea hen gave me feathers,
The duck gave me feathers,
And the hen gave me some, too . . ."

The king, marveling, listened to the song till the end. Then, **apologizing** to Tonton Jean, he counted out the two hundred dollars of the bet. But it was the last time anyone heard of a turtle singing.

apologize to say you are sorry

The Singing Turtle

Philippe Thoby-Marcelin and Pierre Marcelin

Directions Write the answers to these questions using complete sentences.

Comprehension: Identifying Facts

1. Who asks the turtle to go to Tonton Jean's garden?

2. How does the turtle get to the garden?

3. What does the turtle do to encourage his friends as they work?

4. What do the birds gather from the garden?

5. What happens to the turtle's wings after he lays them down?

6. How does the turtle save himself when Tonton Jean catches him in the garden?

7. What happens when Tonton Jean boasts in front of the king that he has a singing turtle?

8. How does the turtle get back to the river?

9. What does Sor Mise put in the jar in place of the turtle?

10. How does the turtle save Tonton Jean?

Comprehension: Understanding Main Ideas

11. How would you describe the character of the turtle?

12. Where in the fable does Tonton Jean show his cleverness?

13. How would you describe the character of Sor Mise?

14. How do you think Sor Mise feels when she sees that the turtle has tricked her into letting him escape?

15. Do you think the bet between Tonton Jean and the king is fair? Why or why not?

16. Who is the hero of this fable? Why do you think so?

17. Why do you think the turtle decides to save Tonton Jean's life?

18. Why do you think the turtle never sings again?

19. What do you think the moral of this fable is?

20. Why do you think the authors did not state a moral?

Review Continued on Next Page

Understanding Literature: Dialect

People who speak the same language often use different words for the same thing. For example, in different parts of the United States, people call soft drinks *soda, pop, soda pop,* or *tonic.* People in the East often say *soda.* People in the Midwest usually say *pop.* People in New England say *tonic.* These differences are all examples of dialect. Dialect is the language spoken by people living in a particular region. The dialect of a region is usually made up of words, expressions, and pronunciations used only in that area or by one social group. Creole, a Haitian language based on French, is often described as a dialect.

21. What are some examples of dialect in "The Singing Turtle"?

22. What effect does the dialect have on the telling of the story?

23. What words or expressions do you use in your everyday speech that older people do not use?

24. What words or expressions do older people use that you and your friends do not use?

25. What words or expressions do you use that people in other areas of the country might not understand?

Critical Thinking

26. How would you compare the way the birds treat the turtle with the way the turtle treats Tonton Jean? How are they the same? How are they different? How does this affect your opinion of the story?

27. Some people might say that this fable has several morals, or messages about life. What do you think?

28. This fable is told with lots of humor. What are several examples of funny descriptions or events? Why do you think writers of fables often include humor along with a moral?

29. The authors are Haitian, growing up and living in the Caribbean. How might this fable be different if the Inuit people of Alaska and Northern Canada told it?

30. What are some other ways this fable might have ended? Would a different ending change the message, or moral?

Writing on Your Own Rewrite this fable with a new hero: the "silly toad" that Sor Mise puts in the jar in place of the turtle.

The King and the Shirt
Adapted from Leo Tolstoy

Leo Tolstoy
1828-1910

Literary Term

irony the difference between what is expected to happen in a story and what does happen

About the Author

Through the years, many well-known authors have created fables of their own. Leo Tolstoy, the famous Russian writer, is one of them. Tolstoy, who was born in 1828, is best known for his novels *Anna Karenina* and *War and Peace*.

Although Tolstoy was a famous novelist, he was not happy. After much thought, he decided that people could make their lives worthwhile only by living simply and serving others. In 1890, he sold all his property, became a vegetarian, and gave up the copyrights on his writing. He worked in the fields and lived simply. Yet he never felt satisfied and continued to look for ways to lead a more pure and worthwhile life until he died in 1910.

Tolstoy wrote fables for the young people of Russia. In one fable, "The Monkey and the Peas," Tolstoy writes about a monkey who drops one pea from the handful he is carrying. As he tries to pick up the pea he dropped, the monkey loses even more peas. As he tries to pick these up, he loses even more. The moral might be: *A bird in the hand is worth two in the bush*. Does this remind you of another fable in this unit?

About the Selection

"The King and the Shirt" is very much like the fables of Aesop. It has a simple plot, tells us a message about life, and features flat characters. As we saw in some of Aesop's fables, the main characters in Tolstoy's fable are people, not animals. Tolstoy does not sum up the message of his fable by stating its moral, but the fable suggests a moral even so.

Unlike many of Aesop's fables, the plot in this fable is ironic. In literature, **irony** is the difference between what a character or the reader expects to happen and what actually does happen.

THE
KING
AND THE
SHIRT

As you read, look for examples of irony.

A king once fell ill.

"I will give half my kingdom to the man who can cure me," he said.

All his wise men gathered together to decide how the king could be cured. But no one knew. Only one of the wise men said what he thought would cure the king.

"If you can find a happy man, take his shirt, put it on the king—and the king will be cured."

The king sent his **emissaries** to search for a happy man. They traveled far and wide, but they could not find a happy man. There was no one who was completely satisfied. If a man was rich, he was ailing; if he was healthy, he was poor. If he was rich and healthy, he had an unhappy marriage; or if he had children, they were sick. Everyone had something to complain of.

Do you think it's true that people always find something to complain about? Do you know anyone you would call truly happy?

Finally, late one night, the king's son was passing by a poor little hut and he heard someone say:

"Now God be praised. I have finished my work. I have eaten my fill, and I can lie down and sleep. What more could I want?"

The king's son rejoiced and gave orders that the man's shirt be taken and carried to the king, and that the man be given as much money as he wanted.

What would you say is the moral of this fable?

The emissaries went in to take off the man's shirt, but the happy man was so poor that he had no shirt.

emissary someone who is sent on a mission

The King and the Shirt
Adapted from Leo Tolstoy

Directions Write the answers to these questions using complete sentences.

Comprehension: Identifying Facts

1. What is wrong with the king?

2. What does the wise man say will cure the king?

3. What happens when the emissaries go in to take off the happy man's shirt?

Comprehension: Understanding Main Ideas

4. Why do the king's emissaries have so much trouble finding a happy man?

5. Why is the poor man happy?

6. Why can't the happy man help the king get well?

Understanding Literature: Irony

In literature, irony results when the reader expects a certain event and a different, or opposite, event occurs. For example, in "The King and the Shirt," the king's messengers expect to find the shirt of a happy man, and so do the readers. The irony is that the only happy man they can find does not even own a shirt. If there were no irony in the story, the happy man would give the king his shirt. The king would get well. As it is, the irony gives the story a different moral than it might have had without the irony.

7. Would you say it is also ironic that the king's messengers have so much trouble finding a happy man in the first place? Why or why not?

8. In a story by the American short-story writer O. Henry, "The Gift of the Magi," a young husband sells his watch to buy a comb for his wife's long hair. Meanwhile, the wife cuts off her hair and sells it to buy a watch chain for her husband's watch. How would you describe the irony in the story?

Critical Thinking

9. What do you think the moral of "The King and the Shirt" is? How can the man be happy if he is so poor that he has no shirt?

10. If the story had no irony, and the happy man's shirt cured the king, what would you say the moral was?

Writing on Your Own Rewrite "The King and the Shirt" using animal characters instead of people. Be sure that your fable has the same plot as Tolstoy's fable does, and that it suggests the same moral.

Setting

Setting describes the place where a story, or an event in a story, happens. The place might be outdoors or indoors. It might be a particular city or region. Whatever the place, the writer usually gives details about it. For example, if a story or event happens outdoors, the writer might tell us about the weather.

A story's setting also describes the time in which the story happens. Stories may happen in the past, the present, or the future. They may happen in the morning, afternoon, or night. Each choice affects the story.

The details of setting do two main things. First, they help readers *see* the story in their own minds. For example, if readers can remember the smells of a rainy night, or the sounds of an old, broken-down house, the details of this setting make the story more real.

Second, the details of setting can tell us something about the story or its characters. Rather than tell readers that a character is having money problems, an author might set the story in a rundown apartment. Rather than say that a girl loves to read, an author can mention the piles of books in her bedroom.

Many fables have an outdoor setting and take place sometime in the past. For example, "The Milkmaid and Her Pail" takes place on the road to the Milkmaid's home. "How the Fly Saved the River" takes place "when the world was new." Often, we do not learn more about a fable's setting than that. Just as they do with characters, the creators of fables depend on the reader's imagination to fill in the details.

Review

1. What is setting?

2. If a story has an outdoor setting, what details might the author describe?

3. How can settings help readers *see* the story?

4. How can the details of setting tell readers something about the characters?

5. What is the setting of many fables?

Writing on Your Own Imagine that you are writing a fable whose moral is, *You can accomplish more with kindness than you can with force* (as in "The North Wind and the Sun"). Describe the setting for your fable. Explain what readers might *see* in this setting. How could the setting help them understand your fable?

UNIT 1 SUMMARY

Unit 1 presents examples of one of the oldest forms of stories: fables. The purpose of most fables is to teach something about life. This lesson is given in the form of a moral, which may either be stated or suggested.

Some of the world's most famous fables come from Aesop, a Greek slave who probably lived between 600 and 500 B.C. Aesop's fables, and many others that came later, share certain characteristics. They were first told orally, rather than written down. They are short and simply told. They usually feature animal characters that think, speak, and behave as human beings would. The characters are flat, meaning that not much is told about them. Each fable ends with a moral, or lesson about life.

Most of the cultures of the world enjoy fables. Fables are still being written today and will probably always be part of the world's literature.

Selections

■ "The Dog and His Reflection" by Aesop tells of a greedy dog who jumps into the river to steal the bone he sees carried by his own reflection.

■ "The Dog in the Manger" by Aesop tells of a selfish dog who tries to keep the hungry cattle from getting to the fresh hay he is sleeping in.

■ "The Milkmaid and Her Pail" by Aesop tells of a milkmaid who is so busy dreaming about all she will gain when she sells the butter churned from her cows' rich milk that she spills the milk.

■ "The North Wind and the Sun" by Aesop tells of an argument between the North Wind and the Sun over who is stronger. The North Wind foolishly agrees to let a traveler settle the question.

■ "How the Fly Saved the River," an Ojibwa fable, tells of a tiny fly that drives away the giant moose who is drinking up the river water.

■ "The Singing Turtle," a fable from Haiti, tells of a man who bets the king that he actually has caught a singing turtle.

■ "The King and the Shirt," by the Russian novelist Leo Tolstoy, tells of a search for a happy man whose shirt will cure the king. The happy man, it turns out, is too poor to own a shirt.

UNIT 1 REVIEW

Directions Write the answers to these questions using complete sentences.

Comprehension: Identifying Facts

1. What is the moral of a fable? Give an example.

2. How are flat characters different from more developed characters?

3. Name at least two authors of fables we still read and enjoy today.

4. List the hero of each fable in this unit.

5. How would you describe a fable for someone who had never read or heard one?

Comprehension: Understanding Main Ideas

6. Does the Dog in "The Dog in the Manger" show the moral of the story by what he *does*, or by what he *doesn't* do? How about the Dog in "The Dog and His Reflection"?

7. In your own words, what is the moral of "The Milkmaid and Her Pail"?

8. Compare the plot of "How the Fly Saved the River" with the plot of "The Singing Turtle." How are they similar? How are they different?

9. Suppose the Dog in "The Dog and His Reflection" crosses the same bridge with another bone the next day. What do you think will happen?

10. In "The King and the Shirt," how do you think the king feels when he learns that the only happy man in his kingdom does not have a shirt?

Understanding Literature: Plot

A plot is the series of events that take place in a story. Each event leads to another, which builds the plot. A plot usually has a beginning, middle, and end. In the beginning of a story, the main ideas, problems, and characters are introduced. During the middle section, the story develops. At the end, the problem is usually resolved, or settled.

11. Define plot.

12. Outline the plot of "The King and the Shirt."

13. The plot of "The Dog and His Reflection," contains a series of events. Could Aesop have left out any of these events without changing the story in important ways? Explain your answer.

14. In your opinion, which fable in this unit has the most believable plot? Why?

15. Sometimes, when you start to read a fable or story, you know what is going to happen in the end. Stories like this have a predictable plot. Did any fables in this unit have a predictable plot? If so, did this make reading the fable more enjoyable or less enjoyable? Explain your opinion.

Critical Thinking

16. Which is your favorite fable in this unit? Explain why.

17. Which fable means the most to you? How can you use it's message or moral in your own life?

18. If you were going to create a fable, which animal would you select as its hero? Explain your choice.

19. Who is your favorite hero in these fables? Explain why.

20. What do you think about the morals of fables? Do people living now need these kinds of messages?

Speak and Listen

Select a fable from this unit that you think would be fun to present to a group of young children. Practice reading the fable aloud, using a lively voice and speaking clearly. You might want to use different voices for different characters. Arrange to read the fable to a group of young children.

Beyond Words

Many famous artists, including Alexander Calder, have created illustrations for fables. Calder also introduced the mobile to the art world. Create a mobile that features characters, objects, or events from a fable in this unit.

Writing on Your Own

Write a fable using one of the following morals:

A stitch in time saves nine.
The squeaky wheel gets the oil.
Don't cry over spilt milk.
There's no place like home.

Your fable should have a setting, plot, and flat characters.

Test-Taking Tip

If you know you will have to define certain words or terms on a test, write each word on one side of a card. Write the definition on the other side. Use the cards as flash cards to test yourself or a partner.

"Myths are early science, the result of men's first trying to explain what they saw around them."
—Edith Hamilton, *Mythology*, 1942

"The ancient people perceived the world and themselves within that world as part of an ancient continuous story composed of innumerable bundles of other stories."
—Leslie Marmon Silko, *Sisters of the Earth*, 1991

Apollo's Chariot,
Odilon Redon

UNIT 2 *Myths*

People from most of the world's cultures have created myths to explain what they did not understand. One important group of myths explains how the world began. Another group explains why events in nature, such as thunderstorms and earthquakes, happen. Myths were often part of people's religion, believed to be true. Unlike the animal characters in fables, the characters in myths are usually gods, goddesses, and heroes. These characters have unusual strengths and powers.

In this unit, you will read myths about the beginning of the world, about some reasons for natural events, and about the experiences of strong, powerful characters.

UNIT 2 ■ ABOUT MYTHS

People from every culture have created, told, and believed in myths. The peoples of ancient India, Greece, Rome, Mexico, North America, Scandinavia, Egypt, Indonesia, Babylon, and many other places had myths related directly to their own history and religious beliefs.

Like fables, myths are one of the oldest forms of stories. Many were first told orally, before being written down. Myths may include a message about life, just as fables do. Myths also have a plot, setting, and characters. However, the characters in myths are not the flat characters of fables. Usually, they are gods, goddesses, or heroes, with great powers and unusual strengths. We find out more about these characters than we do about the characters in fables.

Myths are also different from fables in the way people thought about them. Few people who heard Aesop's fables believed that animals could talk, think, and behave as human beings do. Myths, however, were part of people's religion. They were believed to be true. For example, the people living on the Trobriand Islands in the Pacific Ocean have a myth that explains how death came to be. When people were first created, the Trobriand myth says,

they were immortal, meaning they never died. When they felt themselves growing old, they swam in a special pond and shed their old skin, just like a snake. They came out of the water with a brand new skin. One day, a woman went to the pond and shed her old skin. When she returned to her home in her new skin, her frightened daughter didn't know who she was. Upset, the woman returned to the pond and took back her old skin. Ever since, the Trobriands believe, death has been part of life.

Most myths can be grouped according to the kind of story they tell.

People have always wondered how the world came to be. Before science could supply answers, myths did. One group of myths explains how the world and all its creatures came into being. These are called creation myths. Sometimes, these myths also tell how the world will end. In the myths of the ancient Greeks, the world began from nothingness. In the myths told by the Hopi Indians, all living things came from deep within the earth. The Polynesian creation myths, among others, tell of two parents who bring life to the earth. Still others, such as the myths of India, tell of an animal that dove deep into the sea to bring up a small piece of the earth. This small piece then grew into the world.

A second group of myths explains why natural events such as earthquakes and eclipses happen. People are less afraid once they have reasons for things. For example, in ancient Norse myths, the god Thor created thunder and lightning when he threw a hammer at his enemies. The Greeks believed that thunderbolts were the weapons of the king of the gods, Zeus. For people in these cultures, thunderstorms happened when the gods were fighting. Some of the myths in this group tell us that parts of nature, such as fire and animals, were gifts from the gods.

This unit begins with three myths that were part of ancient Greek culture. "Prometheus" explains how people received one of their most precious gifts, fire. "Demeter and Persephone" offers an explanation of why we have seasons. "Perseus and Medusa" tells of a hero's dangerous mission. "The Beginning and the End of the World," an American Indian myth from the Okanogan culture, explains how the world came to be and how it will end. "Loki and the Master Builder," an ancient Norse myth, tells what happens when the gods put their trust in Loki, a troublemaker. "The Moon Spirit and Coyote Woman," a modern folk myth, tells of the love of the magical Moon Spirit for Coyote Woman.

Sun Tiger, Moon Tiger, **Diego Rivera**

Greek Myths
Anonymous

THE TWELVE OLYMPIANS

Aphrodite
goddess of love
and beauty

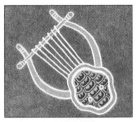

Apollo
god of the arts,
especially poetry
and music

About the Authors

The **myths** in this section come from ancient Greece. The Greeks believed their gods and goddesses looked like human beings. They ate, slept, quarreled, and fell in love, just as people do. However, these gods also had powers that people didn't have. Some could fly. Some could change shape. Some could make people do things against their will. To the Greeks, the gods and goddesses controlled the world. They lived in a place called Olympus. Olympus was believed to be somewhere above a real mountain in Greece, Mount Olympus.

The ancient Greeks recognized the power of their gods and goddesses and included them in almost every part of life. In their homes, they would set up altars to certain gods. They would pray at these altars several times a day. Cooking areas, for example, would often include an altar to Hestia. Hestia was the goddess who tended the hearth in Olympus. In addition, each Greek city chose a certain god or group of gods to honor and respect with temples and festivals. At the festivals, the people would hear the stories of their gods and goddesses retold by their culture's great poets.

Historians believe the Greeks adapted their myths from other ancient cultures that lived near them. At first, ancient Greek myths were told orally, rather than written down. However, their rich stories and complex characters were later collected

Ares
god of war

Artemis
goddess of the hunt and
protector of children

Athena
goddess of wisdom,
war, and crafts

Demeter
goddess of agriculture
and fertility

into three basic works: *Theogony*, by Hesiod, and *The Iliad* and *The Odyssey*, written by Homer. Homer and Hesiod were two of the greatest poets of ancient Greece. All three works were written in the 700s B.C., almost three thousand years ago.

About the Selections

The characters you will meet in these myths are gods, goddesses, and **heroes**. Heroes were a special class of people in Greek mythology. Like all people, they were mortal—meaning they died—unlike the gods and goddesses, who were immortal and never died. However, these heroes had unusual strength and power. They took on the most difficult and dangerous of tasks. Remember that the hero of a story is the main character. In this group of myths, the hero is a god, a goddess, or an especially strong, powerful human being.

As you read these myths, you will begin to see how authors create more complex characters. Writers have many different tools to do this. One of these is called **simile**, which is a way of comparing objects or people using a phrase that includes *like* or *as*.

Zeus
god of the sky and ruler of Olympus

Poseidon
god of the sea and earthquakes

Dionysus
god of wine, mysteries, and the theater

Hephaestus
god of smiths and metal workers

Hera
goddess of marriage

Hermes
god of merchants and Zeus's messenger

As you read, decide what the purpose of this myth is. Why do you think the Greeks told this myth?

In the beginning of time, there was a group of giant gods known as the Titans. The twin brothers Prometheus and Epimetheus were part of this group. The gods gave the brothers the special task of bringing to life all mortal beings—animals and people. They had formed these beings from the soil and fire inside the earth. Still, they were nothing more than clay statues. They needed life.

Prometheus's name means *forethought*. Epimetheus's name means *hindsight*. That was the way the two behaved. Epimetheus acted first and thought later. Prometheus thought carefully first, made plans, and then acted.

Who is the hero of this myth?

As soon as the gods gave him this task, Epimetheus started working. Without a thought, he gave the animals all the best gifts of the gods. He made them strong and nimble, with special coverings to protect them from the wind and cold on earth.

When Prometheus saw what had happened, he was dismayed. There were no special gifts left to protect the humans on whom he had **lavished** so much thought and care. He thought for a long while before he found a solution to this problem. People might not have the protection of furs, feathers, or skins, as the animals to whom Epimetheus had given these gifts. Yet they would have something to keep them warm and safe. They would have fire, and Prometheus would give it to them.

Why was it dangerous for Prometheus to give people fire? Why does he do it anyway?

Fire was a gift that only the gods enjoyed, and Zeus, the leader of the gods, had forbidden any mortal creature from having it. Nevertheless, Prometheus cared deeply about the unprotected people who might not **survive** if they did not have some protection. He sneaked into Olympus at night, and

lavish to provide a great deal of

survive to go on living

lit a torch from the flames of the **Chariot** of the Sun. He **extinguished** the flames, but carried the burning embers back to earth, hiding them in a stalk of fennel. Prometheus gave people his precious gift.

Fennel is an herb of the carrot family.

When Zeus heard of this, he became enraged. How dare Prometheus defy him? How dare he give the **immortal** gods' special treasure to **mere** mortals? Prometheus would have to be punished. He ordered Hephaestus, the god of the blacksmiths and fire, to chain Prometheus to a rock in the Caucasus Mountains for **eternity**. Every day, a giant eagle swept down from the sky and ate the **lobes** of Prometheus' liver. Each night, the lobes would grow back. Prometheus endured this torture for 30,000 years.

The Caucasus Mountains form part of the border between Europe and Asia.

Zeus finally sent Hercules to set Prometheus free. Hercules shot the eagle with a special arrow and released Prometheus from his chains. However, Zeus could not go back on his word. He had ordered that Prometheus be bound for eternity and so he would be. Forevermore, Prometheus carried around a piece of the rock to which he was chained, **embedded** with a link in the chain that had kept him there.

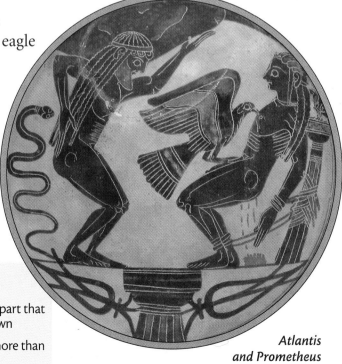

Atlantis and Prometheus

chariot a two-wheeled cart

embed to fix or enclose in something

eternity endless time

extinguish to put out

immortal free from death

lobe a rounded part that sticks out or down

mere nothing more than

DEMETER AND PERSEPHONE

As you read, decide what the purpose of this myth is. Why do you think the Greeks told this myth?

Zeus's sister, Demeter, was a kind and loving goddess who watched carefully over the harvest. She had taught people how to take seeds from fruits and vegetables and plant them. She cared for the young plants and protected them until they grew and bore fruit.

Demeter's daughter, Persephone, was even more beautiful than she. The two were rarely apart. Persephone brought great joy to her mother and all those around her. Everyone noticed her graciousness and beauty, including Hades, god of the underworld and death. He fell in love with the **captivating** girl.

The *underworld* was believed to be the place of departed souls.

One bright morning, Persephone was playing with her friends in a great field of narcissuses. Gaea, the earth mother, had planted these bright yellow flowers to please Hades. As Persephone bent to pick one of these lovely flowers for her mother, the earth suddenly split open. Hades appeared, riding in a **chariot** pulled by horses that were as black as night. He grabbed the terrified girl, and urged his horses back into the **chasm**. As quickly as it had opened, the earth closed over. Persephone was gone.

"As black as night" is a simile. What two things are being compared?

Hades raced to his underground kingdom, a world full of darkness and shadows. As she walked slowly through this **melancholy** place, Persephone felt ever more alone. Nothing here was as it was in her home. In the garden there were only whispering poplars and weeping willows. She could find no trace of the beautiful flowers she and her mother loved so much. The poor souls who lived here had none of the delicious fruits she loved to eat. The garden held only one tree—a **pomegranate**—that bore the food of the dead. The young girl fell to the ground, weeping.

Demeter soon realized that her precious child was missing. For nine long days, she **scoured** the earth, searching

captivating charming	**melancholy** sad	**scour** to search thoroughly
chariot a two-wheeled cart	**pomegranate** a reddish-yellow fruit with thick skin and many seeds	
chasm a large opening		

for her beloved daughter. Finally, the sun god Helios, who sees everything, told her that Hades had taken Persephone to his kingdom. Demeter felt her grief turn to icy anger. Until her daughter returned, her carefully tended plants would not bear fruit. Cursed by the one who had cared so deeply for them, the crops withered and died in the fields. People everywhere starved.

When the gods saw the power of Demeter's curse, they were alarmed. They could not overlook this. The fate of many mortals depended on them. Zeus ordered his brother Hades to let Persephone come back to her mother. Hades knew he had to obey the wishes of his brother. **Reluctantly**, he let Persephone go.

As the young girl started to leave, she heard the wicked laugh of one of Hades's gardeners. She turned as he showed Hades a pomegranate with a few seeds missing. Persephone blushed. She had eaten a few of the seeds. Hades was **jubilant**. She had eaten the food of the dead. Persephone could leave, as Hades had promised his brother, but she would have to return to him.

Demeter was delighted when her lovely daughter came back to her. Yet her joy turned to fury when she found that Persephone had eaten the pomegranate seeds. She knew this meant that her daughter would have to go back to the underworld. The curse would remain. If she could not have her daughter, then people would not have their crops.

Rhea, the oldest and most respected goddess of all, offered a **compromise**. If Demeter agreed, Persephone could spend one part of the year with Hades. During the rest of the year, the girl would live with her mother. Demeter knew this was only fair. With **resignation**, she agreed to the bargain and lifted the curse.

In the spring, summer, and fall, Persephone would be by Demeter's side as she watched over the planting and harvest. In the winter, Persephone would go to the underworld, and the whole world would grieve with the lonely mother.

Proserpine, Dante Gabriel Rossetti

Why does Persephone have to return to Hades?

Why does Demeter lift the curse? Do you think the agreement is fair?

compromise an agreement that attempts to satisfy both sides

jubilant joyful

reluctantly without wanting to

resignation acceptance of one's fate

Medusa,
Caravaggio

This myth is the story of a hero: a human being with unusual strength and power. As you read, notice the ways Perseus shows these characteristics.

PERSEUS AND MEDUSA

When the people gathered at the feast heard his words, they gasped. He, Perseus, would kill the Gorgon Medusa. It was unthinkable. The Gorgons were crude and graceless creatures. Their hair was a mass of **writhing** snakes. One glance from a Gorgon would turn any living thing to stone. The people could not understand why such a handsome and strong man would choose to die in such a terrible way.

Perseus understood the danger, too. Yet, he had no other choice. The king, Polydectes, had tricked him. Polydectes had told his people that he was planning to be married. All the people in the kingdom had brought their king splendid gifts to honor the bride and groom. Perseus had nothing to give. In his shame, he decided to risk everything to bring the king the head of Medusa.

With great determination, Perseus set off on his journey. He asked many people, but no one could tell him how to find the Gorgons. Suddenly, Hermes and Athena appeared to him. They knew of his **quest**. They told him how to find the island where Medusa and her sisters lived. Each had a special gift for

quest a search for something

writhing wiggling

Perseus that he would need to **survive**. Hermes gave him a pair of winged sandals to fly over the sea. Athena presented him with a gleaming shield, warning him to use it as a mirror if he needed to look at the horrible Gorgon. As wonderful as these gifts were, they were not enough for him to succeed, the two warned. Perseus must gather other magical items from the Nymphs of the North.

However, finding the Nymphs of the North was not that easy. Only the Grey Women could tell Perseus where they lived. Living in a world as grey and murky as fog, these sisters were strange creatures who shared only one eye between them. When one of them wanted to look at something, she would snatch the eye and place it in her forehead. Hermes told Perseus that this would be his only chance. He was to grab the eye as they were exchanging it. Only then would the Grey Women tell him how to find the Nymphs.

Perseus followed the plan exactly, and the weird Grey Women told him what he needed to know. He sped to the island where the Nymphs of the North lived. The Nymphs were sympathetic to Perseus's story, and gave him two more gifts: a magic bag and the Cap of Darkness. The Cap would make anyone who wore it invisible. Thanking the Nymphs, Perseus flew once again. He was ready for his **ordeal**.

Even though Perseus was prepared, he still trembled when he saw the island of the Gorgons reflected in his polished shield. Scattered about the barren ground were many strangely shaped stones . . . stones that had once been living creatures. Medusa lay sleeping with her sisters, her hair a mass of snakes with darting tongues. Perseus put on the Cap of Darkness so that no one would see him coming, and swooped down. With one mighty blow, he cut off Medusa's horrific head, threw it quickly into his magic bag, and flew off.

Recall that Hermes is the god of merchants and the messenger of Zeus; Athena is the goddess of wisdom, war, and crafts.

Murky means dim, hard to see through. In the sentence using this word, what is the simile? What two things are being compared?

Why do you think the Greeks told this myth?

ordeal a terrible experience

survive to go on living

Directions Write the answers to these questions using complete sentences.

Comprehension: Identifying Facts

1. To what group of gods do Prometheus and Epimetheus belong?

2. What gift does Prometheus bring to people?

3. How does Zeus punish Prometheus?

4. Who does Zeus send to free Prometheus?

5. As goddess of the harvest, what jobs does Demeter have?

6. Why does Persephone have to return to Hades's underground kingdom?

7. What is the compromise Rhea suggested to make sure Demeter can be with her daughter some of the time?

8. What special gifts does Perseus receive from the gods and the Nymphs of the North?

9. What does Perseus need from the Grey Women?

10. Why can't Perseus look at Medusa?

Comprehension: Understanding Main Ideas

11. How does Prometheus live up to his name, which means "forethought"?

12. Describe Prometheus's attitude toward people.

13. Why is Prometheus's gift of fire so important to people?

14. Why do you think Zeus gives Prometheus such a severe punishment?

15. How would you compare the character of Demeter and the character of Hades in the myth "Demeter and Persephone"?

16. Why do you think the Greeks created the myth of Demeter and Persephone?

17. Why do Hermes, Athena, and the Nymphs of the North help Perseus in his quest to kill Medusa?

18. How does Perseus use each of the gifts he receives to carry out his quest?

19. How would you describe the Gorgon Medusa?

20. Based on what you read in "Perseus and Medusa," what kinds of character traits did the Greeks value?

Understanding Literature: Simile

Writers try to use words in the most effective way possible. Often, by comparing two similar things, a writer can tell the reader something about the characters, setting, or theme of a story. For example, an author might describe a pond this way: "Its surface was as still as a gleaming mirror." What the writer is saying to the reader is: "Think about the pond. Now see its surface in your mind. It looks just like a mirror. It is smooth and glassy. There are no ripples." By using a simile—"as still as a gleaming mirror"—the writer describes the pond clearly in just a few words.

A simile is a descriptive figure of speech that compares two things. A simile includes the words *like* or *as*.

21. In your own words, tell what a simile is.

22. Why do writers use similes?

23. What two things is the writer comparing in this simile: "His horses were black as night"?

24. What two things is the writer comparing in this simile: "She ran like the wind"?

25. Create a simile of your own. Explain what two things your simile is comparing.

Critical Thinking

26. Are you more like Prometheus or Epimetheus? Explain.

27. Which character in these myths do you like the most? Why? How much do we learn about the character?

28. If you were Demeter, what would you have done when your daughter disappeared?

29. What do these three myths tell you about ancient Greece?

30. Which myth did you enjoy reading most? Which parts of it did you particularly enjoy?

Writing on Your Own Write a short poem or paragraph about the relationship between Epimetheus and Prometheus, or the relationship between Demeter and Persephone.

The Beginning and the End of the World
Okanogan Traditional Myth

Literary Terms

character a person or animal in a story, poem, or play

creation myth a myth that tells the story of the beginning of the world

oral literature stories that were first told, rather than being written down

plot the series of events in a story

setting a story's time and place

About the Authors

This myth comes from the Okanogan people, a group belonging to the Plateau Indians who first lived near the Columbia River in the Pacific Northwest. Their name may have come from a word meaning *meeting*. This word was first used as a name for a place on a nearby lake where native peoples from North America gathered to catch fish and exchange goods. The Okanogan were mainly fishers and gatherers. During the winter months, they lived in earth-covered pit houses that were partly underground. When the weather got warmer, the Okanogan moved to homes made of wood. Salmon from the river was an important part of their diet, but the group also hunted bear, deer, and elk, and gathered plants and berries from the nearby plains.

In 1872, the Colville Confederated Tribes (CCT) were set up on a reservation in northeast Washington state. The Okanogan, along with other American Indian groups in the area, moved onto the 1.3 million-acre reservation, larger than the state of Rhode Island. Today, nearly 4,000 Colville Indians live on this reservation, which has a tribal government and operates a fish hatchery.

About the Selection

"The Beginning and the End of the World" is a **creation myth.** It tells the story of how the Okanogan believed their world came to be. It also explains how the world will end. Like most myths, this story was first told orally and not written down. **Oral literature** refers to stories that were first told aloud, passed from generation to generation. This myth is retold by Ella C. Clark from traditional Okanogan tales. Stories from oral literature have the same parts as written stories, including **plot, characters,** and **setting.**

The Beginning and the End of the World

Long, long ago, when the sun was young and no bigger than a star, there was an island far off in the middle of the ocean. It was called Samah-tumi-whoo-lah, meaning White Man's Island. On it lived a race of giants—white giants. Their ruler was a tall white woman called Scomalt. Scomalt was great and strong, and she had Tahmahnawis powers. She could create whatever she wished.

For many years the white giants lived at peace, but at last they quarreled among themselves. Quarreling grew into war. The noise of the battle was heard, and many people were killed. Scomalt was made very, very angry.

"I will drive the wicked ones of these people far from me," she said. "Never again shall my heart be made sick by them. And they shall no longer trouble the peaceful ones of my people."

So she drove the wicked giants to one end of the White Man's Island. When they were gathered together in one place, she broke off that piece of land and pushed it out to sea. For many days the floating island drifted on the water, tossed by waves and wind. All the people on it died except one man and one woman.

They floated and drifted for many more days. The sun beat down upon them, and ocean storms swept over them. They became very hungry, until the man caught a whale. Seeing that their island was about to sink, they built a canoe, put the whale blubber into it, and paddled away.

As you read, think about whether this creation myth is just one story or several stories told together. What is explained by this myth?

Tahmahnawis powers were understood to be supernatural powers.

The *mainland* refers to a continent or the main part of a continent. Which continent do you think this is?

After paddling for many days and many nights, they came to some islands. They steered their way through them and at last reached the mainland. Here they stopped. The mainland was not so large as it is now, because it had not grown much yet. Wandering toward the sunrise, the man and woman came to the country now known as the Okanogan country. They liked that best, and there they stayed.

By this time they were so burned by the sun and whipped by the storm winds that their whiteness was entirely gone. Their skins were tanned a reddish brown. That is why the Indians have that color. All the Indians are the children of this first grandfather and grandmother.

Can you imagine this myth as oral literature, being told to people by a storyteller?

In time to come, the Okanogan Indians say, the lakes will melt the foundations of the world, and the rivers will cut the world loose. Then it will float as the island did many suns and snows ago. That will be the end of the world.

Directions Write the answers to these questions using complete sentences.

Comprehension: Identifying Facts

1. What do we learn about the character of Scomalt?

2. Why does Scomalt send the "wicked giants" away from her?

3. How do the man and the woman survive when their island begins to break apart?

Comprehension: Understanding Main Ideas

4. In this myth, Scomalt drives away the people who made war. What does this say about the Okanogan people's view of war?

5. In the Okanogan tradition, how did their people come to have the skin color they did?

6. How is the story about the beginning of the world similar to the idea about the end of the world? How are the two different?

Understanding Literature: Oral Literature

Long before people developed written language, they told each other stories. Stories helped them preserve their history, values, and culture. Oral literature includes the fables, myths, tales, and legends told from generation to generation. Sometimes the tellers would add, take away, or change details as they told the story. For example, in the myth about Demeter and Persephone, some storytellers said that Persephone has to stay with Hades for half the year, instead of just during the winter. However, even though the details might change, the basic idea remains the same. Persephone always has to spend some of her time in the underworld.

7. Why did people create oral literature?

8. Why might more than one version of the same story exist?

Critical Thinking

9. How is Scomalt different from many female characters we read about in stories?

10. Why do you think this creation myth includes an explanation of the people's skin color?

Writing on Your Own Write a diary entry that Scomalt might have written on the day after she drove the quarreling giants from her land. Be sure to include her thoughts about this event.

Loki and the Master Builder
Snorri Sturluson

About the Author

Like other civilizations, the Norse people of Scandinavia had a rich collection of myths about their gods, goddesses, and other important figures in their culture. As with most myths, Norse myths were first told orally. Snorri Sturluson was one of the first people to collect these myths into a written work.

Snorri Sturluson was born in 1179 in Hvammur, Iceland, where the Norse people had settled. Snorri was a leader of his people. He was elected three times to the highest office in the land, a position much like United States president. However, at that time, the king of Norway wanted to take control of Iceland. Afraid that Snorri might get in his way, he had Snorri killed in 1241.

Literary Term

problem the focus, or main concern, of the plot of a story

Snorri also was a poet and historian. He is best known for two important works. The first, *Heimskringla,* tells the history of the kings of Norway from ancient times until 1177. The second, called *The Prose Edda,* is a handbook for poets. It also contains myths of the Scandinavian people, including "Loki and the Master Builder."

About the Selection

"Loki and the Master Builder" shows how powerful the Norse gods were. In Norse myths, Loki is a character who plays tricks and causes trouble. He can also change shape and sometimes appears as an old woman. Loki was a giant who lived among the gods, even though giants and gods were enemies. The Norse people would have known right away that they could expect trouble from Loki.

The **problem** in this myth is this: a master builder has offered to build the gods a stronghold, which is a kind of fort or protected place. In return, he wants to marry Freyja, goddess of love, and own the sun and the moon.

LOKI and the Master Builder

In the early days of the settlement of the gods, when they had established Midgard and made Valhalla, a builder came to them and offered to make a **stronghold** so excellent that it would be safe and secure against cliff giants and frost **ogres**, even if they got inside Midgard.

He **stipulated** that as his reward he was to have Freyja as his wife and possession of the sun and moon besides.

The Æsir had a conference, and they struck this bargain with the builder. He should receive what he asked for, if he succeeded in building the stronghold in one winter. But if, on the first day of summer, any part of it was unfinished, he was to forfeit his reward; nor was he to receive anyone's help in the work.

When they told him these terms, however, he asked them to let him have the help of his horse, which was called Svadilfari, and acting on the advice of Loki, the gods granted this to him.

Midgard is where the gods live. *Valhalla* is the home of heroes who have died in battle.

The Æsir are gods. They are sworn enemies of giants.

Loki is a trickster, shape-changer, and general troublemaker. Why do you think he gives this advice?

Loki trickster and shape-changer

ogre a monster

Freyja goddess of fertility, death, love, and war

stipulate to demand as a condition of agreement

Thor god of thunder

stronghold a protected place, safe from enemies

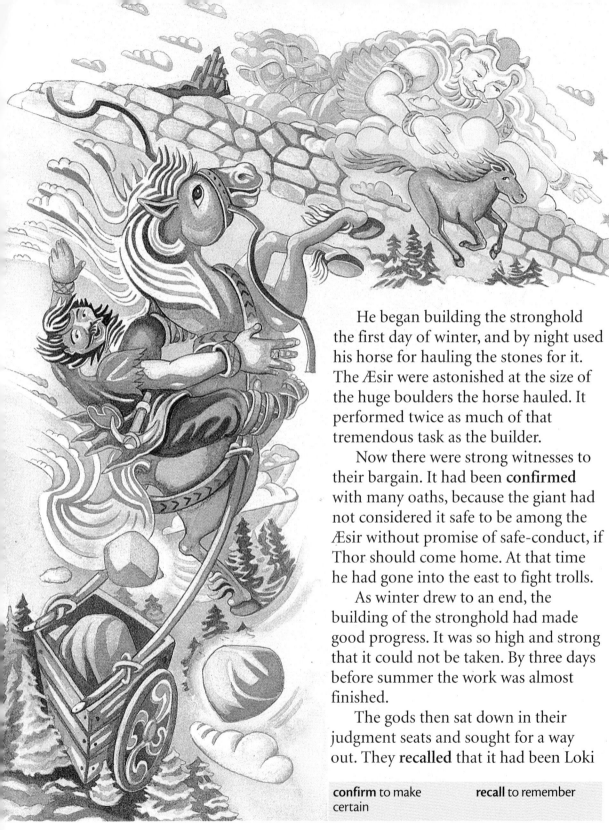

He began building the stronghold the first day of winter, and by night used his horse for hauling the stones for it. The Æsir were astonished at the size of the huge boulders the horse hauled. It performed twice as much of that tremendous task as the builder.

Now there were strong witnesses to their bargain. It had been **confirmed** with many oaths, because the giant had not considered it safe to be among the Æsir without promise of safe-conduct, if Thor should come home. At that time he had gone into the east to fight trolls.

As winter drew to an end, the building of the stronghold had made good progress. It was so high and strong that it could not be taken. By three days before summer the work was almost finished.

The gods then sat down in their judgment seats and sought for a way out. They **recalled** that it had been Loki

confirm to make certain

recall to remember

who had given the advice to marry Freyja into Giantland and also to ruin the sky and heaven by giving the sun and moon to the giants. They threatened him with an evil death if he did not **devise** a plan whereby the builder would forfeit his wages. Loki swore that he would do this, no matter what it might cost him.

That same evening, when the builder was driving out after stones with his stallion Svadilfari, a mare ran out of a wood up to the horse and **whinnied** to him. The stallion became frantic and ran into the wood after the mare. The two horses galloped about all night, and the work was delayed.

The next day, when the builder saw that the work would not be finished, he flew into a rage. As soon as the Æsir saw for certain that it was a giant who had come there, they **disregarded** their oaths and called on Thor.

He came at once and raised the hammer Mjölnir **aloft**. Thor paid the builder his wages, and it was not the sun and the moon. He struck him such a blow that his skull shivered into **fragments**, and he sent him down to Niflhel.

Loki, however, had had such dealings with Svadilfari that some time later he bore a foal. It was gray and had eight legs, and amongst gods and men that horse is the best.

Why do you think the gods want a way out? Why did they make this bargain with the builder in the first place?

Loki has disguised himself as the mare.

aloft overhead	**disregard** to pay no attention to	**whinny** the cry of a horse
devise to think up; to invent	**fragment** a small piece	

Directions Write the answers to these questions using complete sentences.

Comprehension: Identifying Facts

1. What does the builder want as a reward for building a stronghold, or fort, for the Æsir?

2. Whom do the Æsir blame when it looks as if the builder will finish his task by the first day of summer?

3. How does Loki keep the builder from completing the stronghold?

Comprehension: Understanding Main Ideas

4. What part do horses play in this myth?

5. How important is it for the Norse gods to keep their word? Find evidence to support your answer.

6. The builder in this myth seems to be a giant. For what reasons might the Æsir have entered into a bargain with their sworn enemy?

Understanding Literature: Problem

Many stories start with a problem, a dramatic situation that gives the plot its focus. For example, the problem stated in the beginning of the myth of Prometheus is: Prometheus has to give gifts to the mortals, but his brother has taken all the good gifts for the animals. What can Prometheus do to complete his task?

As the plot continues, things often happen that make it difficult for the hero to solve the problem. In the myth of Prometheus, solving his problem was made more difficult because Zeus had said mortals could not have fire.

7. In your own words, what is the problem that focuses the myth about Loki and the master builder?

8. Describe one event in the myth that complicates the problem, or makes it more difficult.

Critical Thinking

9. It appears that the Æsir do not know for sure that the master builder is a giant until he goes into a rage about not finishing his job. How could they not know?

10. In your opinion, is it fair of Thor to punish the builder? Explain your reasoning.

Writing on Your Own What do you think the master builder's stronghold looked like? What clues can you find about this in the myth? Use this information and your imagination to write a short description of the stronghold.

The Moon Spirit and Coyote Woman
Clive Grace

Clive Grace
1964–

About the Author

Many people call themselves storytellers. Few of them are given that title officially. Clive Grace is one of them. In fact, he is qualified as a storyteller by the British library system. He has a Grade B rating, which means he is qualified to tell stories to young people from ages eleven to thirteen.

Clive Grace was born in North London in 1964 and now lives in the city of Bath, England, with his dog, Galen. A computer journalist by trade, Grace is deeply involved in creating and telling stories. Tanais the fox, a thoughtful storyteller himself, is one of Grace's most popular characters. Tanais is the featured character in a series of stories that Grace tells in person and on his Internet Web site. "The Moon Spirit and Coyote Woman" is part of this series. Grace calls this story "a sort of modern folk myth."

About the Selection

"The Moon Spirit and Coyote Woman" has many of the same characteristics as other myths in this unit do. It was created to be told orally; its characters have great powers; and it tells a story about the early days of the earth. However, this is a modern myth, full of descriptions about setting and characters, unlike the other myths in this unit. It is also a love story.

The myth is actually a **story-within-a-story**. This means that a second story is told within another story. In this case, the reader meets a character, Tanais the fox, who then becomes the **narrator**, or storyteller, of another story—the myth of "The Moon Spirit and Coyote Woman".

The Moon Spirit

Why Coyotes Howl at the Moon

As you read, notice how the character of Tanais is developed and described. How is he different from the "flat" animal characters often found in fables?

It was midnight and Tanais the fox was walking alone, deep in thought. It was a beautiful night, a full moon shone high in the sky and he could hear waves crashing against the distant shoreline. He felt a need to look out at the sea, so he decided to walk by himself in the moonlight for a while and maybe smoke his pipe a little. He didn't know *why* he felt this need to be alone, only that he needed it every now and then. Hoping he would feel a lot happier with the sound of waves and the smell of salt, he sniffed **expectantly** at the sea air to catch his bearings and started on his journey.

To *catch your bearings* means to figure out where you are and where you're going.

Leaving a long trail of paw prints behind him, Tanais walked the entire length of the beach occasionally puffing on his pipe. At one point he came across a walking stick tossed upon the sand. It was actually a short length of tree branch or a thick twig that had been **discarded** by the ocean; a few tiny **barnacles** had attached themselves to one end and it was still quite damp from floating in the sea, but it would dry out eventually, so he picked it up, brushed some seaweed off of it and continued on his journey, propping the stick on one shoulder.

Notice the details of setting. How would you describe the location of Tanais's midnight walk?

Tanais especially liked to walk along the shoreline and watch the waves as they crashed against the rocks in the distance. It was a strangely magical night; at one point he thought he heard the sound of fluttering wings somewhere deep in the darkness. Stopping to look around, he saw no one, so he shrugged—snuggling deeper into a scarf he had brought along for the night—continuing on his midnight walk.

---

barnacles small sea animals that attach themselves to rocks or floating objects

discard to throw away or cast off

expectantly as if looking forward to something

& Coyote Woman

Eventually he came upon a rocky cove; it was a favourite haunt of his and he found it ideal as a place of quiet **contemplation**–a place where he could get some thinking done at times like this.

Finding his favourite spot in the cove, Tanais stared for a long while at the moon reflecting off the surface of the sea and felt a **pang** of loneliness. He felt this every now and then and indeed had come to live with it and accept it. He knew that the life of a wanderer is sometimes like that, but he wouldn't have it any other way.

The fox sat down on a smooth rock jutting out over a shallow pool of water; every now and then he puffed on his pipe, sending plumes of smoke into the cold air. Apart from the occasional crash of waves in the distance, all was quiet around him.

Watching the shadows of rocks made by the moon's reflection, Tanais quietly pondered how different everything looked at night; in the daytime the pool was home to tiny sea creatures caught in the low tide, but at night it became something quite different and enchanting. Tanais watched the water in the pool as it caught the moon's reflection, bathing nearby rocks and stones in a shimmering silver light. It was one of the most beautiful places Tanais knew of and he would often return there when he felt sad, lonely or just a little thoughtful.

As he puffed on his pipe Tanais remembered a story he had been told as a cub, a story about the moon and the sea and many other things besides. The moment was perfect for the telling of this particular tale, but there was no one around

Favourite is the British spelling of *favorite*. Later, you will see *colourful* for *colorful* and *centre* for *center*, *realise* for *realize* and *ploughing* for *plowing*. These are all British spellings. A *haunt* is a place someone goes to a lot.

How would you describe Tanais's feelings as he sits on the rock looking at the moon's reflection on the water?

contemplation study; deep thought   **pang** a sharp pain

to hear it! So he sat with his head resting in both paws and looked out at the sea and the moon's reflection, pondering what to do with the story.

After a while, Tanais shrugged a little and looked thoughtfully at the moon. Try as hard as he might he couldn't get the tale out of his head. Suddenly an idea crossed his mind and he paused for a few moments, pondered quietly on his idea before turning his muzzle skywards where he addressed the moon with a smile. "Then I think I shall tell it to you, my friend. You know, I've never told a story to the moon before—I hope you like it." Shifting into a more comfortable position, Tanais paused only to push his scarf a little higher onto his shoulders and he began his tale:

"This story happened years ago," began Tanais a little uncertainly. "It happened many years before I, or anyone I know was born—at a time when this land was still quite young and when there were many places filled with wild magic."

Tanais reached for the stick he had found on the beach and started to draw shapes in the sand in front of him. "Of all the creatures, the most popular, and certainly the most

Here, Tanais becomes the narrator of a story-within-a-story. Who is the audience for his tale?

prolific was the coyote," he said, his sketching rapidly turning into the outline of a coyote.

"Some legends say that the coyotes were the first of the creatures to be made for the new land and that they were told by the creator to look after the land whilst he went off and made the rest of us." Tanais laughed a little. "Others say that the coyote was put here so that none of us would have an easy life." The fox's laugh trailed off into a **wistful** sigh. "I guess we shall never know exactly for sure," he said as he continued drawing. "Back in those days, people just lived by the fact that the sun always followed the moon and that Winter always followed Summer. They didn't have any need for clocks or calendars, choosing to sleep when they were tired and waking when the sun came up." With a flourish, Tanais finished his drawing and stopped for a moment to admire the **likeness**.

With a satisfied nod, Tanais looked back up at the moon. "This story is about one tribe of coyotes in particular," he said. "The other coyote tribes had **dispersed** throughout the land and had fallen into fights and **squabbles** with each other—mainly over land or food, but this tribe was different. Theirs was a peaceful tribe, working hard and quietly living off the land in their own way."

Becoming more elaborate with his drawing, Tanais started to sketch out some more coyotes in the sand; some were ploughing the land, others were harvesting fields or pulling fishing nets in small boats on the sea. Dotted around his picture were small teepee-like tents—out of which poked the faces and noses of coyote mothers with their cubs.

As Tanais drew each coyote he explained to the moon what each one was doing. "None of them were warriors. They lived a peaceful life in spite of their warring cousins," he concluded as he put the stick down. "Some were farmers, others herded cattle or rode horses, whereas a few would catch fish in the ocean."

How do details from the first story help you understand the second story?

Whilst is an old spelling of *while*.

How does Tanais "illustrate" his story-within-a-story?

---

disperse to scatter

likeness a copy or portrait

prolific producing many young

squabble an argument or quarrel

wistful sad

Tanais brushed some sand off of his paws. "The other tribes lived far away and would fight and squabble amongst each other, fouling and spoiling wherever they went. The tribe by the sea was, by contrast, the smallest of all the coyote tribes and their peacefulness didn't interest the others. As they never went attacking or plundering anyone, they never got attacked themselves. After a while they had been all but completely forgotten by the other tribes."

Tanais picked up the stick again and started to very carefully adapt the picture of the first coyote he drew. "Not very far away from the tribe lived a coyote woman," Tanais said. "She was very beautiful and wore a green and purple cape and the feather necklace of a medicine woman. Known only as *Why-ay-looh'*, or 'Coyote Woman,' she loved to take long walks by herself in the plains, searching for herbs and roots that she would later turn into powerful medicines.

As you read the story-within-a-story, look for details of the setting.

How is Medicine Cove like the rocky cove that Tanais himself likes to visit?

"One of her favourite places was a rocky cove; called Medicine Cove, it was shielded on all three sides by a sheer wall of rocks, **accessible** by a secret path that only she knew about. Coyote Woman would often spend many hours sitting in her cove, looking at the moon as it rose over the ocean. Sometimes she would sing to herself or **devise** new magic and medicine, sometimes she would braid colourful beads into her long golden fur or prepare her herbs. In the centre of the cove was a pool of water that she would often use to look into and think about things when she wanted to be by herself and not be disturbed.

An *outcropping* is the part of a rock formation that appears at the surface of the ground.

"One night, Coyote Woman went to her cove and sat on an outcropping of rocks that looked over the pool. As she sat, braiding beads into her hair and humming a song to herself, she looked into the pool and saw to her surprise what looked like a face smiling up at her in the reflection of the moon. With a startled yelp, she jumped back and looked up at the moon shining high in the sky but saw nothing unusual there. Shaking her head, she looked back at the pool and stared into the water."

accessible reachable   **devise** to think up; to invent

Tanais looked down into the pool and saw his reflection looking up at him. The reflection of the moon had slid a little further into the pool and shone behind him, lighting the outline of his ears with an **eerie** glow. He thought about playing with his reflection using the stick he had just been drawing with, but he thought better of it. He paused to remember where he was in the story, then continued.

"At first she thought it must have been some sort of **illusion**—that the reflection in the moon was her *own* face looking up at herself from the pool—so she peered a little closer. Although the face was indistinct and shimmered slightly as it rippled in the water, Coyote Woman found that if she squinted her eyes as she looked into the pool, she could quite clearly see the image of a pure white coyote staring up at her with his deep blue eyes.

"Nothing like this had ever happened before! She had **acknowledged** long ago that this was a very magical place but knowing about magic and coming face to face with it are two very different things."

Tanais looked into the pool again. As he told the story he noticed that the reflection of the moon had slid further into the centre of the pool, bathing even more of the surroundings in its eerie light. This made the rocks appear as if they were formed from glass and made the wet sand glisten with an icy blue **radiance** as the waves crashed and then drew back from the shoreline in a foaming silver-white carpet.

Although entranced by the beauty of the moment, Tanais remembered his audience; hard as it might be, once a story is started, it should always be finished. He took a **refreshing** gulp of sea air to bring him back to his story and continued.

"If Coyote Woman was surprised at what she saw from within the pool she was completely unprepared for what followed," said Tanais, looking around him. "The face in the pool became more real and more solid with each passing

acknowledge to admit; to recognize

eerie spooky

illusion an unreal vision

radiance glowing light

refreshing giving back strength or life

moment until after a minute or so *Hah-ah´*—a moon spirit—was shimmering in the pool, looking up at her with his blue eyes."

Tanais paused for a moment; the hairs on the back of his neck and all along his tail were **bristling** with excitement. The cool sea air had suddenly become as sharp as a razor's edge and seemed to fill the cove with an almost electrifying energy—like the moment just before a thunderstorm. Tanais waited with **bated** breath for something to happen; he half-expected the Coyote Woman or the spirit from the pool to appear at any moment, but the moment passed and nothing appeared—so he gathered his thoughts together and continued a little more cautiously, his whiskers twitching and one ear cocked to catch the slightest change around him.

"The story is a little unclear around this point . . ." said Tanais, scratching at an ear as he observed the pattern of rocks shimmering and glowing under the moon's light, ". . . but the **version** of the story *I* prefer tells of the Coyote Woman and the moon spirit falling in love with each other." Smiling, the fox continued. "You see, the moon spirit loved to look down on this pool from where he lived on one of the moon's highest mountains. When the moon was full and at her most powerful, the moon coyote would shine down on the pool, spreading his magic into the rocks and sand.

"Some say that magic attracts more magic and as the cove was one of the few places still left where wild magic was still very much alive, he naturally felt an **affinity** with the place. The fact that a beautiful Coyote Woman also loved this place merely added to his insistence that he should appear in front of her.

"Without a word, the moon spirit started to lift himself up out of the pool. First a pink nose pushed through the water, followed by a muzzle and then a pair of milky white ears. The moon coyote was pushing very hard against something as he slowly **heaved** more and more of his body out of the pool,

affinity attraction	**bristling** standing erect	**version** a form or type
bated kept low and shallow	**heave** to lift up and out	

pausing every now and then to catch his breath. Water didn't drip off of him, rather the water seemed to solidify and *become* part of him, drawing out into long strands of silver-white hair.

"Coyote Woman stood and watched breathless as Moon Coyote lifted more and more of himself out of the pool. Fighting with all his might, he strained against the water that seemed to cling to him. It was as if it wanted to drag the moon coyote back down, but he continued, straining along with every muscle in his body until he finally leapt free of the pool and stood triumphant in the moonlight.

"The next morning, Coyote Woman and Moon Coyote went into the village. Seeing their medicine woman walking into the village with a stranger, the tribe immediately stopped what they were doing and came rushing to see who her strange new companion was. She padded to the Chief of the tribe's tent and knelt as the Chief of the tribe who was called *Le-ee´-oo* came out to see what was going on.

"'*Le-ee´-oo!*' said Coyote Woman, holding her head down, 'this is *Hah-ah´*,'" pointing at Moon Coyote. 'He came to me

Moon Coyote is the moon spirit.

last night from out of the pool in Medicine Cove. I wish to marry him,' she said rather matter-of-factly. There was a gasp from the villagers as she said this because the medicine women normally didn't marry and when they did, they certainly didn't marry at such a young age.

"The Chief just nodded and looked at Moon Coyote as he slowly walked around him. Every now and then he sniffed and prodded at Moon Coyote and muttered to himself and exchanged words with his **advisers**. Everyone fell silent as he did this until finally the Chief looked deeply into his eyes, snorted to himself and nodded again.

"Turning to Coyote Woman, he looked at her and said rather gruffly, 'Medicine woman, *Hah-ah'* is a spirit, a moon coyote, he is not from this land. Why do you wish to marry him?'

"'Because I love him!' she said, still kneeling '. . . and because he loves me.'

"*Le-ee'-oo* snorted again, but this seemed to be what he wanted to hear, so he looked back at the moon coyote and asked, '. . . and do you love her *Hah-ah'*? Will you stay with her for as long as you live?'

"The moon coyote nodded and padded over to Coyote Woman and gently lifted her up off the ground. 'I do,' he said, 'I will love your medicine woman even after I die.'

"'Then let it be so,' said the Chief. Turning to the villagers the Chief proclaimed in a loud and very formal voice, 'Our medicine woman has a husband. He is *Hah-ah'* of the moon tribe. From now on he shall be known as "Moon Coyote."' With a nod and a gentle smile at the couple, *Le-ee'-oo* walked back into his tent, followed by his advisers. Coyote Woman and Moon Coyote were married."

Tanais frowned a little to himself. Had he ended the story there, it would have been a good place to stop, but even he would be the first to admit that nothing much happened and there was more. ". . . And I suspect you know there's more to the story, don't you?" said Tanais, eyeing the moon

What do you think will happen next?

adviser one who gives advice

suspiciously as he sat down on his rock again. Looking at the shoreline and noticing the water was slowly crawling up the beach toward the pool, the fox reckoned that he would have just enough time to finish telling his tale without getting trapped by the rising tide, so settling down to finish the rest of the story, Tanais took one last puff from his pipe and continued:

"Of course Coyote Woman and Moon Coyote were very happy together; they went back to their home by the sea and watched the waves beating against the shore. Throughout the day they were visited by villagers and friends—bearing gifts and blessings for the newlyweds. Later in the afternoon, they decided to explore the beach and Coyote Woman showed her husband the places she liked to go and things she liked to see. Together they laughed and skipped in the sand, chasing each other up and down the beach as they played games with each other.

"In the evening, Coyote Woman went down to the beach and took her beads and herbs with her. Her husband had gone hunting with his new friends and tribe members, so she thought it would be a good time to sit by herself and **contemplate** how different her life had suddenly become. She thought lovingly about her husband and soon her thoughts drifted towards raising a family together."

Tanais sighed to himself as he pictured the image in his mind. "For the first time in her life Coyote Woman was truly contented."

Tanais stopped and shrugged as he remembered the story. "Coyote Woman was lost in her own dreams and braiding her hair when, all of a sudden, she heard the distant sound of a yelp followed by a cry of pain. Someone was hurt, and it wasn't far away by the sound of it. She rushed to the top of a sandy hillock to see better and, to her horror, saw her husband in the distance lying on the floor twitching.

"As he was the newest member of the tribe and because he had just been married, it was agreed that the hunters were to

contemplate to study
or think about

A *bison* is a buffalo, a large wild animal.

Why do you think the hunters allowed Moon Coyote to go after the first bison, when he had no hunting experience?

go on an expedition and that Moon Coyote was to have the first try at pulling down a bison," explained Tanais, tapping the ashes from his pipe into the sand. "Moon Coyote had never hunted one of these before—being something of a **rarity** where he came from—and it came as no surprise that he had badly **miscalculated**. As he chased after his prey, it **swerved** madly in front of him, trampling him under its powerful hooves, lifting him into the air with its short, but nonetheless **lethal** horns before dashing him on the floor with a sickening crack of bones.

"Seeing her husband lying there, Coyote Woman didn't hesitate, she grabbed her herbs and ran as fast as she could to his side. By the time she arrived, Moon Coyote was barely alive. He was unconscious and his breath was rasping—a thick pool of blood had soaked into the sand and the rear half of his body lay twisted on the floor. You didn't have to be a medicine woman to realise that his back had been broken.

"Nevertheless, Coyote Woman tried to help her husband; she applied her strongest and most powerful medicines—but everything she did to try and heal him was in vain. Moon Coyote's beautiful white coat was now a dull grey and was caked with blood where the bison had tossed him into the air. His deep blue eyes had started to mist over and his rasping breath got fainter with every passing breath. Coyote Woman's instincts told her that he was dying.

"She thought desperately of possible remedies and cures, but this was far beyond her healing capabilities. Eventually, and with tear-filled eyes, she admitted defeat and turned away from her husband to howl a cry so painful and so desperate that everyone for miles around stopped in their tracks and listened with dread at the pain in Coyote Woman's voice.

"There was nothing else to do but to look on helpless as her Moon Coyote's breath faded. She applied what little medicine she could to ease the pain away and just sat, watching Moon Coyote slowly die—lit by the moon as it rose

lethal deadly	**miscalculate** to misjudge or figure out wrong	**rarity** something not usually seen
		swerve to turn sharply

slowly over the sea. Never before had she felt so helpless, if only there was something she could do!

"All of a sudden she had an idea! It was crazy and desperate, but then she *was* desperate. Lifting Moon Coyote's dying body in her paws, *she* ran down to Medicine Cove. The moon coyote was already so far gone that he only moaned **pitifully** and his breath started to rasp and become more ragged again.

"When she finally arrived, Coyote Woman spread her dying husband out in the shallow pool. Propping his head gently on her robes, she watched helpless as his life seemed to **ebb** from his body into the pool.

"Pointing her muzzle towards the moon, the Coyote Woman howled again, a lonely, broken howl. Moon Coyote sagged as the life finally left his body and he breathed his last. Coyote Woman looked on with bated breath, waiting for something to happen, but the moon just carried on its upward ascent into the night sky, shining down on the cove, the moon coyote and his **disconsolately** sobbing widow."

Tanais stared into the pool and sniffed. "The Moon felt that Moon Coyote's death was unfair and although she hadn't the power to bring Coyote Woman's husband back to life, she was, nevertheless, an important part of the wild magic—a magic that was in existence long before death came into the world. She looked down sadly on the sobbing Coyote Woman and decided to do something about it.

"After Coyote Woman had cried herself out, she looked miserably at where her husband lay in the pool and saw, to her astonishment, the ghostly **apparition** of her husband floating above his body. The moon's silver light was shining down on the pool—stronger and brighter than it had ever been before—and his body was still lying in the shallow pool, but the huge ugly blood stain in his side had been washed away by the pool. The spirit of her husband looked down on

Why do you think Coyote Woman brings Moon Coyote to Medicine Cove?

According to this myth, why do coyotes howl at the moon?

---

apparition a vision or appearance

disconsolately impossible to comfort

ebb to flow away

pitifully causing pity

his body and sniffed at it before looking at his wife and, to her amazement, smiled at her."

Tanais stopped. Picking up his stick, he looked at the moon and frowned. "No one really knows what happened as the story ends there. The next day the other tribe members eventually found their way into Medicine Cove and discovered Coyote Woman's drowned body lying next to her husband in the pool.

"Some stories say that Coyote Woman died of a broken heart," Tanais looked carefully at the rising tide, "others say that she had drowned—too heartbroken to notice, or to care—I guess we shall never know," and he kicked a little at the sand. "But the stories all agree on one thing, however. On the night they died, a star appeared next to the moon. It's one of the brightest stars in the sky and is the first to come out in the summer evenings. If you look at it very carefully, you'll see that it appears as if it is two stars joined closely together."

Tanais picked up his hat and looked at his drawings in the sand as the waves crawled closer up the shoreline. The cove was nearly filled with water now and he would have to hurry in order to get out and not get his paws wet. Soon his pictures would be gone—washed away as if they were never there. "Nothing's permanent," muttered the fox as he quickly gathered his belongings together and started on his journey home, his spirit strangely lifted by the telling of such a sad story.

As he turned to walk home, he took one last look at the water rolling **relentlessly** into the cove. The waves were much heavier now and the water was much higher than before. Nodding his head and sniffing the air one last time, Tanais raised his hat to the moon and walked off.

Had he been a little closer to the pool, Tanais would have seen the faces of two shimmering Coyotes—one white, the other golden—holding each other and looking at him as the water washed over them.

What other natural event does this myth explain?

relentlessly without softening or letting up

Directions Write the answers to these questions using complete sentences.

Comprehension: Identifying Facts

1. At what time of day does Tanais tell his story?

2. Where is Tanais when he tells his story?

3. To whom does he tell his story?

4. What details does Tanais give about the way Coyote Woman and Moon Coyote look?

5. What is Coyote Woman's favorite place to go?

6. How does Coyote Woman first meet the moon spirit?

7. How is Moon Coyote injured?

8. How does Coyote Woman try to help her wounded husband?

9. What happens in the heavens the night the two die?

10. What does Tanais fail to notice in the pool as he leaves?

Comprehension: Understanding Main Ideas

11. What kind of mood or feeling does the setting of Tanais's story—a rocky cove at midnight—create?

12. How would you describe Tanais's mood as he begins to tell the story?

13. Tanais says that "knowing about magic and coming face to face with it are two very different things." What do you think this means?

14. Give two examples of the importance of magic in the plot of this myth.

15. In what ways is this myth like a fable?

16. List three details that show that Tanais thinks of the coyotes as a native race, like the Okanogan and other American Indians.

17. Why was one setting—the rocky cove—important to both stories?

18. Why does Coyote Woman bring her dying husband to Medicine Cove?

19. When Tanais realizes the water will wash away his drawings, he remarks that nothing is permanent. What other events in the myth show the truth of this statement?

20. Why do you think Tanais fails to see the faces of the Coyotes in the pool?

Understanding Literature: Story-within-a-story

Storytellers in eastern Europe sometimes use nesting dolls to tell their tales. Nesting dolls are a set of several doll-like figures, each a little smaller than the one before. When you open the largest doll, you find a smaller doll inside. When you open that doll, you find another, even smaller doll, and so on.

A story-within-a-story is somewhat like these dolls. First the reader meets the narrator, whose story has a setting, plot, and characters. Then the narrator begins to tell another story. This second story may have a different plot, setting, and characters. The first story often sets the mood for the second story. The two stories are usually connected in other ways as well. Details of one story can help readers understand the other story better.

21. In your own words, explain what a story-within-a-story is.

22. Why would an author use a story-within-a-story?

23. Outline the basic plot of Tanais's story.

24. Outline the basic plot of the myth of "The Moon Spirit and Coyote Woman."

25. Give two examples of ways in which Tanais's story helps you better understand the myth of "The Moon Spirit and Coyote Woman".

Critical Thinking

26. Does Tanais's story add to or take away from the story of Coyote Woman and Moon Coyote? Explain your thinking.

27. Do you think that Clive Grace wants readers to believe this myth in the same way that ancient Greeks and Norse people believed in their myths? Explain your thinking.

28. According to this myth, how do you explain "why coyotes howl at the moon"?

29. What do you think happened to Coyote Woman?

30. How do you think Tanais would have felt if he had seen the faces in the pool at the end of the story?

Writing on Your Own An obituary is a short article about someone who has died. It gives some details about the person's life as well as his or her death. Write an obituary for Moon Coyote and Coyote Woman.

Point of View

Narrator and Point of View

One of the first decisions writers have to make is who will tell the story. Will the narrator—the storyteller—know everything about the plot? Or should the narrator be a character in the story? If so, how much should the narrator know about the plot as it unfolds? These choices make a difference in the story's point of view. Point of view means the position from which the author or storyteller tells the story. The kind of narrator gives a story its point of view.

If the person telling the story is also a character in it, we say the story is written in first person. First-person narrators use the pronouns *I* and *we*. If the narrator is not a character, the author is using a different point of view: third person. Third-person narrators use the pronouns *he*, *she*, *it*, and *they*. The myths in this unit were all written using the third-person point of view. Tanais, however, in "The Moon Spirit and Coyote Woman," refers to himself as *I* when he tells the story-within-a-story.

When a narrator knows everything about the story, including the thoughts of all the characters, we say the narrator is *omniscient*, meaning all-knowing.

When a narrator sees the story through the eyes of only one character, we say the narrator has limited omniscience. In other words, the narrator does not know everything.

Review

1. What role does the narrator play in a story?

2. What does point of view mean?

3. What does it mean if a story is written from a first-person point of view?

4. What does it mean if a story is written from a third-person point of view?

5. What is the term for a narrator who knows everything?

Writing on Your Own Using the following plot line, write a paragraph that describes the event from both a first-person and a third-person point of view:

A young child pesters his grandmother until she buys him an ice cream cone. Before he has a chance to take even one bite, he drops the cone on the ground.

UNIT 2 SUMMARY

Unit 2 has presented examples of another very old form of story: myth. All cultures have created myths to explain what they didn't understand or what they thought of as holy. Unlike fables, myths were often part of religion. People believed them to be true.

Like fables, many myths were told orally before being written down. Myths include plots, settings, and characters, just as fables do, and they often have messages about life. However, the characters of myths are usually gods, goddesses, or heroes—human beings with unusual strengths and powers. We often find out more about the characters in myths than we do about the flat characters in fables.

Most myths can be grouped based on the kind of story they tell. Some myths explain how the world was created. Others explain events in nature, such as seasons and thunderstorms.

From myths, we can learn what people thought was important. We can also learn how people in different places explained the world, nature, and their own lives.

Selections

■ "Prometheus," a Greek myth, explains what Prometheus suffered in order to give fire to human beings.

■ "Demeter and Persephone," a Greek myth, tells how Demeter's curse explains why we have seasons.

■ "Perseus and Medusa," a Greek myth, describes how a brave hero killed a terrible monster.

■ "The Beginning and the End of the World," from the Okanogan culture, explains how the world began and how it will end.

■ "Loki and the Master Builder," an ancient Norse myth first recorded by Snorri Sturluson, tells what happened when the gods trusted the troublemaker, Loki.

■ "The Moon Spirit and Coyote Woman," by Clive Grace, tells the tragic love story of two magical characters. It also explains why coyotes howl at the moon.

UNIT 2 REVIEW

Directions Write the answers to these questions using complete sentences.

Comprehension: Identifying Facts

1. What are some reasons that people have created myths?

2. We can divide myths into two groups: creation myths and myths that explain events in nature. Describe each group.

3. How are myths different from fables? How are they the same?

4. What is a simile? Give an example.

5. What is a story-within-a-story?

Comprehension: Understanding Main Ideas

6. How is the myth of Prometheus like the myth of Loki and the Master Builder? How are the two myths different?

7. Compare the character of Scomalt with the character of Coyote Woman.

8. What is the problem that focuses the myth of Demeter and Persephone? What happens that makes the problem hard to solve?

9. How would the myth of "The Moon Spirit and Coyote Woman" have been different if it were not told as a story-within-a-story?

10. Why are the characters in myths often gods, goddesses, and heroes with special powers? Does this add to or take away from the stories?

Understanding Literature: Simile and Metaphor

As you have read, similes are tools that writers use to compare objects and people. Similes include the words *like* or *as*. When Clive Grace writes that "The cool sea air had suddenly become as sharp as a razor's edge," he is using a simile. He is telling his readers to think of the air as the sharp edge of a razor, cutting into Tanais's fur. By using a simile, Grace tells us much more than if he had just said, "It was windy."

Metaphors are similar tools. Metaphors also compare two things. However, they do not use *like* or *as*. Metaphors say that one thing *is* another. For example, "the clouds were ghosts" is a metaphor. We are asked to think about the clouds as ghosts—pale, filmy, drifting in space.

Metaphors are different from similes in another important way. In a simile, writers are usually comparing something about an object or person with something about another object or person. For example, "she fell like a rock" is a simile, meaning she fell as a rock would, landing with a heavy thud.

However, "she is a rock," which is a metaphor, tells us much more. It says that she is steady and solid, someone on whom you can depend.

11. How are metaphors like similes?

12. How are metaphors and similes different from each other?

13. Write a simile to describe the rocky cove in "The Moon Spirit and Coyote Woman."

14. Write a metaphor to describe Coyote Woman.

15. Write a metaphor to describe Medusa.

Critical Thinking

16. If you were Perseus, would you have offered to kill Medusa? Why or why not?

17. If Perseus did not have the help of the gods, how might he complete his task?

18. How do you think Scomalt would feel if she were present as the Okanogan world ended?

19. If you were Freyja, how would you feel about being a prize in a contest over which you had no control?

20. Which is your favorite myth in this unit? Explain why you like this work.

Speak and Listen

Prepare a brief oral report on one of the Greek or Norse gods or goddesses. You can use reference materials such as encyclopedias and books on mythology to gather information. Outline what you want to say. Use the outline to present your report to the class.

Beyond Words

Create a collage that represents the characters or plot of the myth of Prometheus. You can use pictures and words from magazines, objects, and your own drawings to complete this project.

Writing on Your Own

Write a creation myth of your own, explaining how school may have been started. Your myth should have a setting, plot, and third-person narrator, as the myths in this unit did. Your characters should be gods, goddesses, or heroes.

Test-Taking Tip

When studying for a test, use a marker to highlight important facts and terms in your notes. For a final review, read over the highlighted areas.

"Americans are overreaching; overreaching is the most admirable and most American of the many American excesses."

—George F. Will, *Statecraft as Soulcraft: What Government Does*, 1984

"These are the stories that never, never die, that are carried like seed into a new country, are told to you and me and make in us new and lasting strengths."

—Meridel Le Sueur, *Nancy Hanks of Wilderness Road*, 1949

Liberty Series VI, **Barbara Cesery**

UNIT 3 *Tall Tales and Legends*

Tall tales and legends are important parts of American folklore. Like fables and myths, many tall tales and legends were first spread by word of mouth. Tall tales feature characters who are larger than life and have fantastic adventures. The stories often come from the American frontier and the colorful people who settled there. Legends are usually based on real people, places, or events. Some details may be true; others come straight from the storyteller's imagination.

In this unit, you will meet two colorful characters from tall tales, two legendary figures from American history, and in a modern legend, a man who has a strange adventure in the middle of the night.

UNIT 3 ■ ABOUT TALL TALES & LEGENDS

In every culture, people develop stories, customs, and traditions that they want to pass on to others. These all become part of the culture's folklore. Folklore includes stories and fairy tales, as well as sayings, games, songs, and dances. People living in a particular area or belonging to the same group preserve important parts of their history through their folklore. Many authors have used folklore as a basis for their work. However, folklore begins with ordinary people, not professional writers.

Tall tales and legends are important parts of American folklore. America's folklore has great variety. As people from different cultures settled here, they brought their folklore with them. Some of their stories found their way into the American folklore that we all share today. For example, stories in African folklore told about the adventures of Trickster Rabbit, who was clever enough to outsmart his enemies. These stories traveled with Africans when they came to this country. Soon, Trickster Rabbit became B'rer Rabbit, a hero of many American folktales.

Folklore is part of oral literature. Most tall tales and legends, like fables and myths, were first told years ago and passed along by word of mouth.

Telling stories, rather than writing them down, has many advantages. When you tell someone a story, you want to keep their attention. You spend time on the more interesting parts of the story and change details to suit your audience. The story is told a little differently each time, depending on who you're telling it to. The basics of plot, character, and setting may stay the same, but the details change.

Tall tales are, first of all, stories. They all have a plot, characters, and setting. Very often, the setting and characters in American tall tales are drawn from the American frontier and the pioneers who settled there. The characters in these tales are larger than life. They tend to be taller, stronger, smarter, and braver than the usual person. For example, Joe Margarec could stir melted iron with his bare hands. Pecos Bill, another tall tale hero, rode a cyclone, creating Death Valley when he crashed as the storm "rained out." Tall tales show these characters using their great strengths to do things most of us could only imagine. In fact, tall tales are stories from the imagination. The ordinary rules of reason do not apply, much to the delight of the people who read or hear tall tales.

Legends are another part of America's folklore. Legends are stories told about real people, places, or events. For example, in some legends, the characters are people who actually lived, such as Daniel Boone and Davy Crockett, or who may have actually lived, such as John Henry. Other legends are built around a real event or a real place. When we listen to legends or read them, we know that some details have been included just to make a good story. We also know that some parts of the story are true.

America's legends and tall tales give people a chance to look back at their past. We'll probably always enjoy these entertaining stories.

This unit includes two tall tales. "Babe the Blue Ox," as told by Esther Shephard, is about Paul Bunyan's huge ox and the wonderful things this animal could do. Walter Blair shows what can happen if you put your mind to it in "Feboldson, Western Scientist." Two legends, "John Henry" and "Life and Adventures of Calamity Jane, by Herself," tell the stories of two real characters from America's past. John Henry was an African-American who helped build railways all along the Atlantic coast. Marthy (Martha)

Cannary Burk had adventures that earned her the name Calamity Jane. The final story in the unit, "The Phantom Hitchhiker" by Daniel Cohen, is a modern urban legend of a driver who picks up a ghostly hitchhiker.

New Eiffel Tower for Paris, **Tsing-Fang Chen**

Babe the Blue Ox
Esther Shephard

Esther Shephard
1891–1975

Literary Terms

dialect the speech of a particular region of a country, or of a certain group of people

exaggeration in literature, making something larger than it is; stretching the truth

folklore stories, customs, and traditions preserved and passed along by people in a particular area or group

tall tale a story from folklore that features exaggerated characters who have fantastic adventures

About the Author

Esther Shephard was born in Minneapolis, Minnesota, in 1891. The age of exploring the American frontier was drawing to a close. However, the spirit of this exciting time lives on in her works.

Her first book, *Paul Bunyan,* retold many of the **tall tales** about this famous imaginary hero of American **folklore.** Shephard drew from many sources to create one of the best collections of Paul Bunyan stories. She also wrote books based on other stories from folklore, including *The Cowherd and the Sky Maiden,* her telling of a Chinese legend that was later produced as an opera. Her other works include *Selected Poems,* a play called *Pierrette's Heart,* and *Walt Whitman's Prose.*

Shephard died in 1975 in San Francisco.

About the Selection

"Babe the Blue Ox" is a chapter in Esther Shephard's book, *Paul Bunyan.* The imaginary folk hero Paul Bunyan was a huge lumberjack (logger) who practiced his trade near the Great Lakes. In fact, according to one tall tale, his footsteps actually created the Great Lakes. Everything about Paul and his equally huge companion, Babe the Blue Ox, is larger than life: their size, their adventures, even their meals. This **exaggeration** is common in tall tales.

Shephard chose to tell this tall tale in **dialect,** meaning in the language of a particular region. To do this, she probably drew heavily on the speech she heard in the logging camps during her childhood in Minnesota. Dialect is more a feature of the way people speak than of the way they write. By writing in dialect, Shephard created a tall tale that sounds as if she is telling the story aloud.

BABE the Blue Ox

Paul Bunyan couldn't of done all the great loggin' he did if it hadn't been for Babe the Blue Ox. I believe I mentioned helpin' to take care of him for a couple of months when I first come to camp, and then I helped measure him once afterwards for a new **yoke** Ole had to make for him. He'd broke the one he had when Paul was doin' an extra quick job haulin' lumber for some millmen down in Muskegon one summer, and Ole had to make him a new one right away and so we had to take Babe's measurements.

I've forgot most of the other figgurs, but I remember he measured forty-two axhandles between the eyes—and a tobacco box—you could easy fit in a Star tobacco box after the last axhandle. That tobacco box was lost and we couldn't never take the measurements again, but I remember that's what it was. And he weighed accordin'. Though he never was weighed that I know of, for there never was any scales made that would of been big enough.

Paul told Ole he might as well make him a new log chain too while he was at it, for the way Babe pulled on 'em, in just about a month or two what had been a chain would be pulled out into a solid bar and wouldn't be any good. And so we measured him up for the chain too.

Babe was so long in the body, Paul used to have to carry a pair of field glasses around with him so as he could see what he was doin' with his hind feet.

One time Babe kicked one of the straw bosses in the head, so his brains all run out, but the cook happened to be handy

As you read, decide why this story is called a tall tale.

Dialect is the way people from a particular region speak. This narrator tends to drop the final 'g' from words like *loggin'* and *helpin'*. The sentences are long, strung together with *and,* the way someone might tell a story out loud.

Many of the exaggerations used in this tall tale concern Babe's great size.

yoke a wooden bar or frame that joins two oxen

Straw bosses were in charge of the work gangs. If the cook replaced this straw boss's brains with hotcake (pancake) batter, what does that say about the man's intelligence?

and he filled the hole up with hotcake batter and plastered it together again and he was just as good as ever. And right now, if I'm not mistaken, that boss is runnin' camp for the Bigham Loggin' Company of Virginia, Minnesota.

Babe was so big that every time they shod him they had to open up a new iron mine on Lake Superior, and one time when Ole the Blacksmith carried one of his shoes a mile and a half he sunk a foot and a half in solid rock at every step.

His color was blue—a fine, pretty, deep blue—and that's why he was called the Blue Ox—when you looked up at him the air even looked blue all around him. His nose was pretty near all black, but red on the inside, of course, and he had big white horns, curly on the upper section—about the upper third—and kind of darkish brown at the tip, and then the rest of him was all that same deep blue.

He didn't use to be always that blue color though. He was white when he was a calf. But he turned blue standin' out in the field for six days the first winter of the Blue Snow, and he never got white again. Winter and summer he was always the same, except probly in July—somewheres about the Fourth— he might maybe've been a shade lighter then.

I've heard some of the old loggers say that Paul brought him from Canada when he was a little calf a few days old— carried him across Lake Champlain in a sack so he wouldn't have to pay duty on him. But I'm thinkin' he must of been a mighty few days old at the time or Paul couldn't of done it, for he must of grown pretty fast when he got started, to grow the size he did. And then besides there's them that says Paul never had him at all when he was a little fellow like that, but that he was a pretty fair-sized calf when Paul got him. A fellow by the name of O'Regan down near Detroit is supposed to of had him first. O'Regan didn't have no more'n about forty acres or so under cultivation cleared on his farm and naturally that wasn't near enough to raise feed for Babe, and so he's supposed to of sold him the year of the Short Oats to Paul Bunyan. I don't know exactly. It's all before my time. When I went to work for Paul, and all the time I knowed him, the Ox was full grown.

Duty is the tax paid on items taken from one country to another.

Babe was as strong as the breath of a tote-teamster, Paul always said, and he could haul a whole section of timber with him at a time—Babe'd walk right off with it—the entire six hundred forty acres at one drag, and haul it down to the landin' and dump it in. That's why there ain't no section thirty-seven no more. Six trips a day six days a week just cleaned up a township, and the last load they never bothered to haul back Saturday night, but left it lay on the landin' to float away in the spring, and that's why there quit bein' section 37's, and you never see 'em on the maps no more.

A *tote-teamster* drove a wagonload of logs to the mill.

The only time I ever saw Babe on a job that seemed to nearly stump him—but that sure did look like it was goin' to for a while, though—durin' all the time I was with Paul was one time in Wisconsin, down on the St. Croix. And that was when he used him to pull the crooks out of eighteen miles of loggin' road; that came pretty near bein' more'n the Ox could handle. For generally anything that had two ends to it Babe could walk off with like nothin'.

But that road of all the crooked roads I ever see—and I've seen a good many in my day—was of all of 'em the crookedest, and it's no wonder it was pretty near too much

for Babe. You won't believe me when I tell you, but it's the truth, that in that stretch of eighteen miles that road doubled back on itself no less than sixteen times, and made four figure 8's, nine 3's, and four S's, yes, and one each of pretty near every other letter in the alphabet.

Of course the trouble with that road was, there was too much of it, and it didn't know what to do with itself, and so it's no wonder it got into mischief.

You'd be walkin' along it, all unsuspectin', and here of a sudden you'd see a coil of it layin' behind a tree, that you never know'd was there, and layin' there lookin' like it was ready to spring at you. The teamsters met themselves comin' back so many times while drivin' over it, that it begun to get on their nerves and we come near havin' a crazy-house in camp there. And so Paul made up his mind that that there road was goin' to be straightened out right then and there, and he went after it accordin'.

What he done was, he went out and told Bill to bring up the Blue Ox right away, and hitch him to the near end of the road.

Then he went up and spoke somethin' kind of low to Babe, and then afterwards he went out kind of to one side himself, and Babe laid hold, and then is the time it come pretty near breakin' the Ox in two, like I said.

Teamsters drive teams of horses.

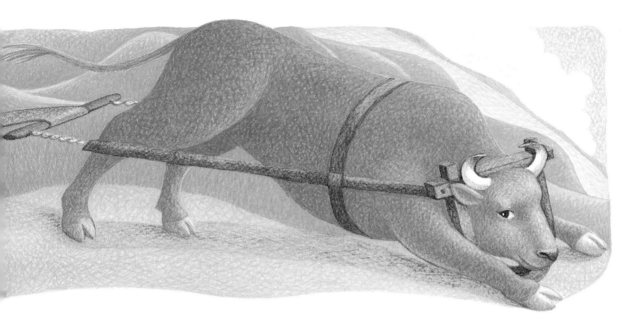

"Come on, Babe! Co-ome on, Ba-abe!" says Paul, and the Ox lays hold and pulls to the last ounce of him. If I live to be a hundred years old I never hope to see an ox pull like that again. His hind legs laid straight out behind him nearly, and his belly was almost down touchin' the ground.

It was one beeg job, as the Frenchmen would of said. And when the crooks finally was all out of that there piece of road, there was enough of it to lay around a round lake we skidded logs into that winter, and then there was enough left in the place where it'd been at first to reach from one end to the other.

I've always been glad I saw Babe on that pull, for it's the greatest thing I ever saw him do—in its way, anyway.

Bill, that took care of the Blue Ox, generally went by the name of Brimstone Bill at camp and the reason was because he got to be so awfully red-hot tempered. But I never blamed him, though. Havin' that Ox to take care of was enough to make a sinner out of the best fellow that ever lived. Of all the scrapin' and haulin' you'd have to do to keep him lookin' anywheres near **respectable** even, no one would ever think.

And the way he ate—it took two men just to pick the balin' wire out of his teeth at mealtimes. Four ton of grain wasn't nothin' for Babe to get away with at a single meal, and

Brimstone is sulfur. Why is this a good nickname for Bill?

Baling wire holds the bales of hay together.

respectable decent; proper; fit to be seen

for the hay—I can't mention quantities, but I know they said at first, before he got Windy Knight onto cuttin' it up for nails to use in puttin' on the cook-house roof, Paul used to have to move the camp every two weeks to get away from the mess of haywire that got collected where Babe ate his dinner. And as for cleanin' the barn and haulin' the manure away—

I remember one night in our bunkhouse as plain as if it'd been yesterday. I can see it all again just like it was then. That was one time afterwards, when we was loggin' down in Wisconsin.

There was a new fellow just come to camp that day, a kind of college fellow that'd come to the woods for his health, and we was all sittin' around the stove that night spinnin' yarns like we almost always done of an evenin' while our socks was dryin'. I was over on one end, and to each side of me was Joe Stiles, and Pat O'Henry—it's funny how I remember it all—and a fellow by the name of Horn, and Big Gus, and a number of others that I don't **recollect** now, and over on the other end opposite me was Brimstone Bill, and up by me was this new fellow, but kind of a little to the side.

Well, quite a number of stories had been told, and some of 'em had been about the Blue Ox and different experiences men'd had with him different times and how the manure used to pile up, and pretty soon that there college chap begun to tell a story he said it reminded him of—one of them there old ancient Greek stories, he said it was, about Herukles cleanin' the Augaen stables, that was one of twelve other hard jobs he'd been set to do by the king he was workin' for at the time, to get his daughter or somethin' like that. He was goin' at it kind of fancy, describin' how the stables hadn't been cleaned for some time, and what a condition they was in as a **consequence**, and what a strong man Herukles was, and how he adopted the plan of turnin' the river right through the stables and so washin' the manure away that way, and goin' on describin' how it was all done. And how the water come through and floated the manure all up on top of the river, and

Spinnin' yarns means telling tall tales.

The "college fellow" is telling about one of the twelve labors of the Greek hero Herakles (Hercules). Later, Brimstone Bill will call him "Herik Lees."

consequence a result or effect   **recollect** to remember

how there was enough of it to spread over a whole valley, and then how the manure rolled up in waves again in the river when it got to where it was swifter—and it was a pretty good story and he was quite a talker too, that young fellow was, and he had all the men listenin' to him.

Well, all the time old Brimstone Bill he sat there takin' it all in, and I could see by the way his jaw was workin' on his tobacco that he was gettin' pretty riled. Everythin' had been quiet while the young fellow was tellin' the story, and some of us was smokin', some of us enjoyin' a little fresh Star or Peerless maybe and spittin' in the sandbox occasionally which was gettin' pretty wet by this time, and there wasn't no sound at all except the occasional sizzle when somebody hit the stove, or the movin' of a bench when somebody's foot or sock would get too near the fire, and the man's voice goin' along describin' about this Herukles and how great he was and how fine the stables looked when he got through with 'em, when all at once Brimstone Bill he busted right into him:

"You shut your blamed mouth about that Herik Lees of yourn," he says. "I guess if your Herik Lees had had the job I've got for a few days, he wouldn't of done it so easy or talked so smart, you young Smart Alec, you—" and then a long string of 'em the way Bill could roll 'em off when he got mad—I never heard any much better'n him—they said he could keep goin' for a good half hour and never repeat the same word twice—but I wouldn't give much for a lumberjack who couldn't roll off a few dozen straight—specially if he's worked with cattle—and all the time he was gettin' madder'n madder till he was fairly sizzlin' he was so mad. "I guess if that Mr. Lees had had Babe to take care of he wouldn't of done it so easy. Tell him he can trade jobs with me for a spell if he wants to, and see how he likes it. I guess if he'd of had to use his back on them one hundred and fifty jacks to jack up the barn the way I got to do he wouldn't of had enough strength left in him to brag so much about it. I just got through raisin' it another sixty foot this afternoon. When this job started we was workin' on the level, and now already Babe's barn is up sixteen hundred foot. I'd like to see the river that could wash

Riled means angry.

Notice all the funny details in this long sentence beginning "Everythin' had been quiet…"

Bill is especially good at rolling off a string of curses and not repeating himself once.

Babe produces so much manure that his barn has to be jacked up higher and higher.

that pile of manure away, and you can just tell that Herik Lees to come on and try it if he wants to. And if he can't, why, then you can just shut up about it. I've walked the old Ox and cleaned 'im and doctored 'im and rubbed 'im ever since he was first invented, and I know what it is, and I ain't goin' to sit here and let you tell me about any Mr. Lees or any other blankety blank liar that don't know what he's talkin' about tellin' about cleanin' barns—not if I know it." And at it he goes again blankety blank blank all the way out through the door, and slams it behind him so the whole bunkhouse shook, and the stranger he sits there and don't know hardly what to make of it. Till I kind of explained to him afterwards before we turned in, and we all, the rest of 'em too, told him not to mind about Bill, for he couldn't hardly help it. After he'd been in camp a few days he'd know. You couldn't hardly blame Bill for bein' **aggravated**—used to be a real good-natured man, and he wasn't so bad even that time I was helpin' him, but the Ox was too much for any man, no matter who.

And so I never held it against Bill much myself. He was fond of Babe too and made quite a pet of him, more so than the rest of us even, and we all did.

"I been with the beast a good long time," he used to say, "and I know the **cantankerous** old reptile most the same's if I had been through him with a

aggravated annoyed; upset

cantankerous hard to deal with

lantern. I know how to do for 'im, and all his little ways and all, and I don't want anybody else botherin' round and messin' things up for me. I can take care of 'im all right. All I want is to be let alone."

Afterwards when Paul got his hay farm down in Wisconsin it made it easier for Bill. Then we'd just rake the hay up in windrows and let it freeze that way layin' out across the fields, and in the winter they'd haul it in one end first in the stable and cut it up in chunks for Babe, just pullin' it up a little each time. That way you could get away from the nuisance of the haywire, and didn't have that to bother with.

Windrows are rows of hay raked up to dry before being baled or stored.

In any of his small camps Paul couldn't never keep Babe but a day or so at a time, because it took the tote-teamsters a year to haul a day's feed for him.

Babe was a kind of playful fellow too. Sometimes he'd step in a river and lay down there and so make the water rise and leave a boom of logs that was below there up high and dry, and again sometimes he'd step on a ridge makin' a lakeshore maybe, and smash it down and let out the water to flood a river and drown out some low water drive.

A *boom* is a chain, cable, or line of connected floating logs. A *drive* is floating logs being guided downstream to a mill.

Around the camp he'd play with almost any of us who was willin' to play with him after the day's work. We used to feed him hotcakes sometimes and he got awful fond of 'em. Them big ones we made on the big griddle we used to fold up in quarters and put clover hay in between and give it to him for a sandwich and he liked that powerful well. But we shouldn't of done it, I know that now. I've thought many times since, it's too bad, for that's what got him started, and once started he seemed he couldn't never stop. Poor old Babe. It proved to be the death of him at last. It was all wrong of us, but of course we didn't think about it then, and had no notion what it would lead to in the end.

Paul Bunyan was sure fond of his Ox, and mighty proud of him too, as he'd a right to be.

"Be faithful" he used to say to him low under his breath as he walked along beside him. "Be faithful, my Babe. Faithful."

Babe the Blue Ox
Esther Shephard

Directions Write the answers to these questions using complete sentences.

Comprehension: Identifying Facts

1. What kind of work does Paul Bunyan do?

2. Babe gets measured once but can't be measured again. Why not?

3. Why does Paul Bunyan have to carry a pair of field glasses (binoculars) around with him when he works with Babe?

4. What has to happen every time they shod Babe (make new shoes for him)?

5. How does Babe get his blue color?

6. How does Paul Bunyan get Babe across Lake Champlain?

7. What job nearly defeats Babe?

8. Why does Paul Bunyan have to move his camp so often?

9. What story does the "college fellow" tell the other loggers?

10. What is Bill's job at camp?

Comprehension: Understanding Main Ideas

11. What happens when Ole the Blacksmith carries one of Babe's shoes a mile and a half? Why does it happen?

12. What are the different stories about the age Babe was when Paul Bunyan got him?

13. Why aren't there any more timber section 37's?

14. What is the trouble with the crooked logging road? Why is it so crooked?

15. Why do the loggers "come near havin' a crazy-house in camp" before Babe straightens the logging road?

16. How does Babe get the crooks out of the road?

17. Why does the college student's story make Brimstone Bill so angry?

18. Why does Bill need to jack up Babe's barn?

19. How do the narrator and the other loggers feel about Babe?

20. Why is it easier for Bill once Paul Bunyan gets his hay farm in Wisconsin?

Understanding Literature: Exaggeration

The storytellers who first created many of America's tall tales knew the value of exaggeration. As they told their yarns, each one tried to outdo the others by coming up with characters and plots that were more and more exaggerated. Characters did not just have breakfast: they ate so much and so fast that they created a tornado that brought down every single tree within twenty miles.

Exaggeration is an important part of the humor in all tall tales. Their characters, plots, and sometimes even settings are often stretched way beyond what could be true. By exaggerating, writers push the limits of truth to create a comic effect. For example, when the narrator talks about a curving road, he reports that "in that stretch of eighteen miles that road doubled back on itself no less than sixteen times, and made four figure 8's, nine 3's, and four S's, yes, and one each of pretty near every other letter in the alphabet." The piling on of one exaggeration after another all through the tall tale keeps us reading and laughing.

21. In your own words, what is exaggeration?

22. Why do storytellers and authors use exaggeration?

23. Give an example of a job that Babe and Paul Bunyan did that shows how exaggeration is used in this tall tale.

24. Is Brimstone Bill an exaggerated character? Explain your thinking.

25. Give an example of exaggeration about something in your own life.

Critical Thinking

26. Why do you think the storyteller's sentences get longer when he reaches especially exciting parts of his tale?

27. In what ways is the myth of "Herukles" told by the college student similar to the tall tales about Babe the Blue Ox? What are some differences between myths and tall tales?

28. Do you think people like Paul Bunyan, Ole the Blacksmith, and Brimstone Bill ever existed? Explain your thinking.

29. What do you learn in this story about logging and the people who work in the industry?

30. Why do you think that feeding Babe hotcakes "proved to be the death of him at last"?

Writing on Your Own Imagine that you are a logger in one of Paul Bunyan's camps. You have just seen Babe. Write a brief description of the Blue Ox, using exaggeration.

Walter Blair

1900–1992

About the Author

Walter Blair was born in Spokane, Washington, and lived through most of the twentieth century. He got to know a number of great storytellers. He listened eagerly to their jokes, yarns, and tall tales.

Wherever he went, Blair collected stories. When he went off to graduate school, all these tales went with him. He began to look at these stories as a scholar would, trying to see how they related to each other and what they showed about America. In fact, he became one of the first Americans to study American humor in a scholarly way.

As he worked, he became a skilled storyteller himself. Walter Blair was especially proud of two of his books: *Davy Crockett: Truth and Legend* and *Tall Tale America*. A special version of *Tall Tale America* was sent by the U. S. Armed Services to military people serving around the world. The book was also chosen as the only example of folklore in the White House Presidential Library.

About the Selection

The story of Febold Feboldson is an **excerpt** from Walter Blair's book *Tall Tale America*. Febold is an imaginary character, a no-nonsense Nebraska farmer. Stories about Febold first appeared in writing in a Nebraska newspaper in 1920. In this selection, Walter Blair's **characterization** of this folk hero is as an inventor whose uncommon sense often made sense.

Febold has certain **character traits** that make him what he is. He always thinks about things and behaves in the same way, no matter what is happening around him. As with real people, a character's traits do not often change, particularly in tall tales. In writing about Febold, Walter Blair had to be true to the character's traits. He could not, for example, portray him as a man who acted first and thought about it later.

Feboldson,
Western Scientist

Nebraska, at the start, was big enough so great hunks could be chopped off and handed over to Colorado, Dakota and Idaho without anybody in Nebraska getting worried. After these gifts had been passed out, it was seen that every dratted mountain in the whole vicinity had been handed over to some other state. Result was that the whole of Nebraska was nothing but valleys, tableland and rolling prairies, all with a southwestern **exposure**. This meant that all the weather and all the wild life that came along had plenty of room to work and play in without natural let or **hindrance**.

Febold Feboldson settled down out there about the time the weather began to feel its strength. He got his farm and his family started, took on the job of Indian Agent, and then started his great work as a natural scientist.

One of the first things he had to cope with was the Great Fog that came along the year of the Great Heat. The Great Heat was bad enough, Heaven knows. Looking back, many people said that one of the most **fiendish** things about it was the way the **mercury** in thermometers everywhere shot up the tubes and spewed out the top like a fountain, so people couldn't *tell* how hot it was. Over in Saline County, though, one fellow with a big thermometer that'd take two hundred

Like all tall tales, this one creates humor by using exaggeration. Look for examples as you read.

Tableland is a broad, level, raised area.

A *let* is a block, or something that gets in the way.

Febold, as a *natural scientist*, studies nature. As you read, notice his character traits.

exposure a position with respect to weather or compass points

fiendish devilish, evil

hindrance something that gets in the way

mercury a heavy, silver-white metal that is liquid at ordinary temperatures

and thirty-two degrees, stood by it day and night with a cake of ice, bound and determined to save his thermometer. And he said the heat never went below a hundred and fifty degrees all those weeks, leastwise when he could see the thermometer with the help either of the sun, the moon or a lantern.

That was bad enough, as you can imagine. But one day Febold looked at the sky, fiddled around with some of his instruments, and made a horrible discovery. "That's bad," he said. "Got to do something **drastic**."

What he did was send a cable to London that read this way: "Send along a gross of your fanciest fog-cutters soon as possible, C.O.D. Febold Feboldson."

A gross is twelve dozen. C.O.D. means cash on delivery.

Being a scientist, you see, Febold had figured out right away what a horrible time Nebraska was in for. He told Mrs. Feboldson about the steps he'd taken that very evening while they were sitting in the sitting room trying to cool off a bit.

"Cabled over to London today for a gross of fog-cutters," he said.

Mrs. Feboldson's eyes stuck out so far they appeared to be on stems. "Fog-cutters?" she said, dazed-like.

"Yes, fog-cutters, Mother," he said. "You see, they have the thickest fogs in London that they have anywhere except on the ocean. And they're inventive there, you know—a right smart race. So they've doubtless got the best fog-cutters you can find anywhere."

"Of course, Febold, but I can't see as we need any fog-cutters. What would we do with them?"

"Cut the fog."

"It's been hot enough to make me wish we could cut the heat," says Mrs. Feboldson. "But if you look out the window there, you'll notice there's no fog—nothing but level land and sky, as far as you can look, with a hundred thousand heat-waves, just what you usually see out that living room window."

"Some unusual things out there, too," says Febold. "What's that dark gray thing up in the sky yonder—a dark gray thing no bigger than a man's hand?"

drastic severe

"Why!" Mrs. Feboldson said. "It's a cloud—first one I've seen since the Great Heat started pestering us. Looks as if it might be a rain cloud."

Febold nodded. "How about that little toe of yours that warns you when we're to have rain? How's it feel?"

Mrs. Feboldson noticed her toe for a minute, then, "I'll swan, it's a-twitching," she told him.

I'll swan means I declare.

"I've fiddled around with my **barometers**, looked at the moon, and listened to the bullfrogs, and they all say the same thing," Febold said. "What's more, they say it's going to be a regular Bible storm—forty days and forty nights. Oh, we'll need those fog-cutters all right, Mother."

"Do they cut rain as well as fogs?"

"No, they just cut fogs, I reckon. But we'll need them. You'll see. Let's turn in."

In the Bible, the flood for which Noah builds his ark lasts forty days and forty nights.

Along toward morning, there was the beginning of that horrible sound that people in Nebraska (and parts of the neighboring territories) kept nearly being driven crazy by for the next forty days and forty nights. People that tried to describe it later said it was like the sound of steam shooting out of three million tea-kettles at once—big kettles, too, boiling like fury—just one long burbling hiss.

As soon as Febold came in from milking, Mrs. Feboldson asked him what that horrible noise was.

"It's working the way I figured it would," he said. "The rain's coming down like a dribbled ocean. But up there ten miles or so, it's spattering down on the hot air that was piled up around here by the Great Heat. As soon as the rain hits the hot air, it turns to steam and makes that hissing noise. The steam will be the fog."

"But the steam's staying up there," Mrs. Feboldson said. "Out the window, all you can see is level land and sky as far as you can look, same as usual, only gray because there's no sun today."

barometer an instrument for measuring air pressure

"Pretty soon, Mother, the rain will hammer the fog down to the ground, and what'll pile up will be the fog. Hope those Englishmen hurry up with those fog-cutters. Things are going to be bad."

Febold was right, as usual. There was a little fog at first, then more and more of it, until taking a walk alone was impossible. At least two people would be needed so one could part the fog and hold it apart while the other one walked through. Cattle didn't have to be watered, because they could drink the fog. But the dirt farmers were scared speechless, because their crops were in a bad way. You see, some of the seeds had figured that the closest sunshine was in China, and had started growing downward.

Around Thanksgiving, when the fog was so thick that portions had turned to three hundred thousand gallons of slush, both farmers and stockmen by the hundreds had about decided to pull out of Nebraska. "Too crowded by this danged fog," they said. "We need elbow room."

It was when things had come to this kind of a pass that the fog-cutters arrived, C.O.D. Febold used one of them to cut red tape so he could pay for them. Then he started to use them on the fog—to slice it into big neat strips. Soon, when he had great piles of these strips, it was needful that he figure out where to put them.

"Can't leave them lying out there on the fields," he told Mrs. Feboldson, "or all the seeds will keep growing downward. I know! I'll lay them out along the roads."

Upshot was that he put those fog strips end to end all along the dirt roads of Nebraska. And before long some of the slush-fog seeped down, and some got so covered with dust that nobody could see where Febold had buried the Great Fog.

Only one serious bad result came of the whole thing. Every spring, when the sun begins to shine and the thaw comes, some of this old fog seeps up on the dirt roads, turning them into the gooiest mess you ever got stuck in.

And if you don't believe this, just go out to Nebraska some spring and try driving on one of those roads.

To cut red tape means to get around rules that slow things up.

Upshot means the final result.

What do you learn about the setting—Nebraska—in this tall tale?

Feboldson, Western Scientist
Walter Blair

Directions Write the answers to these questions using complete sentences.

Comprehension: Identifying Facts

1. What is Febold Feboldson's "great work"?

2. What does Febold order from London?

3. What does Febold do with the strips of fog he cuts?

Comprehension: Understanding Main Ideas

4. How does Febold know it is going to rain?

5. For which natural events and facts of geography does this tall tale give imaginative explanations?

6. What is the "one serious bad result" of Febold's actions?

Understanding Literature: Character Trait

Character traits—ways of behaving, talking, or thinking—show a person's nature. These traits show readers how to see a character's importance in the setting and plot of a story.

Writers do not usually list character traits. Instead, they let characters speak and act for themselves. By reading carefully, we get to know these characters through what they say and do.

When writers use flat characters in a story, as in fables, we learn only one or two of the characters' traits. When writers create round characters, they give readers many clues about the traits of each character. By understanding a character's traits, readers gain a better understanding of the story as a whole.

7. How are flat and round characters different in terms of character traits?

8. What adjectives would you use to describe Febold's character traits?

Critical Thinking

9. Do you think Febold Feboldson is a true scientist? Support your opinion with evidence from the story.

10. Why do you think Walter Blair relates so many conversations between Febold and his wife? What does their conversation tell us about both characters?

Writing on Your Own What if Febold Feboldson saw Babe the Blue Ox? Write a brief skit about what you think might happen.

About the Author

No one knows who first told the story of John Henry, the powerful African-American steel driver. His **legend** began just after the Civil War near the small town of Talcott, West Virginia. There, around 1870, the Chesapeake and Ohio Railroad was building a tunnel straight through a mountain. The work was done by pairs of men, a steel driver and a shaker. The shaker would hold a drill against the rock. The steel driver would strike the drill with a hammer. Then the shaker would turn the drill slightly and the driver would hit it again. When they had drilled a large enough hole, they placed gunpowder in it and blew apart the rock. It took a long time to make progress. When the steam driver machine was invented, some thought it could do a better job of drilling through rock. But John Henry, who may have been an actual person, did not agree.

Some legends say John Henry was born with a hammer in his hand. Some say he was born all grown up—standing over eight feet tall. Others say he had the strength of thirty men. But all agree that John Henry was a hard-working man.

About the Selection

This **ballad** presents one version of the legend of John Henry. It tells about a contest between man and machine.

A ballad is a simple song that usually uses rhyming words, or words with similar sounds. Ballads often include words that are repeated at the end of each section or **stanza**. These repeated words are called a **refrain**. Ballads about John Henry have been sung, read, spoken, and enjoyed for well over a century.

Literary Terms

ballad a form of poetry that tells a story, passed from person to person, often as a simple song with rhyming words and a refrain

legend a story from folklore that features characters who actually lived, or real events or places

refrain repeated words or phrases that create a mood or give importance to something

stanza a group of lines that form a unit in a poem

John Henry

As you read, see what character traits make John Henry the hero of a legend.

When John Henry was a little tiny baby
Sitting on his mama's knee,
He picked up a hammer and a little piece of steel
Saying, "Hammer's going to be the death of me, Lord, Lord,
5   Hammer's going to be the death of me."

John Henry was a man just six feet high,
Nearly two feet and a half across his breast.
He'd hammer with a nine-pound hammer all day

Notice the refrain at the end of each stanza of the ballad. What is the effect of each one?

And never get tired and want to rest, Lord, Lord,
10   And never get tired and want to rest.

John Henry went up on the mountain
And he looked one eye straight up its side.
The mountain was so tall and John Henry was so small,
He laid down his hammer and he cried, "Lord, Lord,"
15   He laid down his hammer and he cried.

John Henry said to his captain,

John Henry's *captain* was his boss.

"Captain, you go to town,
Bring me back a TWELVE-pound hammer, please,
And I'll beat that steam drill down, Lord, Lord,
20   I'll beat that steam drill down."

The captain said to John Henry,
"I believe this mountain's sinking in."
But John Henry said, "Captain, just you stand aside—
It's nothing but my hammer catching wind, Lord, Lord,
25   It's nothing but my hammer catching wind."

John Henry's *shaker* held the drill and gave it a twist by hand after each blow of the steel driver's hammer.

John Henry said to his shaker,
"Shaker, boy, you better start to pray,
'Cause if my TWELVE-pound hammer miss that little piece of steel,
Tomorrow'll be your burying day, Lord, Lord,
30   Tomorrow'll be your burying day."

John Henry said to his captain,
"A man is nothing but a man,
But before I let your steam drill beat me down,
I'd die with this hammer in my hand, Lord, Lord,
35   I'd die with this hammer in my hand."

The man that invented the steam drill,
He figured he was mighty high and fine,
But John Henry sunk the steel down fourteen feet
While the steam drill only made nine, Lord, Lord,
40   The steam drill only made nine.

John Henry hammered on the right-hand side,
Steam drill kept driving on the left.
John Henry beat that steam drill down,
But he hammered his poor heart to death, Lord, Lord,
45   He hammered his poor heart to death.

Well, they carried John Henry down the tunnel
And they laid his body in the sand.
Now every woman riding on a C and O train
Says, "There lies my steel-driving man, Lord, Lord,
50   There lies my steel-driving man."

"C and O" refers to the Chesapeake and Ohio Railroad.

John Henry
Anonymous

Directions Write the answers to these questions using complete sentences.

Comprehension: Identifying Facts

1. As a child, what does John Henry say is going to cause his death?

2. What does John Henry think he can do with a twelve-pound hammer?

3. Who wins the contest: John Henry, or the steam drill?

Comprehension: Understanding Main Ideas

4. How does John Henry feel about the steam drill?

5. Why do you think John Henry dies? Explain your reasoning.

6. Why do you think John Henry has become an American folk hero?

Understanding Literature: Refrain

Ballads are part of the oral literature of a culture. People would learn a ballad by hearing it sung. In turn, they would sing the ballad to others. Like some stories and poems, ballads often include refrains, or words and sentences that are repeated. By repeating, the people who passed these works on to others did two things. First, they helped their audience pay attention to certain details of the story they were telling. Second, repeating made it easier for people to remember the stories.

7. What word, repeated twice, is part of each refrain in the ballad of John Henry? What is the effect of repeating that word?

8. What details of the story do the refrains in this ballad call attention to?

Critical Thinking

9. Recently, the U.S. Postal Service issued a stamp honoring John Henry. Suggest some other ways Americans today could honor his courage and hard work.

10. Imagine that you are nearby when John Henry takes up the captain's challenge to try his strength against the steam drill. Which one would you pick to be the winner? Why?

Writing on Your Own Use the Internet to find out more about the town of Talcott, West Virginia, and the Big Bend Tunnel there. Share your information in a short report for your classmates or for those with whom you correspond through e-mail.

Life and Adventures of Calamity Jane, By Herself
Marthy (Martha) Cannary Burk

Marthy Cannary Burk
"Calamity Jane"
1852–1903

Literary Terms

anecdote a short account of an interesting event in someone's life

autobiography the story of a person's life, written by that person

pamphlet a short printed essay with no cover, or with a paper cover

About the Author

Calamity Jane is a legendary figure of the American West. She was born in Princeton, Missouri, as Marthy Jane Cannary, though some sources call her "Martha." According to her own accounts, Calamity Jane moved west on a wagon train with her family. Her mother died during the trip, and her father soon afterward. She was on her own for most of her life, traveling from Montana to Wyoming and South Dakota. In 1876 Calamity Jane appeared in Deadwood, South Dakota, dressed in men's clothes, and bragged about her adventures as a pony-express rider and army scout. She later married Clinton Burk and, she says, had a child.

Calamity Jane toured with the Wild West shows from 1895 to 1901. These shows featured characters of the old West, including Wild Bill Hickock. During the shows, performers showed off their sharpshooting and expert horseback riding skills. Calamity Jane later returned to Deadwood, the territory she loved. At her request, she is buried there next to Wild Bill Hickock.

About the Selection

In "Life and Adventures of Calamity Jane, by Herself," the author tells how she became Calamity Jane. Claiming to have written this **pamphlet** herself, she sold copies for as little as a dime to support herself. Very few copies of the work exist today.

Although it is supposed to be an **autobiography**—the story of a person's life written by that person—no one really knows if the **anecdotes** it contains are true. Some say that Calamity Jane did not even write this pamphlet herself. They claim it was written by Mrs. Josephine Black.

Whether true or not, the pamphlet paints a lively picture of what it was like to be a woman—a most unusual woman—at this time in the American West.

Life and Adventures of Calamity Jane, by Herself

Missourri is a misspelling of Missouri. *Marthy* may also be a misspelling of Martha.

My maiden name was Marthy Cannary. I was born in Princeton, Missourri, May 1st, 1852. Father and mother were natives of Ohio. I had two brothers and three sisters, I being the oldest of the children. As a child I always had a fondness for adventure and out-door exercise and especial fondness for horses which I began to ride at an early age and continued to do so until I became an expert rider being able to ride the most vicious and stubborn of horses, in fact the greater portion of my life in early times was spent in this manner.

In an autobiography, we usually get a detailed picture of the author, who is also the main character. As you read, decide what kind of a person Calamity Jane was—or, at least, what kind of person she wants us to think she was. How did she think of herself?

In 1865 we **emigrated** from our homes in Missourri by the overland route to Virginia City, Montana, taking five months to make the journey. While on the way the greater portion of my time was spent in hunting along with the men and hunters of the party, in fact I was at all times with the men when there was excitement and adventures to be had. By the time we reached Virginia City I was considered a remarkable good shot and a fearless rider for a girl of my age. I remember many **occurrences** on the journey from Missourri to Montana. Many times in crossing the mountains the conditions of the trail were so bad that we frequently had to lower the wagons over ledges by hand with ropes for they were so rough and rugged that horses were of no use. We also had many exciting times fording

emigrate to leave one's native land

occurrence a happening or event

Calamity Jane on horseback, 1901

streams for many of the streams in our way were noted for quicksands and boggy places, where, unless we were very careful, we would have lost horses and all. Then we had many dangers to **encounter** in the way of streams swelling on account of heavy rains. On occasions of that kind the men would usually select the best places to cross the streams, myself on more than one occasion have mounted my pony and swam across the stream several times merely to amuse myself and have had many narrow escapes from having both myself and pony washed away to certain death, but as the pioneers of those days had plenty of courage we **overcame** all **obstacles** and reached Virginia City in safety.

Mother died at Black Foot, Montana, 1866, where we buried her. I left Montana in Spring of 1866, for Utah, arriving

As you read the anecdotes in this autobiography, decide which you think might have been true. Which do you think the author either made up or greatly exaggerated?

encounter to meet or come upon

obstacle something that gets in the way

overcome to win against or get the better of

at Salt Lake city during the summer. Remained in Utah until 1867, where my father died, then went to Fort Bridger, Wyoming Territory, where we arrived May 1, 1868, then went to Piedmont, Wyoming, with U.P. Railway. Joined General Custer as a scout at Fort Russell, Wyoming, in 1870, and started for Arizona for the Indian Campaign. Up to this time I had always worn the costume of my sex. When I joined Custer I donned the uniform of a soldier. It was a bit awkward at first but I soon got to be perfectly at home in men's clothes.

Was in Arizona up to the winter of 1871 and during that time I had a great many adventures with the Indians, for as a scout I had a great many dangerous missions to perform and while I was in many close places always succeeded in getting away safely for by this time I was considered the most reckless and daring rider and one of the best shots in the western country.

After that campaign I returned to Fort Sanders, Wyoming, remained there until spring of 1872, when we were ordered out to the Muscle Shell or Nursey Pursey Indian outbreak. In that war Generals Custer, Miles, Terry and Crook were all engaged. This campaign lasted until fall of 1873.

It was during this campaign that I was christened Calamity Jane. It was on Goose Creek, Wyoming, where the town of Sheridan is now located. Capt. Egan was in command of the Post. We were ordered out to **quell** an uprising of the Indians, and were out for several days, had numerous **skirmishes** during which six of the soldiers were killed and several severely wounded. When on returning to the Post we were **ambushed** about a mile and a half from our destination. When fired upon Capt. Egan was shot. I was riding in advance and on hearing the firing turned in my saddle and saw the Captain reeling in his saddle as though about to fall. I turned my horse and galloped back with all haste to his side and got there in time to catch him as he was falling. I lifted him onto my horse in front of me and succeeded in getting him safely to the Fort. Capt. Egan on recovering, laughingly

ambush to attack by surprise   **quell** to quiet or put down   **skirmish** a small battle

said: "I name you Calamity Jane, the heroine of the plains." I have **borne** that name up to the present time. We were afterwards ordered to Fort Custer, where Custer city now stands, where we arrived in the spring of 1874; remained around Fort Custer all summer and were ordered to Fort Russell in fall of 1874, where we remained until spring of 1875; was then ordered to the Black Hills to protect miners, as that country was controlled by the Sioux Indians and the government had to send the soldiers to protect the lives of the miners and settlers in that section. Remained there until fall of 1875 and wintered at Fort Laramie. In spring of 1876, we were ordered north with General Crook to join Gen'ls Miles, Terry and Custer at Big Horn river. During this march I swam the Platte river at Fort Fetterman as I was the bearer of important **dispatches**. I had a ninety mile ride to make, being wet and cold, I contracted a severe illness and was sent back in Gen. Crook's ambulance to Fort Fetterman where I laid in the hospital for fourteen days. When able to ride I started for Fort Laramie where I met Wm. Hickock, better known as Wild Bill, and we started for Deadwood, where we arrived about June.

During the month of June I acted as a pony express rider carrying the U.S. mail between Deadwood and Custer, a distance of fifty miles, over one of the roughest trails in the Black Hills country. As many of the riders before me had been held up and robbed of their packages, mail and money that they carried, for that was the only means of getting mail and money between these points. It was considered the most dangerous route in the Hills, but as my reputation as a rider and quick shot was well known, I was **molested** very little, for the toll gatherers looked on me as being a good fellow, and they knew that I never missed my mark. I made the round trip every two days which was considered pretty good riding in that country. Remained around Deadwood all that summer

Calamity Jane, General Crook's Scout, 1895

James Butler (Wild Bill) Hickock, born in Illinois in 1837, was a scout, stagecoach driver, and frontier marshall in Kansas. His shootouts with various outlaws made him a legend.

---

borne carried   **dispatch** a message   **molest** to bother or harm

visiting all the camps within an area of one hundred miles. My friend, Wild Bill, remained in Deadwood during the summer with the **exception** of occasional visits to the camps. On the 2nd of August, while setting at a gambling table in the Bell Union saloon, in Deadwood, he was shot in the back of the head by the **notorious** Jack McCall, a desperado. I was in Deadwood at the time and on hearing of the killing made my way at once to the scene of the shooting and found that my friend had been killed by McCall. I at once started to look for the **assassin** and found him at Shurdy's butcher shop and grabbed a meat cleaver and made him throw up his hands; through the excitement on hearing of Bill's death, having left my weapons on the post of my bed. He was then taken to a log cabin and locked up, well secured as every one thought, but he got away and was afterwards caught at Fagan's ranch on Horse Creek, on the old Cheyenne road and was then taken to Yankton, Dak., where he was tried, sentenced and hung.

I remained around Deadwood locating claims, going from camp to camp until the spring of 1877, where one morning, I saddled my horse and rode towards Crook city. I had gone about twelve miles from Deadwood, at the mouth of Whitewood creek, when I met the overland mail running from Cheyenne to Deadwood. The horses on a run, about two hundred yards from the station; upon looking closely I saw they were **pursued** by Indians. The horses ran to the barn as was their custom. As the horses stopped I rode along side of the coach and found the driver John Slaughter, lying face downwards in the boot of the stage, he having been shot by the Indians. When the stage got to the station the Indians hid in the bushes. I immediately removed all baggage from the coach except the mail. I then took the driver's seat and with all **haste** drove to Deadwood, carrying the six passengers and the dead driver.

A *desperado* is a bandit, or outlaw.

The Black Hills are in southwest South Dakota and northeast Wyoming. Gold mining began there in 1874; Calamity Jane refers to the *camps* and *claims* of the gold prospectors. Deadwood is in present-day South Dakota.

assassin a killer

exception something that is left out

haste speed

notorious well-known, especially for something bad

pursue to chase

Deadwood, South
Dakota, 1876

I left Deadwood in the fall of 1877, and went to Bear Butte Creek with the 7th **Cavalry**. During the fall and winter we built Fort Meade and the town of Sturgis. In 1878 I left the command and went to Rapid city and put in the year prospecting.

In 1879 I went to Fort Pierre and drove trains from Rapid city to Fort Pierre for Frank Witc then drove teams from Fort Pierce to Sturgis for Fred. Evans. This teaming was done with oxen as they were better fitted for the work than horses, owing to the rough nature of the country.

In 1881 I went to Wyoming and returned in 1882 to Miles city and took up a ranch on the Yellow Stone, raising stock and cattle, also kept a way side inn, where the weary traveler could be **accommodated** with food, drink, or trouble if he looked for it. Left the ranch in 1883, went to California, going through the States and territories, reached Ogden the **latter** part of 1883,

Setting describes both place and time. What does Calamity Jane tell us about her times and about the places she lived in?

accommodate to supply someone's needs; to help out

cavalry soldiers on horseback

latter more recent; toward the end

Calamity Jane visits the grave of Wild Bill Hickock.

What would you say is the *temper*—or usual state of mind and feeling—of this baby's mother, Calamity Jane?

and San Francisco in 1884. Left San Francisco in the summer of 1884 for Texas, stopping at Fort Yuma, Arizona, the hottest spot in the United States. Stopping at all points of interest until I reached El Paso in the fall. While in El Paso, I met Mr. Clinton Burk, a native of Texas, who I married in August 1885. As I thought I had travelled through life long enough alone and thought it was about time to take a partner for the rest of my days. We remained in Texas leading a quiet home life until 1889. On October 28th, 1887, I became the mother of a girl baby, the very image of its father, at least that is what he said, but who has the temper of its mother.

When we left Texas we went to Boulder, Colo., where we kept a hotel until 1893, after which we travelled through Wyoming, Montana, Idaho, Washington, Oregon, then back to Montana, then to Dakota, arriving in Deadwood October 9th, 1895, after an absence of seventeen years.

My arrival in Deadwood after an absence of so many years created quite an excitement among my many friends of the past, to such an extent that a vast number of the citizens who had come to Deadwood during my absence who had heard so much of Calamity Jane and her many adventures in former years were anxious to see me. Among the many whom I met were several gentlemen from eastern cities who advised me to allow myself to be placed before the public in such a manner as to give the people of the eastern cities an opportunity of seeing the Woman Scout who was made so famous through her daring career in the West and Black Hill countries.

The Wild West shows of the time were very popular. The most famous was started by "Buffalo Bill," William Frederick Cody, in 1883.

An agent of Kohl & Middleton, the celebrated Museum men came to Deadwood, through the **solicitation** of the gentleman who I had met there and arrangements were made to place me before the public in this manner. My first engagement began at the Palace Museum, Minneapolis, January 20th, 1896, under Kohl and Middleton's management.

Hoping that this little history of my life may interest all readers, I remain as in the older days,

Why is Calamity Jane's story called a legend?

Yours,

Mrs. M. Burk
Better known as Calamity Jane

solicitation an invitation

Life and Adventures of Calamity Jane, By Herself   Marthy (Martha) Cannary Burk

Directions Write the answers to these questions using complete sentences.

Comprehension: Identifying Facts

1. What is Calamity Jane's real name?

2. How does Calamity Jane spend much of her time as a child?

3. When does her family leave Missouri for Montana?

4. When does Calamity Jane start dressing in men's clothing?

5. How does Calamity Jane get her name?

6. Where does Calamity Jane meet Wild Bill Hickock?

7. Between what cities does Calamity Jane say she carried the mail for the pony express?

8. How does Calamity Jane help an overland mail coach reach Deadwood after Indians attack it?

9. What does Calamity Jane say she and her husband did to earn money?

10. What do the "gentlemen from eastern cities" persuade Calamity Jane to do?

Comprehension: Understanding Main Ideas

11. How are Calamity Jane's skills as a horseback rider important to her life?

12. On her way with her family to Montana, Calamity Jane says she forded streams just to amuse herself. What does this tell you about her character?

13. What does Calamity Jane say about her skill as a rider and shooter?

14. How would you describe Calamity Jane's duties as a scout?

15. Do you think Calamity Jane is a good name for this character? Why or why not?

16. Why isn't Calamity Jane robbed when she works as a pony express rider?

17. How does Calamity Jane react to the news of Wild Bill's murder? What does she do?

18. How does Calamity Jane describe her daughter?

19. How does Calamity Jane describe her welcome when she returns to Deadwood after seventeen years?

20. Why does Calamity Jane decide to tour the country toward the end of her life?

Understanding Literature: Anecdote

An anecdote is a brief account of an interesting event in someone's life. "Life and Adventures of Calamity Jane, by Herself" is filled with anecdotes about her adventurous life. These accounts are brief. For example, we learn only certain details about Calamity Jane's time as a pony express rider. She says that she was rarely bothered on her dangerous route and that she made her round trip of fifty miles every two days. We do not know how she felt as she rode along or what the territory looked like. She knew that simply telling people she rode with the pony express would amaze them. Her audience would supply the details as they imagined what it must have been like.

21. In your own words, how would you define an anecdote?

22. How is an anecdote different from a story?

23. Why might an author tell about events through anecdotes?

24. Which of Calamity Jane's anecdotes are funny? Why do you think so?

25. Which anecdote in Calamity Jane's story is most exciting, or well described? How does it hold your interest?

Critical Thinking

26. How might you find out which of Calamity Jane's anecdotes are true? Which stories would be easiest to check?

27. Is it important to you as a reader that Calamity Jane may have invented, rather than lived, some of these anecdotes?

28. Which of Calamity Jane's anecdotes seems the most believable? Which is the most unbelievable? Explain your thinking.

29. How might dressing in men's clothing have helped Calamity Jane? How might her style of dress have hurt her? Explain.

30. Why do you think Calamity Jane wanted to be buried in the same place as Wild Bill Hickock?

Writing on Your Own In some ways, Calamity Jane created her own legend by spreading stories of her adventurous life. Write an anecdote about some event in your life, exaggerating the truth as needed to create your own legend.

The Phantom Hitchhiker
Daniel Cohen

Daniel Cohen
1936–

About the Author

In his twenty-plus years as a writer, Daniel Cohen has written mainly about ghosts. However, he says, "I don't make up ghost stories. I deal with legends and factual accounts." Some of his books on this subject are *The Encyclopedia of Ghosts, Real Ghosts,* and *Ghosts in the House.*

Cohen, born in Chicago, is a former managing editor of *Science Digest* magazine. He and his wife, Susan Cohen, have worked together on a number of science books, including *Where to Find Dinosaurs Today.* They live, with an assortment of cats and dogs, in New Jersey.

About the Selection

"The Phantom Hitchhiker" is probably the best known modern American legend. For over a century, people have told each other this tale. Like the other stories in this unit, the details may change slightly as the tale travels from place to place and person to person. But the basic plot remains the same. You might even have heard the story yourself from a friend, who claims to have heard it from another friend. Like others who have told this legend, your friend may insist it is true. That's the way legends travel today. That's the way they have always traveled.

One of the reasons this legend has remained so popular is that, from the very beginning of the story, readers know that something strange is going to happen. They realize this because the storyteller gives them clues along the way. These clues are called **foreshadowing**. Through foreshadowing, authors build suspense and other elements of a story's **mood**. Mood is the feeling that a piece of writing creates.

The Phantom Hitchhiker

Joel Harris was tired, so tired that he shouldn't have been driving at all. It was nearly three A.M., and he had been up since six o'clock the previous morning.

"Too hard," he muttered to himself. "I'm pushing myself too hard."

To make matters worse it had begun to rain. Joel had to strain his eyes to keep the deserted road in front of him in view.

"Thank God, it's only thirty more miles."

It was the sort of situation in which an ordinary driver might have been tempted to speed a bit, thinking that by getting home faster he could beat the rain and the fatigue. But Joel Harris was one of those instinctively cautious drivers. He automatically slowed his speed to adjust to the **deteriorating** driving conditions. A sense of real danger cut through the weariness and made him more alert.

That's why Joel became aware of the figure at the side of the road before most people would have. First it was just a flash of white in his headlights, but as the car drew closer he could see it was a girl. She was young, about eighteen he guessed, and she was wearing a white party dress. She wasn't actually thumbing a ride, she was just standing there. As the car came closer Joel made eye contact with her. She looked at him pleadingly.

A young girl, alone at night on a deserted road, wearing only a **flimsy** dress, with the rain beginning to really come down. There was no way he was just going to pass her by.

Joel stopped and leaned out the window. "Hey, you need a lift?"

As you read, notice details about time and place that help create the mood. What is the mood of this story?

Why do you think this story is called a modern legend?

---

deteriorate getting worse

flimsy thin, not strongly made

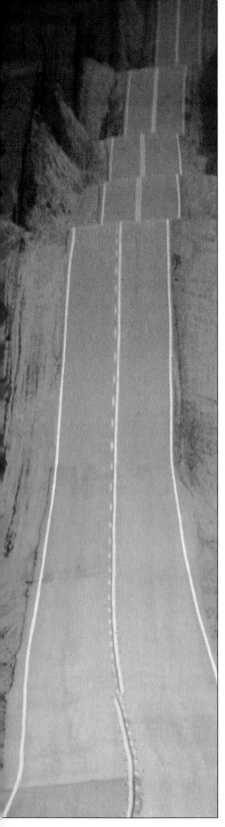

She was already walking toward the car. "Sure do, mister. Thanks."

"You're lucky it's me. You can stand on this road for hours at this time of night without seeing a car. And then you never can tell who is going to stop. You hear about all sorts of terrible things that can happen."

The girl didn't say anything. She just climbed into the back seat of the car.

"Where you going?" Joel asked.

"Middletown."

"This is your lucky day, that's where I'm going too. Where in Middletown do you live? I'll take you right home. No sense in your wandering around town in the dark."

She gave him an address, which Joel recognized as being in one of the older and poorer sections of town. He didn't know that part of town well, but he figured he could find it easily enough.

Joel switched on the interior light and turned to get a look at his passenger. Perhaps he had overestimated her age. She might have been only sixteen, it was hard to tell. She was quite pretty, but looked worn and tired. Her hair, wet from the rain, hung down to her shoulders. Her dress was also wet and rumpled, and had a curiously old-fashioned look. Probably second hand, he thought.

Joel had wanted to ask the girl what she was doing on the road at three in the morning, but there was something about the way she looked at him that made him feel he shouldn't ask that question. It was really none of his business anyway. If she wants to tell me, she'll tell me, he thought.

The girl shivered slightly.

"You must be cold. I'll turn the heater up, and here, take my jacket."

The girl thanked him, wrapped the jacket around her shoulders, and lay back in the seat, her eyes closed. She seemed to fall asleep almost instantly.

Poor kid, thought Joel. She must be exhausted. I wonder what happened.

Joel drove on in silence. He didn't even turn the radio on for fear of waking his sleeping passenger.

It didn't take long to reach town, and he found the address the girl had given him without much trouble. It was the worst house on a bad street. In fact, the house was so **dilapidated** that it looked deserted, and Joel wondered if he had somehow gotten the address wrong.

"Is this the place?"

There was no answer, so he repeated the question more loudly. Still no answer. Sound sleeper, he thought. He turned around. The back seat was empty.

Joel's first **reaction** was surprise, but that was quickly replaced by fear. He hadn't stopped the car since he had first picked up the girl. He checked both back doors, and they were locked from the inside. There was no possible way for anyone to have gotten out of the car. Yet the girl in the white dress was gone.

Joel just wanted to drive away and forget the whole thing. But he couldn't. He had to try and find out what had happened. He went up to the house, half hoping that no one would be there. But as soon as he knocked he saw a light go on inside.

The door was answered by a thin, sad-looking old woman wearing a shabby robe.

"Yes?"

For a moment Joel was startled, for as he stared at the old woman's eyes they reminded him strongly of the eyes of the girl in the white dress.

"I'm sorry to disturb you at this hour," he began haltingly. "I know what I'm going to say will sound crazy. But I've just had the strangest experience of my life."

Joel began to relate the story of the girl he had picked up on the deserted road. As he talked it sounded more and more unbelievable, and he began to feel more and more foolish.

The girl's old-fashioned dress and Joel's jacket are examples of foreshadowing. What other examples of foreshadowing do you find in this story?

To speak *haltingly* means to speak unsurely, without confidence. Why would Joel speak haltingly to the old woman?

dilapidated rundown, in poor condition

reaction a response

But he told the story all the way through, with all the details he could remember.

The woman listened patiently, her lined face registering no **emotion**. Indeed, she looked as if she were listening to a familiar tale. When Joel finished she said, "Where did you say you picked the girl up?"

Joel told her.

"That's my daughter Laura," the old woman said. "She's dead. She was killed in an automobile accident on that road ten years ago. She was coming home from a party.

"You're not the first young man to have had this experience. It usually happens on rainy nights. She was killed on a rainy night like this one. She seems to be trying to get home.

"Laura's buried in Oaklawn Cemetery just outside of town."

Joel had expected to be called crazy, but he never expected to hear a story even crazier than the one he told. He didn't know what to say. He just mumbled something about being terribly sorry, and walked away. Before he did, he caught a glimpse of the name on the door of the house. It was Kearns.

By the time Joel got back into his car and drove away, he had begun to convince himself that the whole experience had never taken place, that it was all a **hallucination** brought on by extreme fatigue. Things like that happen, he thought. That must be it.

He shivered in the cold. Only then did Joel realize that he didn't have his jacket on. He stopped the car and searched for his jacket. It wasn't there. He had given it to the girl in the white dress, and she had taken it away with her.

Now Joel could not let the matter rest. The following day he went to Oaklawn Cemetery. With the help of the caretaker he was able to locate the Kearns family plot. Sure enough, there was the grave of Laura Kearns. She had been just sixteen when she died, ten years earlier.

Draped over the tombstone, neatly folded, was Joel's jacket.

emotion a feeling	**hallucination** a vision that is not real

The Phantom Hitchhiker
Daniel Cohen

Directions Write the answers to these questions using complete sentences.

Comprehension: Identifying Facts

1. As the story begins, what is the time and place?

2. What does Joel do when he sees the girl shiver?

3. Who is Joel's hitchhiker, according to the old woman?

Comprehension: Understanding Main Ideas

4. What does Joel notice about the girl's dress? Why are these details important to the story?

5. Why does Joel go up to the house after the girl disappears?

6. What does Joel find when he visits the cemetery?

Understanding Literature: Foreshadowing

When they use foreshadowing, writers give clues or hints about something that is going to happen. In "The Phantom Hitchhiker," foreshadowing is used to create suspense.

Writers sometimes foreshadow events through their descriptions of setting. For example, Daniel Cohen opens this story by saying it is three A.M.. Readers expect something strange to happen at this time of night. Writers can also foreshadow through the actions of their characters. When the girl wraps Joel's jacket around her shoulders, this foreshadows Joel's discovery of his jacket draped over her tombstone.

7. In your own words, how would you define foreshadowing?

8. How does the description of the girl's dress foreshadow the plot of the story?

Critical Thinking

9. Why do you think this story, in hundreds of local versions, is one of the most popular and widespread of all modern American legends?

10. What do we learn about Joel Harris's character? Use evidence from the story to support your answer.

> **Writing on Your Own** Epitaphs are short sayings written on tombstones. They usually tell something about the person who is buried there, or about death itself. Write an epitaph for Laura Kearns's tombstone.

Skills Lesson: Character Development

The characters of a story bring readers into the story. In one way or another, we see a story through the eyes of its characters. Because of this, authors take great care in creating and developing characters. As we learn more about characters, they become real to us.

Writers develop characters in several ways. They (or their narrators) can tell readers about a character. They can let other characters tell about a character. They can also let characters reveal themselves by what they do, say, and think.

In "The Phantom Hitchhiker," we first meet Joel Harris through the author's description. Daniel Cohen tells us that Joel is tired and knows he has been pushing himself too hard. He also tells us that Joel is not "an ordinary driver," tempted to speed through the rain and his own fatigue. Instead, Joel becomes more alert.

Cohen also tells us about Joel through the other characters in the story. We see that the young girl trusts him enough to accept a ride from him and, later, to fall asleep in his car. Laura's mother opens the door to him, listens patiently to his story, and tells Joel who his hitchhiker is.

Cohen also reveals Joel's character by the things he does, says, and thinks. He feels sorry for the girl alone in the rain and gives her a ride. He gives her his jacket when she's cold. Despite his fear and fatigue, he goes after answers to the mystery of his hitchhiker.

Review

1. In what three ways can an author develop a character?

2. What does Daniel Cohen tell us about Joel?

3. What do the other characters tell us about Joel?

4. What do we learn about Joel through what he does, says, and thinks?

5. Which of these three methods of character development is most important in this story? Why do you think so?

Writing on Your Own Write a character description of a real person or a person you create. Use all three of the techniques mentioned: tell about your character, have another character reveal something about your character, let your character reveal himself or herself.

People everywhere have created folklore: stories, customs, and traditions that they preserve and pass along to their children. American folklore is especially rich in tall tales and legends.

The setting and characters in American tall tales are often drawn from the frontier and the colorful people who lived and worked there. The characters in tall tales are imaginary, larger than life. They are bigger, braver, and smarter than anyone else, and they have fantastic adventures.

Legends are based on real people, real places, or real events. These stories include details that are true and details that are purely imaginary. Part of the fun of reading legends is not knowing which are which!

Most tall tales and legends are part of oral literature, told first not by professional writers but by ordinary people. This folklore tells us a lot about what people over the years have considered important, unique, and funny in their lives.

Selections

- "Babe the Blue Ox," by Esther Shephard, is a tall tale about the great deeds of Paul Bunyan's huge ox.

- "Feboldson, Western Scientist," by Walter Blair, is a tall tale about a no-nonsense Nebraska problem solver during the Great Heat and the Great Fog.

- "John Henry" is a ballad that tells about the legendary contest between a steel-driving man and a machine.

- "Life and Adventures of Calamity Jane, by Herself," by Marthy (Martha) Cannary Burk, is legendary Calamity Jane's own telling of anecdotes from her adventurous life.

- "The Phantom Hitchhiker," by Daniel Cohen, is a modern legend about the adventure of a late-night driver who picks up a mysterious hitchhiker.

UNIT 3 REVIEW

Directions Write the answers to these questions using complete sentences.

Comprehension: Identifying Facts

1. What is a tall tale?

2. Why is exaggeration important to a tall tale?

3. What is a legend?

4. Which of the selections has a refrain?

5. What is a ballad?

Comprehension: Understanding Main Ideas

6. What are some differences between tall tales and legends? What are some similarities? Support your answers with examples from the unit.

7. What characteristics of the ballad of John Henry are similar to the characteristics an anecdote about John Henry might have?

8. Legends feature either real people, real places, or real things. What are some real elements in "Life and Adventures of Calamity Jane" and "The Phantom Hitchhiker"?

9. How does folklore help preserve and pass on people's stories, customs, and history?

10. What have you learned about American culture from these tall tales and legends?

Understanding Literature: Autobiography and Biography

Autobiographies and biographies are two related kinds of literature. The term *biography* means "writing about life." A biography, then, is the story of a person's life, written by another person. The prefix *auto* means "self." An autobiography is the story of a person's life, written by that person. Although both autobiographies and biographies may include exaggerations and untrue details, they don't have the same kinds of plots and character development that stories do.

From its title, we expect "Life and Adventures of Calamity Jane, by Herself" to be an autobiography. However, the work is different from most autobiographies in two ways. First, an autobiography is usually longer, often a whole book. We could call Calamity Jane's brief pamphlet more of an autobiographical sketch. Second, although an autobiography often includes the author's feelings and impressions, we expect that most of its details will be based on fact. People have questioned whether many of the anecdotes in Calamity Jane's pamphlet are true. Calamity Jane became a legendary figure partly because of the wild stories she spread about herself. Her pamphlet shows us how she wanted to be remembered.

11. What is a biography?

12. How is an autobiography different from a biography?

13. How are biographies and autobiographies different from stories?

14. Explain whether a tall tale could be a biography.

15. Imagine that Calamity Jane was the subject of a biography. What are some details you might find out in a biography written about her that you do not find in her pamphlet?

Critical Thinking

16. What tasks would be easier for you to do if you had an ox like Babe?

17. From what you know of Febold Feboldson's character traits, how might he have handled a Great Snowstorm?

18. If you were Joel Harris, what would you have done after you found your jacket on Laura's grave?

19. How would "John Henry" be different if it were written from his boss's point of view?

20. Why do you think people believe some legends are true?

Speak and Listen

On audiotape, tell a scary story that you have heard before. Give the tape to a partner to listen to. After a week, have your partner record his or her version of the story. Listen to both recordings and compare them. Did any details change? How did the changes affect the story?

Beyond Words

Use the Internet to locate several recordings of the ballad of John Henry. Pick the version you like best and record it, using your voice, a musical instrument, or a computer program that creates music.

Writing on Your Own Write a tall tale or legend about the place where you live, or about a character who may have lived there years ago.

Test-Taking Tip

Studying together in small groups, summarizing each selection, and asking questions of one another is one way to review material for literature tests.

"The unread story is not a story; it is little black marks on wood pulp. The reader, reading it, makes it live: a live thing, a story."

—Ursula K. Le Guin, *Dancing at the Edge of the World*, 1989

"Writing the short story is essentially an act of grace. It's not a matter of will so much as trust. I try to let the story do some of the work for me. It knows what it wants to do, say, be. I try not to stand in its way."

—Paulette Bates Alden, 1990

UNIT 4

The Short Story

Short stories are brief works of fiction. They first appeared in the nineteenth century. Because short stories are brief, they usually take place over a short time period, in one main place. Their plots include only the most important descriptive details. They usually have only a few characters. As this form of fiction has developed, authors have changed what the short story is, and what it can do. Readers continue to enjoy the very different kinds of characters, plots, and themes found in the world of the short story.

In this unit, you will read short stories that show how different this form of fiction can be.

A Chat in the Road,
Anna Belle Lee
Washington

The storytelling of fables, myths, tall tales, and legends continues in the short story. People have been telling and writing short stories for many years. Modern short stories first developed in the nineteenth century. At that time, American writers such as Washington Irving, Nathaniel Hawthorne, and Edgar Allan Poe were popular. People became interested in this form of literature. Short stories are still very popular today.

> **Plot:** the series of events in a story
>
> **Setting:** a story's time and place
>
> **Character:** a person or animal in a story
>
> **Point of view:** the relationship of the narrator to the story
>
> **Theme:** the main idea of a story

All short stories have plot, setting, characters, point of view, and theme. The series of events in a short story makes up its plot. The setting is the time and place of the story. There are usually very few characters in a short story. The main character is also called the protagonist or hero. The antagonist is the person or force trying to keep the protagonist from accomplishing his or her goal. Short stories are told by a narrator. The narrator's point of view may be from inside the story (first-person) or as someone who is watching the story happen (third-person). The theme is the story's main idea.

Fables, myths, legends, and tall tales all have these same characteristics. What makes short stories different?

■ Short stories are brief, much shorter than novels, for example. Edgar Allan Poe said these stories should be short enough to read in one sitting. Whether this is true or not, readers can usually finish short stories rather quickly.

■ Because they are brief, short stories usually take place in a short period of time. They may be set in only one place. The time frame of a novel, on the other hand, is often much longer. Novels also may be set in many different places.

■ Writers of short stories focus on the basics of the story. They have less room for description than novelists do. Short-story writers tend to include only the most important details.

■ Short stories are a form of fiction. This means that they did not actually happen. The author creates the characters and the story they live. Writers of fiction may get ideas from the people they meet and the events they observe. However, they change this information to serve the needs of the story.

■ Short stories are included in the kind of literature called prose. Literature can be divided into two forms: prose and poetry. Poetry includes all forms of writing that use special patterns of words and rhythm. Prose includes all other writing, such as short stories, novels, fables, myths, tall tales, and legends. Some people think of prose as writing that sounds like ordinary language, or writing that is organized into paragraphs. (Recall, however, that "John Henry," in Unit 3, tells its legend in a ballad. A ballad is a form of poetry. So, even though the subject of this ballad was originally a legend, its rhyming words and rhythm make it a poem.)

Building on the basic characteristics of short stories, today's authors continue to change what a short story is and does. In the nineteenth century, short stories were often about ghostly or amazing events. Today's short stories often focus on the familiar details of life. The plots of nineteenth-century short stories usually had clear beginnings, middles, and ends. Modern short stories sometimes just

Small Farmers, **Leopoldo Romanach**

stop. The story does not really finish.

Each of the short stories in this unit has a very different style and effect. Mark Twain's "The Celebrated Jumping Frog of Calaveras County" gives readers a funny snapshot of life in one of the California mining towns that sprang up during the Gold Rush. "Everyday Use," by Alice Walker, takes a look at the changing and unchanging world of an African-American family. In "American History," Judith Ortiz-Cofer brings readers into the sometimes painful life of a young Latina girl growing up in Paterson, New Jersey. Langston Hughes's "Thank You, M'am" tells the story of a boy looking for trouble and the woman who makes him stop and think. The last story, "Unfinished Message" by Toshio Mori, deals with a startling event in the life of a Japanese-American family coping with World War II.

The Celebrated Jumping Frog of Calaveras County Mark Twain

Mark Twain
1835–1910

Literary Terms

caricature a character description that is exaggerated to make people laugh

dialogue the between conversation of characters in a story

humorist a writer of humor

novel fiction that is book-length and has more plot and details than a short story

prose all writing that is not poetry

short story a brief work of prose fiction that includes plot, setting, characters, point of view, and theme

story-within-a-story a second story told within another story

About the Author

Samuel Langhorne Clemens, better known as Mark Twain, was born in Missouri. As a young man he traveled west to Nevada and California, and later to Europe and the Middle East.

Clemens picked up his pen name —Mark Twain—on a Steamboat trip to South America. Steamboat pilots had to be sure boats stayed in deep enough water. The phrase *mark twain* means that the river is deep enough—two fathoms, or twelve feet.

Twain's earliest published writings were funny sketches that appeared in newspapers. These were followed by several books about travel, including *Innocents Abroad*. His best-known **novels**—*Tom Sawyer, The Prince and the Pauper,* and *Huckleberry Finn*—are classics of American literature.

Mark Twain is one of America's finest **prose** writers and **humorists**.

About the Selection

"The Celebrated Jumping Frog of Calaveras County" was the **short story** that first made people pay attention to Mark Twain's fiction. An early biography of Twain says that the writer first heard the tale from a prospector (gold miner) he met in California. The story was first published in 1865 as "Jim Smiley and His Jumping Frog." Twain rewrote the story several times.

This story—actually a **story-within-a-story**—features exaggerated **dialogue**, much of it in the dialect of California mining camps, and **caricatures**. Caricature, or exaggerated character description, adds to the story's humor.

The Celebrated Jumping Frog of Calaveras County

In **compliance** with the request of a friend of mine, who wrote me from the East, I called on good-natured, **garrulous** old Simon Wheeler, and inquired after my friend's friend, *Leonidas W.* Smiley, as requested to do, and I hereunto append the result. I have a lurking suspicion that *Leonidas W.* Smiley is a myth; that my friend never knew such a personage; and that he only **conjectured** that, if I asked old Wheeler about him, it would remind him of his **infamous** *Jim* Smiley, and he would go to work and bore me nearly to death with some **infernal reminiscence** of him as long and tedious as it should be useless to me. If that was the design, it certainly succeeded.

I found Simon Wheeler dozing comfortably by the barroom stove of the old, **dilapidated** tavern in the ancient mining camp of Angel's, and I noticed that he was fat and bald-headed, and had an expression of winning gentleness

As you read, note the various parts of a short story: plot, characters, setting, point of view, and theme. Notice that this story uses a first-person narrator.

Hereunto append means that the narrator is about to state the result of his questioning of Simon Wheeler.

compliance the act of doing what is asked

conjecture to guess or suppose

dilapidated rundown, in poor condition

garrulous talkative

infamous well known because of bad or disagreeable things

infernal tiresome, unpleasant

reminiscence remembrance, memory

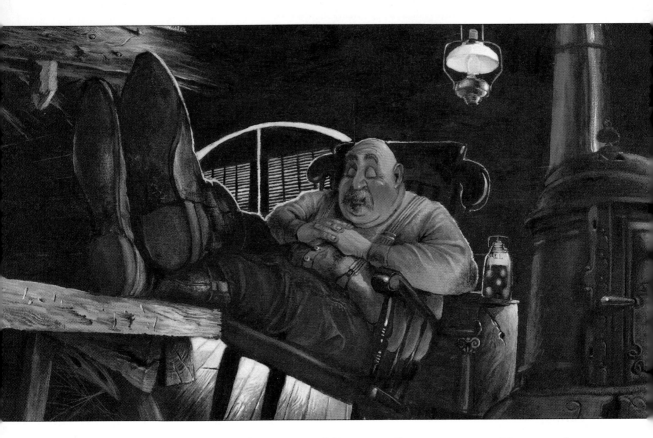

and simplicity upon his **tranquil countenance**. He roused up and gave me good-day. I told him a friend of mine had commissioned me to make some **inquiries** about a cherished companion of his boyhood named *Leonidas W.* Smiley—*Rev. Leonidas W.* Smiley—a young minister of the Gospel, who he had heard was at one time a resident of Angel's Camp. I added, that, if Mr. Wheeler could tell me anything about this Rev. Leonidas W. Smiley, I would feel under many **obligations** to him.

Simon Wheeler backed me into a corner and **blockaded** me there with his chair, and then sat me down and reeled off the **monotonous narrative** which follows this paragraph. He

blockade to prevent escape

countenance face, appearance

inquiry a request for information

monotonous boring, unchanging

narrative a story

obligation a feeling of gratitude

tranquil untroubled

never smiled, he never frowned, he never changed his voice from the gentle-flowing key to which he tuned the initial sentence, he never betrayed the slightest **suspicion** of enthusiasm; but all through the **interminable** narrative there ran a vein of **impressive** earnestness and sincerity, which showed me plainly that, so far from his imagining that there was anything ridiculous or funny about his story, he regarded it as a really important matter, and admitted its two heroes as men of **transcendent** genius in *finesse*. To me, the spectacle of a man drifting **serenely** along through such a queer yarn without ever smiling, was **exquisitely** absurd. As I said before, I asked him to tell me what he knew of Rev. Leonidas W. Smiley, and he replied as follows. I let him go on in his own way, and never interrupted him once:

There was a feller here once by the name of *Jim* Smiley, in the winter of '49—or maybe it was the spring of '50—I don't **recollect** exactly, somehow, though what makes me think it was one or the other is because I remember the big flume wasn't finished when he first came to the camp; but anyway, he was the curiousest man about always betting on anything that turned up you ever see, if he could get anybody to bet on the other side; and if he couldn't, he'd change sides. Any way what suited the other man would suit him—any way just so's he got a bet, *he* was satisfied. But still he was lucky, uncommon lucky—he most always come out winner. He was always ready and laying for a chance; there couldn't be no solit'ry thing mentioned but that feller'd offer to bet on it, and take any side you please, as I was just telling you. If there was a horse-race, you'd find him flush, or you'd find him busted at the end of it; if there was a dog-fight, he'd bet on it; if there was a cat-fight, he'd bet on it; if there was a chicken-fight, he'd bet on it; why, if there was two birds setting on a fence, he would bet you which one would fly first; or if there was a camp meeting, he would be there reg'lar, to bet on

Finesse comes from a French word meaning the end. It usually refers to refinement but can also refer to a technique of card playing. The player tricks the opponent by holding out the highest card in hopes that a lower card will win the hand.

Here begins the story-within-a-story. Notice that the second narrator, Simon Wheeler, talks in dialect.

Gold miners would cut a *flume*, or channel, to run water through for washing the gold.

exquisitely perfectly	**interminable** endless	**suspicion** hint, trace; mistrust, doubt
impressive calling one to pay attention or to wonder	**recollect** to remember	**transcendent** far beyond the usual
	serenely calmly; not at all upset	

A camp meeting was an open-air religious gathering. Parson Walker, a minister, appears to have given the most enthusiastic sermons.

Smiley is a famous Twain caricature. As you read, see which aspects of his personality are exaggerated.

Picture Smiley's horse in a race, lagging behind until the very end. Then, "desperate-like," she'd come up skidding, kicking, coughing, sneezing, her legs going every which way—and win the race!

Parson Walker, which he judged to be the best **exhorter** about here, and so he was, too, and a good man. If he even seen a straddle-bug start to go anywheres, he would bet you how long it would take him to get wherever he was going to, and if you took him up, he would foller that straddle-bug to Mexico but what he would find out where he was bound for and how long he was on the road. Lots of the boys here has seen that Smiley, and can tell you about him. Why, it never made no difference to *him*—he would bet on *any*thing—the dangdest feller. Parson Walker's wife laid very sick once, for a good while, and it seemed as if they warn't going to save her; but one morning he came in, and Smiley asked how she was, and he said she was considerable better—thank the Lord for his inf'nit mercy—and coming on so smart that, with the blessing of Prov'dence, she'd get well yet; and Smiley, before he thought, says, "Well, I'll risk two-and-a-half that she don't, anyway."

Thish-yer Smiley had a mare—the boys called her the fifteen-minute nag, but that was only in fun, you know, because, of course, she was faster than that—and he used to win money on that horse, for all she was so slow and always had the asthma, or the distemper, or the consumption, or something of that kind. They used to give her two or three hundred yards start, and then pass her under way; but always at the fag-end of the race she'd get excited and desperate-like, and come cavorting and straddling up, and scattering her legs around **limber,** sometimes in the air, and sometimes out to one side amongst the fences, and kicking up m-o-r-e dust, and raising m-o-r-e racket with her coughing and sneezing and blowing her nose—and always fetch up at the stand just about a neck ahead, as near as you could cipher it down.

And he had a little small bull pup, that to look at him you'd think he wan't worth a cent but to set around and look ornery and lay for a chance to steal something. But as soon as

exhorter one who strongly urges another to do or believe something

limber moving easily

money was up on him, he was a different dog; his under-jaw'd begin to stick out like the fo'castle of a steamboat, and his teeth would uncover, and shine savage like the furnaces. And a dog might tackle him, and bullyrag him, and bite him, and throw him over his shoulder two or three times, and Andrew Jackson—which was the name of the pup—Andrew Jackson would never let on but what *he* was satisfied, and hadn't expected nothing else—and the bets being doubled and doubled on the other side all the time, till the money was all up; and then all of a sudden he would grab that other dog jest by the j'int of his hind leg and freeze to it—not claw, you understand, but only jest grip and hang on till they throwed up the sponge, if it was a year. Smiley always come out winner on that pup, till he harnessed a dog once that didn't have no hind legs, because they'd been sawed off by a circular saw, and when the thing had gone along far enough, and the money was all up, and he come to make a snatch for his pet holt, he saw in a minute how he'd been imposed on, and how the other dog had him in the door, so to speak, and he 'peared surprised, and then he looked sorter discouraged-like, and didn't try no more to win the fight, and so he got shucked out bad. He give Smiley a look, as much to say that his heart was broke and it was *his* fault for putting up a dog that hadn't no hind legs for him to take holt of, which was his main **dependence** in a fight, and then he limped off a piece and laid down and died. It was a good pup, was that Andrew Jackson, and would have made a name for hisself if he'd lived, for the stuff was in him, and he had genius—I know it, because he hadn't no opportunities to speak of, and it don't stand to reason that a dog could make such a fight as he could under them **circumstances,** if he hadn't no talent. It always makes me feel sorry when I think of that last fight of his'n, and the way it turned out.

Well, thish-yer Smiley had rat-terriers, and chicken-cocks, and tomcats, and all them kind of things, till you couldn't

The *forecastle,* in the forward part of a ship, is where the crew lives.

Bullyrag is an old word for badger, or irritate by teasing.

Smiley's dog, after appearing to lose a fight, would suddenly grab the other dog by its hind leg and hang on until the other dog gave up, no matter how long it took.

circumstance a condition	**dependence** something counted on or necessary

rest, and you couldn't fetch nothing for him to bet on but he'd match you. He ketched a frog one day, and took him home, and said he cal'klated to edercate him; and so he never done nothing for these three months but set in his back yard and learn that frog to jump. And you bet you he *did* learn him, too. He'd give him a little punch behind, and the next minute you'd see that frog whirling in the air like a doughnut—see him turn one summerset, or maybe a couple, if he got a good start, and come down flat-footed and all right, like a cat. He got him up so in the matter of catching flies, and kept him in practice so constant, that he'd nail a fly every time as far as he could see him. Smiley said all a frog wanted was education, and he could do most anything—and I believe him. Why, I've seen him set Dan'l Webster down here on this floor—Dan'l Webster was the name of the frog—and sing out, "Flies, Dan'l, flies!" and quicker'n you could wink, he'd spring straight up, and snake a fly off'n the counter there, and flop down on the floor again as solid as a gob of mud, and fall to scratching the side of his head with his hind foot as **indifferent** as if he hadn't no idea he's been doin' any more'n any frog might do. You never see a frog so modest and straight-for'ard as he was, for all he was so gifted. And when it come to fair and square jumping on the dead level, he could get over more ground at one straddle than any animal of his breed you ever see. Jumping on a dead level was his strong suit, you understand; and when it come to that, Smiley would ante up money on him as long as he had a red. Smiley was monstrous proud of his frog, and well he might be, for fellers that had traveled and been everywhere all said he laid over any frog that ever *they* see.

Well, Smiley kept the beast in a little lattice box, and he used to fetch him downtown sometimes and lay for a bet. One day a feller—a stranger in the camp, he was—come across him with his box, and says:

"What might it be that you've got in the box?"

Summerset is another word for somersault.

To *ante up*, as in poker, means to put your money into the pot.

As you read, see how Twain creates humor with his dialogue.

indifferent uncaring, uninterested, unimpressed

And Smiley says, sorter indifferent like, "It might be a parrot or it might be a canary, maybe, but it ain't—it's only just a frog."

An' the feller took it, and looked at it careful, and turned it round this way and that, and says, "H'm—so 'tis. Well, what's *he* good for?"

"Well," Smiley says, easy and careless, "he's good enough for *one* thing, I should judge—he can outjump any frog in Calaveras county."

The feller took the box again, and took another long, particular look, and give it back to Smiley, and says, very **deliberate,** "Well, I don't see no p'ints about that frog that's any better'n any other frog."

"Maybe you don't," Smiley says. "Maybe you understand frogs, and maybe you don't understand 'em; maybe you've had experience, and maybe you ain't only a amature, as it were. Anyways, I've got *my* opinion, and I'll risk forty dollars that he can outjump any frog in Calaveras county."

By *amature,* Smiley means amateur, in this case someone who doesn't know what he's talking about.

And the feller studied a minute, and then says, kinder sad-like, "Well, I'm only a stranger here, and I ain't got no frog; but if I had a frog, I'd bet you."

And then Smiley says, "That's all right—that's all right—if you'll hold my box a minute, I'll go and get you a frog." And so the feller took the box, and put up his forty dollars along with Smiley's, and set down to wait.

So he set there a good while thinking and thinking to hisself, and then he got the frog out and pried his mouth open and took a teaspoon and filled him full of quail shot—filled him pretty near up to his chin—and set him on the floor. Smiley he went to the swamp and slopped around in the mud for a long time, and finally he ketched a frog, and fetched him in, and give him to this feller, and says:

"Now, if you're ready, set him alongside of Dan'l with his forepaws just even with Dan'l, and I'll give the word." Then he says, "One-two-three-jump!" and him and the feller touched

deliberate carefully saying and meaning every word

up the frogs from behind, and the new frog hopped off, but Dan'l give a heave, and hysted up his shoulders—so—like a Frenchman, but it wasn't no use—he couldn't budge; he was planted as solid as an anvil, and he couldn't no more stir than if he was anchored out. Smiley was a good deal surprised, and he was disgusted too, but he didn't have no idea what the matter was, of course.

The feller took the money and started away; and when he was going out the door, he sorter jerked his thumb over his shoulder—this way—at Dan'l, and says again, very deliberate, "Well, *I* don't see no p'ints about that frog that's any better'n any other frog."

Smiley he stood scratching his head and looking down at Dan'l a long time, and at last he says, "I do wonder what in the nation that frog throw'd off for—I wonder if there ain't something the matter with him—he 'pears to look mighty baggy, somehow." And he ketched Dan'l by the nap of the neck, and lifted him up and says, "Why, blame my cats, if he don't weigh five pounds!" and turned him upside down, and he belched out a double handful of shot. And then he see how it was, and he was the maddest man—he set the frog down and took out after the feller, but he never ketched him. And—

(Here Simon Wheeler heard his name called from the front yard, and got up to see what was wanted.) And turning to me as he moved away, he said: "Just set where you are, stranger, and rest easy—I ain't going to be gone a second."

At this point, the first narrator of the story returns to narrate the end.

But, by your leave, I did not think that a continuation of the history of the enterprising vagabond *Jim* Smiley would be likely to afford me much information concerning the *Rev. Leonidas W.* Smiley, and so I started away.

At the door I met the sociable Wheeler returning, and he buttonholed me and recommenced:

"Well, thish-yer Smiley had a yeller one-eyed cow that didn't have no tail, only jest a short stump like a bannanner, and—"

"Oh, hang Smiley and his **afflicted** cow!" I muttered, good-naturedly, and bidding the old gentleman good-day, I **departed.**

---

afflicted ailing, ill   **depart** to leave

Directions Write the answers to these questions using complete sentences.

Comprehension: Identifying Facts

1. Why does the first narrator call on Simon Wheeler?

2. Where does Wheeler live? Where does the narrator find him?

3. What is Jim Smiley's favorite thing to do?

4. What bet does Smiley offer to Parson Walker?

5. How does Smiley's mare win races?

6. What is Smiley's dog's name?

7. How does the dog win dog fights?

8. What is Smiley's frog's name?

9. What does the stranger do to Smiley's frog while Smiley is away?

10. Who wins the bet: Smiley or the stranger?

Comprehension: Understanding Main Ideas

11. What is "exquisitely absurd" about the way Wheeler tells his tales of Jim Smiley?

12. Why do the other men call Smiley's mare "the fifteen-minute nag"?

13. Why does Smiley's dog lose his last fight?

14. What does Smiley teach his frog to do?

15. Why does Wheeler say Smiley's frog was "modest"?

16. Why does Smiley leave the stranger alone with his frog?

17. How does Smiley feel when he finds out what the stranger has done to his frog?

18. Why does the narrator try to leave when Simon Wheeler is called away?

19. What happens when Wheeler returns before the narrator can leave?

20. From the way Wheeler tells his tales of Smiley, what does he seem to think about the man and his adventures?

Understanding Literature: Caricature

Humorists use many different techniques to make their readers laugh. One is caricature, a way of describing characters. In caricature, authors exaggerate, or stretch the truth about, one or two of a character's traits to amuse readers. People who create comic strips and cartoons often use caricature.

Their drawings may exaggerate one or two features of a person. For example, if a person has large feet in real life, a caricature might show the person with huge feet. Caricature in writing has the same effect.

21. In your own words, what is a caricature?

22. Why do authors use caricature?

23. Mark Twain presents Jim Smiley as a betting man. How does he build his caricature of Smiley, based on this characteristic?

24. How is the description of Smiley's pup, Andrew Jackson, a caricature?

25. Why do you think caricature makes writing funny? Explain.

Critical Thinking

26. How would you describe the first narrator of Twain's story? How good an observer is he? How is his storytelling voice different from Simon Wheeler's storytelling voice?

27. Why do you think Mark Twain presents his tales of Smiley as a story-within-a-story? In what ways does Wheeler's style of storytelling make the events he describes even funnier?

28. "Before he thought," Smiley offers Parson Walker a bet that his wife will die. What does that tell you about Smiley's character?

29. Why do you think Smiley leaves his frog with the stranger while he goes off to find another frog?

30. In what ways is "The Celebrated Jumping Frog of Calaveras County" a tall tale?

Writing on Your Own Rewrite the tale of Smiley's frog's defeat from the point of view of the frog ("Dan'l Webster").

Everyday Use
Alice Walker

Alice Walker
1944–

Literary Terms

first-person a point of view where the narrator is also a character, using the pronouns *I* and *we*

point of view the relationship of the narrator to the story

symbol a person, place, or object that stands for something beyond itself

theme the main idea of a story

About the Author

Alice Walker was the eighth child in a family of Georgia sharecroppers—farmers who work another person's land. She spent her junior year of college in Africa as an exchange student. After graduating, she settled in Mississippi.

Alice Walker has written fiction and poetry about her childhood, about the experiences of African Americans, particularly women, and about her travels in Africa. She is still active in politics, working toward a better life for African Americans and women.

Walker is probably best known for her novel *The Color Purple,* for which she received the Pulitzer Prize and an American Book Award. Her other novels include *The Temple of My Familiar, Possessing the Secret of Joy,* and *Meridian.* She has also published several books of poetry and many essays.

About the Selection

"Everyday Use" is about three African-American women, a mother and her two daughters. The story is told from the **point of view** of the mother. The mother is the **first-person** narrator and an important character. As in most short stories, the time frame is short: a single day. Dee comes to visit her mother and sister at their family home. She has begun a new way of life that she thinks is more suitable for an African-American woman. But is it really? The story explores this question as part of its **theme,** or main idea.

There's more to this story than just what happens during Dee's visit. Look carefully at the details Walker includes in her story. For example, the mother's quilts play an important role, both in the plot and as **symbols**. A symbol in literature is a person, place, or object that stands for something beyond itself.

Everyday Use

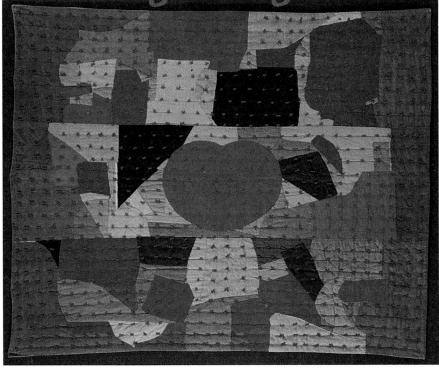

for your grandmama

I will wait for her in the yard that Maggie and I made so clean and wavy yesterday afternoon. A yard like this is more comfortable than most people know. It is not just a yard. It is like an extended living room. When the hard clay is swept clean as a floor and the fine sand around the edges lined with tiny, **irregular** grooves, anyone can come and sit and look up into the elm tree and wait for the breezes that never come inside the house.

Maggie will be nervous until after her sister goes: she will stand hopelessly in corners, homely and ashamed of the burn scars down her arms and legs, eying her sister with a mixture of envy and awe. She thinks her sister has held life always in

As you read, pay attention to the mother's voice and point of view as she narrates the story. Notice how she describes herself and both her daughters.

irregular uneven

the palm of one hand, that "no" is a word the world never learned to say to her.

You've no doubt seen those TV shows where the child who has "made it" is **confronted,** as a surprise, by her own mother and father, tottering in weakly from backstage. (A pleasant surprise, of course: What would they do if parent and child came on the show only to curse out and insult each other?) On TV mother and child embrace and smile into each other's faces. Sometimes the mother and father weep, the child wraps them in her arms and leans across the table to tell how she would not have made it without their help. I have seen these programs.

In the early days of television, there was a popular show called "This Is Your Life," which the narrator describes here.

Sometimes I dream a dream in which Dee and I are suddenly brought together on a TV program of this sort. Out of the dark and soft-seated **limousine** I am ushered into a bright room filled with many people. There I meet a smiling, gray, sporty man like Johnny Carson who shakes my hand and tells me what a fine girl I have. Then we are on the stage and Dee is **embracing** me with tears in her eyes. She pins on my dress a large orchid, even though she has told me once she thinks orchids are tacky flowers.

Johnny Carson hosted the late-night television show "Tonight" from 1962 to 1992.

In real life I am a large, big-boned woman with rough, man-working hands. In the winter I wear flannel nightgowns to bed and overalls during the day. I can kill and clean a hog as mercilessly as a man. My fat keeps me hot in zero weather. I can work outside all day, breaking ice to get water for washing; I can eat pork liver cooked over the open fire minutes after it comes steaming from the hog. One winter I knocked a bull calf straight in the brain between the eyes with a sledge hammer and had the meat hung up to chill before nightfall. But of course all this does not show on television. I am the way my daughter would want me to be: a hundred pounds lighter, my skin like an uncooked barley pancake. My hair glistens in the hot bright lights. Johnny Carson has much to do to keep up with my quick and witty tongue.

The mother believes that Dee would like her to be a "TV mom"— thinner, lighter-skinned, witty. What does this tell you about Dee and her relationship with her mother?

confront to meet face to face	**embrace** to hug	**limousine** a large, fancy car

But that is a mistake, I know even before I wake up. Who ever knew a Johnson with a quick tongue? Who can even imagine me looking a strange white man in the eye? It seems to me I have talked to them always with one foot raised in flight, with my head turned in whichever way is farthest from them. Dee, though. She would always look anyone in the eye. Hesitation was no part of her nature.

"How do I look, Mama?" Maggie says, showing just enough of her thin body **enveloped** in pink skirt and red blouse for me to know she's there, almost hidden by the door.

"Come out into the yard," I say.

Have you ever seen a lame animal, perhaps a dog run over by some careless person rich enough to own a car, sidle up to someone who is ignorant enough to be kind to him? That is the way my Maggie walks. She has been like this, chin on chest, eyes on ground, feet in shuffle, ever since the fire that burned the other house to the ground.

To *sidle* is to move sideways, as if frightened or ashamed. Notice the differences the narrator sees between her two daughters, Dee and Maggie.

Dee is lighter than Maggie, with nicer hair and a fuller figure. She's a woman now, though sometimes I forget. How long ago was it that the other house burned? Ten, twelve years? Sometimes I can still hear the flames and feel Maggie's arms sticking to me, her hair smoking and her dress falling off her in little black papery flakes. Her eyes seemed stretched open, blazed open by the flames reflected in them. And Dee, I see her standing off under the sweet gum tree she used to dig gum out of; a look of concentration on her face as she watched the last **dingy** gray board of the house fall in toward the red-hot brick chimney. Why don't you do a dance around the ashes? I'd wanted to ask her. She had hated the house that much.

I used to think she hated Maggie, too. But that was before we raised the money, the church and me, to send her to Augusta to school. She used to read to us without pity; forcing words, lies, other folks' habits, whole lives upon us two, sitting trapped and ignorant underneath her voice. She washed us in a river of make-believe, burned us with a lot of

Augusta, in eastern Georgia, is the location of Paine College.

dingy dirty, discolored   **envelop** to completely cover

knowledge we didn't necessarily need to know. Pressed us to her with the serious way she read, to shove us away at just the moment, like dimwits, we seemed about to understand.

Dee wanted nice things. A yellow organdy dress to wear to her graduation from high school; black pumps to match a green suit she'd made from an old suit somebody gave me. She was determined to stare down any disaster in her efforts. Her eyelids would not flicker for minutes at a time. Often I fought off the **temptation** to shake her. At sixteen she had a style of her own: and knew what style was.

I never had an education myself. After second grade the school was closed down. Don't ask me why: in 1927 colored asked fewer questions than they do now. Sometimes Maggie reads to me. She stumbles along good-naturedly, but can't see well. She knows she is not bright. Like good looks and money, quickness passed her by. She will marry John Thomas (who has mossy teeth in an earnest face) and then I'll be free to sit here and I guess just sing church songs to myself. Although I never was a good singer. Never could carry a tune. I was always better at a man's job. I used to love to milk till I was hooked in the side in '49. Cows are soothing and slow and don't bother you, unless you try to milk them the wrong way.

I have **deliberately** turned my back on the house. It is three rooms, just like the one that burned, except the roof is tin; they don't make shingle roofs any more. There are no real windows, just some holes cut in the sides, like the portholes on a ship, but not round and not square, with rawhide holding the shutters up on the outside. This house is in a pasture, too, like the other one. No doubt when Dee sees it she will want to tear it down. She wrote me once that no matter where we "choose" to live, she will manage to come see us. But she will never bring her friends. Maggie and I thought about this and Maggie asked me, "Mama, when did Dee ever *have* any friends?"

"Hooked in the side" means kicked by a cow.

deliberately with much thought; knowing exactly what one is doing

temptation an urge to do something

She has a few. **Furtive** boys in pink shirts hanging about on washday after school. Nervous girls who never laughed. Impressed with her they worshiped the well-turned phrase, the cute shape, the **scalding** humor that **erupted** like bubbles in **lye.** She read to them.

When she was courting Jimmy T she didn't have much time to pay to us, but turned all her faultfinding power on him. He *flew* to marry a cheap city girl from a family of ignorant flashy people. She hardly had time to recompose herself.

When she comes I will meet—but there they are!

Maggie attempts to make a dash for the house, in her shuffling way, but I stay her with my hand. "Come back here," I say. And she stops and tries to dig a well in the sand with her toe.

It is hard to see them clearly through the strong sun. But even the first glimpse of leg out of the car tells me it is Dee. Her feet were always neat-looking, as if God himself had shaped them with a certain style. From the other side of the car comes a short, stocky man. Hair is all over his head a foot long and hanging from his chin like a **kinky** mule tail. I hear Maggie suck in her breath. "Uhnnnh," is what it sounds like. Like when you see the wriggling end of a snake just in front of your foot on the road. "Uhnnnh."

Dee next. A dress down to the ground, in this hot weather. A dress so loud it hurts my eyes. There are yellows and oranges enough to throw back the light of the sun. I feel my whole face warming from the heat waves it throws out. Earrings gold, too, and hanging down to her shoulders. Bracelets dangling and making noises when she moves her arm up to shake the folds of the dress out of her armpits. The dress is loose and flows, and as she walks closer, I like it. I hear Maggie go "Uhnnnh" again. It is her sister's hair. It stands

At this point, think about what you have learned about Dee's character. Compare her mother's memories and thoughts with the way Dee behaves when she appears. How is Dee the same kind of person she always was? How has she changed?

Dee seems to be wearing an African-inspired dress, jewelry, and hairdo.

erupt to rise up	**lye** a strong solution that can eat away or destroy by chemical action	**scalding** burning
furtive secretive		
kinky tightly curled		

straight up like the wool on a sheep. It is black as night and around the edges are two long pigtails that rope about like small lizards disappearing behind her ears.

"Wa-su-zo-Tean-o!" she says, coming on in that gliding way the dress makes her move. The short stocky fellow with the hair to his navel is all grinning and he follows up with "Asalamalakim, my mother and my sister!" He moves to hug Maggie but she falls back, tight up against the back of my chair. I feel her trembling there and when I look up I see the perspiration falling off her chin.

"Don't get up," says Dee. Since I am stout it takes something of a push. You can see me trying to move a second or two before I make it. She turns, showing white heels through her sandals, and goes back to the car. Out she peeks next with a Polaroid. She stoops down quickly and lines up picture after picture of me sitting there in front of the house with Maggie **cowering** behind me. She never takes a shot without making sure the house is included. When a cow comes nibbling around the edge of the yard she snaps it and me and Maggie *and* the house. Then she puts the Polaroid in the back seat of the car, and comes up and kisses me on the forehead.

Meanwhile Asalamalakim is going through motions with Maggie's hand. Maggie's hand is as limp as a fish, and probably as cold, despite the sweat, and she keeps trying to pull it back. It looks like Asalamalakim wants to shake hands but wants to do it fancy. Or maybe he don't know how people shake hands. Anyhow, he soon gives up on Maggie.

"Well," I say, "Dee."

"No, Mama," she says. "Not 'Dee,' Wangero Leewanika Kemanjo!"

"What happened to 'Dee'?" I wanted to know.

"She's dead," Wangero said. "I couldn't bear it any longer, being named after the people who **oppress** me."

"You know as well as me you was named after your aunt Dicie," I said. Dicie is my sister. She named Dee. We called her

Wa-su-zo-Tean-o is the greeting used by Black Muslims, the popular name for members of an African-American nationalist religious movement in the United States. *Asalamalakim* is a Muslim greeting that means "Peace be with you."

Dee has taken an African name, as did most followers of the Black Muslims.

cower to hide, as if in fear

oppress to wrong someone; to abuse one's power over someone

"Big Dee" after Dee was born.

"But who was *she* named after?" asked Wangero.

"I guess after Grandma Dee," I said.

"And who was she named after?" asked Wangero.

"Her mother," I said, and saw Wangero was getting tired. "That's about as far back as I can trace it," I said. Though, in fact, I probably could have carried it back beyond the Civil War through the branches.

"Well," said Asalamalakim, "there you are."

"Uhnnnh," I heard Maggie say.

"There I was not," I said, "before 'Dicie' cropped up in our family, so why should I try to trace it that far back?"

He just stood there grinning, looking down on me like somebody inspecting a Model A car. Every once in a while he and Wangero sent eye signals over my head.

"How do you pronounce this name?" I asked.

"You don't have to call me by it if you don't want to," said Wangero.

"Why shouldn't I?" I asked. "If that's what you want us to call you, we'll call you."

"I know it might sound awkward at first," said Wangero.

"I'll get used to it," I said. "Ream it out again."

Well, soon we got the name out of the way. Asalamalakim had a name twice as long and three times as hard. After I tripped over it two or three times he told me to just call him Hakim-a-barber. I wanted to ask him was he a barber, but I didn't really think he was, so I didn't ask.

"You must belong to those beef-cattle peoples down the road," I said. They said "Asalamalakim" when they met you, too, but they didn't shake hands. Always too busy: feeding the cattle, fixing the fences, putting up salt-lick shelters, throwing down hay. When the white folks poisoned some of the herd the men stayed up all night with rifles in their hands. I walked a mile and a half just to see the sight.

Hakim-a-barber said, "I accept some of their **doctrines**, but farming and raising cattle is not my style." (They didn't

The Ford Model A replaced the Model T in the late 1920s. "Asalamalakim" is looking at the mother as a kind of human antique, pleasant but very old-fashioned. The Model A, however, was known for being a finely made and long-lasting car.

Salt-lick shelters were built to keep rain from dissolving the large blocks of salt on poles for cattle.

doctrine a belief or teaching

tell me, and I didn't ask, whether Wangero (Dee) had really gone and married him.)

We sat down to eat and right away he said he didn't eat collards and pork was unclean. Wangero, though, went on through the chitlins and corn bread, the greens and everything else. She talked a blue streak over the sweet potatoes. Everything delighted her. Even the fact that we still used the benches her daddy made for the table when we couldn't afford to buy chairs.

Collards and *chitlins* are foods enjoyed by many people in the American South. Collards are greens; chitlins, or chitterlings, are the intestines of hogs. Muslims don't eat pork.

"Oh, Mama!" she cried. Then turned to Hakim-a-barber. "I never knew how lovely these benches are. You can feel the rump prints," she said, running her hands underneath her and along the bench. Then she gave a sigh and her hand closed over Grandma Dee's butter dish. "That's it!" she said. "I knew there was something I wanted to ask you if I could have." She jumped up from the table and went over in the corner where the churn stood, the milk in it clabber by now. She looked at the churn and looked at it.

Clabber is curdled, or sour, milk.

"This churn top is what I need," she said. "Didn't Uncle Buddy whittle it out of a tree you all used to have?"

"Yes," I said.

"Uh huh," she said happily. "And I want the dasher, too."

The *dasher* on a churn has blades that swirl the milk around.

Notice that these are the first words Maggie has spoken to the visitors.

"Uncle Buddy whittle that, too?" asked the barber.

Dee (Wangero) looked up at me.

"Aunt Dee's first husband whittled the dash," said Maggie so low you almost couldn't hear her. "His name was Henry, but they called him Stash."

"Maggie's brain is like an elephant's," Wangero said, laughing. "I can use the churn top as a centerpiece for the **alcove** table," she said, sliding a plate over the churn, "and I'll think of something artistic to do with the dasher."

When she finished wrapping the dasher the handle stuck out. I took it for a moment in my hands. You didn't even have to look close to see where hands pushing the dasher up and down to make butter had left a kind of sink in the wood. In fact, there were a lot of small sinks; you could see where

alcove a small, set in section of a room

thumbs and fingers had sunk into the wood. It was beautiful light yellow wood, from a tree that grew in the yard where Big Dee and Stash had lived.

After dinner Dee (Wangero) went to the trunk at the foot of my bed and started rifling through it. Maggie hung back in the kitchen over the dishpan. Out came Wangero with two quilts. They had been pieced by Grandma Dee and then Big Dee and me had hung them on the quilt frames on the front porch and quilted them. One was in the Lone Star pattern. The other was Walk Around the Mountain. In both of them were scraps of dresses Grandma Dee had worn fifty and more years ago. Bits and pieces of Grandpa Jarrell's Paisley shirts. And one teeny faded blue piece, about the size of a penny matchbox, that was from Great Grandpa Ezra's uniform that he wore in the Civil War.

Compare the attitudes of the mother, Maggie, and Dee toward the dasher. In what sense can the dasher be considered a symbol in this story—an object standing for something beyond itself?

The mother hears Maggie's reaction to Dee's request for the quilts. Why do you think Maggie is upset?

"Mama," Wangero said sweet as a bird. "Can I have these old quilts?"

I heard something fall in the kitchen, and a minute later the kitchen door slammed.

"Why don't you take one or two of the others?" I asked. "These old things was just done by me and Big Dee from some tops your grandma pieced before she died."

"No," said Wangero. "I don't want those. They are stitched around the borders by machine."

"That'll make them last better," I said.

"That's not the point," said Wangero. "These are all pieces of dresses Grandma used to wear. She did all this stitching by hand. Imagine!" She held the quilts securely in her arms, stroking them.

"Some of the pieces, like those lavender ones, come from old clothes her mother handed down to her," I said, moving up to touch the quilts. Dee (Wangero) moved back just enough so that I couldn't reach the quilts. They already belonged to her.

"Imagine!" she breathed again, clutching them closely to her bosom.

"The truth is," I said, "I promised to give them quilts to Maggie, for when she marries John Thomas."

She gasped like a bee had stung her.

The name of this short story is "Everyday Use." How are these words important to the story? What use are these quilts to Maggie and her mother? What use are they to Dee? Why do you think Dee now wants the quilts she rejected once as old-fashioned?

"Maggie can't appreciate these quilts!" she said. "She'd probably be backward enough to put them to everyday use."

"I reckon she would," I said. "God knows I been saving 'em for long enough with nobody using 'em. I hope she will!" I didn't want to bring up how I had offered Dee (Wangero) a quilt when she went away to college. Then she had told me they were old-fashioned, out of style.

"But they're *priceless*!" she was saying now, furiously; for she has a temper. "Maggie would put them on the bed and in five years they'd be in rags. Less than that!"

"She can always make some more," I said. "Maggie knows how to quilt."

Dee (Wangero) looked at me with hatred. "You just will not understand. The point is these quilts, *these* quilts!"

Passin' It On, Mary Bertoli, SNJM

"Well," I said, stumped. "What would *you* do with them?"

"Hang them," she said. As if that was the only thing you *could* do with quilts.

Maggie by now was standing in the door. I could almost hear the sound her feet made as they scraped over each other.

"She can have them, Mama," she said, like somebody used to never winning anything, or having anything reserved for her. "I can 'member Grandma Dee without the quilts."

I looked at her hard. She had filled her bottom lip with checkerberry snuff and it gave her face a kind of dopey, hangdog look. It was Grandma Dee and Big Dee who taught her how to quilt herself. She stood there with her scarred

Notice that the quilts, also, are symbols in this story. How are they similar to the dasher in their meaning?

What has happened here? What has "hit" the mother to make her do what she does at this point?

hands hidden in the folds of her skirt. She looked at her sister with something like fear but she wasn't mad at her. This was Maggie's portion. This was the way she knew God to work.

When I looked at her like that something hit me in the top of my head and ran down to the soles of my feet. Just like when I'm in church and the spirit of God touches me and I get happy and shout. I did something I never had done before: hugged Maggie to me, then dragged her on into the room, snatched the quilts out of Miss Wangero's hands and dumped them into Maggie's lap. Maggie just sat there on my bed with her mouth open.

"Take one or two of the others," I said to Dee.

But she turned without a word and went out to Hakim-a-barber.

"You just don't understand," she said, as Maggie and I came out to the car.

"What don't I understand?" I wanted to know.

There are differences in the ways Maggie, her mother, and Dee view their heritage as African-American women. What are those differences?

"Your **heritage**," she said. And then she turned to Maggie, kissed her, and said, "You ought to try to make something of yourself, too, Maggie. It's really a new day for us. But from the way you and Mama still live you'd never know it."

She put on some sunglasses that hid everything above the tip of her nose and her chin.

What changes do you notice here in Maggie and in the relationship between Maggie and her mother?

Maggie smiled; maybe at the sunglasses. But a real smile, not scared. After we watched the car dust settle I asked Maggie to bring me a dip of snuff. And then the two of us sat there just enjoying, until it was time to go in the house and go to bed.

heritage a birthright; something one inherits, or gets from someone who came before

Directions Write the answers to these questions using complete sentences.

Comprehension: Identifying Facts

1. What have Maggie and her mother done to prepare for Dee's visit?

2. How does the mother think Maggie will behave during Dee's visit?

3. Why does Maggie have "burn scars down her arms and legs"?

4. What does the mother say about Maggie's future plans?

5. What does the mother notice first when Dee gets out of the car?

6. Whom does Dee bring with her on her visit to her family?

7. Why does Dee say she has changed her name?

8. Why does Dee want the churn top and the dasher?

9. Why does Dee think that Maggie should not have the quilts?

10. What does Dee say her mother doesn't understand?

Comprehension: Understanding Main Ideas

11. What does the mother's dream about going on a game show say about her relationship with Dee?

12. The mother predicts that Maggie will be nervous until her sister leaves. Does this happen?

13. How does the mother describe herself? Maggie? Dee?

14. How did Maggie's experience of the fire compare with Dee's? What does this suggest about each sister's character?

15. What did Dee think about her home when she was younger? What does she think about it now? How would you explain the change?

16. Why do Dee and her friend want to be called by African names?

17. Why are the quilts important to Dee? Why are they important to her mother and Maggie?

18. How does Maggie first react when Dee wants the quilts, based on what her mother hears from the kitchen?

19. What does Maggie's reaction to Dee's wanting the quilts cause her mother to do? Why is this "just like when I'm in church and the spirit of God touches me"?

20. Why does Dee say her mother doesn't understand her heritage?

Review Continued on Next Page

Everyday Use, *Continued*

Understanding Literature: Symbol

A symbol is something that has meaning in itself, and also stands for something else. For example, the American flag is both a special piece of cloth and a symbol of what the United States stands for.

In literature, symbols are real parts of the story. They also stand for or suggest something more. In "Everyday Use," certain objects are parts of Maggie and her mother's everyday life. They see them in one way. Dee sees them in another. These objects are symbols. They help the reader understand the different ways the three women think about their lives.

21. In your own words, what is a symbol?

22. What are the churn top, dasher, and quilts symbols of to Dee? What are they symbols of to Maggie and her mother?

23. In what way is Dee's new name also a symbol in the story?

24. In what ways are Maggie's burn scars used as symbols in the story?

25. Why are the quilts especially good symbols for the theme (main idea) of this story?

Critical Thinking

26. Why do you think Alice Walker dedicates the story "for your grandmama"?

27. In what ways does the last paragraph of the story suggest a change in Maggie? What do you think has caused this change?

28. Dee says that her mother doesn't understand her heritage. Do you agree with Dee? Why or why not?

29. How would you describe the character of the mother in this story? How does her point of view add to the reader's understanding of the story's theme?

30. In an interview, Alice Walker said that her African background was important to her but that her family—her parents and grandparents—was more important. How is this idea part of the story?

Writing on Your Own Is there an object in your life that could be a symbol of what you are and the way you think about things? Write a paragraph describing the object and what it says about you.

American History

Judith Ortiz-Cofer

Judith Ortiz-Cofer

1952–

Literary Terms

epiphany the moment in a story when a character recognizes an important truth

fiction literature in which the author creates the events and characters

flashback a look into the past at some point in a story

image a picture in the reader's mind created by words

About the Author

Judith Ortiz-Cofer was born in Puerto Rico, but moved to Paterson, New Jersey, when she was a child. She spoke Spanish and ate Puerto Rican food bought at local shops. The customs and cultures of both Puerto Rico and the United States became a part of her life. In her writing, she bridges both worlds.

Ortiz-Cofer has written many essays, poems, and short stories. In 1989, the New York City Library System listed her first novel, *The Line of the Sun*, as one of "25 Books to Remember." Her other books include *Silent Dancing: A Partial Remembrance of a Puerto Rican Childhood* and *An Island Like You: Stories of the Barrio*.

Judith Ortiz-Cofer now lives in Georgia and teaches at the University of Georgia. She also travels around the country to share her experiences as a Latina woman.

About the Selection

People often wonder if Judith Ortiz-Cofer is Elena in this story. She says she isn't, since she was only eleven when President Kennedy was assassinated. She drew on her memories to create this short story. Her realistic details help make the events of this **fictional** story come alive.

"American History" is a story about an important day in the life of a Puerto Rican girl living in a rundown part of a New Jersey city. The story is told from Elena's point of view. The narrator provides a **flashback** to some events that happened earlier. In this story, Elena comes to realize a hard truth about her life. In literature, a sudden, important realization is called an **epiphany**. The story ends with a striking **image** of snow falling that tells us something about Elena's epiphany.

American History

As you read, notice what the narrator reveals about herself and her life as a young girl.

Salsa is Latin American popular music.

John F. Kennedy, 35th president of the United States, was shot and killed in Dallas on November 22, 1963. He was the first Roman Catholic president and as such became "a saint" to many Catholics in America, including Puerto Rican immigrants.

I once read in a "Ripley's Believe It or Not" column that Paterson, New Jersey, is the place where the Straight and Narrow (streets) **intersect.** The Puerto Rican **tenement** known as *El Building* was one block up from Straight. It was, in fact, the corner of Straight and Market; not "at" the corner, but *the* corner. At almost any hour of the day, El Building was like a monstrous jukebox, blasting out *salsas* from open windows as the residents, mostly new immigrants just up from the island, tried to drown out whatever they were currently enduring with loud music. But the day President Kennedy was shot there was a **profound** silence in El Building; even the abusive tongues of **viragoes,** the cursing of the unemployed, and the screeching of small children had been somehow **muted.** President Kennedy was a saint to these people. In fact, soon his photograph would be hung alongside the Sacred Heart and over the spiritist altars that many women kept in their apartments. He would become part of the **hierarchy** of **martyrs** they prayed to for favors that only one who had died for a cause would understand.

hierarchy a list in order of importance	**muted** quieted, softened	**tenement** a city apartment for poorer families that is usually unclean, unsafe, uncomfortable
intersect to meet	**profound** deep	
martyr someone who dies for a cause or religious belief		**virago** a loud, harsh-sounding woman

On the day that President Kennedy was shot, my ninth grade class had been out in the fenced playground of Public School Number 13. We had been given "free" exercise time and had been ordered by our P.E. teacher, Mr. DePalma, to "keep moving." That meant that the girls should jump rope and the boys toss basketballs through a hoop at the far end of the yard. He in the meantime would "keep an eye" on us from just inside the building.

It was a cold gray day in Paterson. The kind that warns of early snow. I was miserable, since I had forgotten my gloves, and my knuckles were turning red and raw from the jump rope. I was also taking a lot of abuse from the black girls for not turning the rope hard and fast enough for them.

"Hey, Skinny Bones, pump it, girl. Ain't you got no energy today?" Gail, the biggest of the black girls had the other end of the rope, yelled, "Didn't you eat your rice and beans and pork chops for breakfast today?"

The other girls picked up the "pork chop" and made it into a **refrain**: "pork chop, pork chop, did you eat your pork chop?" They entered the double ropes in pairs and exited without tripping or missing a beat. I felt a burning on my cheeks and then my glasses fogged up so that I could not manage to **coordinate** the jump rope with Gail. The chill was doing to me what it always did; entering my bones, making me cry, **humiliating** me. I hated the city, especially in winter. I hated Public School Number 13. I hated my skinny flatchested body, and I envied the black girls who could jump rope so fast that their legs became a blur. They always seemed to be warm while I froze.

There was only one source of beauty and light for me that school year. The only thing I had **anticipated** at the start of the semester. That was seeing Eugene. In August, Eugene and his family had moved into the only house on the block that had a yard and trees. I could see his place from my window in

The other girls are making fun of Elena for what they assume Puerto Ricans eat for breakfast.

Here, the first-person narrator provides a flashback to an earlier time.

| **anticipate** to look forward to | **coordinate** to move or act smoothly with someone else | **humiliate** to embarrass deeply |
| | | **refrain** repeated words |

El Building. In fact, if I sat on the fire escape I was **literally** suspended above Eugene's backyard. It was my favorite spot to read my library books in the summer. Until that August the house had been occupied by an old Jewish couple. Over the years I had become part of their family, without their knowing it, of course. I had a view of their kitchen and their backyard, and though I could not hear what they said, I knew when they were arguing, when one of them was sick, and many other things. I knew all this by watching them at mealtimes. I could see their kitchen table, the sink, and the stove. During good times, he sat at the table and read his newspapers while she fixed the meals. If they argued, he would leave and the old woman would sit and stare at nothing for a long time. When one of them was sick, the other would come and get things from the kitchen and carry them out on a tray. The old man had died in June. The last week of school I had not seen him at the table at all. Then one day I saw that there was a crowd in the kitchen. The old woman had finally emerged from the house on the arm of a stocky, middle-aged woman, whom I had seen there a few times before, maybe her daughter. Then a man had carried out suitcases. The house had stood empty for weeks. I had had to resist the **temptation** to climb down into the yard and water the flowers the old lady had taken such good care of.

By the time Eugene's family moved in, the yard was a tangled mass of weeds. The father spent several days mowing, and when he finished, from where I sat, I didn't see the red, yellow, and purple clusters that meant flowers to me. I didn't see his family sit down at the kitchen table together. It was just the mother, a red-headed tall woman who wore a white uniform—a nurse's, I guessed it was; the father was gone before I got up in the morning and was never there at dinner time. I only saw him on weekends when they sometimes sat on lawn-chairs under the oak tree, each hidden behind a section of the newspaper; and there was Eugene. He was tall and blond, and he wore glasses. I liked him right away

literally actually, really

temptation an urge to do something

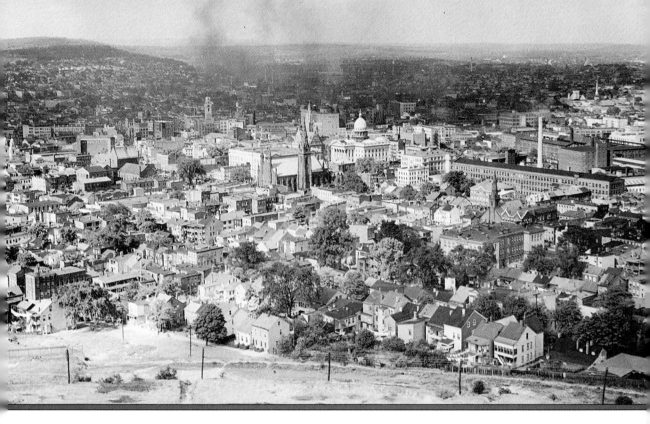

A view of Paterson, New Jersey.

because he sat at the kitchen table and read books for hours. That summer, before we had even spoken one word to each other, I kept him company on my fire escape.

Once school started I looked for him in all my classes, but P.S. 13 was a huge, **over-populated** place and it took me days and many **discreet** questions to discover that Eugene was in honors classes for all his subjects; classes that were not open to me because English was not my first language, though I was a straight A student. After much **maneuvering** I managed "to run into him" in the hallway where his locker was—on the other side of the building from mine—and in study hall at the library where he first seemed to notice me, but did not speak; and finally, on the way home after school one day when I decided to approach him directly, though my stomach was doing somersaults.

discreet careful, showing good judgment	**maneuvering** planning a movement to gain you something	**over-populated** overcrowded

Snobbery means ignoring people considered to be inferior.

I was ready for **rejection**, snobbery, the worst. But when I came up to him, practically panting in my nervousness, and blurted out: "You're Eugene. Right?" he smiled, pushed his glasses up on his nose, and nodded. I saw then that he was blushing deeply. Eugene liked me, but he was shy. I did most of the talking that day. He nodded and smiled a lot. In the weeks that followed, we walked home together. He would **linger** at the corner of El Building for a few minutes then walk down to his two-story house. It was not until Eugene moved into that house that I noticed that El Building blocked most of the sun, and that the only spot that got a little sunlight during the day was the tiny square of earth the old woman had planted with flowers.

I did not tell Eugene that I could see inside his kitchen from my bedroom. I felt dishonest, but I liked my secret sharing of his evenings, especially now that I knew what he was reading since we chose our books together at the school library.

One day my mother came into my room as I was sitting on the window staring out. In her **abrupt** way she said: "Elena, you are acting 'moony'." *Enamorada* was what she really said, that is—like a girl stupidly **infatuated**. Since I had turned fourteen and started menstruating my mother had been more **vigilant** than ever. She acted as if I was going to go crazy or explode or something if she didn't watch me and nag me all the time about being a *señorita* now. She kept talking about **virtue**, **morality**, and other subjects that did not interest me in the least. My mother was unhappy in Paterson, but my father had a good job at the bluejeans factory in Passaic and soon, he kept assuring us, we would be moving to our own house there. Every Sunday we drove out to the suburbs of Paterson, Clifton, and Passaic, out to where people mowed grass on Sundays in the summer, and where children made snowmen in the winter from pure white snow, not like

Being a *señorita* means being a young woman, rather than a child.

---

abrupt said or done suddenly, without much explanation

infatuated foolishly in love

linger to be slow in leaving

morality a system of good conduct

rejection a refusal to accept or hear

vigilant watchful

virtue goodness

the gray slush of Paterson which seemed to fall from the sky in that hue. I had learned to listen to my parents' dreams, which were spoken in Spanish, as fairy tales, like the stories about life in the island paradise of Puerto Rico before I was born. I had been to the island once as a little girl, to grandmother's funeral, and all I remembered was wailing women in black, my mother becoming **hysterical** and being given a pill that made her sleep two days, and me feeling lost in a crowd of strangers all claiming to be my aunts, uncles, and cousins. I had actually been glad to return to the city. We had not been back there since then, though my parents talked constantly about buying a house on the beach someday, retiring on the island—that was a common topic among the residents of El Building. As for me, I was going to go to college and become a teacher.

But after meeting Eugene I began to think of the present more than of the future. What I wanted now was to enter that house I had watched for so many years. I wanted to see the other rooms where the old people had lived, and where the boy spent his time. Most of all, I wanted to sit at the kitchen table with Eugene like two adults, like the old man and his wife had done, maybe drink some coffee and talk about books. I had started reading *Gone With the Wind*. I was **enthralled** by it, with the daring and the **passion** of the beautiful girl living in a mansion, and with her devoted parents and the slaves who did everything for them. I didn't believe such a world had ever really existed, and I wanted to ask Eugene some questions since he and his parents, he had told me, had come up from Georgia, the same place where the novel was set. His father worked for a company that had transferred him to Paterson. His mother was very unhappy, Eugene said, in his beautiful voice that rose and fell over words in a strange, **lilting** way. The kids at school called him "the hick" and made fun of the way he talked. I knew I was his only friend so far, and I liked that, though I felt sad for him

Gone With the Wind, by Margaret Mitchell, is a novel about life in the American South before, during, and after the Civil War.

---

enthralled fascinated

hysterical not able to stop crying

lilting musical

passion strong feeling

sometimes. "Skinny Bones" and the "Hick" was what they called us at school when we were seen together.

The day Mr. DePalma came out into the cold and asked us to line up in front of him was the day that President Kennedy was shot. Mr. DePalma, a short, **muscular** man with slicked-down black hair, was the science teacher, P.E. coach, and **disciplinarian** at P.S. 13. He was the teacher to whose homeroom you got assigned if you were a troublemaker, and the man called out to break up playground fights, and to escort **violently** angry teen-agers to the office. And Mr. DePalma was the man who called your parents in for "a conference."

That day, he stood in front of two rows of mostly black and Puerto Rican kids, **brittle** from their efforts to "keep moving" on a November day that was turning bitter cold. Mr. DePalma, to our complete shock, was crying. Not just silent adult tears, but really sobbing. There were a few titters from the back of the line where I stood shivering.

"Listen," Mr. DePalma raised his arms over his head as if he were about to conduct an orchestra. His voice broke, and he covered his face with his hands. His barrel chest was **heaving.** Someone giggled behind me.

brittle stiff	**muscular** strongly built
disciplinarian one who punishes	**violently** extremely, without control
heaving moving up and down	

"Listen," he repeated, "something awful has happened." A strange gurgling came from his throat, and he turned and spat on the cement behind him.

"Gross," someone said, and there was a lot of laughter.

"The President is dead, you idiots. I should have known that wouldn't mean anything to a bunch of losers like you kids. Go home." He was shrieking now. No one moved for a minute or two, but then a big girl let out a "Yeah!" and ran to get her books piled up with the others against the brick wall of the school building. The others followed in a mad scramble to get to their things before somebody caught on. It was still an hour to the dismissal bell.

A little scared, I headed for El Building. There was an eerie feeling on the streets. I looked into Mario's drugstore, a favorite hangout for the high school crowd, but there were only a couple of old Jewish men at the soda-bar talking with the short order cook in tones that sounded almost angry, but they were keeping their voices low. Even the traffic on one of the busiest intersections in Paterson—Straight Street and Park Avenue—seemed to be moving slower. There were no horns blasting that day. At El Building, the usual little group of unemployed men were not hanging out on the front stoop making it difficult for women to enter the front door. No music spilled out from open doors in the hallway. When I walked into our apartment, I found my mother sitting in front of the grainy picture of the television set.

She looked up at me with a tear-streaked face and just said: "Dios mio," turning back to the set as if it were pulling at her eyes. I went into my room.

Dios mio means "My God."

Though I wanted to feel the right thing about President Kennedy's death, I could not fight the feeling of **elation** that stirred in my chest. Today was the day I was to visit Eugene in his house. He had asked me to come over after school to study for an American History test with him. We had also planned to walk to the public library together. I looked down into his yard. The oak tree was bare of leaves and the ground looked gray with ice. The light through the large kitchen window of

elation great happiness

his house told me that El Building blocked the sun to such an extent that they had to turn lights on in the middle of the day. I felt ashamed about it. But the white kitchen table with the lamp hanging just above it looked cozy and inviting. I would soon sit there, across from Eugene, and I would tell him about my perch just above his house. Maybe I should.

In the next thirty minutes I changed clothes, put on a little pink lipstick, and got my books together. Then I went in to tell my mother that I was going to a friend's house to study. I did not expect her **reaction**.

"You are going out *today*?" The way she said "today" sounded as if a storm warning had been issued. It was said in **utter disbelief**. Before I could answer, she came toward me and held my elbows as I clutched my books.

Hija means daughter.

"*Hija*, the President has been killed. We must show respect. He was a great man. Come to church with me tonight."

She tried to **embrace** me, but my books were in the way. My first impulse was to comfort her, she seemed so **distraught**, but I had to meet Eugene in fifteen minutes.

"I have a test to study for, Mama. I will be home by eight."

Niña means child. Here it is used like "dear."

"You are forgetting who you are, *Niña*. I have seen you staring down at that boy's house. You are heading for humiliation and pain." My mother said this in Spanish and in a resigned tone that surprised me, as if she had no **intention** of stopping me from "heading for humiliation and pain." I started for the door. She sat in front of the TV holding a white handkerchief to her face.

I walked out to the street and around the chain-link fence that separated El Building from Eugene's house. The yard was neatly edged around the little walk that led to the door. It always amazed me how Paterson, the inner core of the city, had no apparent **logic** to its architecture. Small, neat, single

---

disbelief holding something to be untrue

distraught terribly upset

embrace to hug

intention a plan

logic reasoning

reaction a response

utter total; complete

---

residences like this one could be found right next to huge, **dilapidated** apartment buildings like El Building. My guess was that the little houses had been there first, then the immigrants had come in droves, and the **monstrosities** had been raised for them—the Italians, the Irish, the Jews, and now us, the Puerto Ricans and the blacks. The door was painted a deep green: *verde*, the color of hope, I had heard my mother say it: *Verde-Esperanza*.

I knocked softly. A few suspenseful moments later the door opened just a crack. The red, swollen face of a woman appeared. She had a halo of red hair floating over a delicate ivory face—the face of a doll—with freckles on the nose. Her **smudged** eye make-up made her look unreal to me, like a mannequin seen through a **warped** store window.

"What do you want?" Her voice was tiny and sweet-sounding, like a little girl's, but her tone was not friendly.

"I'm Eugene's friend. He asked me over. To study." I thrust out my books, a silly gesture that embarrassed me almost immediately.

"You live there?" She pointed up to El Building, which looked particularly ugly, like a gray prison with its many dirty windows and rusty fire escapes. The woman had stepped halfway out and I could see that she wore a white nurse's uniform with St. Joseph's Hospital on the name tag.

"Yes. I do."

She looked intently at me for a couple of heartbeats, then said as if to herself, "I don't know how you people do it." Then directly to me: "Listen. Honey. Eugene doesn't want to study with you. He is a smart boy. Doesn't need help. You understand me. I am truly sorry if he told you you could come over. He cannot study with you. It's nothing personal. You understand? We won't be in this place much longer, no need for him to get close to people—it'll just make it harder for him later. Run back home now."

dilapidated rundown, in poor condition	**monstrosity** something that is huge and ugly	**smudged** smeared
	residence a place to live in	**warped** curved; out of focus

The narrator has an epiphany here—she recognizes an important truth. What is the truth she sees?

I couldn't move. I just stood there in shock at hearing these things said to me in such a honey-drenched voice. I had never heard an accent like hers, except for Eugene's softer **version**. It was as if she were singing me a little song.

"What's wrong? Didn't you hear what I said?" She seemed very angry, and I finally snapped out of my **trance**. I turned away from the green door, and heard her close it gently.

Our apartment was empty when I got home. My mother was in someone else's kitchen, seeking the **solace** she needed. Father would come in from his late shift at midnight. I would hear them talking softly in the kitchen for hours that night. They would not discuss their dreams for the future, or life in Puerto Rico, as they often did; that night they would talk sadly about the young widow and her two children, as if they were family. For the next few days, we would observe *luto* in our apartment; that is, we would practice **restraint** and silence—no loud music or laughter. Some of the women of El Building would wear black for weeks.

Luto means mourning or sorrow.

That night, I lay in my bed trying to feel the right thing for our dead President. But the tears that came up from a deep source inside me were strictly for me. When my mother came to the door, I pretended to be sleeping. Sometime during the night, I saw from my bed the streetlight come on. It had a pink halo around it. I went to my window and pressed my face to the cool glass. Looking up at the light I could see the white snow falling like a lace veil over its face. I did not look down to see it turning gray as it touched the ground below.

The narrator ends with a visual image—that is, a word picture that appeals to our sense of sight. What does the image suggest about the narrator's feelings?

restraint control

solace comfort

trance a condition in which one can't seem to move

version a form or type

Directions Write the answers to these questions using complete sentences.

Comprehension: Identifying Facts

1. What is El Building?

2. On what day does this story take place? How do you know?

3. Where are Elena and her classmates and what are they doing when they get the news of Kennedy's murder?

4. What is the one thing Elena looks forward to that school year?

5. Why does Elena like Eugene?

6. Why are honors classes not open to Elena?

7. What are Elena's parents' dreams for their future? What are Elena's plans?

8. Why do kids at school call Eugene "the hick"?

9. Why is Mr. DePalma crying?

10. Why doesn't Elena get to study with Eugene?

Comprehension: Understanding Main Ideas

11. Why is El Building usually "like a monstrous jukebox"? How is it on the day Kennedy is shot?

12. How does Elena get along with her classmates?

13. Before Eugene's family moved in, an old couple lived in their house. In what way had Elena become part of the old couple's family?

14. What does Elena notice about El Building after Eugene moves into his house?

15. Why doesn't Elena tell Eugene that she can see inside his kitchen from her bedroom?

16. Why does Elena's mother watch her so closely?

17. Why does Elena think of her parents' dreams as "fairy tales"?

18. Why does Elena say that meeting Eugene made her think more about the present than the future?

19. Why does Elena feel happy even though the president has been shot?

20. Why does Eugene's mother send Elena home after she finds out Elena lives in El Building?

Review Continued on Next Page

Understanding Literature: Epiphany

In fiction, an epiphany is a moment when a character recognizes or realizes an important truth. The epiphany deeply affects the person, sometimes changing him or her forever.

In "American History," the narrator, Elena, has a moment of epiphany that reveals a hard truth about her life. The image at the end of the story—of Elena looking at the snow through the streetlight, rather than watching it fall to the ground—suggests the understanding she has reached from her epiphany on Eugene's doorstep.

21. In your own words, what is an epiphany?

22. What does Elena learn from what Eugene's mother says to her? What makes this moment an epiphany?

23. The narrator says the tears she shed that night "were strictly for me." What does she mean?

24. The day Elena realizes an important truth was also a day of epiphany for the entire country. What truth did America realize that day?

25. Have you ever had a moment that you might call an epiphany? What did you realize about yourself or about life?

Critical Thinking

26. Why do you think this story is called "American History"?

27. Compare Mr. DePalma's reaction to Kennedy's murder with his words to the students. Compare Eugene's mother's reaction with her treatment of Elena. What conclusions can you draw? How are people's feelings about the president different from their feelings about each other?

28. Why do you think Elena's mother does not stop her from going to Eugene's house, even though she knows she is "heading for humiliation and pain"?

29. What details does the narrator give that suggest how Puerto Ricans were treated in her neighborhood?

30. Why do you think Elena chooses to see the snow looking white, "falling like a lace veil," rather than gray as it touches the ground?

Writing on Your Own Have you ever had a moment when you were very happy, but everyone else around you was sad? Write a brief description of the way you were feeling inside and the way you appeared on the outside.

Thank You, M'am
Langston Hughes

Langston Hughes
1902–1967

Literary Terms

antagonist the person or force opposing the protagonist

conflict the struggle of the protagonist against himself or herself, another person, or nature

protagonist the main character; also called the hero

rising action the events of the plot that add to the conflict

sudden fiction brief short stories

About the Author

In the 1920s, a section of New York City called Harlem became the center of a great explosion of African-American art. Today, we call this movement the Harlem Renaissance. Langston Hughes became one of the best-known writers of the Harlem Renaissance.

Hughes was born in Joplin, Missouri. He always knew he loved to write. He enrolled at Columbia University, on the edge of Harlem, in 1921. While Hughes was working in a Washington hotel, the well-known poet Vachel Lindsay took an interest in his writing. Lindsay helped bring attention to Hughes's work. By age twenty-seven, Hughes was making a living with his writing.

Langston Hughes wrote short stories, plays, and novels, but is perhaps best known for his poetry.

About the Selection

"Thank You, M'am" is brief, even for a short story. This kind of story is sometimes called **sudden fiction.** Sudden fiction has all the features of short stories—plot, character, setting, point of view, and theme. However, sudden fiction stories are shorter than other short stories.

Like most stories, this one is about **conflict.** Conflict is a struggle between two forces. In fiction, the main character struggles against himself or herself, another person, or nature. In this story, the **protagonist**, or main character, struggles against an **antagonist**, a person who tries to keep the protagonist from reaching his goal.

Readers learn about the main character's problem at the very beginning of the story: Roger tries and fails to steal a purse. The story moves in unexpected ways from that point on. The plot's twists and turns are part of the **rising action** of the story.

Thank You, M'am

As you read, see if you can find all the elements of a short story in this example of sudden fiction: plot, characters, setting, point of view, and theme.

She was a large woman with a large purse that had everything in it but a hammer and nails. It had a long strap, and she carried it slung across her shoulder. It was about eleven o'clock at night, dark, and she was walking alone, when a boy ran up behind her and tried to snatch her purse. The strap broke with the sudden single tug the boy gave it from behind. But the boy's weight and the weight of the purse combined caused him to lose his balance. Instead of taking off full blast as he had hoped, the boy fell on his back on the sidewalk and his legs flew up. The large woman simply turned around and kicked him right square in his blue-jeaned sitter. Then she reached down, picked the boy up by his shirt front, and shook him until his teeth rattled.

After that the woman said, "Pick up my pocketbook, boy, and give it here."

This story has a clear protagonist and antagonist. Which is which?

She still held him tightly. But she bent down enough to permit him to stoop and pick up her purse. Then she said, "Now ain't you ashamed of yourself?"

Firmly gripped by his shirt front, the boy said, "Yes'm."

The woman said, "What did you want to do it for?"

The boy said, "I didn't aim to."

She said, "You a lie!"

By that time two or three people passed, stopped, turned to look, and some stood watching.

"If I turn you loose, will you run?" asked the woman.

"Yes'm," said the boy.

"Then I won't turn you loose," said the woman. She did not release him.

"Lady, I'm sorry," whispered the boy.

"Um-hum! Your face is dirty. I got a great mind to wash your face for you. Ain't you got nobody home to tell you to wash your face?"

"No'm," said the boy.

"Then it will get washed this evening," said the large woman, starting up the street, dragging the frightened boy behind her.

He looked as if he were fourteen or fifteen, frail and willow-wild, in tennis shoes and blue jeans.

The woman said, "You ought to be my son. I would teach you right from wrong. Least I can do right now is to wash your face. Are you hungry?"

"No'm," said the being-dragged boy. "I just want you to turn me loose."

"Was I bothering *you* when I turned the corner?" asked the woman.

"No'm."

"But you put yourself in contact with *me*," said the woman. "If you think that that contact is not going to last awhile, you got another thought coming. When I get through with you, sir, you are going to remember Mrs. Luella Bates Washington Jones."

Sweat popped out on the boy's face and he began to struggle. Mrs. Jones stopped, jerked him around in front of her, put a half nelson about his neck, and continued to drag him up the street. When she got to her door, she dragged the boy inside, down a hall, and into a large kitchenette-furnished room at the rear of the house. She switched on the light and left the door open. The boy could hear other roomers laughing and talking in the large house. Some of their doors were open, too, so he knew he and the woman were not alone. The woman still had him by the neck in the middle of her room.

She said, "What is your name?"

"Roger," answered the boy.

Notice that much of this very short story is dialogue between the two characters. What is the effect of telling the story through dialogue?

A *half nelson* is a wrestling hold.

"Then, Roger, you go to that sink and wash your face," said the woman, whereupon she turned him loose—at last. Roger looked at the door—looked at the woman—looked at the door—*and went to the sink.*

"Let the water run until it gets warm," she said. "Here's a clean towel."

"You gonna take me to jail?" asked the boy, bending over the sink.

"Not with that face, I would not take you nowhere," said the woman. "Here I am trying to get home to cook me a bite to eat, and you snatch my pocketbook! Maybe you ain't been to your supper either, late as it be. Have you?"

"There's nobody home at my house," said the boy.

"Then we'll eat," said the woman. "I believe you're hungry—or been hungry—to try to snatch my pocketbook!"

"I want a pair of blue **suede** shoes," said the boy.

"Well, you didn't have to snatch *my* pocketbook to get some suede shoes," said Mrs. Luella Bates Washington Jones. "You could of asked me."

"M'am?"

The water dripping from his face, the boy looked at her. There was a long pause. A very long pause. After he had dried his face, and not knowing what else to do, dried it again, the boy turned around, wondering what next. The door was open. He could make a dash for it down the hall. He could run, run, run, *run!*

The woman was sitting on the daybed. After a while she said, "I were young once and I wanted things I could not get."

There was another long pause. The boy's mouth opened. Then he frowned, not knowing he frowned.

The woman said, "Um-hum! You thought I was going to say *but*, didn't you? You thought I was going to say *but I didn't snatch people's pocketbooks.* Well, I wasn't going to say that." Pause. Silence. "I have done things, too, which I would not tell you, son—neither tell God, if He didn't already know.

suede leather with a napped, or soft, surface

Everybody's got something in common. So you set down
while I fix us something to eat. You might run that comb
through your hair so you will look presentable."

In another corner of the room behind a screen was a gas
plate and an icebox. Mrs. Jones got up and went behind the
screen. The woman did not watch the boy to see if he was
going to run now, nor did she watch her purse, which she left
behind her on the daybed. But the boy took care to sit on the
far side of the room, away from the purse, where he thought
she could easily see him out of the corner of her eye if she
wanted to. He did not trust the woman *not* to trust him. And
he did not want to be mistrusted now.

"Do you need somebody to go to the store," asked the boy,
"maybe to get some milk or something?"

"Don't believe I do," said the woman, "unless you just
want sweet milk yourself. I was going to make cocoa out of
this canned milk I got here."

"That will be fine," said the boy.

A *gas plate*, also called a
hot plate, is a heated
iron plate for cooking
in small spaces. An
icebox is a refrigerator.

She heated some lima beans and ham she had in the icebox, made the cocoa, and set the table. The woman did not ask the boy anything about where he lived, or his folks, or anything else that would embarrass him. Instead, as they ate, she told him about her job in a hotel beauty shop that stayed open late, what the work was like, and how all kinds of women came in and out, blonds, redheads, and Spanish. Then she cut him a half of her ten-cent cake.

"Eat some more, son," she said.

When they were finished eating, she got up and said, "Now here, take this ten dollars and buy yourself some blue suede shoes. And next time, do not make the mistake of latching onto *my* pocketbook *nor nobody else's*—because shoes got by devilish ways will burn your feet. I got to get my rest now. But from here on in, son, I hope you will behave yourself."

She led him down the hall to the front door and opened it. "Good night! Behave yourself, boy!" she said, looking out into the street as he went down the steps.

The boy wanted to say something other than, "Thank you, M'am," to Mrs. Luella Bates Washington Jones, but although his lips moved, he couldn't even say that as he turned at the foot of the barren stoop and looked up at the large woman in the door. Then she shut the door.

The protagonist in this story faces more than one conflict. What does Roger struggle against?

Directions Write the answers to these questions using complete sentences.

Comprehension: Identifying Facts

1. What happens when Roger tries to grab Mrs. Jones's purse?

2. What does Roger want to buy with the money from Mrs. Jones's purse?

3. What does Mrs. Jones give Roger after they eat?

Comprehension: Understanding Main Ideas

4. What do we find out about Roger's home life from this story?

5. What do we find out about Mrs. Jones's life?

6. When Mrs. Jones goes behind the screen to prepare supper, why does Roger sit away from the purse, where Mrs. Jones can easily see him?

Understanding Literature: Rising Action

Short stories usually explore a conflict that the main character faces. For example, in "American History," Elena, the protagonist, wants to be friends with Eugene. However, the conflict is that she and Eugene live in two very different worlds. The way the plot of the story moves toward Elena's realizing she can't be friends with Eugene is the rising action of the story. The rising action adds to the conflict.

7. In your own words, what is rising action in a short story?

8. What are some events in the rising action of "Thank You, M'am" that add to Roger's conflict?

Critical Thinking

9. What might Mrs. Jones have done after she caught Roger trying to steal her purse? Why do you think she decides to take him home?

10. In the beginning of the story, Roger thinks it was all right for him to steal money to buy shoes. How do you think he feels at the end of the story? Why do you think so?

Writing on Your Own Imagine that you are Roger. Write a letter to Mrs. Jones. Tell her what you think or how you feel about what she did.

Unfinished Message
Toshio Mori

Toshio Mori

1910-1980

Literary Terms

epilogue a section coming after the story's end

mood the feeling created by a piece of writing

narrator the teller of a story

tone the attitude an author takes toward a subject

About the Author

Toshio Mori was born in Oakland, California, in 1910. Later, he and his family moved to San Leandro, where he attended public school. After the United States entered World War II against Germany and Japan, President Franklin Roosevelt signed an order. It said that all Japanese Americans living on the West Coast had to move. Mori and his family were forced to move to the Topaz Relocation Center in Utah. There, Mori became active in the affairs of the camp. He helped start a newspaper and served as camp historian.

Toshio Mori's first book, *Yokohama, California*, was published in 1949. The book was the first collection of short stories written by a Japanese American to be published in this country. In all his writing, Mori shows what life was like for Japanese Americans in California during the late 1930s and early 1940s.

About the Selection

"Unfinished Message" is from *The Chauvinist and Other Stories*, published in 1979. The details of the story show how Toshio Mori used his experiences in Topaz Relocation Center as a background for his work.

A story's details—setting, characters, point of view, word choice—all contribute to the **mood** it creates. Mood is the feeling created by a story. A story's mood can be happy or sad, edgy or relaxed, scary or funny. "Unfinished Message" creates an edgy, uneasy mood right from the beginning. Readers immediately meet a mother who can't sleep because she keeps seeing her soldier son's face. This first impression sets the **tone** for the rest of the story. Tone is the attitude the author takes toward his or her subject. A writer's tone might be bitter, loving, angry, light-hearted, matter-of-fact. "Unfinished Message" ends with an **epilogue,** which rounds out the story by telling us what happened to the **narrator's** brother.

Unfinished Message

It was on a chilly May night in 1945 in the middle of the Utah desert when my mother sharply called me. "I can't sleep tonight," she said. True, she had been fretting the past few nights, and I knew she was worried over her son at the Italian front.

I reassured her that everything would be all right. Hadn't he, I reasoned with her, come through without a scratch with a full year's service at the front, even with the 442nd Infantry Regiment?

"But I keep seeing Kazuo's face tonight," she said. "Each time I'm about to fall asleep his face keeps coming back."

I tried to calm her fears as best as I could. Nevertheless, she did not sleep that night.

The next night and the night following she slept fitfully more or less. Beneath her outward calm, however, she was under an **ordeal** only a mother could understand. "No news is good news. He's all right," I assured her.

A few days later we received a wire from the War Department that Kazuo had been seriously wounded. The news almost killed her. In the full medical report following we learned that he had a **fractured** skull but was resting peacefully. What struck me as odd was the day my brother was wounded. It was on May 5, the very night my mother was unable to sleep.

When we received word again, it was more cheerful. Kazuo was coming back on the hospital ship destined for home, and we were to decide the hospital nearest our home.

World War II ended with Japan's surrender on August 14, 1945. In May of that year, the fighting was still going on.

As you read, notice how the author creates the mood of the story. Compare the mood with the tone—the author's attitude toward his subject.

fractured broken

ordeal a terrible experience

We were still living in Topaz, Utah Relocation Center at the time, and the nearest available army hospital was the Fitzsimmons in Colorado.

"Let's have him transferred there so we can visit him as soon as he comes home," I said to Mother.

My mother would have none of it. "Do you think this is our real home? Our home is back in San Leandro, California. We'll be moving from here again, and Kazuo too will have to transfer. No, we'll go back and Kazuo can go to a hospital in California."

My mother couldn't get out of the camp soon enough. She counted the days when the next train to California would take us back home. In the meantime we learned that Kazuo was being transferred to DeWitt Army Hospital in Auburn, California.

On our trip home, our train stopped for a few minutes at Auburn, and our first urge was to get off the train and visit Kazuo. My mother stared toward the Auburn interiors. "It must be only a few miles from here. Here we are, so close to him and yet so far."

We heeded our good judgment and did not get off the train. "We must make ready our home. It must be in a mess. We must first go home and get busy cleaning the place. Our home must resemble our old home for Kazuo."

It took us two weeks to clean the house and settle down. My mother had to apply to the United States Attorney's office for a travel permit because she was an enemy alien and Japan and United States were still at war. Secure with a permit my mother accompanied me to Auburn. All the way on the bus to the hospital she nervously weighed the seriousness of Kazuo's **actual** condition. Are his legs all **intact,** are his hands there? she wondered. Can he see, is he normal mentally? It wasn't until she saw him in person did she feel relieved. He could see, his hands were usable, but his legs? Mother talked constantly on everything she could think of but his condition. Before long, she became aware of his actual condition.

In order to relieve ourselves of the hot valley air caught inside of the ward, my brother suggested sitting on the

The mother refuses to think of the internment camp as "home."

Notice that although Kazuo has been wounded serving in the United States Army, his mother is still considered "an enemy alien." What is the author's tone here?

actual true, real   **intact** whole, together

screened porch. It was when the ward boy saw my brother moving on the bed that he came to help him to his wheelchair. The ward boy bodily lifted him on the chair, and Mother saw my brother's spindly legs. He was unable to walk.

Afterwards, Mother asked me to inquire the doctor about Kazuo's condition. Will he ever walk? The doctor I talked to was not too hopeful, but I did not tell Mother.

"He says there's a fifty-fifty **possibility** that Kazuo will walk," I said to Mother.

Coming home, Mother said, "I'm worried over him. If I only could live long enough to see him fully recovered."

Kazuo's head (brain) injury has paralyzed his legs.

After another operation on his head, my brother was transferred to Letterman Hospital in San Francisco, making possible weekly visits for Mother and I. Each time we saw him, she would take me aside and ask, "Do you think he's much improved? Isn't he better?"

That Christmas my brother got a two week **furlough** and came home for the first time since the war had started. I had to help him with his bath and toilet. My brother was confined to his wheelchair.

Time and again, Mother would ask me, "Will he ever walk again? I can't tell him that I worry over him."

Before my brother was released from the hospital, Mother died in her sleep on August 5, 1946. Although she complained of pains in the neck, we were totally unprepared for her death. Her doctor had previously **diagnosed** her **symptoms** as arthritis, but her death was sudden.

After her death our house became dark and silent. Even when my brother returned home for good in a wheelchair, the

---

diagnose to determine the medical condition of someone

furlough a leave of absence

possibility chance

symptom a sign of disease

atmosphere was unchanged. We seemed to be companions in the dark. However, it changed one day.

As I sat quietly in the living room I heard a slight tapping on the window just above the divan where my mother had slept her last. When the taps repeated again, I went outside to check, knowing well that a stiff wind could move a branch of our lemon tree with a lemon or two tapping the wall of our house. There was no wind, no lemon near enough to reach the window. I was puzzled but did not confide in my brother when he joined me in the living room.

I had all but forgotten the incident when my brother and I were quietly sitting in the living room near the spot where our mother had passed away. For a while I was not conscious of the slight tapping on the window. When the repeated taps were loud enough to be heard clearly, I first looked at the window and then glanced at my brother. He too had heard the taps.

"Did you hear that?" I said.

My brother nodded. "Sure," he said. "Did you hear it too? I heard it the other day but I thought it was strange."

We looked at the window. There were no birds in sight, no lemons tapping. Then the taps repeated. After a few moments of silence I was about to comment when we heard the tapping again. This time I looked silently at my brother and on tiptoes approached the window. The tapping continued so I softly touched the window pane. The instant my fingers touched the glass, it stopped.

My brother and I looked at each other, silently aware that it must have been Mother calling our attention. At that instant I became conscious of the purpose of the mysterious taps. I couldn't help but recall Mother's words, "I can't stop worrying over you, my son."

The tappings stopped once and for all after that. We never heard it again after the message had reached us.

Why do you think the author has included an epilogue?

EPILOGUE *This story was written nearly thirty years ago. My brother is alive and well, raising a family in San Leandro, California. He is still **paralyzed** to this day.*

paralyzed unable to move

Unfinished Message
Toshio Mori

Directions Write the answers to these questions using complete sentences.

Comprehension: Identifying Facts

1. Why can't the mother sleep?

2. What does the wire from the War Department say has happened to Kazuo?

3. What do the brothers hear while sitting in the living room?

Comprehension: Understanding Main Ideas

4. Why does the date of Kazuo's injury strike the author as odd?

5. Why does the mother insist that Kazuo go to a hospital in California, rather than one near the camp in Utah?

6. What does the title of this story mean?

Understanding Literature: Mood

The mood in a short story is the feeling it creates. A writer develops a mood by events in the plot, by descriptions of setting, by the use of images, by what characters say and do. Mood can also be affected by point of view and word choice.

A story's mood and its tone can be very different. For example, the mood of "The Celebrated Jumping Frog of Calaveras County" is playful and funny. The tone of Simon Wheeler's narration, however, is sincere, mild, and without any idea that the tales he tells are funny.

7. What are some of the ways a writer develops the mood of a story?

8. How would you describe the mood of "Unfinished Message"?

Critical Thinking

9. Why do you think the narrator and his brother believe that the tapping is their mother trying to contact them? Why do you think the tapping stops after they both realize what it is?

10. Certain events in this story are very eerie (strange). However, the narrator tells about them in a quiet, matter-of-fact way. What effect does the storytelling have on your reaction to the events? Explain.

> **Writing on Your Own** Select a paragraph or two from the story. Rewrite your selection to give more details or to make it more eerie (strange, spooky).

Skills Lesson: Conflict

Conflict is at the heart of a story's plot. Most simply, conflict results when something stands in the way of what the protagonist wants or needs to do.

We can think about conflict as the two sides of a struggle. There are three basic kinds of conflicts in fiction.

■ The first kind of conflict is *person versus (against) person*. Here, the protagonist is stopped from doing something by another character. For example, in "Thank You, M'am," Roger wants money. His attempt to get money is stopped by Mrs. Jones.

■ A second kind of conflict is between people and their environment, or the conditions under which they live. This is called *person versus environment*. In "American History," Elena struggles against what people think of her because she is Puerto Rican and lives in El Building.

■ The third kind of conflict is between a person and his or her own mind, or *person versus self*. This kind of conflict takes place inside a character. In "Everyday Use," the mother struggles to understand and respond to both her daughters.

A short story may have more than one kind of conflict. Sometimes the conflict is both internal (inside the character) and external (outside the character).

For example, in "American History," Elena's struggle against what people think of her reflects the conflict within herself. She feels unsure. She wishes she were more like the other girls in school.

Review

1. What are two examples of conflict within the mind of a character in "Everyday Use"?

2. Give an example of a story in which the conflict is between a character and his or her environment.

3. The very short story "Thank You, M'am" manages to include all three kinds of conflict. What is an example of each?

4. Which kind of conflict do you enjoy most in a short story? Why?

5. Do you think a story has to have some kind of conflict? Why or why not? What if a short story did not contain any conflict? How could the author make it interesting?

Writing on Your Own Choose one of the three kinds of conflict. Develop an outline for the plot of a story that features this kind of conflict.

UNIT 4 SUMMARY

Short stories are among the most popular forms of fiction. Like all fiction, short stories have plot, setting, characters, point of view, and theme. Unlike longer forms, however, short stories tend to feature a brief time period and only one main setting. Writers tend to include only the most important descriptive details. Everything in a short story works to set a mood and to develop one or more themes.

Short stories are part of the kind of literature called prose. Prose—all writing that is not poetry—also includes the fables, myths, tall tales, and legends you have studied in other units.

This unit has presented five short stories with very different styles, moods, and effects. From the set, you get a sense of the wide range offered by this literary form.

Selections

■ "The Celebrated Jumping Frog of Calaveras County," by Mark Twain, describes the funny adventures of a gambling man.

■ "Everyday Use," by Alice Walker, is about an African-American mother and her two daughters, one of whom has come home for a visit.

■ "American History," by Judith Ortiz-Cofer, tells of an important day in American history that becomes important in another way for a Puerto Rican girl living in New Jersey.

■ "Thank You, M'am," by Langston Hughes, is the story of an attempted purse-snatching that does not go at all the way a young man intended.

■ "Unfinished Message," by Toshio Mori, concerns a Japanese-American mother, her two sons, and a strange event that happens after her death.

UNIT 4 REVIEW

Directions Write the answers to these questions using complete sentences.

Comprehension: Identifying Facts

1. What are some ways short stories are different from other kinds of fiction?

2. What kind of conflict is most important in "Unfinished Message"?

3. What is a symbol? In which story do we find symbols?

4. What is the difference between the *mood* of "The Celebrated Jumping Frog of Calaveras County" and its *tone?*

5. Why do humorists like Mark Twain often use caricature in their writing?

Comprehension: Understanding Main Ideas

6. What events are part of the rising action in "Everyday Use"?

7. What is the point of view in each of the stories in this unit?

8. What makes "The Celebrated Jumping Frog of Calaveras County" funny? What are some ways Twain adds humor to the story?

9. How are short stories different from myths and fables? In what ways are they the same?

10. Describe two conflicts in "American History": one between the main character and the conditions of her life, the other inside the main character herself.

Understanding Literature: Fiction and Nonfiction

Prose is usually divided into fiction and nonfiction. In fiction, the author creates the events and characters. Plots and characters come from the writer's imagination. Although fictional stories may be based on real events and real people, writers change information to serve the needs of the story. Fables, myths, tall tales, legends, short stories, plays, and novels are all forms of fiction.

Nonfiction is literature that describes something that actually happened. In nonfiction, readers expect that the author hasn't added anything that isn't true. Nonfiction includes reports, biographies, autobiographies, and essays.

11. In your own words, what is the difference between fiction and nonfiction?

12. What are some responsibilities that a nonfiction writer has that a fiction writer does not have?

13. What are some of the nonfiction elements in "Unfinished Message"?

14. Judith Ortiz-Cofer says that she is not the main character in "American History" because she was only eleven when President Kennedy died. Why might readers think that the story is true, or nonfiction?

15. Which story in this unit do you think comes closest to nonfiction? Why?

Critical Thinking

16. In your opinion, what is the main theme of "Thank You, M'am"?

17. Which protagonist, or main character, in these short stories do you like the best? Why? How does the author make the character come alive for you?

18. With which author do you identify the most? Does this help you understand that author's short story? Explain.

19. How would the effect of "Unfinished Message" be different if it had been told more like a ghost story? Why do you think the author chose to use a matter-of-fact tone?

20. "The Celebrated Jumping Frog of Calaveras County," "Everyday Use," and "Thank You, M'am" all include humor. Compare each narrator's use of amusing details and dialogue.

Speak and Listen

Mark Twain is one of America's finest storytellers. Create your own version of the story he tells in "The Celebrated Jumping Frog of Calaveras County" and tell it to your class.

Beyond Words

Create a series of sketches that might be used to illustrate one of the short stories in this unit.

Writing on Your Own Choose a moral from a fable in Unit 1. Write a short story with that moral as its theme, or main idea.

Test-Taking Tip

Before you begin an exam, skim through the whole test to find out what is expected of you. Try to set aside enough time to complete each section.

"There is no terror in a bang, only in the anticipation of it."
—Alfred Hitchcock, quoted in *Halliwell's Filmgoer's Companion*, 1984

"Nothing gives a fearful man more courage than another's fear."
—Umberto Eco, *The Name of the Rose*, 1980

The Terror,
Jean Baptiste Greuze

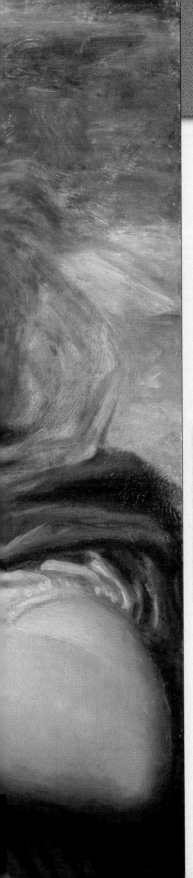

UNIT 5 *Suspense in the Short Story*

Short stories of suspense are among the most popular forms of literature. In this kind of fiction, readers aren't certain what will happen or what some events in the plot mean. This doubt keeps readers interested. Writers of suspense stories like to take what is expected and turn it into something new—and sometimes something scary. In suspense stories, the line between what is real and what is not can be blurred.

In this unit, you will read five stories that will surprise you, play with what you expect, and keep your imagination working even after you've reached a story's end.

Readers everywhere enjoy stories of suspense. They tell each other ghost stories. They line up to see scary movies. Many people enjoy being frightened. They walk through graveyards at night. They visit haunted houses at amusement parks. They suspect that everything will be all right. However, they do not know what will actually happen. People enjoy a little hint of danger and the unexpected.

Suspense in a story keeps readers on edge. As they read, they cannot predict what will happen next. They may think they know, but they can't be sure.

Writers of suspense stories play with what readers expect. They do this by controlling how much readers and characters know about what is happening and what it means.

In some stories, readers know much more than the characters do. Alfred Hitchcock, a film maker who is considered a master of suspense, describes this technique with a simple example. He tells of four characters sitting around a table. The audience sees from the start that there is a bomb under the table. They expect that the bomb will go off. However, they do not know for sure, nor do they know when. They have to wait and see. Waiting creates suspense.

In other stories, characters know more than the readers know. In this kind of suspense story, authors may hint that something strange is about to happen. Yet readers do not know exactly what it is, or when or how it will happen. Characters may know, but readers have to finish the story before they uncover this secret.

In placing these hints or clues in a short story, authors are using the technique of foreshadowing. Foreshadowing may consist of things characters say or do. Authors can also foreshadow events by using a setting that captures the suspenseful nature of the story. For example, in "The Fall of the House of Usher," Edgar Allen Poe foreshadows the events that will occur. He opens his classic short story with these words:

> "During the whole of the chill, dark and soundless day in the autumn of the year, when the clouds hung oppressively low in the heavens, I had been passing alone, on horseback through a singularly dreary tract of country, and at length found myself, as the shadow of the evening drew on, within view of the melancholy house of Usher."

From the beginning, then, readers know that they are in a place of great mystery. They know they must expect the unexpected.

Of course, authors sometimes do just the opposite. They bring readers into a setting that seems completely normal. Nothing seems out of the ordinary. Just as readers become comfortable in this place, writers make the unexpected happen.

As a reader, you just never know. That is what makes short stories with suspense so much fun to read.

The short stories in this unit all have an element of suspense. In "The Lady, or the Tiger?" Frank Stockton keeps his readers involved by leaving them hanging on the edge of that question. In "The Lottery," Shirley Jackson creates a world that only seems ordinary, where the characters know much more than readers do until the horrifying end of the tale. Ray Bradbury's "The Fog Horn" tells a fantastic tale that keeps readers' imaginations racing long after they have finished reading. In W.W. Jacobs's "The Monkey's Paw," readers watch as an elderly couple makes a wish that seems harmless but turns into a disaster. Finally, in Susan Power's "Red Moccasins," readers enter a shadowy world where no one can be sure what is real.

Leap from the Rock, Julius Schnorr Von Carolsfeld

The Lady, or the Tiger?
Frank Stockton

Frank Stockton

1834–1902

Literary Terms

climax the high point of interest or suspense in a story or play

rising action the events of the plot that add to the conflict

satire humorous writing that makes fun of foolishness or evil

suspense a quality in a story that makes the reader uncertain or nervous about what will happen next

About the Author

Born in Philadelphia in 1834, Frank Stockton began his storytelling career when he was just a boy, creating tales for his brothers and sisters. As an adult, he wrote in many different forms, including short stories, novels, fairy tales, humor, and science fiction.

Stockton did some of his writing for popular children's magazines. He and the famous children's author Mary Mapes Dodge started *St. Nicholas* magazine in 1868. Sometimes, Stockton wrote so many stories for an issue that some of them had to be published under a pen name.

In 1876, his health failing, Stockton retired to a small farm in New Jersey and continued to write. He died in 1902. Today he is remembered for his novels, such as *Rudder Grange*, his science fiction works, such as *The Great War Syndicate*, and his collections of children's stories.

About the Selection

Frank Stockton wrote "The Lady, or the Tiger?" in 1882, for a reading at a literary club. The members loved the story. So did the editors of *The Century* magazine. They published it in their November issue that year. It quickly became one of the world's most famous short stories. People everywhere talked about its strange ending. Preachers even used it in their sermons.

The story begins by using humor and **satire** to describe a "semibarbaric" king's system of justice. Then the author presents a problem and begins the **rising action** that makes the problem hard to solve. Just when the problem comes to a **climax**, the story ends. The climax is the highest point of excitement or suspense in a story's plot. Readers expect that after the climax, the story will show how the problem is solved. This story does something else. "The Lady, or the Tiger?" is a story of **suspense**, and readers have to expect the unexpected.

The Lady, or the Tiger?

In the very olden time there lived a semibarbaric king, whose ideas, though somewhat polished and sharpened by the **progressiveness** of distant Latin neighbors, were still large, **florid**, and **untrammeled**, as became the half of him which was **barbaric**. He was a man of **exuberant** fancy, and, withal, of an authority so irresistible that, at his will, he turned his varied fancies into facts. He was greatly given to self-communing; and when he and himself agreed upon any thing, the thing was done. When every member of his domestic and political systems moved smoothly in its appointed course, his nature was **bland** and **genial**; but whenever there was a little hitch, and some of his orbs got out of their orbits, he was blander and more genial still, for nothing pleased him so much as to make the crooked straight, and crush down uneven places.

Semibarbaric means that the king was somewhat civilized and somewhat savage.

Self-communing means thinking deeply about oneself.

This king has absolute power—he does whatever he wants. As you read, notice how the fancy, difficult language pokes fun at a king so sure of himself.

barbaric uncivilized, savage

bland dull, unexciting

exuberant high-spirited

florid healthy

genial friendly

progressiveness the state of being advanced, or accepting of new ideas

untrammeled not bound; free

Semified, a made-up word, shows how the author creates humor and satire. The king's idea of holding public events in arenas has helped make him only *semibarbaric*—only half uncivilized and savage.

The ancient Romans also watched battles to the death between gladiators (slaves trained as fighters) in large public arenas or *amphitheatres.* They too claimed that such public spectacles taught people valuable lessons.

The king did whatever pleased him, no matter where the original idea came from.

Among the borrowed notions by which his barbarism had become semified was that of the public arena, in which, by exhibitions of manly and beastly valor, the minds of his subjects were refined and cultured.

But even here the exuberant and barbaric fancy **asserted** itself. The arena of the king was built not to give the people an opportunity of hearing the **rhapsodies** of dying gladiators, nor to enable them to view the **inevitable** conclusion of a conflict between religious opinions and hungry jaws, but for purposes far better adapted to widen and develop the mental energies of the people. This vast amphitheatre, with its encircling galleries, its mysterious vaults, and its unseen passages, was an agent of poetic justice, in which crime was punished, or virtue rewarded, by the decrees of an **impartial** and **incorruptible** chance.

When a subject was accused of a crime of sufficient importance to interest the king, public notice was given that on an appointed day the fate of the accused person would be decided in the king's arena—a structure which well deserved its name; for, although its form and plan were borrowed from afar, its purpose **emanated** solely from the brain of this man, who, every barleycorn a king, knew no tradition to which he owed more allegiance than pleased his fancy, and who ingrafted on every adopted form of human thought and action the rich growth of his barbaric **idealism**.

When all the people had assembled in the galleries, and the king, surrounded by his court, sat high up on his throne of royal state on one side of the arena, he gave a signal, a door beneath him opened, and the accused subject stepped out into the amphitheatre. Directly opposite him, on the other side of the enclosed space, were two doors, exactly alike and

assert to put oneself or one's ideas forward

emanate to come forth

idealism a belief in the highest standards

impartial fair

incorruptible honorable

inevitable impossible to avoid

rhapsody a joyful song

side by side. It was the duty and the privilege of the person on trial to walk directly to these doors and open one of them. He could open either door he pleased: he was subject to no **guidance** or influence but that of the afore-mentioned impartial and incorruptible chance. If he opened the one, there came out of it a hungry tiger, the fiercest and most cruel that could be **procured**, which immediately sprang upon him and tore him to pieces, as a punishment for his guilt. The moment that the case of the criminal was thus decided, **doleful** iron bells were clanged, great wails went up from the hired mourners posted on the outer rim of the arena, and the vast audience, with bowed heads and downcast hearts, **wended** slowly their homeward way, mourning greatly that one so young and fair, or so old and respected, should have **merited** so **dire** a fate.

Why do you think the king hires mourners?

But if the accused person opened the other door, there came forth from it a lady, the most suitable to his years and station that his Majesty could select among his fair subjects; and to this lady he was immediately married, as a reward of his innocence. It mattered not that he might already possess a wife and family, or that his affections might be engaged upon an object of his own selection: the king allowed no such **subordinate** arrangements to

dire severe, terrible

doleful sad, mournful

guidance direction, instruction

merit to deserve

procure to get or obtain

subordinate lower; lying beneath

wend to make one's way

interfere with his great scheme of **retribution** and reward. The exercises, as in the other instance, took place immediately, and in the arena. Another door opened beneath the king, and a priest, followed by a band of choristers, and dancing maidens blowing joyous airs on golden horns and treading an epithalamic measure, advanced to where the pair stood side by side; and the wedding was promptly and cheerily solemnized. Then the gay brass bells rang forth their merry peals, the people shouted glad hurrahs, and the innocent man, **preceded** by children **strewing** flowers on his path, led his bride to his home.

This was the king's semibarbaric method of **administering** justice. Its perfect fairness is obvious. The criminal could not know out of which door would come the lady: he opened either he pleased, without having the slightest idea whether, in the next instant, he was to be devoured or married. On some occasions the tiger came out of one door, and on some out of the other. The decisions of this **tribunal** were not only fair, they were positively determinate: the accused person was instantly punished if he found himself guilty; and if innocent, he was rewarded on the spot, whether he liked it or not. There was no escape from the judgments of the king's arena.

The **institution** was a very popular one. When the people gathered together on one of the great trial-days, they never knew whether they were to witness a bloody slaughter or a **hilarious** wedding. This element of uncertainty lent an interest to the occasion which it could not otherwise have attained. Thus the masses were entertained and pleased, and the thinking part of the community could bring no charge of unfairness against this plan; for did not the accused person have the whole matter in his own hands?

An *epithalamium,* from the Greek word for bridal chamber, is a song or poem in honor of a bride and bridegroom.

The king considers his system fair because the accused person himself chooses the door to open. What is wrong with this reasoning? What do you think about the king's "justice"?

administering managing, directing	**institution** an important custom	**retribution** revenge; a punishment for crime
hilarious very funny, high-spirited	**precede** to come before	**strew** to scatter widely
		tribunal a court of justice

This semibarbaric king had a daughter as blooming as his most florid fancies, and with a soul as **fervent** and **imperious** as his own. As is usual in such cases, she was the apple of his eye, and was loved by him above all humanity. Among his courtiers was a young man of that fineness of blood and lowness of station common to the conventional heroes of romance who love royal maidens. This royal maiden was well satisfied with her lover, for he was handsome and brave to a degree **unsurpassed** in all this kingdom; and she loved him with an **ardor** that had enough of barbarism in it to make it exceedingly warm and strong. This love-affair moved on happily for many months, until one day the king happened to discover its existence. He did not hesitate nor **waver** in regard to his duty in the premises. The youth was immediately cast into prison, and a day was appointed for his trial in the king's arena. This, of course, was an especially important occasion; and his Majesty, as well as all the people, were greatly interested in the workings and development of this trial. Never before had such a case occurred; never before had a subject dared to love the daughter of a king. In afteryears such things became commonplace enough; but then they were, in no slight degree, novel and startling.

The tiger-cages of the kingdom were searched for the most savage and **relentless** beasts, from which the fiercest monster might be selected for the arena; and the ranks of maiden youth and beauty throughout the land were carefully surveyed by **competent** judges, in order that the young man might have a fitting bride in case fate did not determine for him a different destiny. Of course everybody knew that the deed with which the accused was charged had been done. He had loved the princess, and neither he, she, nor any one else thought of denying the fact; but the king would not think of allowing any fact of this kind to interfere with the workings of

Many stories, especially fairy tales, are about *romance,* or love affairs, between poor young men and royal women.

Here, the rising action of the story begins.

---

ardor deep feeling

competent able to do something

fervent having strong feelings

imperious bossy, acting like royalty

relentless without pity

unsurpassed best, highest

waver to back down

Why does the king use the arena even when everyone agrees the accused is guilty?

the tribunal, in which he took such great delight and satisfaction. No matter how the affair turned out, the youth would be disposed of; and the king would take an **aesthetic** pleasure in watching the course of events, which would determine whether or not the young man had done wrong in allowing himself to love the princess.

The appointed day arrived. From far and near the people gathered, and thronged the great galleries of the arena; and crowds, unable to gain **admittance**, massed themselves against its outside walls. The king and his court were in their places, opposite the twin doors—those fateful **portals**, so terrible in their similarity.

All was ready. The signal was given. A door beneath the royal party opened, and the lover of the princess walked into the arena. Tall, beautiful, fair, his appearance was greeted with a low hum of admiration and anxiety. Half the audience had not known so grand a youth had lived among them. No wonder the princess loved him! What a terrible thing for him to be there!

As the youth advanced into the arena, he turned, as the custom was, to bow to the king: but he did not think at all of that royal personage; his eyes were fixed upon the princess, who sat to the right of her father. Had it not been for the **moiety** of barbarism in her nature it is **probable** that lady would not have been there; but her intense and **fervid** soul would not allow her to be absent on an occasion in which she was so terribly interested. From the moment that the decree had gone forth that her lover should decide his fate in the king's arena, she had thought of nothing, night or day, but this great event and the various subjects connected with it. Possessed of more power, influence, and force of character than any one who had ever before been interested in such a case, she had done what no other person had done—she had possessed herself of the secret of the doors. She knew in

admittance entrance	**fervid** burning, passionate	**portal** a gate
aesthetic artistic		**probable** likely
	moiety half	

which of the two rooms that lay behind those doors stood the cage of the tiger, with its open front, and in which waited the lady. Through these thick doors, heavily curtained with skins on the inside, it was impossible that any noise or suggestion should come from within to the person who should approach to raise the latch of one of them; but gold, and the power of a woman's will, had brought the secret to the princess.

And not only did she know in which room stood the lady ready to emerge, all blushing and **radiant**, should her door be opened, but she knew who the lady was. It was one of the fairest and loveliest of the damsels of the court who had been selected as the reward of the accused youth, should he be proved innocent of the crime of **aspiring** to one so far above him; and the princess hated her. Often had she seen, or imagined that she had seen, this fair creature throwing glances of admiration upon the person of her lover, and sometimes she thought these glances were **perceived** and even returned. Now and then she had seen them talking together; it was but for a moment or two, but much can be said in a brief space; it may have been on most unimportant topics, but how could she know that? The girl was lovely, but she had dared to raise her eyes to the loved one of the princess; and, with all the **intensity** of the savage blood **transmitted** to her through long lines of wholly barbaric ancestors, she hated the woman who blushed and trembled behind that silent door.

When her lover turned and looked at her, and his eye met hers as she sat there paler and whiter than any one in the vast ocean of anxious faces about her, he saw, by that power of quick **perception** which is given to those whose souls are one, that she knew behind which door crouched the tiger, and behind which stood the lady. He had expected her to know it. He understood her nature, and his soul was assured that she would never rest until she had made plain to herself this thing, hidden to all other lookers-on, even to the king. The

The princess has used her wealth and her strong will to discover the secret of the doors.

aspire to hope	**perceive** to understand	**radiant** glowing
intensity strength	**perception** an understanding	**transmit** to send

only hope for the youth in which there was any element of certainty was based upon the success of the princess in discovering this mystery; and the moment he looked upon her, he saw she had succeeded, as in his soul he knew she would succeed.

Then it was that his quick and anxious glance asked the question, "Which?" It was as plain to her as if he shouted it from where he stood. There was not an instant to be lost. The question was asked in a flash; it must be answered in another.

Her right arm lay on the cushioned parapet before her. She raised her hand, and made a slight, quick movement toward the right. No one but her lover saw her. Every eye but his was fixed on the man in the arena.

He turned, and with a firm and rapid step he walked across the empty space. Every heart stopped beating, every breath was held, every eye was fixed immovably upon that man. Without the slightest hesitation, he went to the door on the right, and opened it.

Here is the climax of the story. Suspense is at its highest point. Readers expect the rest of the story to show how the problem is resolved.

Now, the point of the story is this: Did the tiger come out of that door, or did the lady?

The more we reflect upon this question, the harder it is to answer. It involves a study of the human heart which leads us through **devious mazes** of **passion**, out of which it is difficult to find our way. Think of it, fair reader, not as if the decision of the question depended upon yourself, but upon that hot-blooded, semibarbaric princess, her soul at a white heat beneath the combined fires of despair and jealousy. She had lost him, but who should have him?

How often, in her waking hours and in her dreams, had she started in wild horror and covered her face with her hands as she thought of her lover opening the door on the other side of which waited the cruel fangs of the tiger!

But how much oftener had she seen him at the other door! How in her grievous **reveries** had she gnashed her teeth and torn her hair when she saw his start of **rapturous** delight as he opened the door of the lady! How her soul had burned in **agony** when she had seen him rush to meet that woman, with her flushing cheek and sparkling eye of triumph; when she had seen him lead her forth, his whole frame kindled with the joy of recovered life; when she had heard the glad shouts from the **multitude**, and the wild ringing of the happy bells; when she had seen the priest, with his joyous followers, advance to the couple, and make them man and wife before her very eyes; and when she had seen them walk away together upon their path of flowers, followed by the

---

agony great pain

devious crooked; sly

maze web; puzzle

multitude crowd

passion a strong feeling

rapturous extremely happy

reverie a daydream; to be lost in thought

tremendous shouts of the hilarious multitude, in which her one despairing shriek was lost and drowned!

Would it not be better for him to die at once, and go to wait for her in the blessed regions of semibarbaric futurity?

And yet, that awful tiger, those shrieks, that blood!

Her decision had been indicated in an instant, but it had been made after days and nights of **anguished deliberation**. She had known she would be asked, she had decided what she would answer, and, without the slightest hesitation, she had moved her hand to the right.

The question of her decision is one not to be lightly considered, and it is not for me to presume to set myself up as the one person able to answer it. And so I leave it with all of you: Which came out of the opened door—the lady, or the tiger?

Which do you think came out of the opened door? Why do you suppose the author chose to end the story in this way?

anguished distressed, tormented

deliberation careful thought

The Lady, or the Tiger?
Frank Stockton

Directions Write the answers to these questions using complete sentences.

Comprehension: Identifying Facts

1. What does the king use his arena for?

2. What is behind the two doors?

3. What happens after the tiger tears a man to pieces?

4. What happens after the lady comes out of the door?

5. Why does the king throw his daughter's lover into prison?

6. What has the princess done that no one else has ever done before?

7. Why does the princess hate the lady behind the door?

8. What does the princess's lover know instantly when he looks at her?

9. Why does the princess raise her right hand?

10. Why is the princess's decision so hard to make?

Comprehension: Understanding Main Ideas

11. What sort of a ruler is the king? Why is he described as "semibarbaric"?

12. Why is the king's arena called "an agent of poetic justice"?

13. What does the accused subject have to do when he walks into the arena?

14. What do the hired mourners do if the accused picks the door that reveals the tiger?

15. What happens if the accused picks the lady's door but he is already married?

16. Why does the king think he has a system of "perfect fairness"?

17. Why is the arena so popular with the people?

18. Since everyone admits that the young man loves the princess, what question will the events in the arena answer?

19. Why is the question "the lady or the tiger?" so difficult to answer?

20. Why is it important that the princess, like her father, is "semibarbaric"?

Review Continued on Next Page

Understanding Literature: Climax

The climax of a story—sometimes called the turning point—is the highest point of interest or suspense. The rising action of the plot builds to this point. At the climax, the main character either solves the problem of the story, or realizes that the problem will never be solved. From this point on, readers expect the story to end in a certain way. For example, in Unit 4, the climax of "American History" is when Elena understands why she won't be allowed to study with Eugene. The story ends quickly after that, as Elena thinks about what has happened.

21. In your own words, what is the climax of a story?

22. Give an example of the climax in a story you have read.

23. In "The Lady, or the Tiger?" what events in the plot could be considered the rising action of the story?

24. Describe the climax of "The Lady, or the Tiger?"

25. As a reader, how did you feel when the story ended without its problem being solved?

Critical Thinking

26. Do you think the king's system of justice is fair? Why or why not?

27. Since the king loved his daughter dearly, why do you think he threw her lover in prison?

28. Why might the princess not want her lover to open the lady's door?

29. Which do you think came out of the opened door: the lady, or the tiger? Why do you think so?

30. Why do you think this story was so popular?

Writing on Your Own Have you ever had to choose "the lesser of two evils," as the princess did in "The Lady, or the Tiger?" Write a paragraph describing the situation. Explain how and why you made your choice.

The Lottery

Shirley Jackson

Shirley Jackson
1916–1965

Literary Terms

foreshadowing clues or hints that a writer gives about something that has not yet happened

irony the difference between what is expected to happen in a story and what does happen

About the Author

Shirley Jackson, was born in San Francisco in 1916. As a child, she preferred to stay in her room, writing poetry and exploring what she called "other worlds." In 1940 she married Stanley Edgar Hyman and had four children. Jackson once wrote that her family's "major exports [were] books and children, both of which we produce in abundance."

Jackson's work first came to the world's attention in 1948. Her story "The Lottery" was published in *The New Yorker* magazine. Other suspense thrillers soon followed, including her novels *The Haunting of Hill House, Hangsaman,* and *We Have Always Lived in the Castle.* Her fiction is about disturbed states of mind, ghosts, murder, and other dark subjects. However, Shirley Jackson also published two funny accounts of her life with her children, *Life Among the Savages* and *Raising Demons.*

About the Selection

Shirley Jackson's "The Lottery" brought in more mail from readers than any other story *The New Yorker* ever published. People demanded to know what the story meant. When asked for her explanation, Jackson replied that "The Lottery" was just a story.

The real terror of this story begins after readers feel sure they understand what is happening. It is almost as if Shirley Jackson has created a trap for her readers. After reading the story, we look back at examples of **foreshadowing**—hints we didn't notice at the time about what was going to happen.

This story is an excellent example of the use of **irony**. Irony is the difference between what is expected to happen and what does happen.

The Lottery

As you read, ask yourself what each detail adds to what you expect will happen in this story.

The morning of June 27th was clear and sunny, with the fresh warmth of a full-summer day; the flowers were blossoming **profusely** and the grass was richly green. The people of the village began to gather in the square, between the post office and the bank, around ten o'clock; in some towns there were so many people that the **lottery** took two days and had to be started on June 26th, but in this village, where there were only about three hundred people, the whole lottery took less than two hours, so it could begin at ten o'clock in the morning and still be through in time to allow the villagers to get home for noon dinner.

Notice that this lottery happens in other villages too—not just in this one.

The children assembled first, of course. School was recently over for the summer, and the feeling of liberty sat uneasily on most of them; they tended to gather together quietly for a while before they broke into **boisterous** play, and their talk was still of the classroom and the teacher, of books and **reprimands**. Bobby Martin had already stuffed his pockets full of stones, and the other boys soon followed his example, selecting the smoothest and roundest stones; Bobby and Harry Jones and Dickie Delacroix—the villagers pronounced his name "Dellacroy"—eventually made a great pile of stones in one corner of the square and guarded it against the raids of the other boys. The girls stood aside, talking among themselves, looking over their shoulders at the boys, and the very small children rolled in the dust or clung to the hands of their older brothers and sisters.

---

boisterous noisy, wild

lottery a drawing of lots—objects used as counters in a game of chance—used to decide something

profusely generously; in large amounts

reprimand a scolding

Soon the men began to gather, surveying their own children, speaking of planting and rain, tractors and taxes. They stood together, away from the pile of stones in the corner, and their jokes were quiet and they smiled rather than laughed. The women, wearing faded house dresses and sweaters, came shortly after their menfolk. They greeted one another and exchanged bits of gossip as they went to join their husbands. Soon the women, standing by their husbands, began to call to their children, and the children came **reluctantly**, having to be called four or five times. Bobby Martin ducked under his mother's grasping hand and ran, laughing, back to the pile of stones. His father spoke up sharply, and Bobby came quickly and took his place between his father and his oldest brother.

The lottery was conducted—as were the square dances, the teen-age club, the Halloween program—by Mr. Summers, who had time and energy to devote to **civic** activities. He was a round-faced, **jovial** man and he ran the coal business, and people were sorry for him, because he had no children and his wife was a scold. When he arrived in the square, carrying the black wooden box, there was a murmur of conversation among the villagers, and he waved and called, "Little late today, folks." The postmaster, Mr. Graves, followed him, carrying a three-legged stool, and the stool was put in the center of the square and Mr. Summers set the black box down on it. The villagers kept their distance, leaving a space between themselves and the stool, and when Mr. Summers said, "Some of you fellows want to give me a hand?" there was a hesitation before two men, Mr. Martin and his oldest son, Baxter, came forward to hold the box steady on the stool while Mr. Summers stirred up the papers inside it.

The original **paraphernalia** for the lottery had been lost long ago, and the black box now resting on the stool had been put into use even before Old Man Warner, the oldest man in town, was born. Mr. Summers spoke frequently to the

The suspense and, later, the horror of this story builds from matter-of-fact details. Notice that the boys have gathered stones.

civic community	**paraphernalia** equipment	**reluctantly** without wanting to
jovial happy, friendly		

villagers about making a new box, but no one liked to upset even as much **tradition** as was represented by the black box. There was a story that the present box had been made with some pieces of the box that had **preceded** it, the one that had been constructed when the first people settled down to make a village here. Every year, after the lottery, Mr. Summers began talking again about a new box, but every year the subject was allowed to fade off without anything's being done. The black box grew shabbier each year; by now it was no longer completely black but splintered badly along one side to show the original wood color, and in some places faded or stained.

Mr. Martin and his oldest son, Baxter, held the black box securely on the stool until Mr. Summers had stirred the papers thoroughly with his hand. Because so much of the **ritual** had been forgotten or **discarded**, Mr. Summers had been successful in having slips of paper substituted for the chips of wood that had been used for generations. Chips of wood, Mr. Summers had argued, had been all very well when the village was tiny, but now that the population was more than three hundred and likely to keep on growing, it was necessary to use something that would fit more easily into the black box. The night before the lottery, Mr. Summers and Mr. Graves made up the slips of paper and put them in the box, and it was then taken to the safe of Mr. Summers' coal company and locked up until Mr. Summers was ready to take it to the square next morning. The rest of the year, the box was put away, sometimes one place, sometimes another; it had spent one year in Mr. Graves's barn and another year underfoot in the post office, and sometimes it was set on a shelf in the Martin grocery and left there.

At this point, what do we know about the lottery? How often is it held? How do the people feel about it? What do they know of its history?

There was a great deal of fussing to be done before Mr. Summers declared the lottery open. There were the lists to make up—of heads of families, heads of households in each family, members of each household in each family. There was the proper swearing-in of Mr. Summers by the postmaster, as the official of the lottery; at one time, some people

discard to throw away or cast off	**precede** to come before	**ritual** a ceremony
		tradition a custom

Group Expression,
Diana Ong

remembered, there had been a **recital** of some sort, performed by the official of the lottery, a **perfunctory**, tuneless chant that had been rattled off duly each year; some people believed that the official of the lottery used to stand just so when he said or sang it, others believed that he was supposed to walk among the people, but years and years ago this part of the ritual had been allowed to **lapse**. There had been, also, a ritual salute, which the official of the lottery had had to use in addressing each person who came up to draw from the box, but this also had changed with time, until now it was felt necessary only for the official to speak to each person approaching. Mr. Summers was very good at all this; in his clean white shirt and blue jeans, with one hand resting carelessly on the black box, he seemed very proper and important as he talked **interminably** to Mr. Graves and the Martins.

interminably without end

lapse to decline

perfunctory careless; done without much thought

recital a performance of music

Just as Mr. Summers finally left off talking and turned to the assembled villagers, Mrs. Hutchinson came hurriedly along the path to the square, her sweater thrown over her shoulders, and slid into place in the back of the crowd. "Clean forgot what day it was," she said to Mrs. Delacroix, who stood next to her, and they both laughed softly. "Thought my old man was out back stacking wood," Mrs. Hutchinson went on, "and then I looked out the window and the kids were gone, and then I remembered it was the twenty-seventh and came a-running." She dried her hands on her apron, and Mrs. Delacroix said, "You're in time, though. They're still talking away up there."

Mrs. Hutchinson craned her neck to see through the crowd and found her husband and children standing near the front. She tapped Mrs. Delacroix on the arm as a farewell and began to make her way through the crowd. The people separated good-humoredly to let her through; two or three people said, in voices just loud enough to be heard across the crowd, "Here comes your Missus, Hutchinson," and "Bill, she made it after all." Mrs. Hutchinson reached her husband, and Mr. Summers, who had been waiting, said cheerfully, "Thought we were going to have to get on without you, Tessie." Mrs. Hutchinson said, grinning, "Wouldn't have me leave m'dishes in the sink, now, would you, Joe?," and soft laughter ran through the crowd as the people stirred back into position after Mrs. Hutchinson's arrival.

"Well, now," Mr. Summers said soberly, "guess we better get started, get this over with, so's we can go back to work. Anybody ain't here?"

"Dunbar," several people said. "Dunbar, Dunbar."

Mr. Summers consulted his list. "Clyde Dunbar," he said. "That's right. He's broke his leg, hasn't he? Who's drawing for him?"

"Me, I guess," a woman said, and Mr. Summers turned to look at her. "Wife draws for her husband," Mr. Summers said. "Don't you have a grown boy to do it for you, Janey?" Although Mr. Summers and everyone else in the village knew the answer perfectly well, it was the business of the official of the lottery to ask such questions formally. Mr. Summers waited with an expression of polite interest while Mrs. Dunbar answered.

"Horace's not but sixteen yet," Mrs. Dunbar said regretfully. "Guess I gotta fill in for the old man this year."

"Right," Mr. Summers said. He made a note on the list he was holding. Then he asked, "Watson boy drawing this year?"

A tall boy in the crowd raised his hand. "Here," he said. "I'm drawing for m'mother and me." He blinked his eyes nervously and ducked his head as several voices in the crowd said things like "Good fellow, Jack," and "Glad to see your mother's got a man to do it."

"Well," Mr. Summers said, "guess that's everyone. Old Man Warner make it?"

"Here," a voice said, and Mr. Summers nodded.

A sudden hush fell on the crowd as Mr. Summers cleared his throat and looked at the list. "All ready?" he called. "Now, I'll read the names—heads of families first—and the men come up and take a paper out of the box. Keep the paper folded in your hand without looking at it until everyone has had a turn. Everything clear?"

The people had done it so many times that they only half listened to the directions; most of them were quiet, wetting their lips, not looking around. Then Mr. Summers raised one hand high and said, "Adams." A man **disengaged** himself from the crowd and came forward. "Hi, Steve," Mr. Summers said, and Mr. Adams said, "Hi, Joe." They grinned at one another humorlessly and nervously. Then Mr. Adams reached into the black box and took out a folded paper. He held it firmly by one corner as he turned and went hastily back to his place in the crowd, where he stood a little apart from his family, not looking down at his hand.

Why do you think Mr. Adams is nervous?

"Allen." Mr. Summers said. "Anderson. . . . Bentham."

"Seems like there's no time at all between lotteries any more," Mrs. Delacroix said to Mrs. Graves in the back row. "Seems like we got through with the last one only last week."

disengage to pull away from

"Time sure goes fast," Mrs. Graves said.

"Clark. . . . Delacroix."

"There goes my old man," Mrs. Delacroix said. She held her breath while her husband went forward.

"Dunbar," Mr. Summers said, and Mrs. Dunbar went steadily to the box while one of the women said, "Go on, Janey," and another said, "There she goes."

"We're next," Mrs. Graves said. She watched while Mr. Graves came around from the side of the box, greeted Mr. Summers gravely, and selected a slip of paper from the box. By now, all through the crowd there were men holding the small folded papers in their large hands, turning them over and over nervously. Mrs. Dunbar and her two sons stood together, Mrs. Dunbar holding the slip of paper.

"Harburt. . . . Hutchinson."

"Get up there, Bill," Mrs. Hutchinson said, and the people near her laughed.

"Jones."

"They do say," Mr. Adams said to Old Man Warner, who stood next to him, "that over in the north village they're talking of giving up the lottery."

Old Man Warner snorted. "Pack of crazy fools," he said. "Listening to the young folks, nothing's good enough for *them*. Next thing you know, they'll be wanting to go back to living in caves, nobody work any more, live *that* way for a while. Used to be a saying about 'Lottery in June, corn be heavy soon.' First thing you know, we'd all be eating stewed chickweed and acorns. There's *always* been a lottery," he added **petulantly**. "Bad enough to see young Joe Summers up there joking with everybody."

"Some places have already quit lotteries," Mrs. Adams said.

"Nothing but trouble in *that*," Old Man Warner said stoutly. "Pack of young fools."

"Martin." And Bobby Martin watched his father go forward. "Overdyke. . . . Percy."

Why does Old Man Warner call the people over in the north village a "pack of crazy fools"?

petulantly in a grouchy, grumpy way

"I wish they'd hurry," Mrs. Dunbar said to her older son. "I wish they'd hurry."

"They're almost through," her son said.

"You get ready to run tell Dad," Mrs. Dunbar said.

Mr. Summers called his own name and then stepped forward **precisely** and selected a slip from the box. Then he called, "Warner."

"Seventy-seventh year I been in the lottery," Old Man Warner said as he went through the crowd. "Seventy-seventh time."

"Watson." The tall boy came awkwardly through the crowd. Someone said, "Don't be nervous, Jack." Mr. Summers said, "Take your time, son."

"Zanini."

After that, there was a long pause, a breathless pause, until Mr. Summers, holding his slip of paper in the air, said, "All right, fellows." For a minute, no one moved, and then all the slips of paper were opened. Suddenly, all the women began to speak at once, saying, "Who is it?," "Who's got it?," "Is it the Dunbars?," "Is it the Watsons?" Then the voices began to say, "It's Hutchinson. It's Bill," "Bill Hutchinson's got it."

"Go tell your father," Mrs. Dunbar said to her older son.

People began to look around to see the Hutchinsons. Bill Hutchinson was standing quiet, staring down at the paper in his hand. Suddenly, Tessie Hutchinson shouted to Mr. Summers, "You didn't give him time enough to take any paper he wanted. I saw you. It wasn't fair!"

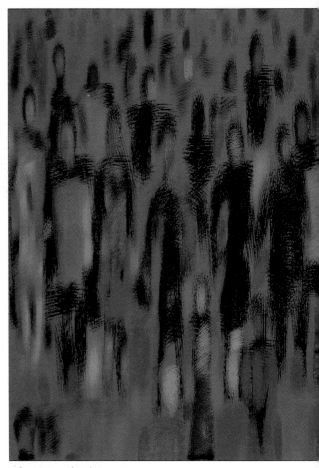

Blue Crowd, Diana Ong

precisely correctly

"Be a good sport, Tessie," Mrs. Delacroix called, and Mrs. Graves said, "All of us took the same chance."

"Shut up, Tessie," Bill Hutchinson said.

"Well, everyone," Mr. Summers said, "that was done pretty fast, and now we've got to be hurrying a little more to get it done in time." He consulted his next list. "Bill," he said, "you draw for the Hutchinson family. You got any other households in the Hutchinsons?"

"There's Don and Eva," Mrs. Hutchinson yelled. "Make *them* take their chance!"

"Daughters draw with their husbands' families, Tessie," Mr. Summers said gently. "You know that as well as anyone else."

"I guess not, Joe," Bill Hutchinson said regretfully. "My daughter draws with her husband's family, that's only fair. And I've got no other family except the kids."

"Then, as far as drawing for families is concerned, it's you," Mr. Summers said in explanation, "and as far as drawing for households is concerned, that's you, too. Right?"

"Right," Bill Hutchinson said.

"How many kids, Bill?" Mr. Summers asked formally.

"Three," Bill Hutchinson said. "There's Bill, Jr., and Nancy, and little Dave. And Tessie and me."

"All right, then," Mr. Summers said. "Harry, you got their tickets back?"

Mr. Graves nodded and held up the slips of paper. "Put them in the box, then," Mr. Summers directed. "Take Bill's and put it in."

"I think we ought to start over," Mrs. Hutchinson said, as quietly as she could. "I tell you it wasn't *fair*. You didn't give him time enough to choose. *Every*body saw that."

Mr. Graves had selected the five slips and put them in the box, and he dropped all the papers but those onto the ground, where the breeze caught them and lifted them off.

"Listen, everybody," Mrs. Hutchinson was saying to the people around her.

"Ready, Bill?" Mr. Summers asked, and Bill Hutchinson, with one quick glance around at his wife and children, nodded.

What do you think will happen next?

"Remember," Mr. Summers said, "take the slips and keep them folded until each person has taken one. Harry, you help little Dave." Mr. Graves took the hand of the little boy, who came willingly with him up to the box. "Take a paper out of the box, Davy," Mr. Summers said. Davy put his hand into the box and laughed. "Take just *one* paper," Mr. Summers said. "Harry, you hold it for him." Mr. Graves took the child's hand and removed the folded paper from the tight fist and held it while little Dave stood next to him and looked up at him wonderingly.

"Nancy next," Mr. Summers said. Nancy was twelve, and her school friends breathed heavily as she went forward, switching her skirt, and took a slip daintily from the box. "Bill, Jr.," Mr. Summers said, and Billy, his face red and his feet over-large, nearly knocked the box over as he got a paper out. "Tessie," Mr. Summers said. She hesitated for a minute, looking around **defiantly**, and then set her lips and went up to the box. She snatched a paper out and held it behind her.

Why does Mrs. Hutchinson hesitate?

"Bill," Mr. Summers said, and Bill Hutchinson reached into the box and felt around, bringing his hand out at last with the slip of paper in it.

The crowd was quiet. A girl whispered, "I hope it's not Nancy," and the sound of the whisper reached the edges of the crowd.

"It's not the way it used to be," Old Man Warner said clearly. "People ain't the way they used to be."

"All right," Mr. Summers said. "Open the papers. Harry, you open little Dave's."

Mr. Graves opened the slip of paper and there was a general sigh through the crowd as he held it up and everyone could see that it was blank. Nancy and Bill, Jr., opened theirs at the same time, and both beamed and laughed, turning around to the crowd and holding their slips of paper above their heads.

defiantly with resistance; with opposition

"Tessie," Mr. Summers said. There was a pause, and then Mr. Summers looked at Bill Hutchinson, and Bill unfolded his paper and showed it. It was blank.

"It's Tessie," Mr. Summers said, and his voice was hushed. "Show us her paper, Bill."

Bill Hutchinson went over to his wife and forced the slip of paper out of her hand. It had a black spot on it, the black spot Mr. Summers had made the night before with the heavy pencil in the coal-company office. Bill Hutchinson held it up, and there was a stir in the crowd.

"All right, folks," Mr. Summers said. "Let's finish quickly."

Although the villagers had forgotten the ritual and lost the original black box, they still remembered to use stones. The pile of stones the boys had made earlier was ready; there were stones on the ground with the blowing scraps of paper that had come out of the box. Mrs. Delacroix selected a stone so large she had to pick it up with both hands and turned to Mrs. Dunbar. "Come on," she said. "Hurry up."

Mrs. Dunbar had small stones in both hands, and she said, gasping for breath, "I can't run at all. You'll have to go ahead and I'll catch up with you."

The children had stones already, and someone gave little Davy Hutchinson a few pebbles.

Tessie Hutchinson was in the center of a cleared space by now, and she held her hands out desperately as the villagers moved in on her. "It isn't fair," she said. A stone hit her on the side of the head.

Old Man Warner was saying, "Come on, come on, everyone." Steve Adams was in the front of the crowd of villagers, with Mrs. Graves beside him.

"It isn't fair, it isn't right," Mrs. Hutchinson screamed, and then they were upon her.

Go back and re-read parts of the story. What details do you notice now that foreshadow the horror of this story?

The Lottery
Shirley Jackson

Directions Write the answers to these questions using complete sentences.

Comprehension: Identifying Facts

1. What do the boys of the village collect as they wait for the lottery to begin?

2. Who conducts the lottery? What other things does he do for the village?

3. What happened to the equipment they used to use for the lottery?

4. In the past, what did the people use instead of slips of paper?

5. What kind of lists have to be made up before the lottery can begin?

6. Why is Mrs. Hutchinson late?

7. Which villagers are called to draw a piece of paper from the black box?

8. Who draws the marked piece of paper?

9. What does Mrs. Hutchinson say about the lottery?

10. How do the people "finish" the lottery?

Comprehension: Understanding Main Ideas

11. What were your first thoughts about the lottery as the story began?

12. At what point in the story did you realize what it meant to "win"?

13. What do the townspeople think about the lottery?

14. Give an example of foreshadowing in the story.

15. Why don't the people want to replace the black box? What is the importance of this object to the story?

16. Describe the story's setting. What details, if any, prepare you for the ending of the story?

17. When does the climax, or turning point, of the story occur?

18. What changes have occurred over the years in the way the lottery is conducted?

19. Why is Old Man Warner an important character in this story?

20. How does Jackson build suspense for the reader? Who knows more: the characters or the reader?

Review Continued on Next Page

Understanding Literature: Irony

There are several different kinds of irony. *Verbal irony* is when a character or the narrator says one thing, but means something else. For example, the conversation among the townspeople while the drawing is going on is ironic when we find out what the lottery really is. Consider Old Man Warner's comment—"Nothing but trouble in *that*"—in response to Mrs. Adams's saying that some villages have stopped holding lotteries.

Dramatic irony is when readers know something that the characters do not realize. *Situational irony*—used in "The Lottery"—is when what readers expect to happen is not what actually occurs.

21. What is the difference between verbal irony and situational irony?

22. What is the irony of the situation described in "The Lottery"?

23. Mrs. Hutchinson, late for the lottery, explains that she "clean forgot what day it was." How is this ironic? How does Mrs. Delacroix's comment add to the irony?

24. How does Old Man Warner's saying "Lottery in June, corn be heavy soon" add to the story's irony?

25. Jackson provides many details in the story. How do these ordinary details add to the irony?

Critical Thinking

26. What do you think this story means? Support your opinion with evidence from the story.

27. Why do you think the people refuse to give up the lottery?

28. How would you feel if you were a Hutchinson and found that you had drawn a blank piece of paper?

29. If you lived in this town, would you have agreed with holding a lottery?

30. The lottery is described as a custom that the townspeople have been following so long that they no longer remember how or why it started. What is a custom you know about that people seem to follow just because they've "always done it that way"? How is this like the situation described in the story?

Writing on Your Own Turn the tables on "The Lottery". Continue the story by writing several paragraphs that add a new and unexpected twist to the ending of the story.

The Fog Horn
Ray Bradbury

Ray Bradbury
1920–

Literary Terms

figurative language language that uses word pictures to compare or describe, and that is not meant to be taken literally

metaphor a figure of speech that says one thing *is* another

personification giving characters such as animals or objects the characteristics of humans

science fiction fiction based on real or imagined facts of science

simile a figure of speech in which two things are compared using a phrase that includes the words *like* or *as*

About the Author

Ray Bradbury is one of the world's most famous writers of **science fiction**. Born in Illinois in 1920, Bradbury has lived in Los Angeles since he was fourteen. From the first, he was interested in movies and comic strips about the future. To date, Bradbury has written more than 500 science fiction and fantasy stories, including the well-known novels *Fahrenheit 451*, *The Martian Chronicles*, and *Something Wicked This Way Comes*. He has also written poetry, plays, essays, and scripts for both television and film.

Bradbury has used his imagination in other ways. As one of Disney's Imagineers (part engineer and part poet), he created the Spaceship Earth exhibit at Epcot Center and worked on the design of Euro-Disney's Orbitron space ride.

About the Selection

Ray Bradbury says that the idea for this short story came to him when he saw the ruins of an old roller coaster in the sand of a southern California beach. He wondered about it for several days. One night, the loud, sad sound of fog horns awakened him. That sound was all he needed to hear. The next morning he got up and wrote "The Fog Horn."

One of the ways Bradbury builds suspense in this story is through its setting. Also, his dialogue—the conversation between characters—shows us what they are like and what they believe.

"The Fog Horn" is also rich in **figurative language**. Bradbury draws word pictures that bring his strange world to life. This kind of language—including **similes, metaphors,** and **personification**—is not meant to be taken literally, or exactly as written. It is meant to paint a picture for the reader.

The Fog Horn

As you read this story, note which details are "science" and which are "science fiction."

Notice the simile: the gulls are scared away by the fog horn "like decks of scattered cards."

How are the details of setting important to this story? What does Bradbury's descrption of the lighthouse foreshadow later in the story?

Out there in the cold water, far from land, we waited every night for the coming of the fog, and it came, and we oiled the brass machinery and lit the fog light up in the stone tower. Feeling like two birds in the gray sky, McDunn and I sent the light touching out, red, then white, then red again, to eye the lonely ships. And if they did not see our light, then there was always our Voice, the great deep cry of our Fog Horn shuddering through the rags of mist to startle the gulls away like decks of scattered cards and make the waves turn high and foam.

"It's a lonely life, but you're used to it now, aren't you?" asked McDunn.

"Yes," I said. "You're a good talker, thank the Lord."

"Well, it's your turn on land tomorrow," he said, smiling, "to dance with the ladies and drink gin."

"What do you think, McDunn, when I leave you out here alone?"

"On the mysteries of the sea." McDunn lit his pipe. It was a quarter past seven of a cold November evening, the heat on, the light switching its tail in two hundred directions, the Fog Horn bumbling in the high throat of the tower. There wasn't a town for a hundred miles down the coast, just a road which came lonely through dead country to the sea, with few cars on it, a stretch of two miles of cold water out to our rock, and rare few ships.

"The mysteries of the sea," said McDunn thoughtfully. "You know, the ocean's the biggest damned snowflake ever? It rolls and swells a thousand shapes and colors, no two alike. Strange. One night, years ago, I was here alone, when all of the fish of the sea surfaced out there. Something made them swim in and lie in the bay, sort of trembling and staring up at

the tower light going red, white, red, white across them so I could see their funny eyes. I turned cold. They were like a big peacock's tail, moving out there until midnight. Then, without so much as a sound, they slipped away, the million of them was gone. I kind of think maybe, in some sort of way, they came all those miles to worship. Strange. But think how the tower must look to them, standing seventy feet above the water, the God-light flashing out from it, and the tower declaring itself with a monster voice. They never came back, those fish, but don't you think for a while they thought they were in the Presence?"

I shivered. I looked out at the long gray lawn of the sea stretching away into nothing and nowhere.

"Oh, the sea's full," McDunn puffed his pipe nervously, blinking. He had been nervous all day and hadn't said why. "For all our engines and so-called submarines, it'll be ten thousand centuries before we set foot on the real bottom of

Why does McDunn think the fish come to "worship" the lighthouse tower?

Comets can be older than the earth. Here, McDunn uses a simile to compare time beneath the sea with the age of a comet's beard, or tail.

the sunken lands, in the fairy kingdoms there, and know *real* terror. Think of it, it's still the year 300,000 Before Christ down under there. While we've paraded about with trumpets, lopping off each other's countries and heads, they have been living beneath the sea twelve miles deep and cold in a time as old as the beard of a comet."

"Yes, it's an old world."

"Come on. I got something special I been saving to tell you."

We ascended the eighty steps, talking and taking our time. At the top, McDunn switched off the room lights so there'd be no reflection in the plate glass. The great eye of the light was humming, turning easily in its oiled socket. The Fog Horn was blowing steadily, once every fifteen seconds.

"Sounds like an animal, don't it?" McDunn nodded to himself. "A big lonely animal crying in the night. Sitting here on the edge of ten billion years calling out to the Deeps, I'm here, I'm here, I'm here. And the Deeps *do* answer, yes they do. You been here not for three months, Johnny, so I better prepare you. About this time of year," he said, studying the murk and fog, "something comes to visit the lighthouse."

"The swarms of fish like you said?"

How is Bradbury building suspense here?

"No, this is something else. I've put off telling you because you might think I'm **daft**. But tonight's the latest I can put it off, for if my calendar's marked right from last year, tonight's the night it comes. I won't go into detail, you'll have to see it yourself. Just sit down there. If you want, tomorrow you can pack your duffel and take the motorboat in to land and get your car parked there at the **dinghy** pier on the cape and drive back to some little inland town and keep your lights burning nights, I won't question or blame you. It's happened three years now, and this is the only time anyone's been here with me to **verify** it. You wait and watch."

Half an hour passed with only a few whispers between us. When we grew tired of waiting, McDunn began describing

---

daft crazy   **dinghy** a small boat   **verify** to prove that something is true

some of his ideas to me. He had some theories about the Fog Horn itself.

"One day many years ago a man walked along and stood in the sound of the ocean on a cold sunless shore and said, 'We need a voice to call across the water, to warn ships; I'll make one. I'll make a voice like all of time and all of the fog that ever was; I'll make a voice that is like an empty bed beside you all night long, and like an empty house when you open the door, and like trees in autumn with no leaves. A sound like the birds flying south, crying, and a sound like November wind and the sea on the hard, cold shore. I'll make a sound that's so alone that no one can miss it, that whoever hears it will weep in their souls, and hearths will seem warmer, and being inside will seem better to all who hear it in the distant towns. I'll make a sound and an **apparatus** and they'll call it a Fog Horn and whoever hears it will know the sadness of **eternity** and the briefness of life.'"

The Fog Horn blew.

"I made up that story," said McDunn quietly, "to try to explain why this thing keeps coming back to the lighthouse every year. The Fog Horn calls it, I think, and it comes. . ."

"But—" I said.

"Sssst!" said McDunn. "There!" He nodded out to the Deeps.

Something was swimming toward the lighthouse tower.

It was a cold night, as I have said; the high tower was cold, the light coming and going, and the Fog Horn calling and calling through the raveling mist. You couldn't see far and you couldn't see plain, but there was the deep sea moving on its way about the night earth, flat and quiet, the color of gray mud, and here were the two of us alone in the high tower, and there, far out at first, was a ripple, followed by a wave, a rising, a bubble, a bit of **froth**. And then, from the surface of the cold sea came a head, a large head, dark-colored, with immense eyes, and then a neck. And then—not a body—but more neck and more! The head rose a full forty feet above the water on a

> Notice the figurative language used to describe the lonely sound of the Fog Horn: like an empty bed, an empty house, trees with no leaves.

> *Raveling* means tangling up.

apparatus a device   eternity endless time   froth foam

slender and beautiful dark neck. Only then did the body, like a little island of black coral and shells and crayfish, drip up from the **subterranean**. There was a flicker of tail. In all, from head to tip of tail, I estimated the monster at ninety or a hundred feet.

I don't know what I said. I said something.

"Steady, boy, steady," whispered McDunn.

"It's impossible!" I said.

How does McDunn "explain" the monster?

"No, Johnny, *we're* impossible. *It's* like it always was ten million years ago. *It* hasn't changed. It's *us* and the land that've changed, become impossible. *Us!*"

It swam slowly and with a great dark majesty out in the icy waters, far away. The fog came and went about it, **momentarily** erasing its shape. One of the monster eyes caught and held and flashed back our immense light, red, white, red, white, like a disk held high and sending a message in **primeval** code. It was as silent as the fog through which it swam.

"It's a dinosaur of some sort!" I crouched down, holding to the stair rail.

"Yes, one of the tribe."

"But they died out!"

"No, only hid away in the Deeps. Deep, deep down in the deepest Deeps. Isn't *that* that a word now, Johnny, a real word, it says so much: the Deeps. There's all the coldness and darkness and deepness in the world in a word like that."

"What'll we do?"

"Do? We got our job, we can't leave. Besides, we're safer here than in any boat trying to get to land. That thing's as big

A *destroyer* is a warship.

as a destroyer and almost as swift."

"But here, why does it come *here?*"

The next moment I had my answer.

The Fog Horn blew.

And the monster answered.

A cry came across a million years of water and mist. A cry so **anguished** and alone that it shuddered in my head and my

anguished distressed, tormented	**momentarily** for a moment	**subterranean** beneath the earth
	primeval ancient	

body. The monster cried out at the tower. The Fog Horn blew. The monster roared again. The Fog Horn blew. The monster opened its great toothed mouth and the sound that came from it was the sound of the Fog Horn itself. Lonely and vast and far away. The sound of **isolation**, a viewless sea, a cold night, apartness. That was the sound.

"Now," whispered McDunn, "do you know why it comes here?"

I nodded.

"All year long, Johnny, that poor monster there lying far out, a thousand miles at sea, and twenty miles deep maybe, **biding** its time, perhaps it's a million years old, this one creature. Think of it, waiting a million years; could *you* wait that long? Maybe it's the last of its kind. I sort of think that's true. Anyway, here come men on land and build this lighthouse, five years ago. And set up their Fog Horn and sound it and sound it, out toward the place where you bury yourself in sleep and sea memories of a world where there were thousands like yourself, but now you're alone, all alone in a world not made for you, a world where you have to hide.

"But the sound of the Fog Horn comes and goes, comes and goes, and you stir from the muddy bottom of the Deeps, and your eyes open like the lenses of two-foot cameras and you move, slow, slow, for you have the ocean sea on your shoulders, heavy. But that Fog Horn comes through a thousand miles of water, faint and familiar, and the furnace in your belly stokes up, and you begin to rise, slow, slow. You feed yourself on great slakes of cod and minnow, on rivers of jellyfish, and you rise slow through the autumn months, through September when the fogs started, through October with more fog and the horn still calling you on, and then, late in November, after pressurizing yourself day by day, a few feet higher every hour, you are near the surface and still alive. You've got to go slow. If you surfaced all at once you'd explode. So it takes you all of three months to surface, and then a number of days to swim through the cold waters to the

McDunn imagines himself as the monster. What does this add to the story?

---

bide to wait   **isolation** aloneness

lighthouse. And there you are, out there, in the night, Johnny, the biggest damn monster in **creation**. And here's the lighthouse calling to you, with a long neck like your neck sticking way up out of the water, and a body like your body, and, most important of all, a voice like your voice. Do you understand now, Johnny, do you understand?"

The Fog Horn blew.

The monster answered. I saw it all, I knew it all—the million years of waiting alone, for someone to come back who never came back. The million years of isolation at the bottom of the sea, the insanity of time there, while the skies cleared of reptile-birds, the swamps dried on the continental lands, the sloths and saber-tooths had their day and sank in tar pits, and men ran like white ants upon the hills.

The Fog Horn blew.

"Last year," said McDunn, "that creature swam round and round, round and round, all night. Not coming too near, puzzled, I'd say. Afraid, maybe. And a bit angry after coming all this way. But the next day, unexpectedly, the fog lifted, the sun came out fresh, the sky was as blue as a painting. And the monster swam off away from the heat and the silence and didn't come back. I suppose it's been brooding on it for a year now, thinking it over from every which way."

The monster was only a hundred yards off now, it and the Fog Horn crying at each other. As the lights hit them, the monster's eyes were fire and ice, fire and ice.

"That's life for you," said McDunn. "Someone always waiting for someone who never comes home. Always someone loving some thing more than that thing loves them. And after a while you want to destroy whatever the thing is, so it can't hurt you no more."

The monster was rushing at the lighthouse.

The Fog Horn blew.

"Let's see what happens," said McDunn.

He switched the Fog Horn off.

"The Fog Horn blew" is repeated a number of times. How does this add to the suspense?

creation the world

The **ensuing** minute of silence was so intense that we could hear our hearts pounding in the glassed area of the tower, could hear the slow greased turn of the light.

The monster stopped and froze. Its great lantern eyes blinked. Its mouth gaped. It gave a sort of rumble, like a volcano. It twitched its head this way and that, as if to seek the sounds now **dwindled** off into the fog. It peered at the lighthouse. It rumbled again. Then its eyes caught fire. It reared up, **threshed** the water, and rushed at the tower, its eyes filled with angry torment.

"McDunn!" I cried. "Switch on the horn!"

McDunn fumbled with the switch. But even as he flicked it on, the monster was rearing up. I had a glimpse of its gigantic paws, fishskin glittering in webs between the fingerlike **projections**, clawing at the tower. The huge eye on the right side of its anguished head glittered before me like a **caldron** into which I might drop, screaming. The tower shook. The Fog Horn cried; the monster cried. It seized the tower and gnashed at the glass, which shattered in upon us.

McDunn seized my arm. "Downstairs!"

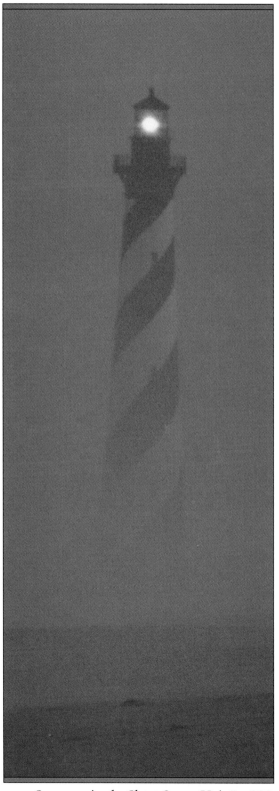

caldron a large pot, usually used for boiling

dwindle to fade away

ensuing following

projection something that juts out

thresh to strike, or toss about

The tower rocked, trembled, and started to give. The Fog Horn and the monster roared. We stumbled and half fell down the stairs. "Quick!"

We reached the bottom as the tower buckled down toward us. We ducked under the stairs into the small stone cellar. There were a thousand **concussions** as the rocks rained down; the Fog Horn stopped **abruptly**. The monster crashed upon the tower. The tower fell. We knelt together, McDunn and I, holding tight, while our world exploded.

Then it was over, and there was nothing but darkness and the wash of the sea on the raw stones.

That and the other sound.

"Listen," said McDunn quietly. "Listen."

We waited a moment. And then I began to hear it. First a great vacuumed sucking of air, and then the **lament**, the bewilderment, the loneliness of the great monster, folded over and upon us, above us, so that the sickening **reek** of its body filled the air, a stone's thickness away from our cellar. The monster gasped and cried. The tower was gone. The light was gone. The thing that had called to it across a million years was gone. And the monster was opening its mouth and sending out great sounds. The sounds of a Fog Horn, again and again. And ships far at sea, not finding the light, not seeing anything, but passing and hearing late that night, must've thought: There it is, the lonely sound, the Lonesome Bay horn. All's well. We've rounded the cape.

And so it went for the rest of that night.

The sun was hot and yellow the next afternoon when the rescuers came out to dig us from our stoned-under cellar.

"It fell apart, is all," said Mr. McDunn gravely. "We had a few bad knocks from the waves and it just crumbled." He pinched my arm.

Why doesn't McDunn tell the rescuers what really happened?

---

abruptly suddenly, without warning

concussion a blow; a shock

lament a crying out in grief

reek a terrible smell

There was nothing to see. The ocean was calm, the sky blue. The only thing was a great **algaic** stink from the green matter that covered the fallen tower stones and the shore rocks. Flies buzzed about. The ocean washed empty on the shore.

The next year they built a new lighthouse, but by that time I had a job in the little town and a wife and a good small warm house that glowed yellow on autumn nights, the doors locked, the chimney puffing smoke. As for McDunn, he was

algaic coming from algae or water plants such as seaweed

master of the new lighthouse, built to his own **specifications**, out of steel-**reinforced** concrete. "Just in case," he said.

The new lighthouse was ready in November. I drove down alone one evening late and parked my car and looked across the gray waters and listened to the new horn sounding, once, twice, three, four times a minute far out there, by itself.

The monster?

It never came back.

"It's gone away," said McDunn. "It's gone back to the Deeps. It's learned you can't love anything too much in this world. It's gone into the deepest Deeps to wait another million years. Ah, the poor thing! Waiting out here, and waiting out there, while man comes and goes on this **pitiful** little planet. Waiting and waiting."

I sat in my car, listening. I couldn't see the lighthouse or the light standing out in Lonesome Bay. I could only hear the Horn, the Horn, the Horn. It sounded like the monster calling.

I sat there wishing there was something I could say.

Recall that when the narrator first saw the sea monster, he reports, "I don't know what I said. I said something." Why do you think the narrator has difficulty putting his thoughts into words?

---

pitiful causing pity

reinforced made stronger

specification a set of directions

Directions Write the answers to these questions using complete sentences.

Comprehension: Identifying Facts

1. Who narrates this story?

2. What is the job of the two men?

3. What is the setting (location and time) of the story?

4. What strange experience does McDunn talk about at the beginning of the story?

5. How does McDunn describe the sound of the fog horn?

6. Why has McDunn been nervous all day?

7. Describe the monster.

8. What does the monster do when it hears the fog horn?

9. What happens when McDunn switches off the fog horn?

10. How do the men escape being killed?

Comprehension: Understanding Main Ideas

11. How would you describe the location of the lighthouse?

12. What are two examples of ways Bradbury foreshadows the coming of the monster?

13. What mental picture did you have of the monster's appearance? What parts of the picture were created by the words of the story? What parts did you create with your imagination?

14. Who would you consider to be the protagonist, or main character, in this story? Why?

15. How did McDunn feel about the monster? Was he afraid of it? Support your opinion with evidence from the story.

16. How do McDunn and the narrator describe the feelings and thoughts of the monster? How are these different from what you might expect in a story about a monster?

17. Why does the monster come to the lighthouse?

18. What happened when the monster came last year? Why is its behavior different this year?

19. What would you say is the climax, or turning point, of this story? Do you think what happens after the climax adds to or takes away from the effect of the story? Explain your answer.

20. In your opinion, what is the theme, or main idea, of this story?

Review Continued on Next Page

Understanding Literature: Dialogue

The words that characters say to one another make up a story's dialogue. Most writers signal dialogue with quotation marks. Just as conversations do in life, dialogue allows the characters in a short story to relate to one another. Through dialogue, fiction writers can let readers know how the characters feel about each other, about themselves, and about life itself. Dialogue can also tell us parts of the plot.

21. Which character in "The Fog Horn" has the most words of dialogue? How does this affect your understanding of the story?

22. What does McDunn's dialogue tell you about his character?

23. The narrator tells the story, but he doesn't have nearly as much dialogue as McDunn does. What do the narrator's few words of dialogue tell you about him and his opinion of McDunn?

24. Are the sounds the monster makes part of the dialogue? What is the monster saying? Who is the monster talking to?

25. How would the story be different if it did not have any dialogue?

Critical Thinking

26. In your opinion, why did the monster never return to the lighthouse?

27. Why do you think McDunn stayed in the lighthouse on that November night, knowing that the monster would probably return?

28. Compare the way Ray Bradbury creates suspense in this story with the way Frank Stockton creates suspense in "The Lady, or the Tiger?" How are they similar? How are they different?

29. At the end of the story, the narrator wishes there were something he could say. What do you think he means?

30. Do you think this story was more suspenseful or less suspenseful than "The Lottery"? Why?

> **Writing on Your Own** Pretend you are McDunn. Write a diary entry for the night you return to the rebuilt lighthouse.

The Monkey's Paw
W. W. Jacobs

W. W. Jacobs

1863–1943

Literary Terms

foreshadowing clues or hints that a writer gives about something that has not yet happened

mood the feeling created by a piece of writing

setting a story's time and place

About the Author

W. W. (William Wymark) Jacobs was born in London in 1863. He grew up in an area near the docks of London, where he saw ships and sailors from all over the world. He never forgot the stories he heard there. In fact, they gave him ideas for most of the stories and novels he went on to write.

Jacobs was in his twenties, working as a clerk, when he began to publish stories in magazines. The success of his first collection of stories, *Many Cargoes*, in 1896 led to his becoming a full-time writer. He wrote several novels, but he is mainly known for his short stories. Most of his stories are about sailors and the sea. Some are humorous and some, like "The Monkey's Paw," are tales of suspense and horror.

About the Selection

"The Monkey's Paw" is W. W. Jacobs's most famous story. No doubt he had heard tales like it as a boy on the London docks from sailors returning from mysterious ports of call. The story first appeared in *Harper's Monthly* in 1902. It was also included in a later collection of Jacobs's short stories called *The Lady and the Barge*. The story has also been used as the basis of other stories and plays.

Jacobs begins by bringing the reader to a lonely spot on the outskirts of an English town. By using such a lonely **setting**, Jacobs focuses our attention on the strange events that are about to unfold. In contrast, Jacobs describes the cozy, warm living room where the elderly couple and their son sit. The difference between the two places becomes even more important as the story goes on. Another important way the author builds the **mood** of this story is through **foreshadowing**. Foreshadowing, as discussed earlier, refers to clues or hints about something that has not yet happened.

The Monkey's Paw

As you read, notice how details of setting slowly increase the mood of horror and suspense.

Without, the night was cold and wet; but in the small parlor of Laburnam Villa the blinds were drawn and the fire burned brightly. Father and son were at chess, the former, who possessed ideas about the game involving **radical** changes, putting his king into such sharp and unnecessary perils that it even **provoked** comment from the white-haired old lady knitting **placidly** by the fire.

"Hark at the wind," said Mr. White, who, having seen a fatal mistake after it was too late, was **amiably desirous** of preventing his son from seeing it.

"I'm listening," said the latter, grimly surveying the board as he stretched out his hand. "Check."

"I should hardly think that he'd come tonight," said his father, with his hand **poised** over the board.

"Mate," replied the son.

"That's the worst of living so far out," bawled Mr. White, with sudden and unlooked-for violence; "of all the beastly, slushy, out-of-the-way places to live in, this is the worst. Pathway's a bog, and the road's a **torrent**. I don't know what people are thinking about. I suppose because only two houses in the road are let, they think it doesn't matter."

"Never mind, dear," said his wife, soothingly; "perhaps you'll win the next one."

Notice how Mr. White describes the setting of their house. Only two houses in the road are *let*, meaning rented—theirs and one other. Otherwise, they are alone.

amiably kindly	**poise** to hold steady	**radical** extreme
desirous anxious for	**provoke** to cause someone to take action	**torrent** a flood
placidly calmly		

Mr. White looked up sharply, just in time to **intercept** a knowing glance between mother and son. The words died away on his lips, and he hid a guilty grin in his thin gray beard.

"There he is," said Herbert White, as the gate banged to loudly and heavy footsteps came toward the door.

The old man rose with **hospitable haste**, and opening the door, was heard **condoling** with the new arrival. The new arrival also condoled with himself, so that Mrs. White said, "Tut, tut!" and coughed gently as her husband entered the room, followed by a tall, burly man, beady of eye and rubicund of visage.

Sergeant-Major Morris is described as tall, strongly built, with small, shiny eyes and a red (rubicund) face (visage).

"Sergeant-Major Morris," he said, introducing him.

The sergeant-major shook hands, and taking the proffered seat by the fire, watched contentedly while his host got out whiskey and tumblers and stood a small copper kettle on the fire.

Proffered means offered.

At the third glass his eyes got brighter, and he began to talk, the little family circle regarding with eager interest this visitor from distant parts, as he squared his broad shoulders in the chair and spoke of wild scenes and doughty deeds; of wars and **plagues** and strange peoples.

"Twenty-one years of it," said Mr. White, nodding at his wife and son. "When he went away, he was a slip of a youth in the warehouse. Now look at him."

"He don't look to have taken much harm," said Mrs. White politely.

"I'd like to go to India myself," said the old man, "just to look round a bit, you know."

"Better where you are," said the sergeant-major, shaking his head. He put down the empty glass, and sighing softly, shook it again.

"I should like to see those old temples and fakirs and jugglers," said the old man. "What was that you started telling me the other day about a monkey's paw or something, Morris?"

"Nothing," said the soldier hastily. "Leastways nothing worth hearing."

Fakirs are men of India who claim to work miracles and wonders.

condole to soothe; to sympathize with	**hospitable** welcoming	**plague** a disease
haste speed	**intercept** to catch, block, or cut off	

"Monkey's paw?" said Mrs. White curiously.

"Well, it's just a bit of what you might call magic, perhaps," said the sergeant-major offhandedly.

His three listeners leaned forward eagerly. The visitor absentmindedly put his empty glass to his lips and then set it down again. His host filled it for him.

"To look at," said the sergeant-major, fumbling in his pocket, "it's just an ordinary little paw, dried to a mummy."

He took something out of his pocket and proffered it. Mrs. White drew back with a **grimace**; but her son, taking it, examined it curiously.

"And what is there special about it?" inquired Mr. White as he took it from his son, and having examined it, placed it upon the table.

"It had a spell put on it by an old fakir," said the sergeant-major, "a very holy man. He wanted to show that fate ruled people's lives and that those who interfered with it did so to their sorrow. He put a spell on it so that three separate men could each have three wishes from it."

His manner was so **impressive** that his hearers were conscious that their light laughter jarred somewhat.

"Well, why don't you have three, sir?" said Herbert White, cleverly.

The soldier regarded him in the way that middle age is wont to regard **presumptuous** youth. "I have," he said quietly; and his blotchy face whitened.

"And did you really have the three wishes granted?" asked Mrs. White.

"I did," said the sergeant-major; and his glass tapped against his strong teeth.

"And has anybody else wished?" **persisted** the old lady.

"The first man had his three wishes. Yes," was the reply; "I don't know what the first two were, but the third was for death. That's how I got the paw."

The fakir's spell is the first of several foreshadowings of evil connected with the monkey's paw.

grimace an expression of disgust	**impressive** grand, convincing	**presumptuous** overconfident
	persist to continue	

His tones were so grave that a hush fell upon the group.

"If you've had your three wishes, it's no good to you now, then, Morris," said the old man at last. "What do you keep it for?"

The soldier shook his head. "Fancy, I suppose," he said slowly. "I did have some idea of selling it, but I don't think I will. It has caused enough mischief already. Besides, people won't buy. They think it's a fairy tale, some of them; and those who do think anything of it want to try it first and pay me afterward."

"If you could have another three wishes," said the old man, eyeing him keenly, "would you have them?"

"I don't know," said the other. "I don't know."

He took the paw, and dangling it between his forefinger and thumb, suddenly threw it upon the fire. White, with a slight cry, stooped down and snatched it off.

"Better let it burn," said the soldier solemnly.

"If you don't want it, Morris," said the other, "give it to me."

"I won't," said his friend **doggedly**. "I threw it on the fire. If you keep it, don't blame me for what happens. Pitch it on the fire again like a sensible man."

> Why does Sergeant-Major Morris want to destroy the monkey's paw?

doggedly stubbornly

The other shook his head and examined his new possession closely. "How do you do it?" he inquired.

"Hold it up in your right hand and wish aloud," said the sergeant-major, "but I warn you of the **consequences**."

"Sounds like the Arabian Nights," said Mrs. White as she rose and began to set the supper. "Don't you think you might wish for four pairs of hands for me?"

A talisman is a charm, something with magical powers.

Her husband drew the talisman from his pocket; and then all three burst into laughter as the sergeant-major, with a look of alarm on his face, caught him by the arm.

"If you must wish," he said, gruffly, "wish for something sensible."

Mr. White dropped it back in his pocket, and placing chairs, motioned his friend to the table. In the business of supper the talisman was partly forgotten, and afterward the three sat listening in an **enthralled** fashion to a second **installment** of the soldier's adventures in India.

"If the tale about the monkey's paw is not more truthful than those he has been telling us," said Herbert as the door closed behind their guest, just in time for him to catch the last train, "we shan't make much out of it."

"Did you give him anything for it, Father?" inquired Mrs. White, regarding her husband closely.

"A trifle," said he, coloring slightly. "He didn't want it, but I made him take it. And he pressed me again to throw it away."

"Likely," said Herbert with pretended horror. "Why, we're going to be rich and famous and happy. Wish to be an emperor, Father, to begin with: then you can't be henpecked."

Henpecked means nagged.

An antimacassar is a cover to protect the back of a chair.

He darted round the table, **pursued** by the **maligned** Mrs. White armed with an antimacassar.

Mr. White took the paw from his pocket and eyed it **dubiously**. "I don't know what to wish for, and that's a fact," he said slowly. "It seems to me I've got all I want."

consequence a result or effect	**enthralled** fascinated	**maligned** unfairly accused
dubiously with doubt; suspiciously	**installment** one part	**pursue** to chase

"If you only cleared the house, you'd be quite happy, wouldn't you?" said Herbert with his hand on his father's shoulder. "Well, wish for two hundred pounds, then; that'll just do it."

His father, smiling shamefacedly at his own **credulity**, held up the talisman, as his son, with a solemn face, somewhat marred by a wink at his mother, sat down at the piano and struck a few impressive chords.

"I wish for two hundred pounds," said the old man distinctly.

Pounds are English money. This is the amount Mr. White needs to pay the mortgage on his house.

A fine crash from the piano greeted the words, interrupted by a shuddering cry from the old man. His wife and son ran toward him.

"It moved," he cried with a glance of disgust at the object as it lay on the floor.

"As I wished, it twisted in my hand like a snake."

"Well, I don't see the money," said his son as he picked it up and placed it on the table, "and I bet I never shall."

"It must have been your fancy, Father," said his wife, regarding him anxiously.

He shook his head. "Never mind, though; there's no harm, but it gave me a shock all the same."

They sat down by the fire again while the two men finished their pipes. Outside, the wind was higher than ever; and the old man started nervously at the sound of a door banging upstairs. A silence unusual and **depressing** settled upon all three, which lasted until the old couple rose to retire for the night.

How is the mood of the story changing?

"I expect you'll find the cash tied up in a big bag in the middle of your bed," said Herbert, as he bade them good night, "and something horrible squatting up on top of the wardrobe watching you as you pocket your ill-gotten gains."

He sat alone in the darkness, gazing at the dying fire and seeing faces in it. The last face was so horrible and so simian that he gazed at it in amazement. It got so vivid that, with a little uneasy laugh, he felt on the table for a glass containing a

Simian means apelike.

credulity willingness to believe   depressing saddening

little water to throw over it. His hand grasped the monkey's paw, and with a little shiver he wiped his hand on his coat and went up to bed.

In the brightness of the wintry sun next morning as it streamed over the breakfast table he laughed at his fears. There was an air of **prosaic** wholesomeness about the room which it had lacked on the previous night; and the dirty, shriveled little paw was pitched on the sideboard with a carelessness which betokened no great belief in its **virtues**.

"I suppose all old soldiers are the same," said Mrs. White. "The idea of our listening to such nonsense! How could wishes be granted in these days? And if they could, how could two hundred pounds hurt you, Father?"

"Might drop on his head from the sky," said the **frivolous** Herbert.

"Morris said the things happened so naturally," said his father, "that you might if you so wished **attribute** it to **coincidence**."

"Well, don't break into the money before I come back," said Herbert as he rose from the table. "I'm afraid it'll turn you into a mean, **avaricious** man; and we shall have to **disown** you."

His mother laughed, and following him to the door, watched him down the road, and returning to the breakfast table, was very happy at the expense of her husband's credulity. All of which did not prevent her from scurrying to the door at the postman's knock, nor prevent her from referring somewhat shortly to retired sergeants-major of bibulous habits when she found that the post brought a tailor's bill.

Bibulous habits means a fondness for drinking whiskey.

"Herbert will have some more of his funny remarks, I expect, when he comes home," she said as they sat at dinner.

attribute to credit something to	**coincidence** chance	**frivolous** playful
avaricious greedy	**disown** to deny one's connection with	**prosaic** everyday
		virtue goodness

"I dare say," said Mr. White, pouring himself out some beer; "but for all that, the thing moved in my hand; that I'll swear to."

"You thought it did," said the old lady soothingly.

"I say it did," replied the other. "There was no thought about it; I had just—What's the matter?"

His wife made no reply. She was watching the mysterious movements of a man outside, who, peering in an undecided fashion at the house, appeared to be trying to make up his mind to enter. In mental connection with the two hundred pounds, she noticed that the stranger was well dressed and wore a silk hat of glossy newness. Three times he passed at the gate, and then walked on again. The fourth time he stood with his hand upon it, and then with sudden resolution flung it open and walked up the path. Mrs. White at the same moment placed her hands behind her, and hurriedly unfastening the strings of her apron, put that article of **apparel** beneath the cushion of her chair.

She brought the stranger, who seemed ill at ease, into the room. He gazed at her **furtively** and listened in a **preoccupied** fashion as the old lady apologized for the appearance of the room, and her husband's coat, a garment which he usually reserved for

apparel clothing

furtively secretly, as if ashamed

preoccupied thinking of something else

the garden. She then waited as patiently as her sex would permit, for him to **broach** his business; but he was at first strangely silent.

"I—was asked to call," he said at last and stooped and picked a piece of cotton from his trousers. "I come from Maw and Meggins."

The old lady started. "Is anything the matter?" she asked, breathlessly. "Has anything happened to Herbert? What is it? What is it?"

Her husband interposed. "There, there, Mother," he said. "Sit down, and don't jump to conclusions. You've not brought bad news, I'm sure, sir"; and he eyed the other **wistfully**.

"I'm sorry—," began the visitor.

"Is he hurt?" demanded the mother wildly.

The visitor bowed in **assent**. "Badly hurt," he said quietly, "but he is not in any pain."

"Oh, thank God!" said the old woman, clasping her hands. "Thank God for that! Thank—"

She broke off suddenly as the **sinister** meaning of the **assurance** dawned upon her and she saw the awful **confirmation** of her fears in the other's **averted** face. She caught her breath, and turning to her slower-witted husband, laid her trembling old hand upon his. There was a long silence.

"He was caught in the machinery," said the visitor at length in a low voice.

"Caught in the machinery," repeated Mr. White in a dazed fashion, "yes."

He sat staring blankly out at the window, and taking his wife's hand between his own, pressed it as he had been wont to do in their old courting-days nearly forty years before.

"He was the only one left to us," he said, turning gently to the visitor. "It is hard."

To *interpose* is to come between. Mr. White steps in to reassure his wife.

assent agreement	**broach** to begin a topic	**sinister** evil
assurance a promise	**confirmation** proof	**wistfully** sadly
avert to turn away		

The other coughed and, rising, walked slowly to the window. "The firm wished me to **convey** their sincere sympathy with you in your great loss," he said, without looking round. "I beg that you will understand I am only their servant and merely obeying orders."

There was no reply; the old woman's face was white, her eyes staring, and her breath **inaudible**; on the husband's face was a look such as his friend the sergeant might have carried into his first action.

"I was to say that Maw and Meggins disclaim all responsibility," continued the other. "They admit no **liability** at all; but in consideration of your son's services, they wish to present you with a certain sum as **compensation**."

Mr. White dropped his wife's hand, and rising to his feet, gazed with a look of horror at his visitor. His dry lips shaped the words. "How much?"

"Two hundred pounds," was the answer.

Unconscious of his wife's shriek, the old man smiled faintly, put out his hands like a sightless man, and dropped, a senseless heap, to the floor.

In the huge new cemetery, some two miles distant, the old people buried their dead, and came back to a house steeped in shadow and silence. It was all over so quickly that at first they could hardly realize it and remained in a state of **expectation** as though of something else to happen—something else which was to lighten this load, too heavy for old hearts to bear.

But the days passed, and expectation gave place to resignation—the hopeless resignation of the old, sometimes miscalled **apathy**. Sometimes they hardly exchanged a word, for now they had nothing to talk about and their days were long to weariness.

It was about a week after that the old man, waking suddenly in the night, stretched out his hand and found himself alone. The room was in darkness, and the sound of

> Why does this question and its answer cause such horror?

---

apathy a lack of concern

compensation a payment for damages

convey to pass along

expectation what is expected or looked forward to

inaudible unheard

liability debt

subdued weeping came from the window. He raised himself in bed and listened.

"Come back," he said tenderly. "You will be cold."

"It is colder for my son," said the old woman, and wept afresh.

The sound of her sobs died away on his ears. The bed was warm, and his eyes heavy with sleep. He dozed fitfully and then slept until a sudden wild cry from his wife awoke him with a start.

"The paw!" she cried wildly. "The monkey's paw!"

He started up in alarm. "Where? Where is it? What's the matter?"

She came stumbling across the room toward him. "I want it," she said quietly. "You've not destroyed it?"

"It's in the parlor, on the bracket," he replied marveling. "Why?"

She cried and laughed together, and bending over, kissed his cheek.

"I only just thought of it," she said **hysterically**. "Why didn't I think of it before? Why didn't you think of it?"

"Think of what?" he questioned.

"The other two wishes," she replied rapidly. "We've only had one."

"Was not that enough?" he demanded fiercely.

"No," she cried triumphantly; "we'll have one more. Go down and get it quickly, and wish our boy alive again."

The man sat up in bed and flung the bedclothes from his **quaking** limbs. "Good God, you are mad!" he cried, **aghast**.

"Get it," she panted; "get it quickly, and wish—Oh, my boy, my boy!"

Her husband struck a match and lit the candle. "Get back to bed," he said unsteadily. "You don't know what you are saying."

"We had the first wish granted," said the old woman feverishly; "why not the second?"

"A coincidence," stammered the old man.

> **Why do you think Mrs. White wants the monkey's paw?**

---

aghast shocked

hysterically in wild excitement

quaking shaking, trembling

subdued muffled

"Go and get it and wish," cried his wife, quivering with excitement.

The old man turned and regarded her, and his voice shook. "He has been dead ten days, and besides he—I would not tell you else, but—I could only recognize him by his clothing. If he was too terrible for you to see then, how now?"

"Bring him back," cried the old woman and dragged him toward the door. "Do you think I fear the child I have nursed?"

He went down in the darkness and felt his way to the parlor and then to the mantelpiece. The talisman was in its place, and a horrible fear that the unspoken wish might bring his **mutilated** son before him ere he could escape from the room seized upon him, and he caught his breath as he found that he had lost the direction of the door. His brow cold with sweat, he felt his way round the table and groped along the wall until he found himself in the small passage with the unwholesome thing in his hand.

Even his wife's face seemed changed as he entered the room. It was white and **expectant** and to his fears seemed to have an unnatural look upon it. He was afraid of her.

"Wish!" she cried in a strong voice.

"It is foolish and wicked," he **faltered**.

"Wish!" repeated his wife.

He raised his hand. "I wish my son alive again."

The talisman fell to the floor, and he regarded it fearfully. Then he sank trembling into a chair as the old woman, with burning eyes, walked to the window and raised the blind.

He sat until he was chilled with the cold, glancing occasionally at the figure of the old woman peering through the window. The candle end, which had burned below the rim of the china candlestick, was throwing pulsating shadows on the ceiling and walls, until, with a flicker larger than the rest, it **expired**. The old man, with an unspeakable sense of relief at the failure of the talisman, crept back to his bed; and

Why is Mr. White afraid to wish for his son's return?

---

expectant expecting or waiting for something

expire to go out

falter to hesitate

mutiliated to tear apart, damage

a minute or two afterward the old woman came silently and apathetically beside him.

Neither spoke but lay silently listening to the ticking of the clock. A stair creaked, and a squeaky mouse scurried noisily through the wall. The darkness was **oppressive**; and after lying for some time screwing up his courage, he took the box of matches, and striking one, went downstairs for a candle.

At the foot of the stairs the match went out, and he paused to strike another; and at the same moment a knock, so quiet and **stealthy** as to be scarcely **audible**, sounded on the front door.

The matches fell from his hand and spilled in the passage. He stood motionless, his breath suspended until the knock was repeated. Then he turned and fled swiftly back to his room and closed the door behind him. A third knock sounded through the house.

"What's that?" cried the old woman, starting up.

"A rat," said the old man in shaking tones—"A rat. It passed me on the stairs."

His wife sat up in bed listening. A loud knock resounded through the house.

"It's Herbert!" she screamed. "It's Herbert!"

She ran to the door; but her husband was before her and, catching her by the arm, held her tightly.

"What are you going to do?" he whispered hoarsely.

"It's my boy; it's Herbert!" she cried, struggling mechanically. "I forgot it was two miles away. What are you holding me for? Let go. I must open the door."

"For God's sake, don't let it in," cried the old man, trembling.

"You're afraid of your own son," she cried, struggling. "Let me go. I'm coming, Herbert; I'm coming."

There was another knock, and another. The old woman with a sudden wrench broke free and ran from the room. Her husband followed to the landing and called after her appealingly as she hurried downstairs. He heard the chain rattle back and the bottom bolt drawn slowly and stiffly from the socket. Then the old woman's voice, strained and panting.

Who do you think is at the door?

The fakir wanted to show that fate rules people's lives and those who interfere do so to their sorrow. How have the Whites interfered with fate?

audible loud enough to be heard   **oppressive** heavy, burdensome   **stealthy** secretive

"The bolt," she cried loudly. "Come down. I can't reach it."

But her husband was on his hands and knees groping wildly on the floor in search of the paw. If he could only find it before the thing outside got in. A perfect fusillade of knocks **reverberated** through the house, and he heard the scraping of a chair as his wife put it down in the passage against the door. He heard the creaking of the bolt as it came slowly back; and at the same moment he found the monkey's paw and frantically breathed his third and last wish.

The knocking ceased suddenly, although the echoes of it were still in the house. He heard the chair drawn back, and the door opened. A cold wind rushed up the staircase, and a long loud wail of disappointment and **misery** from his wife gave him courage to run down to her side and then to the gate beyond. The street lamp flickering opposite shone on a quiet and deserted road.

The knocks sound like bullets hitting the house.

What do you think his third wish is?

misery suffering   **reverberate** to echo

Directions Write the answers to these questions using complete sentences.

Comprehension: Identifying Facts

1. What are Mr. White, Mrs. White, and their son doing as the story opens?

2. Describe the outdoor setting of the story.

3. Describe the indoor setting of the story.

4. Who comes to visit the White family?

5. What does the sergeant-major say is special about the monkey's paw?

6. What was the third wish of the first man to use the paw?

7. What is Mr. White's first wish?

8. What news does the stranger bring?

9. What is Mr. White's second wish?

10. What is Mr. White's third wish?

Comprehension: Understanding Main Ideas

11. Who is the protagonist, or main character, in this story? Why do you think so?

12. Who or what is the antagonist?

13. How do the members of the White family seem to feel about each other? How well do they seem to know each other? Why is this important to the story?

14. What are several foreshadowings of evil before Mr. White gets the monkey's paw?

15. Why did the fakir put a spell on the paw? What did he want to show?

16. How much does Mr. White really need the two hundred pounds?

17. What is the face that Herbert sees in the fire?

18. Why is the amount of money that the son's company pays in damages for his death a source of horror to Mr. and Mrs. White?

19. Why is Mr. White so afraid to make the second wish his wife wants?

20. Why does Mr. White see nothing but "a quiet and deserted road" when he runs out to the gate?

Understanding Literature: Setting

Setting is an important part of every short story. Details of setting can make a story believable by helping the reader form a mental picture of the story's time and place. Setting is more than simply time and place, however. Setting also includes the objects that surround the characters. In this way, the monkey's paw, which is so important to this story, can be considered part of the setting.

Writers use setting to add richness to their stories. Details of setting help create a story's mood, mirror the plot, and define characters.

21. In your opinion, why are the objects in a story important to readers?

22. How does the description of the weather and of the neighborhood at the beginning of "The Monkey's Paw" help set the mood of the story?

23. How does the monkey's paw change the feeling in the White's house? Find evidence in the story to support your answer.

24. In what ways is the setting of the White's house important to the plot of the story?

25. How did Mr. White, Mrs. White, and Herbert White differ in their feelings about the monkey's paw? How do these differences help you understand the characters?

Critical Thinking

26. How would "The Monkey's Paw" be different in mood and effect if there were no foreshadowings of evil?

27. In what ways, if any, does the story prove the fakir's view of the role of fate in people's lives?

28. What are some ways that Jacobs builds suspense in this story? Support your answer with examples.

29. Just before he makes his second wish, why do you think Mr. White feels afraid as he looks at his wife's face?

30. What is the effect of Mrs. White's difficulty with the bolt on the door?

Writing on Your Own What becomes of the monkey's paw? Three men made three wishes on it, so its magic powers are gone. Imagine that Mrs. White finds the paw one day as she is cleaning. Write a brief description of what she does with it.

Red Moccasins
Susan Power

Susan Power
1961–

Literary Terms

flashback a look into the past at some point in a story

image a picture in the reader's mind created by words

symbol a person, place, or object that stands for something beyond itself

unreliable narrator a first-person narrator whose views cannot be depended on to be completely true

About the Author

Susan Power's life is strongly rooted in the culture of the Standing Rock Sioux people. As was her mother, she is an enrolled member of this North Dakota group. Before her mother died, she gave Power her own Sioux name, Wakca Wastewin, which means *prairie flower*. Like her Indian name, Power's writing is grounded in her past—the stories and traditions of her ancestors.

Susan Power was born in Chicago in 1961. She earned a law degree but then enrolled in the University of Iowa's Writers' Workshop. She spent two years "living, eating, sleeping, dreaming, and breathing fiction." At Iowa, she began to explore the things that united her to her people and their traditions.

Her first novel, *The Grass Dancer*, received the 1995 PEN/ Hemingway Award for First Fiction. A second novel, *Strong Heart Society*, soon followed. Her short stories have been published in many magazines and were included in the 1993 and 1997 editions of *The Best American Short Stories*.

About the Selection

Susan Power builds her suspense story "Red Moccasins" carefully. Each detail of mood, plot, setting, and character contributes to a growing sense of terror. As you read, pay careful attention to all these details. The **symbols**, the color **images**, the characters' names, the **flashbacks**, even the words that are repeated are all clues that enrich this frightening story.

The story is told by a first-person narrator, Anna Thunder, who is also the main character. Anna Thunder suffers the deaths of the two people she loves most. Because of the effects of these deaths on her, she can be called an **unreliable narrator**. That is, readers gradually realize that the way she sees events may not be the "true" or most complete way to see them. Readers must decide for themselves what really happens.

Red Moccasins

My niece Bernardine Blue Kettle, the one I called Dina, was thirteen—too old to be sitting on my lap. But there she was, her long legs draped over mine and her feet scraping the ground. Our fingers were laced together, both sets of arms wrapped around her pole waist. My four-year-old son, Chaske, was sitting on the floor, drumming a pillow with my long wooden cooking spoon. He covered one ear with his hand and twisted his face to imitate the Sioux singers he worshipped, old men who **singed** their vocal cords on high notes. He pounded his song into the pillow, making the Sioux **lullaby** sound **energetic** as a powwow song.

"Dance for me," I told Dina. I wanted her to play along with Chaske. Dina left my lap and danced around her cousin as if he were a drummer at the powwow grounds. She was serious, aware of her posture, light on her feet, tucking sharp elbows into her sides. Max, my son's pet owlet, watched Dina circle the room. He bobbed forward on the offbeat from his perch atop the mantel clock. My husband had discovered him wandering through a prairie dog town.

As you read, notice the point of view of this first-person narrator. In what ways might she be unreliable in her view of what happens and why?

This image of Dina dancing around Chaske foreshadows a later event in the story.

---

energetic lively   **lullaby** a bedtime song   **singe** to burn

"Look at Max," I told the children. "You've got him dancing, too." But Max quickly tired of the game and used his long legs to turn himself around, so all we could see were his feathered back and hunched shoulders.

I clapped and clapped when the song ended, and Chaske gave up the spoon so I could stir his supper, another batch of the watery potato soup we'd been eating for weeks.

It was 1935 and a good portion of North Dakota had dried up and blown away. Grit peppered our food, coated our teeth, and silted our water. We heard that cities as distant as Chicago and New York were sprinkled with Plains topsoil. I thought it was fitting, somehow. I imagined angry ancestors fed up with Removal grabbing fistfuls of **parched** earth to fling toward Washington, making the president choke on dust and ashes. We prayed for rain, and when it did not come, when instead we were **strangled** by **consumption,** many people said the end of the world had come to the Standing Rock Sioux Reservation. I was not a doomsday **disciple.** I wouldn't let the world end while my son, Chaske, still had so much living to do.

"Bet you can't guess what's for supper," I teased Chaske, who was perched on Dina's shoulders.

consumption tuberculosis, a lung disease easily spread from person to person	**disciple** a follower **parched** dried out **strangle** to choke

"Potato soup!" he shouted, delighted to be suddenly taller than me. Dina rolled her eyes but didn't say anything. She bounced Chaske up and down, stooped over and then lifted on her toes like a horse rearing on its hind legs.

They looked like two opposites, like people with blood running from separate rivers. Chaske, whose **baptism** name was Emery Bauer, Jr., after his German father, was sturdy and tall for his age, his powerful calf muscles bulging like little crab apples under the skin. His hair was creamy yellow, the color of beeswax, and his eyes were a silvery gray, so pale they were almost white.

I couldn't trace Chaske's Sioux blood or find evidence of his father in his features and coloring. It was as if he came from his own place, having sidestepped all the family tracks laid out before him. Dina, on the other hand, was a blueprint of the women in our family, long-legged and graceful, thick braids grazing her narrow hips. Her little heart-shaped face was dark brown, the color of a full-blood, and her eyes black as onyx studs. Dina had been with me when I delivered Chaske, holding my hand while old women assisted me. Dina was the one who placed him in my arms, and I remember thinking, as she held him, that he looked like a bundle of sunflowers, yellow against her dusky skin. I placed the children together in my mind, couldn't imagine one without the other.

After supper Dina washed the dishes. It was so easy it was like a game to her because in my modern house, fit for a white woman, she could pump water directly into my kitchen sink and watch it drain away. She didn't have to go outside and haul buckets. I pulled out my sewing basket and let Chaske play with a jar full of buttons.

"Have you finished my costume?" Dina called over her shoulder.

The *Removal* on page 264 refers to the forced movement of American Indians to reservations. Many were removed to the Dust Bowl, areas of the prairie states that get dust storms. In these storms, strong winds remove the topsoil.

This close connection in the narrator's mind between her son and her niece is another important bit of foreshadowing.

baptism Christian ceremony for naming and for coming into the faith

"You'll be the first to know," I said. I laughed because she was so impatient, more impatient every day. I was sewing Dina her first complete Sioux costume. Ordinarily a mother would do this, but Dina's was the next thing to useless. Joyce Blue Kettle had never gotten close enough to a needle to stick herself, let alone sew a costume. As a child she'd been restless and boy-crazy, so she never learned to tan hides or do beadwork. If her mother scolded her, saying, "Look at your little cousin. Look at her fine beadwork," Joyce would puff out her bottom lip and squeeze round tears onto her flat cheeks. She would say, "You know I can't see right," pointing to her left eye, which was crossed, permanently focused on her nose. Of course, she managed to see well enough to paint her face and read movie magazines she swiped from the Lugers' store. Joyce and I were first cousins, which in our tribe made us sisters, **despite** our differences.

When Dina finished stacking the clean plates, I called her into the sitting room. "I'm almost ready to start your moccasins," I said. I traced the outline of her foot onto a scrap of cardboard so that the soles would match perfectly her fine narrow feet.

"Will you make me rattlesnake hair ties?" Dina asked. I dropped the **paring** knife I was using to cut the pattern from cardboard.

"Where did you see hair ties like that?" I was careful to leave the blade in my lap because my hands were shaking.

"I've dreamt about the Red Dress woman," she whispered. "And she had rattlesnake rattles tied in her hair. She shook them at me. She told me I could wear my hair like that."

"You can't," I said. I knew I sounded too angry. "When she comes after you, you should turn the other way."

"Have you seen her?" asked Dina, staring at me.

"Yes. But I discouraged her from coming." I didn't tell my niece that at her age I had dreamt about Čuwígnaka Ša, Red Dress, my dead grandmother. I had heard her insistent voice, crackling with energy, whispering promises of a deadly power

The relationship between Joyce and the narrator is important to the story. How would you describe their relationship as children?

---

despite in spite of   **paring** peeling

passed on through the bloodlines from one woman to the next. I had seen her kneeling beside a fire, feeding it with objects stolen from her victims: buttons, letters, twists of hair. She sang her spells, replacing the words of an ancient honor song with those of her own choosing. She **doused** the flames.

"Could she really control people?" Dina asked.

"That's what they say. But it didn't do her any good. She spelled one too many and he killed her."

My niece held her unfinished costume in her hands. She stroked the blue trade cloth material and pinched the cowrie shells sprinkled across the dress and leggings. I'd hidden the beaded belt and the flour-sack cape covered with inch-long bugle beads to surprise her with later.

There was a knock at the kitchen door. Dina's father, Clifford Blue Kettle, poked his head into the kitchen and waved at me.

"Come on in," I said. He shook his head and twisted the doorknob like he was trying to wring it loose. Black bangs hid his eyes.

"Dina here?" he asked me, so whispery he had to clear his throat and ask me again. Dina stepped into the doorway between the sitting room and kitchen. "Your ma says to get home now," he told her.

"He's so shy around you," Dina said, laughing softly.

I waved off her comment as if I disagreed, but she was right; my cousin's husband had feelings for me. When we were children, he had followed me everywhere, helping me with my chores and bringing me little treasures he'd discovered: seashells, fool's gold, ripe chokecherries. One time he brought me a round glass eye he'd poked from the socket of his sister's doll. It was too much for Joyce. She **intercepted** the gift, snatched it from the palm of my hand as I studied the green iris. She took Clifford over the same way, ordering him around, demanding his attention, and because I didn't love Clifford, I let her keep him. It never seemed to occur to him that he could protest. He was **amiable** and slow-minded. He

What sort of person was Red Dress, the narrator's grandmother?

Why is Clifford Blue Kettle shy around the narrator?

---

amiable friendly, good-natured

douse to put out

intercept to catch, block, or cut off

longed to please. Even now he brought me little gifts or
fashioned toys for Chaske, like my son's first baby rattle, and I
could see he had something for me. One hand was hidden
behind his back.

"What have you got there?" I asked. I walked to the door
and tried to peek over his shoulder, which made him grin.

"Got these in a giveaway. Know Joyce can't use them." He
handed me a mason jar full of red beads tiny as poppy seeds. I
poured a few of them into my hand and admired their rich
color, scarlet as a fresh wound sliced into my palm. I spilled
them back into the jar.

"Thank you. I can put these to good use."

Having given me the gift, Clifford relaxed. He kicked the
back steps with the toe of his foot. "Come on now," he called
to his daughter.

Dina kissed Chaske's plump cheek before she left, and he smiled at her, kissing his fist and popping it against her arm.

I meant to stay up late to finish sewing Dina's leggings, but Chaske started coughing. He clenched his hands over his chest as if he had captured something between them, a sawing cricket or fluttering moth. I knew the odd gesture was a way he dealt with pain, trying to hammer it down. I carried Chaske to my lumpy brass bed and curled beside him. His coughing finally tapered off and he murmured, "Max."

"Max is fine," I said. "Go to sleep." I rubbed Chaske's back, my hand moving in circles, unable to relax while I listened to his breathing. His hair smelled like sweet grass, and his little body, changing too quickly from plump to wiry, warmed the bed. I guarded his sleep, forcing my breath into a perfect rhythm as if I could breathe for him, and in the morning I was weary but triumphant, having kept the world in orbit.

Chaske's coughing and breathing worry the narrator.

I had been a widow for two months, since the end of November. Dr. Kessler, a **notorious alcoholic** but the only doctor on the reservation, had **diagnosed** Emery as consumptive and told him he should go to the white **sanatorium** in Rapid City, South Dakota.

"I better not," my husband said, **terse** as always. But after seven years of marriage, I could practically read Emery's mind. He didn't want to split up our family. If I became ill, I would never be admitted to the hospital Dr. Kessler had suggested; I would be sent to the **inferior** Sioux sanatorium where few patients recovered. And our son Chaske wasn't really an appropriate candidate for either place. Who knew where he would end up?

"We'll take our chances," Emery said, and so we did. Emery remained at home where I was to keep him well fed and well rested. Consumption was **rampant** by this time,

Emery has tuberculosis. There was no cure or drug to treat the disease. The hospital for white people was better than the one for the Sioux. Rather than go where his wife would not be admitted, Emery chooses to stay home.

alcoholic a problem drinker

diagnose to determine the medical condition of someone

inferior second-rate

notorious well known, especially for something bad

rampant existing everywhere

sanatorium a hospital for treating certain illnesses

terse using few words

hitting nearly every family on our reservation, and no attempts were made to quarantine the sick from the healthy. My husband was a successful rancher, in partnership with his two brothers, and I couldn't keep him from work for very long. In the end it wasn't consumption that killed him but a wild horse he called Lutheran. Emery's two brothers brought my husband's body to me, stumbling beneath his bear weight. They were crying, promising me they would shoot that devil horse who had thrown Emery and broken his neck.

"No!" I said, and they looked suddenly **wary**. They grabbed my arms as if they expected me to pitch forward. "That horse did him a kindness." I wanted them to leave so I could comb Emery's hair and wash his face. "He didn't waste away from the consumption. He went quickly."

Later that night I sat on the edge of Chaske's cot. I told him that his sleeping father, laid out in the next room on our brass bed, was having such good dreams he didn't want to wake up.

"Is he dreaming about Max?" Chaske asked me.

"Yes," I said. "He's dreaming about all of us."

I panicked that night when I realized I didn't own a single photograph of my husband. It wasn't my memory I worried about, but Chaske's. He was so young I couldn't trust that he would remember Emery, the shape of his black beard, his tremendous wingspan and silent laugh. As Chaske slept I told him about his father, chanting our history until it became a song-story I hoped he would follow in his dreams.

I told him about the day I met Emery Bauer. It was the winter of 1928, and I was eighteen years old. I had been snowbound for several days in my family's cabin and was desperate to be outdoors where I could work the cramps out of my legs and fill my lungs with fresh air. I went for a long walk, fighting through high drifts, pausing only to search for **landmarks**.

I wandered onto the **leased** land of the Bauer ranch, thinking I was heading toward town. I came to a shallow

Here the narrator provides a flashback to the time, seven years earlier, when she met her future husband.

---

landmark a marker that shows location   **lease** to rent   **wary** suspicious

frozen pond. The ice was uneven, marred by tangled clumps of weeds, but I noticed a man skimming across it as if on a smooth pane of glass. He balanced on silver blades slim as butter knives, **propelling** his barrel body forward and then magically backward, skirting the weeds and chiseling the ice with his skates. I had heard about ice-skating, but I'd never seen it done. I'd never seen a man spin like a top. I hunched beside a frozen bush, hoping he wouldn't notice me. But I was framed in white and difficult to miss. The graceful man suddenly skated toward me, stopping so quickly his blades spit a spray of ice. He towered over me, smiling, alternately fingering his black beard and tapping the heavy workboots slung around his neck.

"You like to dance on water?" he asked me. I shook my head. I didn't know what else to do. "I'm Emery," he said. He waited, staring directly into my eyes, which made me uncomfortable.

"I'm Anna Thunder," I finally answered.

"Now *that's* a name to live up to." He clapped his large hands together. "Come here, this will be fun." Emery removed his skates, which I saw were metal blades screwed onto a pair of workboots. He donned the shoes he'd been carrying and knelt in the snow. Even down on one knee he was tall.

"Give me your foot," he said. He was the only white man other than the doctor and reservation priest I had ever spoken to, but I trusted him completely. **Ironically**, I think it was his size that calmed me. He was such a giant he seemed uncomfortable in his body; his posture, an **accommodating** stoop, and his gestures, apologetic. Off the ice he shambled awkwardly. So I did as he requested. I watched him stuff one of his mittens in the toe of each boot and then fit the skates on my feet. He held my hands and pulled me across the ice. At first I was rigid and tottered on the slippery surface, but eventually I relaxed and pushed off the blades, cutting the ice with confident strokes.

accommodating making up for; making allowance for	**ironically** unlike what one would expect	**propel** to push forward or onward

Notice that the narrator again refers to dancing. Here, she describes the time before she and Emery married as "an ice dance." This image will take on importance later in the story.

"God made you to skate," Emery breathed in my ear.

Our **courtship** was an ice dance, and Emery's wedding present to me was my own set of silver blades he'd ordered from the Sears catalogue. He attached them to a new pair of ankle-high laced boots cut out of fancy thin leather.

Emery and I married despite **disapproval** from both sides. Joyce Blue Kettle protested the loudest, flapping her tongue so much I thought she might wear it thin as a hair ribbon. Joyce had been married for several years by that time and was already a mother, but she was jealous.

"People will say you're greedy," Joyce confided to me the night before my wedding.

"What do you mean?" I only half listened, distracted as I was by the last minute details of polishing my shoes and combing my damp hair with a clump of sage to scent it.

"They say you're marrying him to get things. What about the seven new dresses, one for each day of the week, he bought you? What about the horsehair sofa and the brass bed? Didn't he even build you a house?"

Earlier that day I had taken Joyce on a tour of the new house, a neat clapboard structure made of planed lumber. I felt guilty as we moved through the rooms, the number of my possessions suddenly **overwhelming** me. All my life I had been taught that material goods were **dispensable**, things to be shared with friends and family. We were not supposed to have more than we needed, so there were endless rounds of giveaways at our dances, where people unburdened themselves of **accumulated** objects. But Emery was not Sioux, and his affection for me resulted in **lavish** offerings.

Let them say what they want, I decided. I repeated this aloud to my cousin Joyce, who was pinching the ivory-colored velvet **fabric** of my wedding cap.

"They know Emery has different ways," I said.

Why does the narrator feel guilty about the number of possessions in her new house?

accumulate to collect	**dispensable** easily done without	**overwhelm** to take over one's thoughts or feelings
courtship the period before marriage	**fabric** material	
disapproval objections	**lavish** abundant	

"Whatever you say." Joyce shrugged her shoulders, and the next day when I pinned the elegant cap to my newly bobbed black hair, I noticed sharp **creases** in the pile that no amount of smoothing could repair.

On our first wedding anniversary, Emery and I gave a feast for my Sioux relatives. I'd thought time would set things right for Joyce, but she remained bitter about the match. She trailed after me at the feast, pretending to help me in the kitchen where she sat idle, letting her mouth do all the work.

"Čuwígnaka Ša, was really looking out for you," she said, fighting a sly smile. She was referring to our grandmother, Red Dress. Joyce liked to tell people that Emery hadn't fallen for me, but for the old magic I had used to spell him. I ignored her, knowing that I'd never tested these powers. If they really existed, I figured they must have **atrophied** like an unused muscle. Besides, I'd heard people say the same thing about Joyce and her conquest of Clifford. I struggled for something pleasant to say.

> The narrator has never tried to use the powers her grandmother said were passed on to all the women in the family.

"That Bernardine's getting smarter every day, and Clifford looks like he's doing real good."

"That's because I keep him happy." Joyce smoothed a narrow hand across her wiry hair.

"You know, it works differently in my house," I said. "Emery comes up with so many ways to please me." I ran my own narrow hand from my waist to the round edge of my hip.

Later, I forgave Joyce because when she heard about my husband's sudden death she sent Bernardine to the house to watch over Chaske. Clifford accompanied his daughter, offering to take Emery's personal stock of two horses and one cow to his own place where he could tend them. I was grateful to my cousin for letting her family assist me.

Before his brothers buried him, I bathed Emery's face and trimmed his beard. I filled his pockets with the lemon drop candies he favored and the deck of cards we used to play gin rummy. Then I packed both pairs of ice skates in the coffin so

atrophy to wither   **crease** a fold; a wrinkle

Here again, the narrator refers to dancing—this time, dancing after death.

that he would be waiting for me by a shallow frozen pond, ready to strap skates on my feet and take me ice-dancing.

The first day of February was mild, so I opened the windows to air out the house. I'd traded two of my dresses for a scrawny chicken, and I was relieved to be cooking something other than potato soup. Max pecked at the chicken's liver, winking at me from his perch beside the stove.

I overheard Chaske talking to Max. "Atéwaye," my father, he called the young owl. I understood then that this was Chaske's way of keeping his father alive. "Atéwaye, look at this," he said, holding up a blue-and-white-swirled marble. He chattered for a long time, disturbing Max's sleep, until he started coughing. I moved to hold him, murmuring, "You aren't sick," because his eyes looked afraid, round as the owlet's.

He was racked by coughing fits most of the day, and his cheeks were flushed. By the time we finished supper, I considered bundling him up and trying to get him to Dr. Kessler's place, three miles away. But the wind changed. The sky was suddenly a heavy gray, and it seemed to be lowering itself, ready to flatten our reservation. Without the horses, I was afraid to set out on foot.

"Close the windows!" I shouted and felt foolish. I was the only one who could heed the command. So I sealed our house against a kicking wind and a crushing mantle of snow. Chaske and I went to bed early. I slept through the night for the first time in many weeks.

Chaske was worse the next day. The pain in his chest made him cry. I gave him castor oil, which Dr. Kessler had recommended for my husband, but it didn't seem to help. No one I knew had a phone, so I put on several layers of clothes and started to walk the half mile to Dina's place, thinking someone there could contact the doctor. But I realized it would take a long time to make it through such deep snow. I couldn't leave Chaske alone for very long.

I told him stories to take his mind off the pain. I even unpacked the baby rattle he'd given up years before, the rattlesnake rattle Clifford had made for him. I shook it beside his ear, **punctuating** my singing with its sliding rasp. I sang him funny songs, even dirty songs, and when the pain had exhausted him, I sang the Sioux lullaby he had so recently performed. He was too weak to raise his own voice, but he **wielded** the wooden cooking spoon in his hand and banged it against the wall. The brass bed rocked with our desperate rhythm, we churned the air with our noise. For a moment, I wondered if I could save Chaske myself, summon a healing magic. But I remembered Joyce's **futile** attempts to cure her crossed eye, the hours she spent as a child pointing her finger at the offending organ while staring at her reflection in a cracked mirror. I knew we did not have the healing touch.

The grandmother, Red Dress, had evil powers. The narrator realizes that the family magic, if it exists, will not heal.

The house was dark and my voice was almost gone when I heard a knock at the front door.

"Coming!" I croaked.

It was my cousin Joyce, standing on my front porch. I could see Emery's sorrel mare at the gate and Dina seated on my slender palomino. I waved to her.

"I come about the costume," Joyce said. At first I didn't know what she was talking about. "There's that powwow tonight," she continued, "up at the hall. Dina was hoping her costume was ready so she could wear it."

"Chaske is real sick. He needs the doctor. Could you stop at Kessler's place and tell him to come?"

Joyce promised to fetch him. She patted my arm.

I returned to Chaske warm with confidence. "Everything will be okay," I crooned, my voice clear and strong again. I rocked Chaske in the brass bed, held his body against mine as if I could absorb the tearing coughs. At least an hour passed. I was sinking into the dark and feeling hope drain away. I could actually *feel* it, a trickle of heat on my hands.

All this time I had pictured Joyce driving the horse through wet snow as high as its chest. I could see the horse swimming across snowfields to reach Dr. Kessler. But the

---

futile useless **punctuate** to mark at regular intervals **wield** to hold; to use

The narrator is imagining that, instead of fetching the doctor, Joyce and her daughter are dancing at the powwow.

picture changed. I saw my cousin and her daughter break through snow walls, pound the flakes to slush beneath the horses' hooves, but only as far as the community hall. They were inside the flat building, their cheeks pink and fingers warming in their jacket pockets. They were dancing together around the drum, their feet moving in a perfect mother-daughter **symmetry.** Then it was Dina, dancing alone as her mother watched from the sidelines, tracking the girl with the eye she could control. Her lips were pinched with satisfaction, she held herself stiff and straight in the wooden folding chair, proud. The picture dazzled my eyes as I sat in the dark room, burned itself against the backs of my eyelids. I imagined I could even hear the song that moved Bernardine's feet. It

symmetry balance

swept across the snow and spilled its notes against the bedroom window. The glass shrieked.

Finally I lit the lamp. I saw my reflection in the windowpane and noticed new lines etched in my face, drawn from nose to chin. I lifted the lamp high to regard the rest of the room. I nearly dropped it. Patches of brilliant red speckled the walls beside my bed and the faded quilts. My own hands were covered with blood from Chaske's lungs. His eyes were truly white now, as if his spirit were the only thing that had given them **pigmentation**. I knew I had lost him. But before I moved to wash his body, I poked my finger in his mouth, deep in a pool of black blood. I swallowed the fluid because wherever he had gone I wanted to follow close behind.

Why does the narrator swallow her son's blood?

My son's coffin was carried to town and stored in an icehouse. The ground was frozen, so we couldn't bury him just yet. Joyce Blue Kettle showed up at my door with small pails of food and wet eyes. She said Dina was so upset she couldn't get out of bed. I didn't let her inside the house.

"Get away," I said. I refused to open the door wider than an inch.

"I'm just sick about it. I didn't know how bad he was."

"You were dancing, weren't you? You were dancing."

Why didn't Joyce tell the doctor to come?

Her eyes sparkled and lit like a flash fire. "Who do you think you are? If Dina was sick you know that doctor wouldn't lift a finger to make it over here. He'd tell me to bring her in. What makes you think he'd come for yours? Is yours better than mine?"

I left the door cracked open and went to my room. I removed every dress from the wardrobe, even stepped out of the blue calico I was wearing. I rushed down the stairs in my cotton slip.

"Here!" I said, throwing the dresses at my cousin who waited, curious, on my front porch. "You always wanted them. Take them! Take them!"

Joyce backed down the steps and hurried away. She nearly tripped over the skirt of one dress, the one I wore at my

pigmentation color

wedding. I watched her run across the frozen yard, my five remaining dresses clutched to her chest.

I was as frozen as the ground, frost on my upper lip, my tongue a chunk of ice. My mind was numb, but my fingers still worked. I dug out the red beads Clifford had given me. Originally I'd planned to find dark blue beads as well, intending to decorate Dina's moccasins with the two contrasting colors. But now I just wanted to finish the slippers.

It took me three full days to bead the moccasins. I beaded the upper half, the sides, the leather tongue, even the soles, using all but a handful of beads. The moccasins were pure red. In those three days, I didn't eat a single **morsel** of food. I kept my stomach filled with water. The pump had frozen so I had to drink gritty, melted snow. I let Max pick at the meals the community had cooked for me.

I remember the night I finished beading Dina's moccasins the way I remember stories I have read in books—from a distance, from behind a **barrier**, perhaps a sheet of ice. I folded Dina's costume and placed the moccasins on top. Then I wrapped the bundle in a pillowcase. I dressed to go outdoors, wearing Emery's workboots, and I fastened Chaske's baby rattle to my braid with a leather thong. I tossed the braid over my shoulder and heard its warning rasp. It was after midnight, but I didn't take a lantern; the moon was a chilly night-light. I picked up the package and was about to set off when something stopped me, a sudden prick of heat deep inside my body. The snow attracted my gaze as I paused in the doorway. It looked clean, as though it could deaden the spark. So I covered my head and arms with snow, molding it to my thighs. I didn't feel the chill or the moisture. I moved on like a snow queen.

I can still hear my footsteps crackling through the drifts. I stopped several feet from the door of the Blue Kettle place.

The moccasins are red, the color connected with Red Dress, the grandmother with evil powers.

What does this way of remembering suggest about the narrator's state of mind on this night?

barrier something that blocks the way

morsel a small piece

"Čuwígnaka Ša, you help me now," I **implored**. I hunched in the snow.

Bernardine, I called with my mind. *Bernardine*. I didn't speak aloud, but my head buzzed with her name, the syllables filled my throat. My teeth clicked her name. *Bernardine*.

She was wearing the flannel nightdress I'd given her for Christmas, and she was barefoot. She came right up to me. *We must dress you*, I said, still silent. She was obedient, her eyes glazed and swollen from crying. She lifted her arms so I could remove the nightdress. Her skin **shriveled** in the cold, but she didn't shiver. I dressed her then, in the trade cloth dress and leggings. I tied the belt around her waist and slipped the cape over her head. I smoothed her thick braids. Finally I knelt before her and fit the beaded moccasins on her feet. I tied the laces.

"You dance," I hissed. The words were white smoke in the air.

No one will ever know how many hours Bernardine danced in the snow. She danced herself into another world. Clifford found her the next day about a mile from their house, at the edge of a circular track she'd worn through high snowdrifts. People said she was frozen to a young hackberry tree, **embracing** it as if she had given up on her powwow steps and commenced waltzing.

I heard Joyce wanted someone to remove the shreds of leather and beads, all that remained of Dina's red moccasins. But the pieces were fused to her daughter's skin. One old woman started to cut them off, slicing into flesh, which was the moment Joyce stumbled out of her mind. So they left them on Dina's feet.

For two months she and my son, Chaske, rested side by side in the icehouse. People avoided me and my cousin after an initial round of visits. But everyone turned out for the joint burial.

The narrator calls upon her grandmother for help. What does this tell you about what she's planning to do?

Notice that the children are together again, as the narrator always thought of them.

embrace to hug	**implore** to beg	**shrivel** to wither; to dry out

Joyce and Clifford and I stood near the open graves. I noticed everyone else had pulled back. I don't remember a single word **uttered** by the Catholic priest. I don't even remember walking to the tiny cemetery behind the church. But I can hear the sound of Joyce's laughter. She giggled into a white handkerchief, tears rolling down her flat cheeks. Her short hair was patchy, singed in several places, and I guessed that Clifford had tried to set her hair with a curling iron. She looked years younger, her face smooth and empty, so different from my own face, which I hardly recognized anymore. My skin was parched and lined as the bottom of a dry creek bed.

That spring, after the children were buried, I discovered that magic let loose can take on a life of its own. I had made my niece dance, and there was no one to tell her to stop. Bernardine Blue Kettle was still dancing, this time around my pretty clapboard house. I didn't actually see her; I was too afraid to look, afraid I would see Chaske riding on her shoulders. But I heard the stamp and shuffle of her steps. She never visited at the same time, teasing me with her **unpredictability**, and there were no footprints in the dirt. But each time the noise ended and I found the courage to step onto my porch, I saw the flash of red beads that had fallen on the ground. I didn't touch them. I kicked the dirt to hide their gleam.

I noticed that even the magpies, always greedy for shimmering objects, **scavenged** in some other yard. They did not **covet** the sparkling red beads scattered outside my house.

What does the narrator mean by "magic let loose can take on a life of its own?"

covet to want

scavenge to search for

unpredictability impossible to tell in advance

uttered said

Directions Write the answers to these questions using complete sentences.

Comprehension: Identifying Facts

1. What kind of song is Chaske playing as the story opens?

2. What is the setting of the story?

3. The narrator, Anna Thunder, refers to Dina as her niece. However, how is Anna related to Dina's mother, Joyce Blue Kettle?

4. What is Anna sewing for Dina?

5. What does Dina say that Red Dress, in a dream, told her she could do?

6. Who was Red Dress?

7. What does Dina's father give to Anna?

8. How does Anna know that Joyce did not go to get the doctor for Chaske?

9. What does Anna do with the costume she made for Dina to wear at the powwow?

10. What happens to Dina?

Comprehension: Understanding Main Ideas

11. Why are people saying the end of the world has come to the reservation?

12. How are Dina and Chaske different in the way they look?

13. Why is Anna frightened when she hears Dina talk about Red Dress?

14. In her mind, what does Anna think makes Joyce jealous of her?

15. Why does Emery decide not to go to the hospital in Rapid City to treat his consumption (tuberculosis)?

16. Why does Anna pack both her husband's and her ice skates in his coffin?

17. What events cause the narrator to seek revenge against her cousin?

18. What is the narrator wearing when she goes to the Blue Kettle house? Why is this important?

19. Why are the red moccasins an important symbol in this story? What do you think they stand for?

20. Why does the narrator believe that "Bernardine Blue Kettle was still dancing, this time around my pretty clapboard house"?

Understanding Literature: Unreliable Narrator

A story's narrator plays an important part in the way readers see a story. Readers see only the details that the narrator presents. Sometimes the narrator is a character in the story. At other times, the narrator seems to look in on the story as if watching a play.

"Red Moccasins" is told from the point of view of the main character, Anna Thunder. She has faced two terrible events. Two months before the story opens, her husband died. In the course of the story, she loses her son. These kinds of events strongly affect people. In their grief, they may not think clearly. Because of Anna's grief, readers do not know if she is presenting all the facts of the story. She is an unreliable narrator. Readers must decide for themselves what really happens in the story and what it means.

21. What are the effects on a story of having an unreliable first-person narrator?

22. Which stories in this unit have third-person narrators that observe from a point outside the story? Which stories have first-person narrators who are characters in the story?

23. Anna Thunder can be considered unreliable because of her emotional state. For what other reasons might a narrator be considered unreliable?

24. Do you think the narrator in "The Fog Horn" is reliable? Explain your reasoning.

25. How might "Red Moccasins" be different if it had a third-person narrator?

Critical Thinking

26. Why do you think Anna Thunder gives her cousin all her dresses?

27. The narrator says she remembers the night she finished beading Dina's moccasins "the way I remember stories I have read in books—from a distance, from behind a barrier, perhaps a sheet of ice." What does she mean?

28. What role does Red Dress, the narrator's dead grandmother, play in Dina's death?

29. Why do you think Anna Thunder causes the death of her niece, a thirteen-year-old girl she loves?

30. What does the narrator mean when she says, "I discovered that magic let loose can take on a life of its own"?

Writing on Your Own Imagine the scene as Bernardine Blue Kettle "danced herself into another world." Write a paragraph describing what happened, narrated by Dina herself.

Skills Lesson Plot Development

The plot of a short story includes the events of the story. Authors can develop their plots in several different ways.

A *chronological* plot moves forward in time until the story ends. Fables, myths, tall tales, and legends are usually told in chronological order. Shirley Jackson's "The Lottery" also uses a chronological plot. The story starts as people gather for their town's annual lottery and ends as they "finish" the event. In fact, the story's movement from calm beginning to horrible end adds to its powerful effect.

Another way authors develop their plots is by using *flashbacks*. Remember that a flashback interrupts chronological order to tell readers something important that happened earlier. The narrator of "Red Moccasins" offers flashbacks several times in her story, especially when she describes meeting her husband.

Review

1. Why might flashbacks be especially useful tools for people who write suspense stories?

2. What are the chronological events of "Red Moccasins"?

3. What background information do you learn in "The Lady, or the Tiger?" as the story opens?

4. What important past events are told in "The Fog Horn"?

5. What might be the effect of rewriting "The Lottery" as a flashback remembered by one of the townspeople? Would the story be as powerful? Why or why not?

Writing on Your Own Think about a suspense story you know. Outline the events of the story in chronological (time) order. Then pick a point close to the climax of the story. Using this as your new starting point, briefly rewrite the story.

UNIT 5 SUMMARY

Short stories of suspense hold readers' interest by keeping them in doubt about what will happen, when, and why. In some stories, readers know more than the characters do. Suspense is created as readers wait to see when characters will realize the situation, or when the expected will happen. In other stories, the characters know more than readers do. Suspense rises as readers try to guess what is happening, what will happen, or what the events really mean.

To create a mood of suspense, writers depend on such techniques as foreshadowing and irony. Foreshadowing gives the reader clues or hints about something that hasn't happened yet. Irony lies in the difference between what is expected to happen and what does happen.

Many suspense writers also use details of setting to build suspense. Some stories are set in lonely, dark places where readers feel strange events are likely. Other stories are set in ordinary, everyday places that gradually become settings for the unexpected.

Readers everywhere enjoy the way writers of suspense stories play with what is expected. Not knowing what will happen, not being sure what events

mean, waiting for something surprising or strange, feeling a bit scared—these are all reading experiences that make suspense stories so popular.

Selections

■ "The Lady, or the Tiger?" by Frank Stockton, builds to the climax suggested by the story's title and then ends without answering the question.

■ "The Lottery," by Shirley Jackson, sets a trap for readers by describing what seems an ordinary small town with a little custom the townspeople enjoy—until shocked readers begin to understand what that custom really is.

■ "The Fog Horn," by Ray Bradbury, takes readers to a lonely lighthouse where two working men have a narrow escape from a meeting with a creature from another world.

■ "The Monkey's Paw," by W.W. Jacobs, describes members of a loving family who allow an evil object into their home and then suffer the horrible results.

■ "Red Moccasins," by Susan Power, builds to a scary climax as a grief-stricken woman calls on dark magic to help her take revenge.

UNIT 5 REVIEW

Directions Write the answers to these questions using complete sentences.

Comprehension: Identifying Facts

1. What are some ways authors build suspense in a short story?

2. What is the climax of "The Lottery"?

3. In your own words, what is dialogue?

4. How can setting add to the suspense in a short story?

5. What can readers learn about characters through their dialogue?

Comprehension: Understanding Main Ideas

6. How does Shirley Jackson use irony in "The Lottery"?

7. How are flashbacks used in "Red Moccasins"?

8. What effect does ending "The Lady, or the Tiger?" right before the climax have on readers?

9. Why might readers consider the narrator in "Red Moccasins" to be unreliable?

10. How is the theme of "The Fog Horn" different from the theme of "The Monkey's Paw"?

Understanding Literature: Character Names

Parents take great care in naming their children. Authors do the same thing when they name their characters. Sometimes, they choose a name that reflects the character's role in the story. For example, in "The Lottery," Old Man Warner does "warn" the townspeople about what will happen if they stop the lottery. Think also of the importance of the names in "Red Moccasins": Anna Thunder, Red Dress, Blue Kettle.

11. In "The Lady, or the Tiger?" none of the characters have names. Readers know them by their titles ("king," "princess"). What effect does this have on you as a reader?

12. In "The Lottery," readers know many characters' names. How does this affect you as a reader? How does it add to the suspense and horror of the story?

13. The two characters in "The Fog Horn" are known only as McDunn and Johnny. Why do you think Ray Bradbury chose such simple names for characters in a story about a sea monster? If you met someone who introduced himself as "McDunn," what would your impressions be?

14. What do you think of when you hear the name "Sergeant-Major Morris"? How do your impressions of the name compare with the character's role in "The Monkey's Paw"?

15. Why do you think Susan Power calls her narrator "Anna Thunder"? Recall that when Anna's husband, Emery, first hears her name, he says, "Now *that's* a name to live up to." Does Anna "live up" to her name? Explain your answer.

Critical Thinking

16. Which kind of suspense story do you enjoy more: one in which readers know more than the characters, or one in which the characters know more than the readers? Why?

17. In your opinion, which short story in this unit is most suspenseful? Explain your reasoning.

18. Are suspense stories easier or harder to read than fables? Why do you feel this way?

19. In what ways is it important for all parts of a suspense story to be believable? In what ways is it not important? Support your opinion with evidence from the stories in this unit.

20. In what ways is "Unfinished Message," from Unit 4, a suspense story? Explain your reasoning.

Speak and Listen

Imagine that you are a television reporter. You have been asked to give a one-minute report about the events in "The Lottery." Write the report and time yourself reading it to be sure it isn't longer than one minute. Present your report to the class.

Beyond Words

Anna Thunder had a talent for beading. Learn more about this skill. If time permits, make a beading project and display it in your classroom.

Writing on Your Own The myth of Prometheus could be considered a tale of suspense. Rewrite the myth as a suspense story, using some of the techniques for creating suspense found in this unit, such as setting and irony.

Test-Taking Tip

If you are having trouble answering a question on a test, go on to the next question. Come back to any skipped questions once you finish your first pass.

Above: *Peasant in Blue Shirt*, Paul Cezanne
Above Center: *Regina*, Bernardita Zegers
Above Right: *Portrait of a Steelworker*, Aaron Henry Gorson
Below: *The Way It Is*, G.G. Kopilak
Below Right: *Fatima*, Elizabeth Barakah Hodges

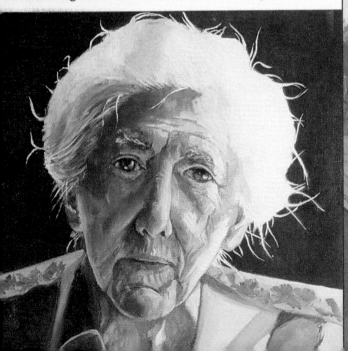

UNIT 6 *Nonfiction*

Nonfiction is factual prose writing. Since all prose that isn't fiction is called nonfiction, nonfiction takes many forms. Three of the most important are essays, biographies, and autobiographies. Nonfiction writers may use many of the techniques of fiction. However, readers expect nonfiction to present facts. Readers also expect nonfiction to have one or more specific purposes: to describe, explain, persuade, entertain, tell, or do several of these.

In this unit, you will read about a real sea monster, a wise grandfather, a dignified businessman, an embarrassing experience, an awakening, and a dangerous adventure on the highest mountain in the world.

"The responsibility of a writer is to excavate the experience of the people who produced him."

—James Baldwin, *A Dialogue*, 1973

"Character cannot be developed in ease and quiet. Only through experiences of trial and suffering can the soul be strengthened, vision cleared, ambition inspired and success achieved."

—Helen Keller, *Helen Keller's Journal*, 1938

UNIT 6 ▪ ABOUT NONFICTION

Nonfiction is a very broad category of literature. In general, every form of prose writing that is not fiction is nonfiction. A work of fiction comes from the author's imagination. Nonfiction concerns real people, facts, and true experiences.

Nonfiction writers use many of the techniques found in fiction. Nonfiction works may have suspense, irony, imagery, conflict, symbols, repetition, and humor. Authors may interpret experiences in personal ways and give personal opinions. However, readers expect nonfiction to deal with real events that happened to real people.

Readers also expect that nonfiction literature will have one or more specific purposes. The purpose of a nonfiction work is its central idea: the author's reason for writing. Works may describe, tell a story, persuade, explain, entertain, or do several of these at once.

Biographies and autobiographies are forms of nonfiction. They are true accounts of people's lives. A biography is written by someone other than the person whose life is being described. An autobiography is written by the person. From both, readers expect to learn about the actual events of a person's life, and how that person feels and thinks about what happened.

Essays are another kind of nonfiction literature. The form of the essay was developed by the sixteenth-century French writer Michel de Montaigne. For his short, nonfiction works intended to explain his ideas, Montaigne used the French term *J'essai*, which means "I try." Like short stories, essays are brief. In essays, authors try to communicate an idea, explain information, express an opinion, or explore how they feel. Reflective essays explore many sides of a topic about which an author has deep feelings. Biographical essays select a few important events from a person's life that show the person's character.

A nonfiction narrative tells a true story, usually in chronological order. A personal account, which can be longer than an essay, is written by someone who has had an experience he or she wants to explain and interpret. Two people who have had the same experience may see that experience in very different ways. Sometimes, personal accounts are in the form of a diary.

The nonfiction literature in this unit shows how today's authors continue to use essays and other forms to communicate their own thoughts on many different subjects. A never-before-seen world of strange fish and stranger experiences awaits readers of the excerpt from Thor Heyerdahl's book *Kon-Tiki*. Rudolfo Anaya, in "A Celebration of Grandfathers," presents a touching reflective essay about what his grandfather and all older people can teach us. Yoshiko Uchida's "Of Dry Goods and Black Bow Ties" is a biographical essay about an unusual man with unusual dignity. An excerpt from Maya Angelou's autobiography, *Gather Together in My Name*, describes an embarrassing experience that proved important to the course of her life. In the excerpt from Helen Keller's autobiography, *The Story of My Life*, readers learn how Anne Sullivan awoke young Helen's desire to learn about the world around her. The final selection, an excerpt from Jon Krakauer's *Into Thin Air*, is a personal account of one of the greatest disasters in the history of climbing Mount Everest.

Left: *Self-Portrait*, Tsing-Fang Chen
Below: *America*, Maria Angelica Ruiz-Tagle

Kon-Tiki
Thor Heyerdahl

Thor Heyerdahl
1914–

Literary Terms

excerpt a short passage from a longer piece of writing

narrative a story, usually told in chronological order

nonfiction prose writing about real people and true experiences

sequence the order of events

About the Author

Thor Heyerdahl is an explorer and an adventurer. Born in southern Norway in 1914, he studied zoology—animal science—in college. In 1936, he traveled to the islands of Polynesia to study the wildlife there. As he worked, Heyerdahl wondered how people first came to these islands. At the time, it was believed that the first settlers in Polynesia came from Asia. Heyerdahl noticed that the winds and water currents ran from east to west. Because of this, he decided the first settlers could have come from South America.

In 1947, he and five friends set out to test his theory. They built a balsa-wood raft, named the *Kon-Tiki*, that was like the rafts used by ancient South Americans. The crew set sail from Peru. After 101 days and more than four thousand miles, they arrived in Polynesia. Heyerdahl had the proof he needed: South Americans might have settled Polynesia.

Heyerdahl led other voyages. In one he sailed a papyrus boat to prove that ancient Egyptians could have sailed to South America and founded the Aztec and Incan cultures there.

Heyerdahl has written about these and other adventures in his books *Kon-Tiki, Aku-Aku, The Secret of Easter Island*, and *Expedition of the Ra.*

About the Selection

This selection is an **excerpt**, or short passage, from Heyerdahl's **nonfiction** account of the voyage of the *Kon-Tiki*. It tells of the crew's sightings of strange ocean wildlife as they sailed across the Pacific in their raft.

Heyerdahl's book is a **narrative**, or story. Like most narratives, its **sequence** is chronological, or in time order.

FROM Kon-Tiki

Not a day passed but we, as we sat floating on the surface of the sea, were visited by **inquisitive** guests which wriggled and waggled about us, and a few of them, such as dolphins and pilot fish, grew so familiar that they accompanied the raft across the sea and kept round us day and night.

When night had fallen and the stars were twinkling in the dark tropical sky, a phosphorescence flashed around us in **rivalry** with the stars, and single glowing plankton resembled round live coals so vividly that we involuntarily drew in our bare legs when the glowing pellets were washed up round our feet at the raft's stern. When we caught them, we saw that they were little brightly shining species of shrimp. On such nights we were sometimes scared when two round shining eyes suddenly rose out of the sea right alongside the raft and glared at us with an unblinking **hypnotic** stare. The visitors were often big squids which came up and floated on the surface with their devilish green eyes shining in the dark like phosphorus. But sometimes the shining eyes were those of deep-water fish which came up only at night and lay staring, fascinated by the glimmer of light before them. Several times, when the sea was calm, the black water round the raft was suddenly full of round heads two or three feet in diameter, lying motionless and staring at us with great glowing eyes. On other nights balls of light three feet and more in diameter would be visible down in the water, flashing at **irregular** intervals like electric lights turned on for a moment.

As you read, notice how Heyerdahl shapes his narrative.

Phosphorescence is glowing light coming from something that has absorbed heat or light. *Plankton* are the tiny animal and plant life found in the ocean. The *stern* is the back of the raft.

hypnotic causing a dreamlike state

inquisitive curious

irregular uneven

rivalry a struggle to win

Subterranean means being underground. In this case, from deep in the ocean.

We gradually grew accustomed to having these subterranean or submarine creatures under the floor, but nevertheless we were just as surprised every time a new species appeared. About two o'clock on a cloudy night, when the man at the helm had difficulty in distinguishing black water from black sky, he caught sight of a faint **illumination** down in the water which slowly took the shape of a large animal. It was impossible to say whether it was plankton shining on its body, or whether the animal itself had a phosphorescent surface, but the glimmer down in the black water gave the ghostly creature **obscure, wavering** outlines. Sometimes it was roundish, sometimes oval, or triangular, and suddenly it split into two parts which swam to and fro under the raft independently of each other. Finally there were three of these large shining phantoms wandering round in slow circles under us.

A *fathom* is equal to six feet. Five fathoms is thirty feet.

The *starboard* side is the right, the *port* side is the left.

They were real monsters, for the visible parts alone were some five fathoms long, and we all quickly collected on deck and followed the ghost dance. It went on for hour after hour, following the course of the raft. Mysterious and noiseless, our shining companions kept a good way beneath the surface, mostly on the starboard side where the light was, but often they were right under the raft or appeared on the port side. The glimmer of light on their backs **revealed** that the beasts were bigger than elephants but they were not whales, for they never came up to breathe. Were they giant ray fish which changed shape when they turned over on their sides? They took no notice at all if we held the light right down on the surface to **lure** them up, so that we might see what kind of creatures they were. And, like all proper goblins and ghosts, they had sunk into the depths when the dawn began to break.

We never got a proper explanation of this **nocturnal** visit from the three shining monsters, unless the solution was afforded by another visit we received a day and a half later in the full midday sunshine. It was May 24, and we were lying

A *swell* is a long wave.

drifting on a leisurely swell in exactly 95° west by 7° south. It

illumination a light	**nocturnal** nighttime	**reveal** to show
lure to tempt	**obscure** unclear	**wavering** quivering

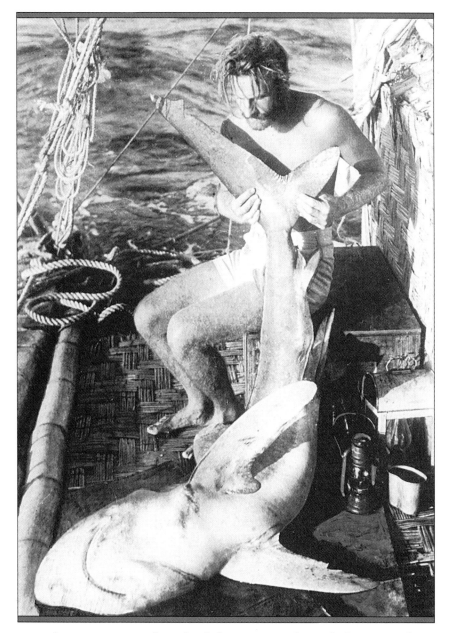

Heyerdahl has just hauled this shark on deck by grabbing its rough tail fin. The shark is helpless once the tail fin is above the water.

was about noon, and we had thrown overboard the guts of two big dolphins we had caught earlier in the morning. I was having a refreshing plunge overboard at the bow, lying in the water but keeping a good lookout and hanging on to a rope end, when I caught sight of a thick brown fish, six feet long, which came swimming inquisitively toward me through the crystal-clear sea water. I hopped quickly up on to the edge of

The *bow* is the front of the raft.

the raft and sat in the hot sun looking at the fish as it passed quietly, when I heard a wild war whoop from Knut, who was sitting aft behind the bamboo cabin. He bellowed "Shark!" till his voice cracked in a falsetto, and, as we had sharks swimming alongside the raft almost daily without creating such excitement, we all realized that this must be something extra-special and flocked astern to Knut's assistance.

Knut had been squatting there, washing his pants in the swell, and when he looked up for a moment he was staring straight into the biggest and ugliest face any of us had ever seen in the whole of our lives. It was the head of a **veritable** sea monster, so huge and so hideous that, if the Old Man of the Sea himself had come up, he could not have made such an impression on us. The head was broad and flat like a frog's, with two small eyes right at the sides, and a toadlike jaw which was four or five feet wide and had long fringes drooping from the corners of the mouth. Behind the head was an enormous body ending in a long thin tail with a pointed tail fin which stood straight up and showed that this sea monster was not any kind of whale. The body looked brownish under the water, but both head and body were thickly covered with small white spots.

The monster came quietly, lazily swimming after us from astern. It grinned like a bulldog and lashed gently with its tail. The large round dorsal fin projected clear of the water and sometimes the tail fin as well, and, when the creature was in the trough of the swell, the water flowed about the broad back as though washing round a submerged reef. In front of the broad jaws swam a whole crowd of zebra-striped pilot fish in fan formation, and large remora fish and other **parasites** sat firmly attached to the huge body and traveled with it through the water, so that the whole thing looked like a curious zoological collection crowded round something that resembled a floating deep-water reef.

Aft is near the stern, or back, of the raft.

In mythology, the Old Man of the Sea is a god who rose out of his home at the bottom of the sea to give advice to sailors.

parasite an animal that depends on another for its life, giving nothing in return

veritable true

A twenty-five-pound dolphin, attached to six of our largest fishhooks, was hanging behind the raft as bait for sharks, and a swarm of the pilot fish shot straight off, nosed the dolphin without touching it, and then hurried back to their lord and master, the sea king. Like a mechanical monster it set its machinery going and came gliding at leisure toward the dolphin which lay, a beggarly trifle, before its jaws. We tried to pull the dolphin in, and the sea monster followed slowly, right up to the side of the raft. It did not open its mouth but just let the dolphin bump against it, as if to throw open the whole door for such an **insignificant** scrap was not worth while. When the giant came close up to the raft, it rubbed its back against the heavy steering oar, which was just lifted up out of the water, and now we had **ample** opportunity of studying the monster at the closest quarters—at such close quarters that I thought we had all gone mad, for we roared stupidly with laughter and shouted overexcitedly at the completely fantastic sight we saw. Walt Disney himself, with all his powers of imagination, could not have created a more hair-raising sea monster than that which thus suddenly lay with its terrific jaws along the raft's side.

Why do the men laugh? Do you think they are afraid?

The monster was a whale shark, the largest shark and the largest fish known in the world today. It is exceedingly rare, but scattered specimens are observed here and there in the tropical oceans. The whale shark has an average length of fifty feet, and according to zoologists it weighs fifteen tons. It is said that large specimens can attain a length of sixty feet; one harpooned baby had a liver weighing six hundred pounds and a collection of three thousand teeth in each of its broad jaws.

Our monster was so large that, when it began to swim in circles round us and under the raft, its head was visible on one side while the whole of its tail stuck out on the other. And so **incredibly grotesque, inert,** and stupid did it appear when seen fullface that we could not help shouting with laughter, although we realized that it had strength enough in its tail to

ample sufficient	**incredibly** unbelievably	**insignificant** unimportant
grotesque hideous	**inert** unmoving	

Kon-Tiki had an open bamboo cabin and two masts lashed together with a square sail between. The raft was named for the Peruvian sun-god, who vanished across the sea to the west.

smash both balsa logs and ropes to pieces if it attacked us. Again and again it described narrower and narrower circles just under the raft, while all we could do was to wait and see what might happen. When it appeared on the other side, it glided **amiably** under the steering oar and lifted it up in the air, while the oar blade slid along the creature's back.

We stood round the raft with hand harpoons ready for action, but they seemed to us like toothpicks in relation to the mammoth beast we had to deal with. There was no indication that the whale shark ever thought of leaving us again; it circled

amiably kindly

round us and followed like a faithful dog, close up to the raft. None of us had ever experienced or thought we should experience anything like it; the whole adventure, with the sea monster swimming behind and under the raft, seemed so completely unnatural that we could not really take it seriously.

In reality the whale shark went on **encircling** us for barely an hour, but to us the visit seemed to last a whole day. At last it became too exciting for Erik, who was standing at a corner of the raft with an eight-foot hand harpoon, and, encouraged by ill-considered shouts, he raised the harpoon above his head. As the whale shark came gliding slowly toward him and its broad head moved right under the corner of the raft, Eric thrust the harpoon with all his giant strength down between his legs and deep into the whale shark's gristly head. It was a second or two before the giant understood properly what was happening. Then in a flash the **placid** half-wit was **transformed** into a mountain of steel muscles.

We heard a swishing noise as the harpoon line rushed over the edge of the raft and saw a **cascade** of water as the giant stood on its head and plunged down into the depths. The three men who were standing nearest were flung about the place, head over heels, and two of them were flayed and burned by the line as it rushed through the air. The thick line, strong enough to hold a boat, was caught up on the side of the raft but snapped at once like a piece of twine, and a few seconds later a broken-off harpoon shaft came up to the surface two hundred yards away. A shoal of frightened pilot fish shot off through the water in a desperate attempt to keep up with their old lord and master. We waited a long time for the monster to come racing back like an **infuriated** submarine, but we never saw anything more of him.

> Why do you think the whale shark's visit seemed to last all day?

> A *shoal* is a large group.

cascade a waterfall	**infuriated** very angry	**transformed** greatly changed
encircle to circle	**placid** calm; peaceful	

Directions Write the answers to these questions using complete sentences.

Comprehension: Identifying Facts

1. What are two of the "inquisitive guests" that stay with the raft day and night?

2. After dark, what glows in the water as brightly as the stars?

3. What are the "shining eyes" that sometimes frighten the sailors at night?

4. What do the three "monsters" look like to the men on the raft?

5. How do the men know that the "monsters" are not whales?

6. At what time of day does the whale shark first appear?

7. How does Heyerdahl describe the whale shark?

8. What swims on and around the whale shark?

9. What does Erik do to the whale shark?

10. How does the whale shark's behavior change after it is attacked?

Comprehension: Understanding Main Ideas

11. What would you say is the author's main purpose in writing this excerpt?

12. What is the tone of this excerpt: serious, humorous, matter-of-fact, or a combination of these?

13. How does the *Kon-Tiki*'s crew feel about the strange fish they see?

14. Why do the men draw in their bare legs when the glowing "pellets" are washed up around their feet?

15. How do the three "monsters" the crew sees one night behave like "goblins and ghosts"?

16. Why does the crew laugh at the sight of the "hair-raising sea monster"?

17. What details make the whale shark come alive for readers?

18. What does Heyerdahl think about Erik's attempt to harpoon the whale shark? Support your answer.

19. What are some details of everyday life aboard the *Kon-Tiki*?

20. What does this excerpt suggest about Thor Heyerdahl's view of nature?

Understanding Literature: Narrative

Forms of nonfiction writing can be grouped by looking at the way the author organizes the material. In this excerpt from his book, Heyerdahl describes events chronologically. He presents a narrative, or nonfiction story.

A nonfiction narrative is different from the narrative of a short story. In both cases, a narrative is a story. However, in writing nonfiction narratives, authors present a series of actual events, told from their own point of view. In writing short stories, authors use an imagined plot and characters. Point of view depends on who narrates the story.

21. How is a nonfiction narrative different from the narrative in a short story?

22. What would be the effect if Heyerdahl wrote his narrative from a third-person point of view?

23. What would be the effect if Heyerdahl presented the events of his narrative in another order (starting, for example, with the whale shark plunging to the bottom of the ocean), as short story authors sometimes do?

24. If you were writing a short story based on the events Heyerdahl describes, how would you organize the narrative? Explain your reasoning.

25. Would you rather read a nonfiction narrative or a short story on the same topic? Explain.

Critical Thinking

26. Why do people sometimes laugh when something scary happens, as the crew did when the whale shark appeared?

27. How might Heyerdahl have written this part of his book differently if the whale shark had seriously damaged the *Kon-Tiki*?

28. How do you think the sailors would have reacted if they had seen the whale shark appear, not on a sunny afternoon, but on a dark night?

29. How would you have felt about being part of the crew on this adventure? Explain your answer.

30. Compare this nonfiction narrative about a kind of sea monster with Ray Bradbury's short story in Unit 5, "The Fog Horn." How are they the same? How are they different?

Writing on Your Own Imagine that you are on the *Kon-Tiki* and you just saw the whale shark. Write a letter to your best friend describing the experience.

Rudolfo A. Anaya

1937–

Literary Terms

essay a short nonfiction work on any subject

imagery the use of word pictures that appeal to the five senses

purpose a nonfiction writer's main idea or goal

reflective essay a personal essay exploring an author's feelings

repetition using a phrase or image more than once, for emphasis

About the Author

Rudolfo Anaya has been called the father of modern Chicano, or Mexican-American, literature. He was born in Pastura, New Mexico, in 1937. Pastura is twenty miles south of the Pecos River. The stories and customs of the Mexican-American community in this part of America's Southwest have been important in Anaya's work. He has said that he has always "used the technique of the *cuento* (story). I am an oral storyteller, but now I do it on the printed page."

Anaya is probably best known for his first novel, *Bless Me, Ultima*. Published in 1972, this work received several awards. In addition to his other novels, Anaya has also written poetry, plays, essays, short stories, and children's books.

About the Selection

"A Celebration of Grandfathers" is an **essay**. Essays are short nonfiction works on any subject. A writer's **purpose** in an essay may be to tell a story, to describe, to explain, to persuade, to entertain, or to do several of these at once. Essays do not require one particular kind of order, and they don't have to have a plot, as short stories do. Instead, authors can present events in the order that seems best to them.

In his essay, Rudolfo Anaya thinks back on his grandfather's life and what it meant. He moves back and forth from this personal story to reflect on what all old people should mean to us. Anaya's writing is rich in **imagery**, word pictures that appeal to the five senses. He also draws attention to his Mexican-American background by the **repetition** of Spanish phrases. "A Celebration of Grandfathers" is a **reflective essay**. In such an essay, the author explores many sides of a topic about which he or she has deep personal feelings.

A Celebration of Grandfathers

"Buenos días le de Dios, abuelo." God give you a good day, grandfather. This is how I was taught as a child to greet my grandfather, or any grown person. It was a greeting of respect, a **cultural** value to be passed on from generation to generation, this respect for the old ones.

The old people I remember from my childhood were strong in their beliefs, and as we lived daily with them we learned a wise path of life to follow. They had something important to share with the young, and when they spoke the young listened. These old abuelos and abuelitas had worked the earth all their lives, and so they knew the value of **nurturing,** they knew the **sensitivity** of the earth. The daily struggle called for cooperation, and so every person contributed to the social fabric, and each person was respected for his contribution.

The old ones had looked deep into the web that connects all **animate** and **inanimate** forms of life, and they recognized the great design of the **creation.**

These *ancianos* from the cultures of the Rio Grande, living side by side, sharing, growing together, they knew the rhythms and cycles of time, from the preparation of the earth in the spring to the digging of the acequias that brought the water to the dance of harvest in the fall. They shared good

As you read, try to decide what the author's main purpose is in this reflective essay.

Abuelos and *abuelitas* are grandfathers and grandmothers.

Anaya uses imagery to describe the *web* connecting everything in the world. As you read, look for other images.

Ancianos are old people. *Acequias* are irrigation ditches.

animate living, conscious

creation the world

cultural relating to the beliefs and customs of a group

inanimate nonliving, unconscious, unmoving

nurture to feed or care for

sensitivity able to be easily hurt

times and hard times. They helped each other through the **epidemics** and the personal **tragedies,** and they shared what little they had when the hot winds burned the land and no rain came. They learned that to **survive** one had to share in the process of life.

Hard workers all, they tilled the earth and farmed, ran the herds and spun wool, and carved their saints and their kachinas from cottonwood late in the winter nights. All worked with a deep faith which perplexes the modern mind.

Their faith shone in their eyes; it was in the strength of their grip, in the **creases** time wove into their faces. When they spoke, they spoke plainly and with few words, and they meant what they said. When they prayed, they went straight to the source of life. When there were good times, they knew how to dance in celebration and how to prepare the foods of the fiestas. All this they passed on to the young, so that a new generation would know what they had known, so the string of life would not be broken.

Today we would say that the old abuelitos lived **authentic** lives.

Newcomers to New Mexico often say that time seems to move slowly here. I think they mean they have come in contact with the inner strength of the people, a strength so solid it causes time itself to pause. Think of it. Think of the high, northern New Mexico villages, or the lonely ranches on the open llano. Think of the Indian pueblo which lies as solid as rock in the face of time. Remember the old people whose eyes seem like windows that peer into a distant past that makes absurdity of our **contemporary** world. That is what one feels when one **encounters** the old ones and their land, a pausing of time.

We have all felt time stand still. We have all been in the presence of power, the knowledge of the old ones, the majestic peace of a mountain stream or an aspen grove or red

Kachinas are small wooden dolls that represent the spirit of an ancestor or a god.

Fiestas are feasts.

The *llano* is a plain. A *pueblo* is an Indian village in the Southwest.

---

authentic genuine; of true value

contemporary modern

crease a fold; a wrinkle

encounter to meet or come upon

epidemic widespread disease

survive to go on living

tragedy misfortune, suffering

buttes rising into blue sky. We have all felt the light of dusk **permeate** the earth and cause time to pause in its flow.

A *butte* is a steep hill.

I felt this when first touched by the spirit of Ultima, the old *curandera* who appears in my first novel, *Bless Me, Ultima*. This is how the young Antonio describes what he feels:

A *curandera* is a medicine woman.

> When she came the beauty of the llano
> unfolded before my eyes, and the gurgling waters
> of the river sang to the hum of the turning earth.
> The magical time of childhood stood still, and the
> pulse of the living earth pressed its mystery into my
> living blood. She took my hand, and the silent,
> magic powers she possessed made beauty from the
> raw, sun-baked llano, the green river valley, and the
> blue bowl which was the white sun's home. My
> bare feet felt the throbbing earth, and my body
> trembled with excitement. Time stood still . . .

At other times, in other places, when I have been privileged to be with the old ones, to learn, I have felt this inner reserve of strength upon which they draw. I have been held motionless and speechless by the power of curanderas. I have felt the same power when I hunted with Cruz, high on the Taos mountain, where it was more than the **incredible** beauty of the mountain bathed in morning light, more than the shining of the quivering aspen, but a connection with life, as if a shining strand of light connected the particular and the **cosmic**. That feeling is an epiphany of time, a standing still of time.

Remember that an *epiphany* is a moment when a character discovers an important truth. Here, Anaya experiences "a standing still of time."

But not all of our old ones are curanderos or hunters on the mountain. My grandfather was a plain man, a farmer from Puerto de Luna on the Pecos River. He was probably a descendent of those people who spilled over the mountain from Taos, following the Pecos River in search of farmland. There in that river valley he settled and raised a large family.

Bearded and walrus-mustached, he stood five feet tall, but to me as a child he was a giant. I remember him most for his silence. In the summers my parents sent me to live with him

At this point, Anaya moves from general reflections on the wisdom of old people to specific memories of his own grandfather.

cosmic the universe	**incredible** hard to believe	**permeate** to enter; to soak into

on his farm, for I was to learn the ways of a farmer. My uncles also lived in that valley, the valley called Puerto de Luna, there where only the flow of the river and the whispering of the wind marked time. For me it was a magical place.

I remember once, while out hoeing the fields, I came upon an anthill, and before I knew it I was badly bitten. After he had covered my **welts** with the cool mud from the irrigation ditch, my grandfather calmly said: "Know where you stand." That is the way he spoke, in short phrases, to the point.

One very dry summer, the river dried to a trickle, there was no water for the fields. The young plants withered and died. In my sadness and with the impulses of youth I said, "I wish it would rain!" My grandfather touched me, looked up in the sky and whispered, "Pray for rain." In his language there was a difference. He felt connected to the cycles that brought the rain or kept it from us. His prayer was a meaningful action, because he was a **participant** with the forces that filled our world, he was not a bystander.

A young man died at the village one summer. A very **tragic** death. He was dragged by his horse. When he was found I cried, for the boy was my friend. I did not understand why death had come to one so young. My grandfather took me aside and said: "Think of the death of the trees and the fields in the fall. The leaves fall, and everything rests, as if dead. But they bloom again in the spring. Death is only this small **transformation** in life."

These are the things I remember, these fleeting images, few words.

I remember him driving his horse-drawn wagon into Santa Rosa in the fall when he brought his harvest produce to

participant one who takes part in	**transformation** a major change
tragic sad, unfortunate	**welt** a bruise

sell in the town. What a tower of strength seemed to come in that small man huddled on the seat of the giant wagon. One click of his tongue and the horses obeyed, stopped or turned as he wished. He never raised his whip. How unlike today when so much teaching is done with loud words and threatening hands.

I would run to greet the wagon, and the wagon would stop. "Buenos días le de Dios, abuelo," I would say. This was the **prescribed** greeting of **esteem** and respect. Only after the greeting was given could we approach these **venerable** old people. "Buenos días le de Dios, mi hijo," he would answer and smile, and then I could jump up on the wagon and sit at his side. Then I, too, became a king as I rode next to the old man who smelled of earth and sweat and other deep **aromas** from the orchards and fields of Puerto de Luna.

Mi hijo means my son.

We were all sons and daughters to him. But today the sons and daughters are breaking with the past, putting aside los abuelitos. The old values are threatened, and threatened most where it comes to those relationships with the old people. If we don't take the time to watch and feel the years of their final transformation, a part of our **humanity** will be **lessened.**

I grew up speaking Spanish, and oh! how difficult it was to learn English. Sometimes I would give up and cry out that I couldn't learn. Then he would say, "Ten paciencia." Have patience. *Paciencia,* a word with the strength of centuries, a word that said that someday we would **overcome.** *Paciencia,* how soothing a word coming from this old man who could still sling hundred-pound bags over his shoulder, chop wood for hours on end, and hitch up his own horses and ride to town and back in one day.

"You have to learn the language of the Americanos," he said. "Me, I will live my last days in my valley. You will live in a new time, the time of the gringos."

Gringos are foreigners— North Americans.

aroma a fragrance	**lessened** made less; taken away	**prescribed** required
esteem honor		**venerable** aged; respected
humanity human beings	**overcome** to win against or get the better of	

A new time did come, a new time is here. How will we form it so it is fruitful? We need to know where we stand. We need to speak softly and respect others, and to share what we have. We need to pray not for **material** gain, but for rain for the fields, for the sun to nurture growth, for nights in which we can sleep in peace, and for a harvest in which everyone can share. Simple lessons from a simple man. These lessons he learned from his past which was deep and strong as the currents of the river of life, a life which could be stronger than death.

He was a man; he died. Not in his valley, but nevertheless cared for by his sons and daughters and flocks of grandchildren. At the end, I would enter his room which carried the smell of medications and Vicks, the faint **pungent** odor of urine, and cigarette smoke. Gone were the aroma of the fields, the strength of his young manhood. Gone also was his patience in the face of crippling old age. Small things bothered him; he shouted or turned sour when his **expectations** were not met. It was because he could not care for himself, because he was returning to that state of childhood, and all those wishes and desires were now wrapped in a crumbling old body.

"Ten paciencia," I once said to him, and he smiled. "I didn't know I would grow this old," he said. "Now, I can't even roll my own cigarettes." I rolled a cigarette for him, placed it in his mouth and lit it. I asked him why he smoked, the doctor had said it was bad for him. "I like to see the smoke rise," he said. He would smoke and doze, and his quilt was spotted with little burns where the cigarettes dropped. One of us had to sit and watch to make sure a fire didn't start.

I would sit and look at him and remember what was said of him when he was a young man. He could mount a wild horse and break it, and he could ride as far as any man. He could dance all night at a dance, then work the acequia the following day. He helped neighbors, they helped him. He

Why does Anaya repeat the phrase, "Ten paciencia," to his grandfather?

expectation what is expected or looked forward to   **material** physical, real   **pungent** sharp

married, raised children. Small legends, the kind that make up everyman's life.

He was 94 when he died. Family, neighbors, and friends gathered; they all agreed he had led a rich life. I remembered the last years, the years he spent in bed. And as I remember now, I am reminded that it is too easy to romanticize old age. Sometimes we forget the pain of the transformation into old age, we forget the natural breaking down of the body. Not all go gentle into the last years, some go crying and cursing, forgetting the names of those they loved the most, withdrawing into an **internal anguish** few of us can know. May we be granted the patience and care to deal with our ancianos.

For some time we haven't looked at these changes and needs of the old ones. The American image created by the mass media is an image of youth, not of old age. It is the beautiful and the young who are praised in this society. If **analyzed** carefully, we see that same damaging thought has crept into the way society views the old. In response to the old, the mass media have just created old people who act like the young. It is only the healthy, pink-cheeked, outgoing, older persons we are shown in the media. And they are always selling something, as if an entire generation of old people were salesmen in their lives. Commercials show very lively old men, who must always be in excellent health according to the new myth, selling insurance policies or real estate as they are out golfing; older women selling coffee or toilet paper to those just married. That image does not **illustrate** the real life of the old ones.

Real life takes into account the natural cycle of growth and change. My grandfather pointed to the leaves falling from the tree. So time brings with its transformation the often painful, wearing-down process. Vision blurs, health **wanes**; even the act of walking carries with it the painful reminder of the

Do you agree that the mass media has created an image of youth, even when we see older people?

---

analyze to study in detail

anguish great pain

illustrate to show; to picture

internal inside; unspoken

wane to fade

autumn of life. But this process is something to be faced, not something to be hidden away by false images. Yes, the old can be young at heart, but in their own way, with their own dignity. They do not have to copy the always-young image of the Hollywood star.

My grandfather wanted to return to his valley to die. But by then the families of the valley had left in search of a better future. It is only now that there seems to be a return to the valley, a revival. The new generation seeks its roots, that value of love for the land moves us to return to the place where our ancianos formed the culture.

I returned to Puerto de Luna last summer, to join the community in celebration of the founding of the church. I drove by my grandfather's home, my uncles' ranches, the neglected adobe washing down into the earth from whence it came. And I wondered, how might the values of my grandfather's generation live in our own? What can we **retain** to see us through these hard times? I was to become a farmer, and I became a writer. As I plow and plant my words, do I nurture as my grandfather did in his fields and orchards? The answers are not simple.

"They don't make men like that anymore," is a phrase we hear when one does honor to a man. I am glad I knew my grandfather. I am glad there are still times when I can see him in my dreams, hear him in my **reverie.** Sometimes I think I catch a whiff of that earthy aroma that was his smell, just as in lonely times sometimes I catch the fragrance of Ultima's herbs. Then I smile. How strong these people were to leave such a lasting impression.

So, as I would greet my abuelo long ago, it would help us all to greet the old ones we know with this kind and respectful greeting: "Buenos días le de Dios."

What is the effect of the repetition of this Spanish greeting at the beginning, middle, and end of the essay?

retain to keep   **reverie** a daydream

Directions Write the answers to these questions using complete sentences.

Comprehension: Identifying Facts

1. According to Anaya, what is the proper greeting for a young person to say to a grownup?

2. List three things that the *ancianos* learn from working with the earth.

3. Who is Ultima?

4. Why does the author spend his summers with his grandfather?

5. How does his grandfather help Anaya accept the death of his young friend?

6. How does Anaya feel when he rides beside his grandfather in his wagon?

7. What Spanish phrase does the author repeat to the old man when he is ill? What does it mean?

8. How does the mass media present old people, according to the author?

9. What question does the author ask in comparing his writing with the work his grandfather did?

10. Through which of his senses does Anaya sometimes feel the presence of his grandfather and Ultima? Why?

Comprehension: Understanding Main Ideas

11. What clues does the title of this essay give you about what to expect?

12. Anaya says that old people pass their knowledge to younger people. How is this like his essay?

13. Where is the author and what is he doing when he has "an epiphany of time, a standing still of time"? What do you think this experience means?

14. Through which event do you learn the most about Anaya's grandfather?

15. How was Anaya's time as a young boy with his grandfather the same as his experience with him when the old man was ill? How was it different?

16. What values learned from his grandfather and other old people does Anaya bring to the present?

17. Why does Anaya feel that the media's image of old age is not a true picture?

18. Anaya repeats two Spanish phrases: a greeting and his grandfather's advice about learning English. What does this add to his essay?

19. How does Anaya use the idea of cooperation throughout the essay?

20. In one sentence, how would you sum up the purpose of this essay?

Understanding Literature: Reflective Essay

Essays can be grouped according to their purpose. Some tell a story, some describe, some explain, some persuade, some entertain. Many essays have more than one purpose.

Reflective essays such as "A Celebration of Grandfathers" have one main purpose: to share with readers an author's personal thoughts and feelings about something. If they also describe, explain, or entertain, so much the better.

21. For what main purpose do authors write reflective essays?

22. What kinds of things would you expect to read about in a reflective essay?

23. In what ways is "A Celebration of Grandfathers" different from Heyerdahl's excerpt from *Kon-Tiki*?

24. What are some thoughts Anaya shares about the way his grandfather led his life? Which details show that he has thought about what his grandfather's life meant? Explain.

25. One of Anaya's purposes is to persuade readers that young people have much to learn from old people. What does he say old people can teach younger people?

Critical Thinking

26. If you were Anaya's grandfather, how do you think you would feel about this essay? Why?

27. Why do you think Anaya includes information about Ultima in "A Celebration of Grandfathers"?

28. How do you think Anaya feels about his grandfather's death? Explain your answer.

29. If you were to write a reflective essay on someone who has influenced your life, who would you write about? Explain how your life has been changed by this person.

30. How do you want to be remembered by your grandchildren?

Writing on Your Own Write two reflective paragraphs about the lessons your grandparents or other older people have taught you.

Of Dry Goods and Black Bow Ties
Yoshiko Uchida

Yoshiko Uchida
1921–1992

Literary Terms

biographical essay an essay about true events in a person's life

biography the story of a person's life, written by someone other than the person

symbol a person, place, or object that stands for something beyond itself

About the Author

On December 7, 1941, the day Japan bombed Pearl Harbor, Yoshiko Uchida was a senior at the University of California, Berkeley. Even though she had been born in California, Uchida, her family, and more than 100,000 other Japanese Americans were now considered a risk to the safety of the United States. They were all forced to move to internment camps in the desert Southwest.

At the camp, Yoshiko Uchida opened a school for the children. She began gathering details of her experiences. These would inspire many of her fiction and nonfiction works. Uchida once said that she wrote "to give young Asians a sense of their own history." Her first book, *The Dancing Kettle and Other Japanese Folk Tales*, is a collection of stories she heard as a child. Traveling to Japan after the war, she gathered more stories. These became part of two other collections of folk tales, *The Magic Listening Cap* and *The Sea of Gold*.

Writing gave Yoshiko Uchida a way to remember and celebrate the experiences of her people.

About the Selection

A **biography** is the story of a person's life, written by someone other than that person. "Of Dry Goods and Black Bow Ties" is a **biographical essay**. In it, Yoshiko Uchida shows what she called "the strength of spirit and the sense of hope and purpose" in the Japanese Americans she knew. She does this in part by using an unusual **symbol**—a black bow tie.

Biographers make their subjects come alive in many of the same ways fiction writers do. Writers of biographical essays choose events and details that reveal people's personalities and values. The characters in this essay are Japanese immigrants who came to this country believing in the promise of America.

Of Dry Goods and Black Bow Ties

Long after reaching the age of sixty, when my father was persuaded at last to wear a **conservative** four-in-hand tie, it was not because of his family's urging, but because Mr. Shimada (I shall call him that) had died. Until then, for some forty years, my father had always worn a plain black bow tie, a formality which was required on his first job in America and which he had continued to observe as faithfully as his father before him had worn his samurai sword.

My father came to America in 1906 when he was not yet twenty-one. Sailing from Japan on a small six-thousand-ton ship which was buffeted all the way by rough seas, he landed in Seattle on a **bleak** January day. He revived himself with the first solid meal he had enjoyed in many days, and then allowed himself one day of rest to restore his sagging spirits. Early on the second morning, wearing a stiff new bowler, he went to see Mr. Shozo Shimada to whom he carried a letter of introduction.

At that time, Shozo Shimada was Seattle's most successful Japanese business man. He owned a chain of dry goods stores which extended not only from Vancouver to Portland, but to cities in Japan as well. He had come to America in 1880, penniless but enterprising, and sought work as a laborer. It wasn't long, however, before he saw the **futility** of trying to **compete** with American laborers whose bodies were twice his

A *four-in-hand tie* is a necktie.

As you read, notice the details the author has chosen to describe Mr. Shimada, the subject of this biographical essay.

A *bowler* is a derby hat.

Dry goods include cloth, lace, thread, buttons, and so on.

bleak gloomy

compete to be a rival for

conservative usual, typical

futility uselessness

in muscle and bulk. He knew he would never go far as a laborer, but he did possess another skill that could give him a start toward better things. He knew how to sew. It was a matter of **expediency** over masculine pride. He set aside his shovel, bought a second-hand sewing machine, and hung a dressmaker's sign in his window. He was in business.

In those days, there were some Japanese women in Seattle who had neither homes nor families nor sewing machines, and were delighted to find a friendly Japanese person to do some sewing for them. They flocked to Mr. Shimada with bolts of cloth, **elated** to discover a dressmaker who could speak their native tongue and, although a male, sew western-styled dresses for them.

Mr. Shimada acquainted himself with the fine points of turning a seam, fitting sleeves, and coping with the slippery folds of silk, and soon the women told their friends and gave him enough business to keep him thriving and able to establish a healthy bank account. He became a trusted friend and **confidant** to many of them and soon they began to bring him what money they earned for safekeeping.

-san added to Japanese names and titles shows respect.

"Keep our money for us, Shimada-san," they urged, refusing to go to American banks whose tellers spoke in a language they could not understand.

At first the money **accumulated** slowly and Mr. Shimada used a pair of old socks as a **repository,** stuffing them into a far corner of his drawer beneath his union suits. But after a time, Mr. Shimada's private bank began to overflow and he soon found it necessary to **replenish** his supply of socks.

---

accumulate to collect

confidant someone to confide in

elated delighted, thrilled

expediency practicality

replenish to fill up

repository place for safekeeping

He went to a small dry goods store downtown, and as he glanced about at the buttons, threads, needles and laces, it occurred to him that he owed it to the women to **invest** their savings in a business venture with more future than the dark recesses of his bureau drawer. That night he called a group of them together.

"Think, ladies," he began. "What are the two basic needs of the Japanese living in Seattle? Clothes to wear and food to eat," he answered himself. "Is that not right? Every man must buy a shirt to put on his back and pickles and rice for his stomach."

Why does Mr. Shimada call the women together?

The women marveled at Mr. Shimada's cleverness as he spread before them his fine plans for a Japanese dry goods store that would not only carry everything available in an American dry goods store, but Japanese foodstuff as well. That was the beginning of the first Shimada Dry Goods Store on State Street.

By the time my father appeared, Mr. Shimada had long since abandoned his sewing machine and was well on his way to becoming a business tycoon. Although he had opened cautiously with such stock items as ginghams, flannel, handkerchiefs, socks, shirts, overalls, umbrellas and ladies' silk and cotton stockings, he now carried tins of salt rice crackers, bottles of soy sauce, vinegar, ginger root, fish-paste cakes, bean paste, Japanese pickles, dried mushrooms, salt fish, red beans, and just about every item of canned food that could be shipped from Japan. In addition, his was the first Japanese store to install a U.S. Post Office Station, and he thereby attained the right to fly an American flag in front of the large sign that bore the name of his shop.

When my father first saw the big American flag fluttering in front of Mr. Shimada's shop, he was **overcome** with admiration and awe. He expected that Mr. Shozo Shimada would be the finest of Americanized Japanese gentlemen, and when he met him, he was not disappointed.

Although Mr. Shimada was not very tall, he gave the **illusion** of height because of his erect carriage. He wore a

illusion an unreal vision; a false impression	**invest** to put money into something, hoping for a profit	**overcome** to make weak or helpless

An *alpaca* suit was made from the wool of the alpaca, an animal similar to a llama.

spotless black alpaca suit, an **immaculate** white shirt and a white collar so stiff it might have overcome a lesser man. He also wore a black bow tie, black shoes that buttoned up the side and a gold watch whose thick chain looped grandly on his vest. He was probably in his fifties then, a ruddy-faced man whose hair, already turning white, was parted carefully in the center. He was an imposing figure to **confront** a young man fresh from Japan with scarcely a future to look forward to. My father bowed, summoned as much dignity as he could muster, and presented the letter of introduction he carried to him.

Mr. Shimada was quick to sense his need. "Do you know anything about bookkeeping?" he inquired.

"I intend to go to night school to learn this very skill," my father answered.

Mr. Shimada could **assess** a man's qualities in a very few minutes. He looked my father straight in the eye and said, "Consider yourself hired." Then he added, "I have a few basic rules. My employees must at all times wear a clean white shirt and a black bow tie. They must answer the telephone promptly with the words, 'Good morning or good afternoon, Shimada's Dry Goods,' and they must always treat each customer with respect. It never hurts to be polite," he said thoughtfully. "One never knows when one might be **indebted** to even the lowliest of beggars."

My father was impressed with these modest words from a man of such success. He accepted them with a sense of mission and from that day was committed to white shirts and black bow ties, and treated every customer, no matter how humble, with respect and courtesy. When, in later years, he had his own home, he never failed to answer the phone before it could ring twice if at all possible.

My father worked with Mr. Shimada for ten years, becoming first the buyer for his Seattle store and later, manager of the Portland branch. During this time Mr. Shimada continued on a course of **exhilarated expansion.** He

assess to determine the value of	**confront** to meet face to face	**expansion** growth
		immaculate very clean
	exhilarated excited	**indebted** in debt to

established two Japanese banks in Seattle, bought a fifteen-room house outside the dreary confines of the Japanese community and dressed his wife and daughter in velvets and ostrich feathers. When his daughter became eighteen, he sent her to study in Paris, and the party he gave on the eve of her departure, hiring musicians, as well as **caterers** to serve roast turkey, **venison**, baked ham and **champagne**, seemed to **verify** rumors that he had become one of the first Japanese **millionaires** of America.

In spite of his **phenomenal** success, however, Mr. Shimada never forgot his early friends nor lost any of his generosity, and this, **ironically** enough, was his undoing. Many of the

Why was Mr. Shimada so loyal to his friends?

caterer someone who supplies food	**ironically** unlike what one would expect	**venison** deer meat
champagne a sparkling wine	**millionaire** a very rich person	**verify** to prove that something is true
	phenomenal amazing	

women for whom he had once sewn dresses were now well established, and they came to him requesting loans with which they and their husbands might open grocery stores and laundries and shoe repair shops. Mr. Shimada helped them all and never demanded any **collateral.** He operated his banks on faith and trust and gave no thought to such common **prudence** as maintaining a reserve.

When my father was called to a new position with a large Japanese firm in San Francisco, Mr. Shimada came down to Portland to extend personally his good wishes. He took Father to a Chinese dinner and told him over the peanut duck and chow mein that he would like always to be considered a friend.

"If I can ever be of assistance to you," he said, "don't ever hesitate to call." And with a firm shake of the hand, he wished my father well.

That was in 1916. My father wrote regularly to Mr. Shimada telling him of his new job, of his bride, and later, of his two children. Mr. Shimada did not write often, but each Christmas he sent a box of Oregon apples and pears, and at New Year's a slab of heavy white rice paste from his Seattle shop.

1929 was the year the stock market crashed and the Great Depression began. Many banks and businesses failed.

In 1929 the letters and gifts stopped coming, and Father learned from friends in Seattle that both of Mr. Shimada's banks had failed. He immediately **dispatched** a letter to Mr. Shimada, but it was returned unopened. The next news he had was that Mr. Shimada had had to sell all of his shops. My father was now manager of the San Francisco branch of his firm. He wrote once more asking Mr. Shimada if there was anything he could do to help. The letter did not come back, but there was no reply, and my father did not write again. After all, how do you offer help to the head of a fallen empire? It seemed almost **irreverent.**

It was many years later that Mr. Shimada appeared one night at our home in Berkeley. In the dim light of the front porch my mother was startled to see an elderly gentleman

collateral money as protection for payment of a debt	**dispatch** to send **irreverent** not offering the proper respect	**prudence** wisdom, common sense

wearing striped pants, a morning coat and a shabby black hat. In his hand he carried a small black **satchel.** When she invited him inside, she saw that the morning coat was faded, and his shoes badly in need of a shine.

"I am Shimada," he announced with a courtly bow, and it was my mother who felt **inadequate** to the occasion. She hurriedly pulled off her apron and went to call my father. When he heard who was in the living room, he put on his coat and tie before going out to greet his old friend.

Mr. Shimada spoke to them about Father's friends in Seattle and about his daughter who was now married and living in Denver. He spoke of a **typhoon** that had recently swept over Japan, and he drank the tea my mother served and ate a piece of her chocolate cake. Only then did he open his black satchel.

"I thought your girls might enjoy these books," he said, as he drew out a brochure describing *The Book of Knowledge.*

"Fourteen volumes that will tell them of the wonders of this world." He spread his arms in a magnificent gesture that recalled his **eloquence** of the past. "I wish I could give them to your children as a personal gift," he added softly.

Without asking the price of the set, my father wrote a check for one hundred dollars and gave it to Mr. Shimada.

Mr. Shimada glanced at the check and said, "You have given me fifty dollars too much." He seemed troubled for only a moment, however, and quickly added, "Ah, the balance is for a deposit, is it? Very well, yours will be the first deposit in my next bank."

"Is your home still in Seattle then?" Father asked cautiously.

"I am living there, yes," Mr. Shimada answered.

And then, suddenly overcome with memories of the past, he spoke in a voice so low he could scarcely be heard.

"I paid back every cent," he murmured. "It took ten years, but I paid it back. All of it. I owe nothing."

> A morning coat is a jacket with tails in back, worn for daytime formal events.

> How would you describe the character of Mr. Shimada?

eloquence ability to speak with great feeling and expressiveness

inadequate unable to do what is required

satchel a small suitcase

typhoon a powerful storm

How is the black bow tie used as a symbol in this story?

"You are a true gentleman, Shimada-san," Father said. "You always will be." Then he pointed to the black tie he wore, saying, "You see, I am still one of the Shimada men."

That was the last time my father saw Shozo Shimada. Some time later he heard that he had returned to Japan as penniless as the day he set out for America.

It wasn't until the Christmas after we heard of Mr. Shimada's death that I ventured to give my father a silk, four-in-hand tie. It was charcoal gray and flecked with threads of silver. My father looked at it for a long time before he tried it on, and then fingering it gently, he said, "Well, perhaps it is time now that I put away my black bow ties."

Directions Write the answers to these questions using complete sentences.

Comprehension: Identifying Facts

1. What does Mr. Shimada do to earn money when he decides he is not suited for work as a laborer?

2. At first, what does Mr. Shimada do with the money people give him for safekeeping?

3. How does Mr. Shimada suggest the women invest their money?

4. How is Mr. Shimada dressed when Uchida's father first meets him?

5. What are Mr. Shimada's rules for his employees?

6. When and why does Mr. Shimada stop sending letters and gifts to the Uchida family?

7. How does Mr. Shimada lose all his money?

8. What happens during Mr. Shimada's last visit?

9. What does Mr. Shimada say about his past business troubles?

10. When does Uchida's father finally put on a necktie?

Comprehension: Understanding Main Ideas

11. How is a black bow tie used as a symbol in this story?

12. How does the Uchida family feel about Mr. Shimada? Give examples.

13. What would you say is the main purpose of this essay?

14. Why is Mr. Shimada so successful in business before 1929?

15. How does Mr. Shimada show his wealth?

16. When Mr. Shimada visits for the last time, how is his dress different from when Mr. Uchida worked for him? What does this say about him?

17. Why do you think Mr. Shimada is the only person in the essay who receives the honor of adding -san to his name?

18. Do you believe Mr. Shimada when he says he has paid all the money back? How do you know?

19. Compare the main purpose of this essay with "A Celebration of Grandfathers."

20. How are Mr. Shimada and Rudolfo Anaya's grandfather similar? How are they different?

Review Continued on Next Page

Of Dry Goods and Black Bow Ties, *Continued*

Understanding Literature: Biographical Essay

In writing a biography, authors describe not only people's lives, but also the times in which they lived. These details help readers understand the person being written about.

"Of Dry Goods and Black Bow Ties," is set in Seattle, Washington. Many Japanese-American immigrants settled there in the late 1800s and early 1900s. People like the author's father and Mr. Shimada came to America looking for the opportunity to improve their lives. In her biographical essay, Uchida recreates this world through details and carefully selected events.

21. What did Japanese immigrants at this time think about America? What evidence can you find in the story?

22. What kind of dresses does Mr. Shimada sew? What does this say about Japanese-American women of the time?

23. In his first store, Mr. Shimada sells Japanese food products. What does this tell you about Japanese-American culture at this time?

24. How does Mr. Shimada's appearance show his character and values? What details does the author provide about the way he looks?

25. List two other details of early Japanese-American culture that you learn in this essay.

Critical Thinking

26. Why does the author's father finally decide "it is time" to put away his black bow ties?

27. Do you think the Uchida family could have helped Mr. Shimada more than they did? Explain.

28. How would this essay be different if it were written as an autobiography?

29. Uchida uses the black bow tie as a symbol of Japanese-American workers. What symbol might she use for American workers today? Explain.

30. Uchida says she writes "to give young Asians a sense of their own history." What can they learn from this essay?

Writing on Your Own Create a poster or flyer that Mr. Shimada might have used to announce the opening of his first store.

Gather Together in My Name
Maya Angelou

Maya Angelou
1928–

Literary Terms

autobiography the story of a person's life, written by that person

humor writing intended to amuse

tone the attitude an author takes toward a subject

About the Author

On a clear, cold January day in 1993, Maya Angelou read her poem "On the Pulse of Morning" at the inauguration of President Bill Clinton. She was the first African American and the first woman to present her work at such an occasion.

Angelou was born Marguerite Johnson in 1928. She was born in St. Louis but spent most of her troubled childhood in Stamps, Arkansas. At sixteen she left home, determined to find her own way.

For a while, Angelou took any job she could find. She cooked. She served food in a restaurant. She was a dancer. She adopted her new name, the one by which people know her today. In the 1960s, she married a South African freedom fighter and moved to Cairo, Egypt. There she became the editor of the only English-language newspaper in the Middle East. Returning to New York, she began to publish her writing.

Maya Angelou has written poetry, novels, short stories, plays, and articles. She is probably best known for her **autobiography**, in five volumes. In it, she tells of her life and times as an African-American woman.

About the Selection

This excerpt comes from the second in Maya Angelou's series of autobiographical books, *Gather Together in My Name*, published in 1974. The book tells of her life from her late teens through her twenties, as she struggled to leave childhood behind and become her own person. At this point in the story, she calls herself Rita Johnson. She is living with her mother and young son. She dreams of a "knight in shining armor" who will lead her to a new life. R.L. Poole isn't quite that person.

With lots of **humor**, Angelou describes a highly embarrassing moment. Notice the **tone** she adopts toward this material.

from Gather Together in My Name

A *cornucopia* is also called a horn of plenty. The author uses this image and the "charming prince" to suggest that she was hoping for a better life.

My charming prince was going to appear out of the blue and offer me a cornucopia of goodies. I would only have to smile to have them brought to my feet.

R.L. Poole was to prove my dreams at least **partially prophetic.** When I opened the door to his ring and informed him that I was Rita Johnson, his already long face **depressed** another inch.

"The ... uh ... dancer?" His voice was slow and cloudy.

Dancer? Of course. I had been a cook, waitress, madam, bus girl—why not a dancer? After all, it was the only thing I had studied.

"Yes, I'm a dancer." I looked at him boldly. "Why?"

"I'm looking for a dancer, to work with me."

I thought he might be a talent scout for a chorus line or maybe the big stage show, featuring colored dancers, called "Change Your Luck."

"Come in."

We sat at the dining-room table and I offered a coffee. He looked me over, one feature at a time. My legs (long), my hips (spare), my breasts (nearly **nonexistent**). He drank the coffee slowly.

"I've studied since I was fourteen," I said. . . .

Poole doesn't brag, and Rita is sure this means he is polished and worldly, everything she wants to be.

"I'm Poole. From Chicago." His announcement held no boast, and I was sure that represented sophistication rather than false modesty. "I do rhythm tap and I want a girl

depress to fall

nonexistent not there

partially partly

prophetic able to foretell the future

partner. She doesn't have to do much but flash. Are you agva?" ("Flash" and A.G.V.A." were words unknown to me.)

I sat quietly and looked at him. Let him figure it out for himself.

"I met the woman at the record shop and she told me about you. Said all you talked about was dancing. She gave me your address.

"Some cats from the Local, musicians, straightened me out with the contacts for a few gigs. Scale is twenty-two fifty, but I'll do a few under scale to get some ends together."

I hadn't the slightest notion of what he was talking about. Scale. Agva. Gigs. Local. Ends.

"More coffee?" I went into the kitchen, walking like a model, chin down and **sternum** up, and my tail bone tucked under like white women.

I put on a fresh pot of coffee and tried desperately to decide on a role for myself. Should I be mysterious and **sultry,** asking nothing, answering all questions with a knowing smirk, or should I be the open, friendly, palsy every-boy's-sister girl-next-door type? No decision came to my mind, so I went back into the dining room, my legs stuck together with fine **decorum**.

"What did you study?"

"Ballet. Modern Ballet and the Theory of Dance." I made it sound like Advanced Thermonuclear Propulsion.

His face fell again.

"Any tap-dancing?"

"No."

"Jazz?"

"No."

"Acrobatics?"

To *flash* means to frame or highlight another dancer. A.G.V.A. stands for American Guild of Variety Artists, a performers' union.

Scale means the minimum union wage: $22.50 an hour. *Gigs* are jobs. The *Local* is the union office. *Ends* means money.

---

decorum proper behavior

jazz popular dance with strong rhythms

sternum the breastbone

sultry sexy

Rita mentions some of the popular dances of the time.

"No." I was losing him, so I jumped in the gap. "I used to win every jitterbug contest. I can do the Texas Hop. The Off Time. The boogie-woogie. The Camel Walk. The New Coup de Grâce. And I can do the split."

With that I stood up, straddle-legged, and looked down into his sad face, then I began to slide down to the floor.

I was unprepared for the movement (I had on a straight skirt), but R.L. was less ready than I. As my legs slipped apart and down, I lifted my arms in the graceful ballet position number 1 and watched the **impresario's** face race from mild interest to **incredulous**. My hem caught mid-thigh and I felt my **equilibrium** teeter. With a quick slight of hand I jerked up my skirt and continued my downward glide. I hummed a little snatch of song during the last part of the slither, and kept my mind on Sonja Henie in her cute little tutus.

Ballet is dance that combines different poses and steps with leaps and turns. There are five basic positions, or poses, in ballet—Rita has raised her arms in the correct pose for first position.

Unfortunately, I hadn't practiced the split in months, so my pelvic bones resisted with force. I was only two inches from the floor, and I gave a couple of little bounces. I accomplished more than I planned. My skirt seams gave before my bones surrendered. Then my left foot got caught between the legs of Mother's heavy oak table, and the other foot jumped at the gas heater and captured the pipe that ran from the jets into the wall. Pinned down at my **extremities** with the tendons in my legs screaming for ease, I felt as if I were being crucified to the floor, but in true "show must go on" fashion I kept my back straight and my arms uplifted in a position that would have made Pavlova proud. Then I looked at R.L. to see what impression I was making. Pity at my **predicament** was drawing him up from his chair, and **solicitude** was written over his face with a brush wider than a kitchen mop.

Pavlova was a famous ballet dancer.

My independence and **privacy** would not allow me to accept help. I lowered my arms and balanced my hands on the

equilibrium balance	**impresario** someone who manages or directs a show	**predicament** a problem
extremities limbs of the body; legs		**privacy** desire to be alone
	incredulous not believing	**solicitude** concern

floor and jerked my right foot. It held on to the pipe, so I jerked again. I must have been in excellent shape. The pipe came away from the stove, and gas hissed out steadily like ten fat men resting on a summer's day.

R.L. stepped over me and looked down into the gas jet. . . . He **swiveled** over to the window and opened it as wide as it would go, then back down to the stove. Near the wall at the end of the pipe, he found a tap and turned it. The hissing died and the thick sweetish odor **diluted**.

I had still to **extricate** my other leg from the avaricious table.

Avaricious means greedy. Here, the table didn't want to give up Rita's leg.

R.L. lifted an edge of the table, and my ankle was **miraculously** free. I could have gotten up, but my feelings were so hurt by the stupid clumsiness that I just rolled over on my stomach, beat my hands on the floor and cried like a baby.

There was no doubt that R.L. Poole had just witnessed his strangest **audition**. He could have walked down the hall and out the door, leaving me breathing in the dust of the ancient rug, but he didn't. I heard the chair creak, announcing that he had sat back down.

I was sure he was doing his best to hold in his laughter. I tried for more tears, to irritate him and force him to leave, but the tear **ducts** had closed and the sound I made was as false as a show girl's eyelashes. Nothing for it but to get up.

I dried my face with dusty hands and lifted my head. R.L. was sitting at the table in the same chair, his head propped up with his hand. The dark-brown face was **somber** and he said quietly, "Well, anyway, you've got nice legs."

Do you think Rita got the job?

---

audition a tryout

dilute to water down; to make weak

duct an opening; a tube

extricate to untangle

miraculously magically

somber gloomy

swivel to turn suddenly

Directions Write the answers to these questions using complete sentences.

Comprehension: Identifying Facts

1. Who is R. L. Poole? Why does he come to see Rita?

2. What does Rita tell him she knows about dancing?

3. What happens when Rita tries to do a split?

Comprehension: Understanding Main Ideas

4. What does Rita want Poole to think of her? Why does she try to do a split for him?

5. How would you describe Poole's reaction to Rita's accident?

6. Angelou describes this embarrassing experience with a great deal of humor. How does she create humor in her writing?

Understanding Literature: Autobiography

An autobiography is the story of a person's life, written by the person. The author tells about events and about his or her reaction to these events. An autobiography is a deeply personal work. Authors decide which experiences were most important in shaping their lives.

As writers look back on certain events, they may see them differently than they did at the time they happened. Readers need to decide what the author's tone is toward the material. An experience that seemed earth-shaking at the time may be told using a humorous tone.

7. What do you think Angelou remembers most clearly about her first meeting with R. L. Poole? How does she show this in her writing?

8. What is the tone of this excerpt? What is Angelou's attitude toward her younger self? How do you know?

Critical Thinking

9. Have you ever tried so hard to impress someone that you embarrassed yourself? How does Angelou make her feelings clear to the reader?

10. What do you think happened after Rita's strange audition? Do you think she got the job? Why or why not?

Writing on Your Own Write a brief description about an event that happened when you were younger. Ask someone who was there to read it. Do they remember the event in the same way? Would they add or change any details? What does this tell you about autobiographies?

Helen Keller

1880–1968

Literary Terms

analogy a comparison between two otherwise different objects that share some of the same characteristics

autobiography the story of a person's life, written by that person

imagery the use of word pictures that appeal to the five senses

About the Author

Helen Keller led a normal life for her first nineteen months. Then, before her second birthday, she got very sick. As a result, she lost her sight and hearing. It was as if someone had drawn a curtain between her and the life she was just beginning to know.

Helen Keller's teacher, Anne Sullivan, was the person who drew that curtain aside. The two remained together until Sullivan's death in 1936. Anne Sullivan was herself partly blind from a childhood infection. She taught Helen by spelling words into her hand using a system she had learned at the famous Perkins Institution for the Blind in Boston.

Helen Keller went on to graduate from Radcliffe College. She became a famous writer and lecturer, raising money for the education of blind people and for other social causes. She published seven books, including *Out of the Dark* and *The Story of My Life*. Her meeting with Anne Sullivan and her triumph over great misfortune became the subject of a well-known play, *The Miracle Worker*.

About the Selection

Helen Keller's **autobiography**, *The Story of My Life*, appeared first as a series of monthly selections in *Ladies Home Journal*. At first, she typed on a regular typewriter. When she stopped, she had to remember the exact words she had ended with before she could begin again.

In this excerpt, Keller describes how her love for learning grew from roots planted and cared for by her teacher. She uses **analogies**, or word comparisons, to make this part of her life clear for her readers. Her writing is also rich in **imagery**, or word pictures. Since she was blind and deaf, her images call on the other senses, especially touch and smell.

from
The Story of My Life

As you read, notice how Helen Keller describes Anne Sullivan's teaching methods.

For a long time I had no regular lessons. Even when I studied most earnestly it seemed more like play than work. Everything Miss Sullivan taught me she **illustrated** by a beautiful story or a poem. Whenever anything delighted or interested me she talked it over with me just as if she were a little girl herself. What many children think of with dread, as a painful plodding through grammar, hard sums and harder definitions, is today one of my most precious memories. . . .

We read and studied out of doors, preferring the sunlit woods to the house. All my early lessons have in them the breath of the woods—the fine, **resinous** odour of pine needles, blended with the perfume of wild grapes. Seated in the gracious shade of a wild tulip tree, I learned to think that everything has a lesson and a suggestion. "The loveliness of things taught me all their use." Indeed, everything that could hum, or buzz, or sing, or bloom, had a part in my education—noisy-throated frogs, katydids and crickets held in my hand until, forgetting their **embarrassment,** they **trilled** their reedy note, little downy chickens and wildflowers, the dogwood blossoms, meadow-violets and budding

Anne Sullivan became Helen Keller's teacher in 1887, shortly before Helen was seven years old.

embarrassment self-consciousness

illustrate to show; to picture

resin a sticky, yellow or brown substance that flows from some trees

trill two alternating musical tones

fruit trees. I felt the bursting cotton-bolls and fingered their soft fiber and fuzzy seeds; I felt the low **soughing** of the wind through the cornstalks, the silky rustling of the long leaves, and the indignant snort of my pony, as we caught him in the pasture and put the bit in his mouth—ah me! how well I remember the spicy, clovery smell of his breath! . . .

Our favourite walk was to Keller's Landing, an old tumble-down lumber-wharf on the Tennessee River, used during the Civil War to land soldiers. There we spent many happy hours and played at learning geography. I built dams of pebbles, made islands and lakes, and dug river-beds, all for fun, and never dreamed that I was learning a lesson. I listened with increasing wonder to Miss Sullivan's descriptions of the great round world with its burning mountains, buried cities, moving rivers of ice, and many other things as strange. She made raised maps in clay, so that I could feel the mountain ridges and valleys, and follow with my fingers the **devious** course of rivers. . . .

Notice all the sensory images in this paragraph.

Arithmetic seems to have been the only study I did not like. From the first I was not interested in the science of numbers. Miss Sullivan tried to teach me to count by stringing beads in groups, and by arranging kindergarten straws I learned to add and subtract. I never had patience to arrange more than five or six groups at a time. When I had accomplished this my conscience was at rest for the day, and I went out quickly to find my playmates. . . .

Once there were eleven tadpoles in a glass globe set in a window full of plants. I remember the eagerness with which I made discoveries about them. It was great fun to plunge my hand into the bowl and feel the tadpoles frisk about, and to let them slip and slide between my fingers. One day a more **ambitious** fellow leaped beyond the edge of the bowl and fell on the floor, where I found him to all appearance more dead than alive. The only sign of life was a slight wriggling of his tail. But no sooner had he returned to his element than he darted to the bottom, swimming round and round in joyous

---

ambitious determined   **devious** crooked; sly   **sough** to sigh or moan

Hellen Keller graduated *cum laude* from Radcliffe College in 1904.

Trace this analogy between a shallow brook and a child's mind. What does each reflect? How do the reflections change when the brook becomes a deep river? How does a human mind change as it is educated?

activity. He had made his leap, he had seen the great world, and was content to stay in his pretty glass house under the big fuchsia tree until he attained the dignity of froghood. Then he went to live in the leafy pool at the end of the garden, where he made the summer nights musical with his quaint love-song.

Thus I learned from life itself. At the beginning I was only a little mass of possibilities. It was my teacher who unfolded and developed them. When she came, everything about me breathed of love and joy and was full of meaning. She has never since let pass an opportunity to point out the beauty that is in everything, nor has she ceased trying in thought and action and example to make my life sweet and useful.

It was my teacher's genius, her quick sympathy, her loving **tact** which made the first years of my education so beautiful. It was because she seized the right moment to **impart** knowledge that made it so pleasant and acceptable to me. She realized that a child's mind is like a shallow brook which ripples and dances merrily over the stony course of its education and reflects here a flower, there a bush, yonder a fleecy cloud; and she attempted to guide my mind on its way, knowing that like a brook it should be fed by mountain streams and hidden springs, until it broadened out into a deep river, capable of reflecting in its **placid** surface, billowy hills, the **luminous** shadows of trees and the blue heavens, as well as the sweet face of a little flower.

impart to tell; to make known

luminous filled with light

placid calm; peaceful

tact skill and grace in dealing with others

Directions Write the answers to these questions using complete sentences.

Comprehension: Identifying Facts

1. Where do Helen Keller and her teacher read and study?

2. What smells does Helen remember from her lessons? What does she remember touching?

3. What happens to the tadpole that leaps out of the bowl?

Comprehension: Understanding Main Ideas

4. Why is it so valuable for Helen Keller to study outside, in the woods?

5. What does Keller learn from the tadpoles she keeps in a glass globe?

6. Keller writes that "everything that could hum, or buzz, or sing, or bloom" taught her something. How could this be, since she was deaf and blind?

Understanding Literature: Analogies

An analogy is a comparison between two things. The two things are alike in some ways, but are mainly different from each other. Writers use analogies to explain an unfamiliar thing by comparing it to something familiar.

Helen Keller uses the image of a shallow brook growing into a deep river as an analogy for a child's mind as it learns about the world. The brook and the child's mind are very different. However, the child's mind grows when new information is added. This education, Keller is saying, is like what happens to a brook when it is fed by "mountain streams and hidden springs."

7. In your own words, what is an analogy?

8. What do readers learn from Keller's analogy comparing a child's mind with a shallow brook?

Critical Thinking

9. What would you say made Anne Sullivan such a wonderful teacher?

10. Not once in this selection does Keller mention being blind and deaf. Why do you think she leaves out that information?

> **Writing on Your Own** Helen Keller did not describe how things looked because she could not see. She could touch, smell, taste, and also feel vibrations. Select a paragraph from this selection and add details that Keller might have included if she could see.

Into Thin Air
Jon Krakauer

About the Author

Jon Krakauer had an unusual childhood hero: Willi Unsoeld. Unsoeld, a friend of Jon's father, was part of the first American climbing expedition to Mount Everest. He helped Krakauer climb his first mountain when he was only eight years old.

After college, Jon Krakauer became, in his own words, a "climbing bum." He worked some of the time as a carpenter and climbed the rest of the time. Often, he was asked to write articles about his adventures.

In 1996, *Outside* Magazine asked him to write a story about a new business. Companies had been set up to guide people to the top of Mount Everest, the highest mountain in the world. These people, some of whom had never climbed before, paid as much as $65,000 for this experience. Krakauer was to see what this alarming business was all about.

About the Selection

Near Everest, Krakauer joined a group of climbers led by Andy Harris, one of the best guides in the business. Krakauer took careful notes in **diary** form, both in base camp and as they climbed. One danger in climbing is the lack of oxygen or *hypoxia*. At high altitudes, the air is very thin. Breathing is difficult. Climbers can lose awareness and judgment. Just as part of Krakauer's group was "summiting," or reaching the top, a terrible storm hit the mountain. Before it was over, four of the climbers in his group were dead. *Into Thin Air* is Krakauer's **personal account** of what turned out to be Everest's deadliest climbing season ever.

Krakauer uses many of the same techniques used in fiction to tell his story. His writing is filled with **irony**, **suspense**, and **conflict**. This excerpt includes all three. Krakauer tells how the accomplishment of reaching the summit quickly turned to disaster.

Jon Krakauer
1954–

Literary Terms

conflict the struggle of the protagonist against himself or herself, another person, or nature

diary a daily record of events and feelings

irony the difference between what is expected to happen in a story and what does happen

personal account a nonfiction narrative about an experience, told by a person who lived through it

suspense a quality in a story that makes the reader uncertain or nervous about what will happen next

from Into Thin Air

Mount Everest is on the border between Tibet and Nepal in the Himalayas. At 29,028 feet, it is the highest mountain in the world.

from Chapter Thirteen
Southeast Ridge
May 10, 1996
27,600 feet

Bottled oxygen does not make the top of Everest feel like sea level. Climbing above the South Summit with my regulator delivering just under two liters of oxygen per minute, I had to stop and draw three or four lungfuls of air after each **ponderous** step. Then I'd take one more step and have to pause for another four heaving breaths—and this was the fastest pace I could manage. Because the oxygen systems we were using delivered a lean mix of **compressed** gas and **ambient** air, 29,000 feet with gas felt like **approximately** 26,000 feet without gas. But the bottled oxygen **conferred** other benefits that weren't so easily quantified.

Climbing along the blade of the summit ridge, sucking gas into my ragged lungs, I enjoyed a strange, **unwarranted** sense of calm. The world beyond the rubber mask was **stupendously** vivid but seemed not quite real, as if a movie were being projected in slow motion across the front of my goggles. I felt

Climbing Mount Everest is a classic conflict between human beings and nature. As you read, notice how Krakauer explains the two "sides" of the contest.

---

ambient surrounding on all sides

approximately nearly

compressed compact, dense

confer to supply

ponderous heavy

stupendously amazingly

unwarranted uncalled-for

drugged, **disengaged,** thoroughly **insulated** from **external stimuli.** I had to remind myself over and over that there was 7,000 feet of sky on either side, that everything was at stake here, that I would pay for a single bungled step with my life.

Half an hour above the South Summit I arrived at the foot of the Hillary Step. One of the most famous pitches in all of mountaineering, its forty feet of near-vertical rock and ice looked **daunting,** but—as any serious climber would—I'd wanted very badly to take the "sharp end" of the rope and lead the Step. It was clear, however, that Boukreev, Beidleman, and Harris all felt the same way, and it was hypoxic **delusion** on my part to think that any of them was going to let a client hog such a **coveted** lead.

In the end, Boukreev—as senior guide and the only one of us who had climbed Everest previously—claimed the honor; with Beidleman paying out the rope, he did a masterful job of leading the pitch. But it was a slow process, and as he painstakingly ascended toward the crest of the Step, I nervously studied my watch and wondered whether I might run out of oxygen. My first canister had expired at 7:00 A.M. on the Balcony, after lasting about seven hours. Using this as a benchmark, at the South Summit I'd calculated that my second canister would expire around 2:00 P.M., which I stupidly assumed would allow plenty of time to reach the summit and return to the South Summit to retrieve my third oxygen bottle. But now it was already after 1:00, and I was beginning to have serious doubts. . . .

The Hillary Step is named for Sir Edmund Hillary of New Zealand. In 1953, he and Tenzing Norgay of Nepal were the first to reach the summit of Everest. A *pitch* is a slope. The summit lies about 20 to 30 minutes beyond the Hillary Step.

Notice how Krakauer builds suspense.

covet to want	**disengage** to pull away	**stimuli** agents of change or activity
daunting frightening	**external** outside	
delusion a trick; an error	**insulated** protected from	

Plodding slowly up the last few steps to the summit, I had the sensation of being underwater, of life moving at quarter speed. And then I found myself atop a slender wedge of ice, **adorned** with a discarded oxygen cylinder and a battered aluminum survey pole, with nowhere higher to climb. A string of Buddhist prayer flags snapped furiously in the wind. Far below, down a side of the mountain I had never laid eyes on, the dry Tibetan plateau stretched to the horizon as a boundless **expanse** of dun-colored earth.

Reaching the top of Everest is supposed to trigger a **surge** of intense **elation**; against long odds, after all, I had just attained a goal I'd coveted since childhood. But the summit was really only the halfway point. Any impulse I might have felt toward self-congratulation was **extinguished** by **overwhelming apprehension** about the long, dangerous descent that lay ahead.

The summit is less than 10 feet in diameter.

To Buddhists and Hindus of Tibet and Nepal, Everest is a sacred mountain. The Tibetans call it *Chomolungma*— Mother Goddess of the World.

Krakauer's feelings upon reaching the summit are ironic. Instead of happiness, he fears the *descent*, or downward journey.

Everest Summit 29,028 feet

The Hillary Step

The South Summit

The Balcony 27,600 feet

Camp Four 26,000 feet

adorned decorated

apprehension fear, dread

elation great happiness

expanse something vast, spread out

extinguish to put out

overwhelming extreme

surge a rush or flow

Krakauer is dazed and confused—*punch drunk*—because of lack of oxygen.

A storm has begun. The suspense builds as Krakauer fights his way back down to camp.

from Chapter Fourteen
Summit
1:12 P.M., May 10, 1996
29, 028 feet

From the Balcony I descended a few hundred feet down a broad, gentle snow gully without incident, but then things began to get sketchy. The route **meandered** through outcroppings of broken shale blanketed with six inches of fresh snow. **Negotiating** the puzzling, **infirm** terrain demanded unceasing concentration, an all-but-impossible feat in my punch-drunk state. . . .

I sat down to rest on a broad, sloping ledge, but after a few minutes a deafening BOOM! frightened me back to my feet. Enough new snow had accumulated that I feared a massive slab avalanche had released on the slopes above, but when I spun around to look I saw nothing. Then there was another BOOM!, accompanied by a flash that momentarily lit up the sky, and I realized I was hearing the crash of thunder.

In the morning, on the way up, I'd made a point of continually studying the route on this part of the mountain, frequently looking down to pick out **landmarks** that would be helpful on the descent, **compulsively** memorizing the terrain: "Remember to turn left at the **buttress** that looks like a ship's prow. Then follow that skinny line of snow until it curves sharply to the right." This was something I'd trained myself to do many years earlier, a drill I forced myself to go through every time I climbed, and on Everest it may have saved my life. By 6:00 P.M., as the storm **escalated** into a full-scale

buttress part of a mountain that sticks out

compulsively unable to stop

escalate to get stronger

infirm not solid or stable

landmark a marker that shows location

meander to wander

negotiate to manage

blizzard with driving snow and winds gusting in excess of 60 knots, I came upon the rope that had been fixed by the Montenegrins on the snow slope 600 feet above the Col. Sobered by the force of the rising **tempest,** I realized that I'd gotten down the trickiest ground just in the nick of time.

Wrapping the fixed line around my arms to rappel, I continued down through the blizzard. Some minutes later I was overwhelmed by a disturbingly familiar feeling of **suffocation,** and I realized that my oxygen had once again run out. Three hours earlier when I'd attached my regulator to my third and last oxygen canister, I'd noticed that the **gauge** indicated that the bottle was only half full. I'd figured that would be enough to get me most of the way down, though, so I hadn't bothered exchanging it for a full one. And now the gas was gone.

I pulled the mask from my face, left it hanging around my neck, and pressed onward, surprisingly unconcerned. However, without **supplemental** oxygen, I moved more slowly, and I had to stop and rest more often. . . .

I was so far beyond ordinary exhaustion that I experienced a queer **detachment** from my body, as if I were observing my descent from a few feet overhead. I imagined that I was dressed in a green cardigan and wingtips. And although the gale was generating a windchill in excess of seventy below zero Fahrenheit, I felt strangely, disturbingly warm.

At 6:30, as the last of the daylight seeped from the sky, I'd descended to within 200 vertical feet of Camp Four. Only one obstacle now stood between me and safety: a bulging incline of hard, glassy ice that I would have to descend without a rope. Snow pellets **borne** by 70-knot gusts stung my face; any exposed flesh was instantly frozen. The tents, no more than 650 horizontal feet away, were only **intermittently** visible through the whiteout. There was no margin for error.

Montenegro is part of the former Yugoslavia. A *col* is a pass.

To *rappel* is to descend by sliding down a rope passed under one thigh, across the body, and over the opposite shoulder.

Wingtips are fancy, pointed shoes. Krakauer's mind is playing tricks on him.

Climbers begin their summit attempt at midnight, hoping to reach the summit by noon. It takes four to six hours to descend from the summit back to Camp Four.

borne carried

detachment a separation from

gauge a device for measuring

intermittently off and on

suffocation not being able to breathe

supplemental additional, extra

tempest a bad storm

Worried about making a critical blunder, I sat down to **marshal** my energy before descending further.

Once I was off my feet, **inertia** took hold. It was so much easier to remain at rest than to summon the **initiative** to tackle the dangerous ice slope; so I just sat there as the storm roared around me, letting my mind drift, doing nothing for perhaps forty-five minutes.

I'd tightened the drawstrings on my hood until only a tiny opening remained around my eyes, and I was removing the useless, frozen oxygen mask from beneath my chin when Andy Harris suddenly appeared out of the gloom beside me. Shining my headlamp in his direction, I reflectively **recoiled** when I saw the **appalling** condition of his face. His cheeks were coated with an armor of frost, one eye was frozen shut, and he was **slurring** his words badly. He looked in serious trouble. "Which way to the tents?" Andy blurted, frantic to reach shelter.

I pointed in the direction of Camp Four, then warned him about the ice just below us. "It's steeper than it looks!" I yelled, straining to make myself heard over the tempest. "Maybe I should go down first and get a rope from camp—" As I was in midsentence, Andy **abruptly** turned away and moved over the lip of the ice slope, leaving me sitting there dumbfounded.

Scooting on his butt, he started down the steepest part of the incline. "Andy," I shouted after him, "it's crazy to try it like that! You're going to blow it for sure!" He yelled something back, but his words were carried off by the screaming wind. A second later he lost his purchase, . . . and was suddenly rocketing headfirst down the ice.

Two hundred feet below, I could just make out Andy's motionless form slumped at the foot of the incline. I was sure he'd broken at least a leg, maybe his neck. But then, incredibly, he stood up, waved that he was O.K., and started

Krakauer does not discover until later that this climber was not Andy Harris, his guide. Andy Harris died on the mountain.

abruptly suddenly, without warning	**inertia** not able to move	**recoil** to draw back in horror
appalling dreadful	**initiative** drive; energy	**slur** to leave out or substitute sounds
	marshal to collect	

lurching toward Camp Four, which, at the moment was in plain sight, 500 feet beyond.

I could see the shadowy forms of three or four people standing outside the tents; their headlamps flickered through curtains of blowing snow. I watched Harris walk toward them across the flats, a distance he covered in less than ten minutes. When the clouds closed in a moment later, cutting off my view, he was within sixty feet of the tents, maybe closer. I didn't see him again after that, but I was certain that he'd reached the **security** of camp, where Chuldum and Arita would doubtless be waiting with hot tea. Sitting out in the storm, with the ice bulge still standing between me and the tents, I felt a pang of envy. I was angry that my guide hadn't waited for me.

My backpack held little more than three empty oxygen canisters and a pint of frozen lemonade; it probably weighed no more than sixteen or eighteen pounds. But I was tired, and worried about getting down the incline without breaking a leg, so I tossed the pack over the edge and hoped it would come to rest where I could retrieve it. Then I stood up and started down the ice, which was as smooth and hard as the surface of a bowling ball.

Fifteen minutes of **dicey**, fatiguing crampon work brought me safely to the bottom of the incline, where I easily located my pack, and another ten minutes after that I was in camp myself. I lunged into my tent with my crampons still on, zipped the door tight, and sprawled across the frost-covered floor too tired to even sit upright. For the first time I had a sense of how wasted I really was: I was more exhausted than I'd ever been in my life. But I was safe. Andy was safe. The others would be coming into camp soon. We'd . . . done it. We'd climbed Everest. It had been a little sketchy there for a while, but in the end everything had turned out great.

It would be many hours before I learned that everything had not in fact turned out great—that nineteen men and women were stranded up on the mountain by the storm, caught in a desperate struggle for their lives.

Camp Four, at 26,000 feet, is in a windy, lonely pass the size of a football field. The air above this altitude is dangerously thin.

Crampons are climbing irons—steel spikes attached to the climber's boots.

dicey risky   **security** safety

Into Thin Air
Jon Krakauer

Directions Write the answers to these questions using complete sentences.

Comprehension: Identifying Facts

1. Why does Krakauer climb so slowly above the South Summit of Everest?

2. How does the "lean mix" of oxygen he gets make him feel?

3. What is the Hillary Step?

4. Why is Boukreev given the honor of leading the climb over the Step?

5. How high is the summit of Mount Everest?

6. Why does Krakauer have trouble finding his way down from the summit?

7. What does he hear after he sits down to rest?

8. After he runs out of oxygen, how does he feel?

9. What is the last obstacle Krakauer faces to get back to camp?

10. How does Andy Harris get by this obstacle?

Comprehension: Understanding Main Ideas

11. How does Krakauer feel when he finally reaches the summit?

12. Climbing mountains like Everest is made even more dangerous by the thin air at such high altitudes. How does Krakauer make his readers aware of this danger?

13. Why does Krakauer nervously study his watch as he and his party ascend the Step? How does his concern help build suspense in his writing?

14. What is ironic about Krakauer's feelings when he reaches the summit?

15. Krakauer makes his way back from the summit alone. What does this say about him as a person?

16. What do you learn about the storm that hits just as Krakauer begins his descent?

17. How does Krakauer's habit of memorizing the terrain as he climbs save his life on Everest?

18. Why could it be said that Andy Harris's sudden appearance after Krakauer has been sitting in the storm for nearly an hour helped save Krakauer's life?

19. Why do you think Krakauer chooses to rappel down the ice slope using his crampons, when Andy Harris just slides down?

20. What is ironic about Krakauer's thoughts when he reaches his tent?

Understanding Literature: Personal Account

A personal account is a narrative, or story, about an event told by a person who lived through it. Personal accounts are nonfiction, but authors shape events as they remember them. When more than one person has an experience, each may see the event in a different way.

Jon Krakauer's story of this Everest expedition first appeared as a magazine article. After it came out, several other survivors of the expedition complained that Krakauer had not been entirely truthful. He had not written the story in exactly the way others remembered it. He had, however, written it as well and as truthfully as he could.

21. Why might two people who shared an experience tell different stories of what happened?

22. How do you think an account of this expedition by one of the professional guides might be different from Krakauer's account?

23. What are some ways readers can tell this selection is a personal account?

24. Why do you think people like to read personal accounts about dangerous adventures like this one?

25. What challenges do you think the author faced in writing this account?

Critical Thinking

26. What is surprising about Krakauer's feelings when he reaches the summit of Mount Everest?

27. How might you compare reaching the top of Mount Everest with standing on the surface of the moon?

28. Do you think you would like to be Jon Krakauer's friend? Explain.

29. What else would you like to know about this part of the expedition, other than what Krakauer tells you?

30. There have been about 4,000 attempts to climb Mount Everest. Fewer than 700 climbers have succeeded. Why do you think people are driven to attempt such a dangerous experience? If you had a chance to climb Everest, would you?

Writing on Your Own Imagine that you are a weather observer at the foot of Mount Everest. Write a weather bulletin advising climbers that you have just spotted a large storm approaching. Use details from Krakauer's account to describe the weather climbers might expect.

Imagery

Authors use imagery to appeal to readers' five senses. Images in literature are most often visual—creating mental pictures that help us see an essay, story, or poem more completely. For example, in the excerpt from *Into Thin Air*, Jon Krakauer presents the visual image he himself had while suffering from altitude sickness. He pictured himself looking ridiculous, climbing the mountain in a sweater and wingtip shoes. Sharing this image helps readers understand his mental state. In "Of Dry Goods and Black Bow Ties," the visual image of Mr. Shimada is important. We need to see him in his "spotless black alpaca suit, an immaculate white shirt and a white collar so stiff it might have overcome a lesser man."

Authors also create images appealing to the other senses. Rudolfo Anaya remembers the powerful smells of earth and sweat when he describes his grandfather. Helen Keller writes of the "spicy, clovery smell" of her pony's breath. In the excerpt from Maya Angelou's *Gather Together in My Name*, the only sound readers *hear* after Rita's attempt to impress Mr. Poole is the gas "hiss[ing] out steadily like ten fat men

resting on a summer's day." The image shows how ridiculous Rita felt at that point.

In appealing to the five senses, writers add realistic details that help readers become involved on more than one level.

Review

1. In your own words, explain what imagery in literature is.

2. Why do authors use imagery?

3. To which sense does this image appeal? "I felt the bursting cotton-bolls and fingered their soft fiber and fuzzy seeds."

4. List three other images used in the selections in this unit. Explain to which sense each appeals.

5. Find an image from this unit that you think is especially powerful. Explain your choice.

Writing on Your Own Write a paragraph describing a baby. Use images that appeal to each of the five senses.

UNIT 6 SUMMARY

Nonfiction includes every form of prose writing that concerns real people, facts, and true experiences. Unlike fiction, nonfiction doesn't have to have a plot, character development, setting, or theme. Writers present and shape real events as their memory and understanding demand.

The purpose of a nonfiction work may be to explain, persuade, tell, describe, entertain, or to do several of these at once. Writers use many of the techniques of fiction—suspense, irony, imagery, symbols, conflict, repetition, humor— but readers expect nonfiction to be about real events that happened to real people.

Biographies and autobiographies, true accounts of people's lives, are popular forms of nonfiction. Another popular form is the essay, a short nonfiction work on any subject. Nonfiction narratives tell true stories, usually in chronological order. Personal accounts, which can be longer than essays, are written by people who have had experiences they want to explain.

Nonfiction books and essays are as popular as fiction. Readers turn to nonfiction for many reasons. One is the desire to understand human experience and the world through facts and their interpretation.

Selections

■ The excerpt from Thor Heyerdahl's book *Kon-Tiki*, the story of a 4,000-mile trip across the Pacific by raft, describes a strange encounter with a real-life sea monster.

■ In his reflective essay "A Celebration of Grandfathers," Rudolfo Anaya honors his grandfather, his Mexican-American traditions, and all old people.

■ Yoshiko Uchida's biographical essay, "Of Dry Goods and Black Bow Ties," gives readers a glimpse into the life of Japanese immigrants to the United States. The rise and fall of Mr. Shimada's fortunes did not cause him to lose his dignity.

■ In the excerpt from Maya Angelou's autobiography, *Gather Together in My Name*, the author looks back with humor at an embarrassing moment.

■ Helen Keller, in the excerpt from her autobiography, *The Story of My Life*, describes how her gifted teacher, Anne Sullivan, awakened her to the joys of learning about the world.

■ In the excerpt from *Into Thin Air*, Jon Krakauer's personal account of a Mount Everest expedition that turned deadly, readers get a vivid sense of what it means to risk your life for an adventure.

Directions Write the answers to these questions using complete sentences.

Comprehension: Identifying Facts

1. What are some forms of nonfiction literature?

2. What is meant by the purpose of a nonfiction work?

3. What is a reflective essay?

4. For what reasons do authors write essays?

5. What is an excerpt?

Comprehension: Understanding Main Ideas

6. In what basic ways is nonfiction different from fiction?

7. What do readers expect from nonfiction literature?

8. How does a reflective essay differ from a biographical essay?

9. What is the difference between an autobiography, a biography, and a personal account?

10. How is a nonfiction narrative different from a short story, even though they may tell a very similar story?

Understanding Literature: Essays

Many essays follow a pattern: introduction, body, and conclusion. In the introduction, usually the first paragraph, authors may announce or suggest their purpose for writing. The body of the essay includes paragraphs that support the purpose. The conclusion sums up the essay's major ideas. The conclusion may also include the author's opinion or view of the topic.

Although this order works for many authors, others have used different patterns. Their purposes for writing may not fit into a three-part pattern. When they want to communicate clearly with readers, modern essay writers are often more concerned with content than with following a pattern.

11. Which essays or excerpts in this unit have the basic three-part pattern: introduction, body, conclusion?

12. Which essays or excerpts use different patterns?

13. Other than their order, what else is similar about the pieces with introductions, bodies, and conclusions (e.g., their subject matter, their purpose)?

14. What do you see that is similar in the other essays or excerpts?

15. Which is more important to you as a reader: the pattern or content? Why?

Critical Thinking

16. Some people say that calling nonfiction anything that is "not fiction" is like calling Shakespeare's plays "not novels." Do you think it is useful to call so many types of writing "nonfiction"? Explain.

17. Why do you think Rudolfo Anaya decided to write about his grandfather within a reflective essay, rather than writing a biographical essay about him, as Yoshiko Uchida does about Mr. Shimada?

18. Why do you think people still like to write and read essays—more than 400 years since this literary form was invented?

19. Would you rather read nonfiction or fiction? Why?

20. Which selection in this unit do you enjoy reading the most? What makes this work especially interesting to you?

Speak and Listen

Choose one of the selections in this unit. Make a list of questions to ask people in your class about their reactions to this work. Interview several people. Present what you learn in an oral presentation.

Beyond Words

Helen Keller learned geography from the clay maps that Anne Sullivan made for her. In this spirit, create a work of art that could be appreciated by a person who is blind. Experiment with a blindfold to see if your creation has meaning to someone who cannot see.

Writing on Your Own

Diaries and journals are important forms of nonfiction writing. Keep a personal diary or journal for a week. Each day, write down a few sentences about what happens and what it means to you. Be sure to date each entry.

Test-Taking Tip

Look for specifics in each test question that tell you in what form your answer is to be. For example, some questions ask for a paragraph, and others may require only a sentence.

"To read a poem is to hear it with our eyes; to hear it is to see it with our ears."

—Octavio Paz, *Alternating Current*, 1967

"I don't go get a poem. It calls me and I accept it."

—Lucille Clifton, *A View From the Loft*, 1994

Tulip Field in Arles,
Tsing-Fang Chen

UNIT 7 *Poetry*

Poets express ideas, share memories, create beautiful or startling images, or entertain. Poetry is a short form of literature that has its own forms and depends on certain rhythms. Poets, more than most prose writers, must pay close attention to both the sound and the meaning of each word. They use writing tools that help them get the most out of every word. Poetry is known for creating powerful or beautiful impressions with words.

In this unit, you will meet poets from many parts of the world and from many life experiences. You will read poems in four groups: ballads and songs, rhyme and rhythm, imagery, and voices.

UNIT 7 ■ ABOUT POETRY

The first thing readers notice about most poems is that they look different from prose. Although one poem can look very different from another, in general we can say that poetry is literature in verse form. That is, poems have particular kinds of rhythm and are often divided into stanzas. A stanza is a group of lines that forms a unit of a poem. Poetry is also known for painting powerful or beautiful impressions with words.

Like all writers, poets want to communicate ideas and impressions. They have a purpose and they want to entertain readers or get them thinking. However, compared with most prose literature, poems are short. Poets have to condense their ideas. Each word they select has to be exactly right.

Writers of both prose and poetry use many "tools of the trade" to communicate in words. Because poets try to get the most out of few words, they use these tools, or techniques, more often. As you'll see in the Writer's Tool Chest that follows, the poet's tools depend on the fact that each word has both sound and meaning. As babies, we learn about the sounds of words. As we grow older, we learn that those sounds have meaning. We come to know that the sounds making up the word *parade* mean a group of people marching, often as part of a celebration. We also learn that we can use the same word in different ways to mean different things. For example:

Pilar marched in the Founder's Day <u>*Parade*</u>.

Diego and his bears <u>*parade*</u> *through the yard every morning.*

Writers—poets especially—are very aware of both the sound and the meaning of words. Poets often use sound to create mood and meaning. They use techniques such as alliteration—repeating beginning sounds—and onomatopoeia—words that sound like their meaning. They expand the meanings of words with techniques you've met before in prose, tools such as imagery and figurative language.

As mentioned, poetry takes a different form than prose. Short stories, novels, and other kinds of prose are written in sentences and paragraphs. Poets usually use another structure. They use lines instead of sentences, and stanzas instead of paragraphs.

Within that general structure, poets often use patterns of rhyming words. Rhyming words are words that end in the same sound. For example *bit* and *wit* are rhyming words. Both end with the *it* sound. Some kinds of poems have specific rules of rhyme and rhythm. For example, limericks are five-line poems, usually humorous, with a certain pattern of rhyming words at the end of each line. In a limerick, the first, second, and fifth lines of the poem rhyme. The third and fourth lines have a different rhyme. We show the pattern by giving rhyming lines the same letter. For example, the rhyming pattern of a limerick is shown by *a a b b a*.

There are many kinds of rhyme, but many poems don't rhyme at all. Poems can also have a special rhythm. Rhythm is the pattern created by the stressed (accented) and unstressed (unaccented) syllables in a line of poetry. However, poets do not necessarily have to use rhythm either.

If all this is true, then what makes poetry *poetry*? People have been trying to answer that question for many years. The American poet Robert Frost said that poetry is what gets lost in the translation. What he meant was that a poem is not just a string of words. It is a personal impression of what those words together mean to the poet and to each reader.

The poems in this unit have been grouped into four sections: ballads and songs, rhyme and rhythm, imagery, and voices. Within each section are poems with very different tones, purposes, forms, and techniques. You'll meet poets from many ethnic groups, writing from a wide range of life experiences.

Que Pasa en el Fondo, **Maria Angelica Ruiz-Tagle**

A Writer's Tool Chest

Tools that Use the Meaning of Words

Imagery the use of word pictures that appeal to the five senses

Example: *December. Frost crackling*
Beneath my steps, my breath
Before me, then gone,

These words paint a word picture of winter. Readers *hear* the crackling frost, *see* a puff of breath, and *feel* the cold air. In this way, the poet allows readers to hear, see, and feel winter.

Figurative Language language that uses word pictures to compare or describe, and that is not meant to be taken literally

Example: *In the August grass*
Struck by the last rays of sun
The cracked teacup screams.

In this example, the poet has a cracked teacup screaming, an image that is not meant to be taken literally. The language gives readers a sense of strangeness, danger, and violence. It is hot (*August*), and when the sun's last rays strike the cracked teacup, it *screams*. Figurative language usually includes metaphor, simile, personification, and hyperbole.

Metaphor a figure of speech that says one thing *is* another

Example: *Hold fast to dreams*
For if dreams die
Life is a broken-winged bird
That cannot fly.

In this example, life without dreams is compared to a bird with broken wings.

Personification giving characters such as animals and objects the characteristics of humans

Example: *Stormy, husky, brawling,*
City of the Big Shoulders:

In this example, the poet describes a city as if it were a person.

Simile a figure of speech in which two things are compared using a phrase that includes the words *like* or *as*

Example: *O, my luve's like a red, red rose,*
That's newly sprung in June,

In this example, the loved one is compared to a red rose that has just bloomed, using the word *like*.

Hyperbole using exaggeration to show that something is important

Example: *And I will luve thee still, my dear,*
Till a' the seas gang dry.

In this example, the lover says he will love his dear one until all the seas run dry. He overstates his case to prove his love.

Tools that Use the Sound of Words

Alliteration repeating sounds by using words whose beginning sounds are the same

Example: *Be the caller, the called,*
The singer, the song, and the sung.

In this example, the beginning *c* sounds are repeated in the first line. The beginning *s* sounds are repeated in the second line.

Assonance repeating sounds by using words with the same vowel sounds

Example: *We real cool. We*
Left school.

In this example, the *oo* vowel sound is repeated.

Onomatopoeia using words that sound like their meaning

Example: *How they tinkle, tinkle, tinkle,*
In the icy air of night!

In this example, the word *tinkle* sounds like the small, silver bells being described. *Tinkle* also means a series of short, high sounds from a bell. Other words that sound like their meaning are *buzz* and *hiss*.

Repetition using a word, phrase, or image more than once, for emphasis

Example: *this morning*
this morning
i met myself

Using this technique in a poem about an amazing experience reflects the speaker's excitement as she begins to tell her story.

Rhyme words that end with the same or similar sounds

Example: *'Twas brillig, and the slithy toves*
Did gyre and gimble in the wabe;
All mimsy were the borogoves,
And the mome raths outgrabe.

Despite the nonsense words, notice that the first and third lines and the second and fourth lines rhyme.

End rhyme a rhyming pattern in which the ends of lines contain the same sound

Example: *"Mother dear, may I go downtown*
Instead of out to play,
And march the streets of Birmingham
In a Freedom March today?"

The second and fourth lines of this poem show end rhyme.

Internal rhyme rhyme that occurs within one line of a poem. *Internal* means inside.

Example: *He left it dead, and with its head*
He went galumphing back.

Dead and *head* have the same ending sound. This means that they are rhyming words. Since both appear in the same line of the poem, they are an example of internal rhyme.

Rhyme scheme the pattern created by the ending sounds of the lines of a poem

Example: *Two roads diverged in a yellow wood,*   a
And sorry I could not travel both   b
And be one traveler, long I stood   a
And looked down one as far as I could a
To where it bent in the undergrowth;   b

The rhyme scheme for this poem is: **a b a a b**. This is a way of showing that the first, third, and fourth lines rhyme, and the second and fifth lines rhyme.

Rhythm a pattern created by the stressed and unstressed syllables in a line of poetry

Example: *As I walked out in the streets of Laredo,*
As I walked out in Laredo one day,

The rhythm pattern of these lines can be heard by breaking the words into syllables and reading the lines aloud, noticing which syllables you stress, or put the accent on:

*As **I** walked **OUT** in the **STREETS** of La-**RE**-do,*
(11 syllables)

*As **I** walked **OUT** in La-**RE**-do one **DAY**,*
(10 syllables)

Ballads and Songs

Robert Burns
1759–1796

Dudley Randall
1914–

Literary Terms

ballad a form of poetry
that tells a story, passed
from person to person,
often as a simple song
with rhyming words
and a refrain

dialect the speech of a
particular region of a
country, or of a certain
group of people

hyperbole using
exaggeration to show
that something is
important

poetry literature in
verse form that usually
has rhythm and paints
powerful or beautiful
impressions with
words

repetition using a
word, phrase, or image
more than once, for
emphasis

stanza a group of lines
that forms a unit in a
poem

About the Authors and Selections

Ballads and songs have long been popular forms of **poetry.** You may recall from Unit 3 that a ballad tells a story. Ballads usually use rhyming words. They often include **repetition,** words or phrases repeated at various places in the poem, sometimes as a refrain. The repetition calls attention to these words or phrases and helps create the poem's effect. Many ballads are arranged in four-line **stanzas.** A stanza is a group of lines that forms a unit in a poem.

Ballads and songs are part of the oral tradition of a culture, passed from person to person. "A Red, Red Rose" was first published as a song written by Robert Burns in the eighteenth century. The song is written in Burns's native Scots **dialect.** Among other language tools, Burns uses **hyperbole,** meaning exaggeration. Burns's other work includes "Auld Lang Syne," the song many people sing on New Year's Eve.

"The Streets of Laredo" is a traditional American ballad. We don't know who first told about the death of a cowboy in Laredo, Texas. Traditional folk ballads tell simple stories and probably were sung as well as spoken. "The Streets of Laredo" is a cowboy ballad about a young gambler shot in a "card house."

Ballads are still used by poets to tell new stories. In "Ballad of Birmingham," Dudley Randall tells the tragic true story of the 1963 bombing of a church in Birmingham, Alabama. Four young girls were killed. Randall's poem was also set to music and recorded. Many people first heard this chilling ballad as a song. The bombing horrified the American people and focused attention on the sometimes-violent struggle for civil rights.

Ellen Terry, **George Frederic Watts**

A Red, Red Rose

O, my luve's like a red, red rose,
That's newly sprung in June,
O, my luve's like the melodie,
4   That's sweetly play'd in tune.

As fair art thou, my bonnie lass,
So deep in luve am I,
And I will luve thee still, my dear,
8   Till a' the seas gang dry.

Till a' the seas gang dry, my dear,
And the rocks melt wi' the sun!
And I will luve thee still, my dear,
12   While the sands o' life shall run.

And fare thee weel, my only luve,
And fare thee weel a while!
And I will come again, my luve,
16   Tho' it were ten thousand mile!

—*Robert Burns*

Notice the two similes used by the speaker to describe his love (*luve*).

A *bonnie lass* is a pretty girl. *A'* means all. *Gang* means go.

Weel means well.

The Streets of Laredo

As I walked out in the streets of Laredo,
As I walked out in Laredo one day,
I spied a poor cowboy wrapped up in white linen,
4 Wrapped in white linen as cold as the clay.

Oh, beat the drums slowly, and play the fife lowly,
Play the dead march as you carry me along,
Take me to the green valley, there lay the sod o'er me,
8 For I'm a young cowboy, and I know I've done wrong.

Let sixteen **gamblers** come handle my **coffin,**
Let sixteen cowboys come sing me a song,
Take me to the graveyard, and lay the sod o'er me,
12 For I'm a poor cowboy, and I know I've done wrong.

It was once in the saddle I used to go dashing,
It was once in the saddle I used to go gay,
First to the dram house, and then to the card house,
16 Got shot in the breast, and I'm dying today.

Get six jolly cowboys to carry my coffin,
Get six pretty maidens to bear up my **pall,**
Put bunches of roses all over my coffin,
20 Put roses to deaden the sods as they fall.

Oh, bury me beside my knife and my six-shooter,
My spurs on my heel, my rifle by my side,
And over my coffin put a bottle of brandy,
24 That's the cowboy's drink, and carry me along.

We beat the drums slowly and played the fife lowly,
And bitterly wept as we bore him along,
For we all loved our comrade, so brave, young, and
    handsome,
28 We all loved our comrade, although he'd done wrong.

— *Traditional American Ballad*

There is a change of speakers between the first and second stanzas. Who is the speaker from here until the last stanza?

A *dram house* is a bar, or saloon. A *card house* is a place to gamble.

The Bolter, Charles M. Russell

coffin a box that holds a dead body

gambler someone who plays games for money

pall a coffin

Ballad of Birmingham

(On the bombing of a church in Birmingham, Alabama, 1963)

"Mother dear, may I go downtown
Instead of out to play,
And march the streets of Birmingham
4 In a Freedom March today?"

"No, baby, no, you may not go,
For the dogs are fierce and wild,
And clubs and hoses, guns and jails
8 Aren't good for a little child."

"But, mother, I won't be alone.
Other children will go with me,
And march the streets of Birmingham
12 To make our country free."

"No, baby, no, you may not go,
For I fear those guns will fire.
But you may go to church instead
16 And sing in the children's choir."

She has combed and brushed her night-dark hair,
And bathed rose petal sweet,
And drawn white gloves on her small brown hands,
20 And white shoes on her feet.

The mother smiled to know her child
Was in the sacred place,
But that smile was the last smile
24 To come upon her face.

For when she heard the explosion,
Her eyes grew wet and wild.
She raced through the streets of Birmingham
28 Calling for her child.

She clawed through bits of glass and brick,
Then lifted out a shoe.
"O, here's the shoe my baby wore,
32 But, baby, where are you?"

—Dudley Randall

In 1963, Dr. Martin Luther King, Jr., led nonviolent civil rights demonstrations—Freedom Marches—in Birmingham, Alabama. Demonstrators were met with attack dogs, tear gas, cattle prods, and fire hoses.

What is the irony in this poem?

Outside Sixth Avenue Baptist Church where funeral services were held for the bombing victims.

Ballads and Songs

Directions Write the answers to these questions using complete sentences.

Comprehension: Identifying Facts

1. To what two things does the poet compare his love ("luve") in Robert Burns's poem?

2. The poet gives three examples of how long he will love his "bonnie lass." What are the three?

3. Why does the poet say these words to his beloved? What does the last stanza mean?

4. What is the setting for "The Streets of Laredo"?

5. What is happening to the "poor cowboy"?

6. What requests does the cowboy make about his funeral and burial?

7. How did the cowboy die?

8. Who is the narrator of "Ballad of Birmingham"?

9. Why does the mother send her daughter to church, instead of to the Freedom March?

10. What happens to the young girl?

Comprehension: Understanding Main Ideas

11. From "A Writer's Tool Chest" on pages 354–355, find at least three tools used by Robert Burns in his poem. List each with an example.

12. Why do you think the lover uses exaggerated examples (hyperbole) about the strength of his love?

13. Why do you think the cowboy in "The Streets of Laredo" wants his funeral and burial to be as he describes them in the poem?

14. How do the townspeople in "The Streets of Laredo" feel about the young cowboy? Give some evidence.

15. What is the irony in "Ballad of Birmingham"? Irony is the difference between what is expected to happen and what does happen.

16. Why do you think Dudley Randall uses the ballad form to write about this tragic church bombing?

17. What is the mood of "A Red, Red Rose"? Compare it with the mood of "Ballad of Birmingham."

18. Both "The Streets of Laredo" and "Ballad of Birmingham" feature two different speakers. Who are they?

19. Which ballad in this section created the clearest pictures in your mind? How did the poet do that?

20. Repetition is important to ballads. Give an example of repetition from each poem in this section.

Understanding Literature: Rhythm

Rhythm in poetry is similar to rhythm in music. It is the beat behind the words. The rhythm of poetry is built on the syllables—the individual sounds—of words. For example, *umbrella* has three syllables, or beats: *um, brel,* and *la.* The second syllable—*brel*—is stressed, or accented. The first and third syllables are unstressed, or unaccented. We say *um-BREL-la.*

Poets often use special patterns of rhythm in their poetry to achieve certain effects.

21. How many syllables are in each line of the first stanza of "The Streets of Laredo"?

22. Which syllables are stressed?

23. Does this pattern of syllables continue throughout the ballad? Explain.

24. How does this pattern of syllables compare with the pattern of syllables in "Ballad of Birmingham"?

25. How does the rhythm—the pattern of syllables—in "Ballad of Birmingham" compare with the pattern of syllables in a song you particularly like?

Critical Thinking

26. Do all of these poems tell a story? Explain your thinking.

27. The narrator of "The Streets of Laredo," and the cowboy himself say the cowboy "done wrong." What do you think he did? Explain.

28. The speaker in Burns's poem compares his love to a rose and a melody. What would you use to compare with a person you love? Explain your choice.

29. Which songs that you listen to today tell a story, as the ballads in this section do? Describe the songs.

30. If you were going to write a ballad about a real event that was as important and terrible as the Birmingham church bombing, which event would you select? Why?

Writing on Your Own Write a ballad telling a story you think should be told. Include at least four stanzas. Use the poems in this section as models.

Rhyme and Rhythm

David McCord
1897–1997

Gwendolyn Brooks
1917–

About the Authors and Selections

The poems in this unit were selected to show you how poets create patterns of **rhyme** and **rhythm** in their work.

David McCord was a poet, essayist, and artist. He published 550 poems. Most of them were written for young readers. McCord's poem "Blesséd Lord, what it is to be young" uses a poetry pattern called the **limerick**. A limerick is a five-line poem. Its first, second, and fifth lines end with words that rhyme, or have the same sounds. Its third and fourth lines also end with rhyming words. Most limericks are light verse, written to amuse. McCord's poem is unusual, because it uses the limerick form for a serious purpose.

In 1950, Gwendolyn Brooks became the first African American to win a Pulitzer Prize (for *Annie Allen*, a verse narrative). She grew up in Chicago and most of her poetry is about African-American life. "WE REAL COOL" captures the rhythms of Chicago's pool halls and city streets, and of the young African-American men who make this world their own. The poem is made up of eight rhyming, three-word sentences. The jazzy style gives the last, shocking sentence a powerful effect.

Lewis Carroll, the pen name of Charles Lutwidge Dodgson, was a nineteenth-century British mathematician and writer. He gave the world *Alice's Adventures in Wonderland,* and *Through the Looking-Glass,* two classic books of fantasy. The poem "Jabberwocky," from *Through the Looking-Glass,* was written in part as a gift for Carroll's brothers and sisters. Carroll was famous for playing with language and inventing words.

To help his brothers and sisters understand the nonsense words of "Jabberwocky," he gave them a few definitions:

> **brillig** the time for broiling dinner; the end of the afternoon
>
> **slithy** a word that combines the words *slimy* and *lithe,* and means smooth and active
>
> **toves** a kind of badger
>
> **gyre** to scratch like a dog
>
> **gimble** to make holes in everything
>
> **wabe** a side of a hill

Lewis Carroll
1832–1898

Using these definitions, the first stanza of "Jabberwocky" means: "It was late afternoon, and the smooth, active badgers were scratching themselves and making holes in the side of the hill." With his nonsense words, however, Carroll also used several writer's tools, especially rhyme and rhythm, that turn the words into poetry. "Jabberwocky" shows how important the sounds and arrangement of words can be to a poem.

Edgar Allan Poe is one of America's most famous writers of suspense and horror. However, Poe chose to describe himself as a poet. "The Raven," "Annabelle Lee," and "The Bells" are three of his most famous poems. "The Bells" shows how poets can use sound to create different moods. Using the techniques of **onomatopoeia, alliteration,** and **assonance,** the poem presents four ways in which the sound of bells can influence mood. Poe's language creates the sounds of sleigh bells, wedding bells, alarm bells, and funeral bells. Many people feel that this poem needs to be read out loud to be truly appreciated.

Edgar Allan Poe
1809–1849

Literary Terms

alliteration repeating sounds by using words whose beginning sounds are the same

assonance repeating sounds by using words with the same vowel sounds

limerick a five-line poem in which the first, second, and fifth lines, and the third and fourth lines, rhyme

onomatopoeia using words that sound like their meaning

rhyme words that end with the same or similar sounds

rhythm a pattern created by the stressed and unstressed syllables in a line of poetry

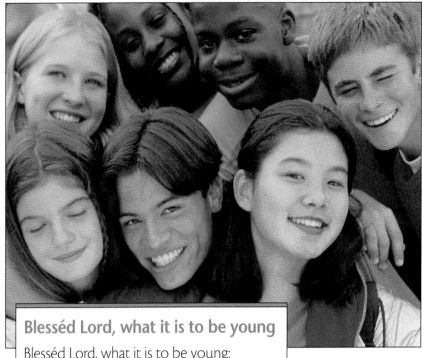

■ The rhyme scheme here is the same as in all limericks: a a b b a. Here, however, the poet has a serious message.

Blesséd Lord, what it is to be young

Blesséd Lord, what it is to be young:
To be of, to be for, be among—
       Be enchanted, **enthralled,**
       Be the caller, the called,
The singer, the song, and the sung.

—*David McCord*

■ Brooks uses both alliteration and assonance. *Lurk late* and *strike straight* are examples of alliteration. *Cool* and *school* are examples of assonance.

WE REAL COOL

*The Pool Players.
Seven at the Golden Shovel.*

We real cool. We
Left school. We

Lurk late. We
Strike straight. We

Sing sin. We
Thin gin. We

Jazz June. We
Die soon.

—*Gwendolyn Brooks*

enthralled fascinated

Jabberwocky

'Twas brillig, and the slithy toves
   Did gyre and gimble in the wabe;
All mimsy were the borogoves,
4   And the mome raths outgrabe.

"Beware the Jabberwock, my son!
   The jaws that bite, the claws that catch!
Beware the Jubjub bird, and **shun**
8   The frumious Bandersnatch!"

He took his vorpal sword in hand:
   Long time the manxome foe he sought—
So rested he by the Tumtum tree,
12   And stood awhile in thought.

And as in uffish thought he stood,
   The Jabberwock, with eyes of flame,
Came whiffling through the tulgey wood,
16   And burbled as it came!

One, two! One, two! And through and through
   The vorpal blade went snicker-snack!
He left it dead, and with its head
20   He went galumphing back.

"And hast thou slain the Jabberwock?
   Come to my arms, my beamish boy!
O frabjous day! Callooh! Callay!"
24   He chortled in his joy.

'Twas brillig, and the slithy toves
   Did gyre and gimble in the wabe;
All mimsy were the borogoves,
28   And the mome raths outgrabe.

—*Lewis Carroll*

'Twas means it was.

How does the poet help us understand what all these nonsense words might mean?

The Jabberwock, illustration by John Tenniel from the first edition, 1872

shun to avoid

The Bells

I

Sledges are sleighs, or sleds.

Hear the sledges with the bells—
　　Silver bells!
What a world of merriment their melody **foretells**!
　　How they tinkle, tinkle, tinkle,
　　　In the icy air of night!

6 　　While the stars that oversprinkle
All the heavens, seem to twinkle
　　With a crystalline delight;
　　Keeping time, time, time,
　　In a sort of Runic rhyme,

Runic means songlike, or poem-like. Tintinnabulation is the ringing of bells.

To the tintinnabulation that so musically wells

12 　　From the bells, bells, bells, bells,
　　　Bells, bells, bells—
From the jingling and the tinkling of the bells.

II

Hear the mellow wedding bells—
　　Golden bells!
What a world of happiness their **harmony** foretells!

Poe uses onomatopoeia, imitating the sound of silvery sleigh bells with words like *tinkle, oversprinkle, twinkle*. In what other ways does he use sound to create the music of these bells?

18 　　Through the **balmy** air of night
　　How they ring out their delight!—
　　From the **molten**-golden notes,
　　　And all in tune,
　　What a liquid ditty floats
To the turtle-dove that listens, while she **gloats**

24 　　　On the moon!
Oh, from out the sounding cells,
What a gush of **euphony voluminously** wells!

---

balmy mild	**foretell** to tell the future	**molten** heated until liquid
euphony a pleasing sound	**gloat** to delight in	**voluminously** hugely
	harmony melody	

How it swells!
How it dwells
On the future!—how it tells
Of the **rapture** that **impels**
To the swinging and the ringing
Of the bells, bells, bells—
Of the bells, bells, bells, bells,
Bells, bells, bells—
To the rhyming and the chiming of the bells!

30

III

36

Hear the loud **alarum** bells!
Brazen bells!
What a tale of terror, now their turbulency tells!
In the startled ear of night
How they scream out their affright!
Too much horrified to speak,
They can only shriek, shriek,
Out of tune,
In a clamorous appealing to the mercy of the fire,
In a mad **expostulation** with the deaf and frantic fire,
Leaping higher, higher, higher,
With a desperate desire,
And a **resolute endeavor**
Now—now to sit, or never,
By the side of the pale-faced moon.
Oh, the bells, bells, bells!
What a tale their terror tells

42

48

alarum alarm, warning	**endeavor** attempt; effort	**impel** to urge forward
brazen made of brass; bold	**expostulation** objection; complaint	**rapture** great happiness
		resolute determined

Of Despair!

54 How they clang, and clash, and roar!

What a horror they outpour

On the **bosom** of the **palpitating** air!

Yet the ear, it fully knows,

By the twanging

And the clanging,

60 How the danger **ebbs** and flows;

Yet the ear distinctly tells,

In the jangling,

And the wrangling,

How the danger sinks and swells,

By the sinking or the swelling in the anger of the bells—

66 Of the bells—

Of the bells, bells, bells, bells,

Bells, bells, bells—

In the clamor and the clanging of the bells!

IV

Hear the tolling of the bells—

Iron bells!

72 What a world of solemn thought their monody **compels**!

In the silence of the night,

How we shiver with affright

At the **melancholy** menace of their tone!

For every sound that floats

From the rust within their throats

78 Is a groan.

And the people—ah, the people—

They that dwell up in the **steeple**,

All alone,

And who, tolling, tolling, tolling,

In that muffled **monotone**,

Poe uses sounds like the long *a* in *twanging, clanging, jangling,* and *wrangling* to give a sense of these alarm bells.

A *monody* is a poem of grief; it is also a steady sound of one instrument or voice in music.

bosom a breast; a heart	**ebb** to slow down; to get lower	**palpitating** breathing in and out
compel to make happen	**melancholy** sad	**steeple** a church tower
	monotone sameness; on one note	

84   Feel a glory in so rolling
     On the human heart a stone—
They are neither man nor woman—
They are neither **brute** nor human—
     They are Ghouls:—
And their king it is who tolls:—

90   And he rolls, rolls, rolls,
     Rolls
A pæan from the bells!
And his merry bosom swells
With the pæan of the bells!
And he dances, and he yells;

96   Keeping time, time, time,
    In a sort of Runic rhyme,
     To the pæan of the bells:—
     Of the bells:
    Keeping time, time, time,
    In a sort of Runic rhyme,

102   To the throbbing of the bells—
     Of the bells, bells, bells—
To the sobbing of the bells:—
Keeping time, time, time,
    As he **knells,** knells, knells,
In a happy Runic rhyme,

108   To the rolling of the bells—
     Of the bells, bells, bells:—
    To the tolling of the bells—
Of the bells, bells, bells, bells,
    Bells, bells, bells—
To the moaning and the groaning of the bells.

—Edgar Allan Poe

Ghouls are evil spirits that rob graves.

A *pæan* is a song of triumph or thanksgiving; the king of the ghouls is happy to grieve human beings with his bells.

brute an animal

knell to ring for a death, funeral, or disaster

Rhyme and Rhythm

Directions Write the answers to these questions using complete sentences.

Comprehension: Identifying Facts

1. What is the topic of McCord's poem?

2. Who is speaking in "WE REAL COOL"? Who is "we"?

3. According to Brooks's poem, what makes the speakers "real cool"?

4. Why does the father warn his son to "beware the Jabberwock"?

5. What two other creatures is the boy warned about?

6. How does the boy slay the Jabberwock?

7. What kind of bells are described in the first stanza of "The Bells"?

8. What feelings do the wedding bells in the second stanza create?

9. In the third stanza, which words describe the sounds of the bells?

10. According to the fourth stanza, who sounds the church bells at night?

Comprehension: Understanding Main Ideas

11. In David McCord's poem, being young is like being "the singer, the song, and the sung." What do you think he means?

12. How are McCord's poem and Brooks's poem similar? How are they different?

13. What is the effect of the short, rhymed lines of "WE REAL COOL"?

14. Retell the story of "Jabberwocky" in your own words.

15. What is the rhyme scheme, or pattern of rhyming words, in the first stanza of "Jabberwocky"? Does Lewis Carroll use the same rhyme scheme in every stanza? Explain.

16. How are the sounds—especially the vowel sounds—of the words in the first stanza of "The Bells" different from the sounds of the words in the fourth stanza? How do the different sounds help readers "hear" the different bells?

17. What are some words Poe repeats throughout "The Bells"? What do the repetitions add to the poem?

18. Give three examples of how Poe uses onomatopoeia to imitate the sounds of the bells in "The Bells".

19. How does the mood of "The Bells" change in each stanza of the poem?

20. Which stanza of "The Bells" do you think is most similiar to the climax of a story?

Understanding Literature: Alliteration, Consonance, and Assonance

Using words with similar sounds helps create rhyme, rhythm, and "music" in a poem. The sounds can be matched in several ways.

When poets use words whose first sound matches, as in David McCord's "The singer, the song, and the sung," they are using a tool called alliteration. This kind of alliteration can also be called consonance. Gwendolyn Brooks uses alliteration and consonance in "We/ Lurk late. We/strike straight." Notice the matching sounds at the beginning and ending of the words.

When poets use words that have the same vowel sounds, they are using a tool called assonance. In Brooks's poem, "cool" and "school" have the same vowel sound.

21. In this line from a nursery rhyme, which words show alliteration?

    Jack and Jill went up a hill

22. Which words show assonance?

23. Find two examples of alliteration in "Jabberwocky."

24. Find two examples of both alliteration and assonance in "The Bells."

25. Why do you think poets use tools like alliteration and assonance? What are some of their effects on poems?

Critical Thinking

26. Would you say that your life is more like the youth described in "Blesséd Lord, what it is to be young," or more like the pool players' lives in "WE REAL COOL"? Explain.

27. Just as Lewis Carroll did, create five words that others would not find in a dictionary. Define each word and use it in a sentence.

28. If you were going to write a poem about the sound of bells, what images would you use?

29. What is a sound that you hear every day, as people during Poe's time heard bells? What are some words that describe the sound?

30. Which poem in this section would you most like to read aloud to someone? Explain your choice.

Writing on Your Own What pictures did you see in your mind as you read each of the four stanzas of "The Bells"? Write a two-sentence description for each stanza.

Gary Soto
1952–

Victor Hugo
1802–1885

Langston Hughes
1902–1967

About the Authors and Selections

Sometimes poets use the writing tool called **imagery**. They create word pictures that appeal to the five senses: sight, smell, taste, touch, hearing. Through imagery, poets ask readers to remember the sweetness of a ripe pear or the mournful sound of a train whistle in the night. Imagery helps readers to see, hear, taste, touch, and smell a poem—rather than just think about it. All the poems in this section include striking images. Many depend on **figurative language**, word pictures that are not meant to be taken literally.

Born in Fresno, California, Gary Soto is a poet and teacher. He draws many of his images from his Mexican heritage. His poem "Oranges" comes from his 1985 collection *Black Hair*. In the poem, Soto remembers when he was twelve and walking with a girl for the first time. His images help us see, hear, touch, smell, and taste his memory.

Victor Hugo was the leading literary figure in France during the nineteenth century. He is considered a master of French poetry. He published many books of poetry and wrote many plays. He is best known in the United States for his two great novels, *The Hunchback of Notre Dame* and *Les Misérables*. The six short lines of his poem "Be Like the Bird" gives readers a clear image of a bird singing in spite of danger.

Langston Hughes wrote short stories, plays, and novels, but he is best known for his poetry. He wrote several poems about dreams. These poems all have clear images that describe how important it is to keep dreams and goals alive. The poem in this section, "Dreams," uses two powerful **metaphors** to describe what happens when dreams die.

Lance Henson grew up in the Southern Cheyenne culture near Calumet, Oklahoma. He has published 17 volumes of poetry. Much of his work is about American Indian experiences. In "flock," he creates a sharp image drawn directly from his life on a farm in Oklahoma. The poem ends with a striking **simile.**

William Carlos Williams lived all his life in Rutherford, New Jersey. He was a pediatrician as well as one of the twentieth century's most important poets. Williams's poetry is known for its clear images and simple language. "The Red Wheelbarrow" is one of his most famous short poems. In it, he asks readers to see a truth about life by seeing clearly with their eyes.

Lady Sei Shonagon was a lady-in-waiting in the court of Japan in the tenth century. "The rooster's crowing" is in a traditional form of Japanese poetry, the **tanka.** This poem was included in an anthology of Japanese poetry collected in the thirteenth century. The image in the poem uses mainly the sense of hearing.

Another form of Japanese poetry, the **haiku,** has been used by many Western writers. "Haiku," by Etheridge Knight, is a series of nine haikus. Each paints a clear image. Knight wrote this poem during his term in prison. Later, the poem became part of Knight's first book, *Poems from Prison,* published in 1969. After he served his term, Knight went on to write and teach at the University of Pittsburgh.

Lance Henson
1944–

William Carlos
Williams
1883–1963

Etheridge Knight
1931–1991

Literary Terms

figurative language language that uses word pictures to compare or describe, and that is not meant to be taken literally

haiku a form of Japanese poetry having three lines with five syllables in the first, seven in the second, and five in the third

imagery the use of word pictures that appeal to the five senses

metaphor a figure of speech that says one thing *is* another

simile a figure of speech in which two things are compared using a phrase that includes the words *like* or *as*

tanka a form of Japanese poetry having five lines with five syllables in the first, seven in the second, five in the third, and seven in the fourth and fifth

Oranges

The first time I walked
With a girl, I was twelve,
Cold, and weighted down
With two oranges in my jacket.
December. Frost crackling
6 Beneath my steps, my breath
Before me, then gone,
As I walked toward
Her house, the one whose
Porch light burned yellow
Night and day, in any weather.
12 A dog barked at me, until
She came out pulling
At her gloves, face bright
With rouge. I smiled,
Touched her shoulder, and led
her down the street, across
18 A used car lot and a line
Of newly planted trees,
Until we were breathing
Before a drugstore. We
Entered, the tiny bell
Bringing a saleslady
24 Down a narrow aisle of goods.
I turned to the candies
Tiered like bleachers,
And asked what she wanted—
Light in her eyes, a smile
Starting at the corners

Color is important in this poem. Notice the oranges, the yellow porch light, the girl's face "bright with rouge"—reddish makeup on her cheeks. Where else does color stand out?

tiered arranged in rows, one above the other

30 Of her mouth. I fingered
A nickel in my pocket,
And when she lifted a chocolate
That cost a dime,
I didn't say anything.
I took the nickel from
36 My pocket, then an orange,
And set them quietly on
The counter. When I looked up,
The lady's eyes met mine,
And held them, knowing
Very well what it was all
42 About.

     Outside,
A few cars hissing past,
Fog hanging like old
Coats between the trees.
I took my girl's hand
48 In mine for two blocks,
Then released it to let
Her unwrap the chocolate.
I peeled my orange
That was so bright against
The gray of December
54 That, from some distance,
Someone might have thought
I was making a fire in my hands.

—*Gary Soto*

Which images help you see, hear, touch, smell, and taste the poet's memory?

Which senses does Hugo appeal to in this image of a bird? Why should we "be like the bird"?

Hughes uses two images to describe life without dreams. What is he saying about the importance of holding on to your dreams?

The images in "flock" create a cold, empty feeling as the land and animals pass through winter. What picture do you get in your mind from the last two lines?

Williams paints a kind of "picture" with words. His imagery depends on color and on the shininess of a wheelbarrow glazed with rain water.

Be Like the Bird

Be like the bird, who
Halting in his flight
On limb too slight
Feels it give way beneath him,
Yet sings
Knowing he hath wings.

— *Victor Hugo*

Dreams

Hold fast to dreams
For if dreams die
Life is a broken-winged bird
That cannot fly.

Hold fast to dreams
For when dreams go
Life is a **barren** field
Frozen with snow.

— *Langston Hughes*

flock

across the road
ice huddles against the trees

there is only a whisper of
leaves among the cottonwoods

and over the joyless valley

snow moves
like an ancient herd

— *Lance Henson*

The Red Wheelbarrow

so much depends
upon

a red wheel
barrow

glazed with rain
water

beside the white
chickens.

— *William Carlos Williams*

barren without life   **glazed** glassy; smooth and shiny

376   *Unit 7 Poetry*

Haiku

–1–

Eastern guard tower
glints in sunset; **convicts** rest
like lizards on rocks.

–2–

The piano man
is sitting at 3 am
his songs drop like plum.

–3–

Morning sun slants cell.
Drunks stagger like cripple flies
On the Jailhouse floor.

–4–

To write a blues song
Is to regiment **riots**
and pluck gems from graves.

–5–

A bare pecan tree
slips a pencil shadow down
a moonlit snow slope.

–6–

The falling snow flakes
Can not **blunt** the hard aches nor
Match the steel stillness.

–7–

Under moon shadows
A tall boy flashes knife and
Slices star bright ice.

–8–

In the August grass
Struck by the last rays of sun
The cracked teacup screams.

–9–

Making **jazz** swing in
Seventeen syllables AIN'T
No square poet's job.

—*Etheridge Knight*

The rooster's crowing

The rooster's crowing
In the middle of the night
Deceived the hearers;
But at Osaka's gateway
The guards are never fooled.

—*Lady Sei Shonagon*

■ In this tanka, Osaka is a major Japanese city. The rooster may deceive some people into thinking it is morning, but never the guards at the gate.

■ *Blues* are a form of jazz. Blues songs are about the dark, sad parts of life. In this haiku, Knight compares writing a blues song to giving order to chaos and to taking something bright and beautiful from a dead place—something from nothing. What would "the blues" have to do with prison life?

■ What sense does Knight mainly appeal to with his images?

blunt to soften

convict a person in prison

glint to gleam

jazz popular dance music with strong rhythms

riot a public disturbance

Imagery

Directions Write the answers to these questions using complete sentences.

Comprehension: Identifying Facts

1. What does the boy in Gary Soto's poem carry in his jacket?

2. How does the boy in "Oranges" pay for the ten-cent candy?

3. Why does the bird in Victor Hugo's poem sing, even though the limb gives way beneath him?

4. What does the speaker in "Dreams" encourage readers to do?

5. According to Langston Hughes's poem, what happens if dreams die?

6. In "flock," how does the poet describe the valley?

7. What color images do you find in Williams's poem?

8. In Lady Sei Shonagon's poem, what does the rooster's crowing do to the hearers, but not to the guards?

9. In Knight's first haiku, what are the resting convicts compared to?

10. In Knight's last haiku, what does he say about the job of writing haiku (which he calls "Making jazz swing in/Seventeen syllables")?

Comprehension: Understanding Main Ideas

11. What images of touch do you find in "Oranges"?

12. Why might someone think the boy was "making a fire in [his] hands" in "Oranges"? Why is an image of fire effective at the end of this poem?

13. In Hugo's poem, what lesson does the bird have to teach?

14. How is a life without dreams like "a broken-winged bird" and "a barren field" as described in "Dreams"?

15. How does the image "ice huddles against the trees" make you feel?

16. What sound image do you find in "flock"?

17. Why is color important in "The Red Wheelbarrow"?

18. How is Williams's poem like a still life painting?

19. How does the rooster's crowing fool those who hear it?

20. In Knight's fourth haiku, what does he compare with writing a blues song? What do you think he means?

Understanding Literature: Tanka and Haiku

Tanka and haiku are old forms of poetry that began in Japan. They are both brief. Both have a special pattern of rhythm. Tanka has five lines: five syllables in the first line, seven in the second, five in the third, and seven in the fourth and fifth. The pattern is 5–7–5–7–7.

Haiku has three lines: five syllables in the first line, seven in the second, and five in the third. The pattern is 5–7–5. The lines of haiku and tanka do not usually rhyme.

Tanka and haiku from old Japan were mainly about nature. Poets created images of the mountains, rivers, and trees they saw around them. Poets today use these forms to express many different thoughts and emotions.

21. How are tanka and haiku alike? How are they different?

22. Count the syllables in each of Knight's haikus. Do they all follow the 5–7–5 syllable pattern?

23. What subjects does Etheridge Knight explore in his haiku?

24. Why do you think a modern writer like Knight would be interested in the haiku form? What does such a short form, with such strict rules for line and syllable count, ask of a poet?

25. In your opinion, why do tanka and haiku poets use images to express their thoughts?

Critical Thinking

26. In "Oranges," when the girl chooses candy that costs a dime, the boy puts his nickel and one orange on the counter. Does the lady accept the payment? How do you know?

27. Compare the images of birds in Hugo's poem and in Hughes's poem. What does each mean? What picture does each create in your mind?

28. Reread "Dreams." Write a simile or metaphor that shows how you would feel if one of your dreams died.

29. Study the simile that ends the poem "flock." What is Henson saying about the snow? What pictures do his words create in your mind?

30. In what ways is "The Red Wheelbarrow" like haiku in its subject matter and effect?

> **Writing on Your Own** Create a haiku about nature and a more modern haiku about the future.

Voices

Jane Hirschfield
1953–

Robert Frost
1874–1963

Luis Omar Salinas
1937–

About the Authors and Selections

In this section, you'll meet poets from a wide range of ethnic groups and life experiences. Each has a special way of seeing the world. Each uses the tools of poetry in individual ways. In short, each poet has a clear, individual **voice.**

In "The Poet," Jane Hirshfield explores the quiet, rather lonely world of poets. She writes especially about women poets, whose life and work remain unknown to the wider world. Hirshfield first published this poem in *The Atlantic Monthly* in 1997. She has published four collections of her poems and written many essays about poets and poetry.

Robert Frost is one of the twentieth century's most important and honored poets. "The Road Not Taken" is one of Frost's best-known poems. In it, the poet tells how the course of his life was set when he was forced to choose between two roads in a wood. This choice becomes an image of the hard decisions people have to make in life.

Luis Omar Salinas is a noted poet whose main subject is the experience of Hispanic people in the United States. His poem "In a Farmhouse" is about a little boy who has worked all day in the cotton fields for two dollars and thirty cents. Salinas shows how poets can bring the world's attention to those who might otherwise be forgotten.

One of Lucille Clifton's main subjects for poetry is African-American girls and women. Clifton's poem "this morning" describes an experience many adults have: seeing themselves as they used to be. The poem, with its skillful use of **repetition,** shows Clifton's love for the sounds of words.

Lan Nguyen was born in Vietnam in 1960. She spent her childhood in a country torn apart by war. "My Life Story" describes what it is like to be a young person surrounded by war and death. In simple terms, she tells how difficult it is to feel powerless—"only a sand in the big desert."

Gu Cheng, author of "A Headstrong Boy," was born in China in 1956. In 1974, he helped start a magazine to publish poetry and fiction, but the Chinese government did not approve. Today, Gu Cheng lives in exile from China. In his poem, Gu Cheng speaks in the voice of a "headstrong" boy, meaning a willful person who doesn't listen to others. The poem is rich in **figurative language.**

Lucille Clifton
1936–

Nikki Giovanni has devoted much of her career to helping other African-American writers find their way into the spotlight. In her poem "Nikki-Rosa," Giovanni comments on how the white culture tends to view the childhoods of African Americans who become famous. She makes it clear that "all the while I was quite happy."

Carl Sandburg first earned national attention as a poet when *Poetry* magazine published "Chicago." In all his work, Sandburg tries to capture the special ways of talking and thinking found in America's Midwest. In this poem, Sandburg uses **personification,** giving human characteristics to a city.

Nikki Giovanni
1943–

As you read the poems in this section, see how each voice creates a particular **mood** and **tone.**

Carl Sandburg
1878–1967

Literary Terms

figurative language language that uses word pictures to compare or describe, and that is not meant to be taken literally

mood the feeling created by a piece of writing

personification giving characters such as animals or objects the characteristics of humans

repetition using a word, phrase, or image more than once, for emphasis

tone the attitude an author takes toward a subject

voice the way a writer expresses ideas through style, form, content, and purpose

The Poet

She is working now, in a room
not unlike this one,
the one where I write, or you read.
Her table is covered with paper.
The light of the lamp would be
6 tempered by a shade, where the bulb's
single harshness might dissolve,
but it is not; she has taken it off.
Her poems? I will never know them,
though they are the ones I most need.
Even the alphabet she writes in
12 I cannot **decipher**. Her chair—
let us imagine whether it is leather
or canvas, vinyl or wicker. Let her
have a chair, her shadeless lamp,
the table. Let one or two she loves
be in the next room. Let the door
18 be closed, the sleeping ones healthy.
Let her have time, and silence,
enough paper to make mistakes and go on.

—*Jane Hirshfield*

The poet has taken the shade off her lamp, so nothing "tempers" the "harshness" of the light. Why do you think she has done this?

At the Writing Desk, **Frederick Childe Hassam**

decipher to make clear; to explain

Edge of the Forest,
Paul Ranson

The Road Not Taken

Two roads **diverged** in a yellow wood,
And sorry I could not travel both
And be one traveler, long I stood
And looked down one as far as I could
To where it bent in the undergrowth;

6 Then took the other, as just as fair,
And having perhaps a better claim,
Because it was grassy and wanted wear;
Though as for that the passing there
Had worn them really about the same.

And both that morning equally lay
12 In leaves no step had trodden black.
Oh, I kept the first for another day!
Yet knowing how way leads on to way,
I doubted if I should ever come back.

I shall be telling this with a sigh
Somewhere ages and ages **hence:**
18 Two roads diverged in a wood, and I—
I took the one less traveled by,
And that has made all the difference.

—Robert Frost

diverge to branch off   **hence** in the future

Notice the rhyme scheme Frost uses in every stanza: a b a a b. He uses end rhyme throughout the poem.

The speaker made a choice of path that "made all the difference" in his life. What important choices have you made in your life?

In a Farmhouse

Fifteen miles
out of Robstown
with the Texas sun
4 fading in the distance
I sit in the bedroom
profoundly,
animated by the day's work
8 in the cottonfields.

I made two dollars and
thirty cents today
I am eight years old
12 and I wonder
how the rest of the Mestizos
do not go hungry
and if one were to die
16 of hunger
what an odd way
to leave for heaven.

—*Luis Omar Salinas*

■ Are you surprised to learn that the speaker is eight years old? How does this fact change the tone of the poem?

■ *Mestizos* are persons of mixed Spanish and American ancestry.

■ Notice the sound of Clifton's poem. How do the sounds, short lines, and simple words help the reader see the young, lively girl being described?

this morning
(for the girls of eastern high school)

this morning
this morning
    i met myself

coming in

5 a bright
jungle girl
shining
quick as a snake
a tall
10 tree girl a
me girl

    i met myself

this morning
coming in

15 and all day
i have been
a black bell
ringing
i **survive**

20   survive
survive

—*Lucille Clifton*

animated made lively, happy

profoundly strongly

survive to go on living

My Life Story

What shall I tell about my life?

a life of changes
a life of losing
remembering
eighteen years ago
6   a little child was born
surrounded by the love of family
so warm and tender
surrounded by mountains and rivers
so free and beautiful

But life was not
12   the dearest father passed away
and left a big scar in the child's head

She grew up with something missing in her
She had seen the people born and dying
   born from the war
   dying from guns and bombs

18   Sometimes she wished
she could do something
for herself and her people

But what could she do?

Nothing but watch and watch
for she is too small
24   only a sand in the big desert
no power
nothing at all

She is only herself
an ordinary person
carrying a dream
30   that seems so far, far, far away

The only thing she can do
is keep hoping
one day her dream will come true

God cannot be mean to her forever.

—Lan Nguyen

Here the poet
describes very simply
the horrors of growing
up in a country at war.

In a metaphor, the poet
compares herself to "a
sand in the big
desert"—one of
millions, with no power.

A Headstrong Boy

Headstrong means willful—not willing to listen to anyone.

> I guess my mother spoiled me—
> I'm a headstrong boy. I want every instant
> to be lovely as crayons.

The boy wants to draw "eyes that never wept". Then, he wants to draw a love "who's never seen a mournful cloud". What do these two images have in common?

> 4 I'd like to draw—on **chaste** white paper—
> a clumsy freedom, eyes that never wept,
> a piece of sky, a feather, a leaf,
> a pale green evening, and an apple.
>
> 8 I'd like to draw dawn, the smile dew sees,
> the earliest, tenderest love—an imaginary love
> who's never seen a mournful cloud,
> whose eyes the color of sky will gaze at me
> 12 forever, and never turn away.
> I'd like to draw distance, a bright horizon,

Furze is a shrub.

> carefree, rippling rivers, hills **sheathed** in green furze.
> I want the lovers to stand together in silence,
> 16 I want each breathless moment to **beget** a flower.

beget to breed   **chaste** pure   **sheathe** to cover with something that protects

I want to draw a future I've never seen—
nor ever can—though I'm sure she'll be beautiful.
I'll draw her an autumn coat the color of candle flame,
20 and maple leaves, and all the hearts that ever loved her.
I'll draw her a wedding, an early morning garden party,
swathed in candy-wrappers decked with winter scenes.

Notice how the poet personifies the future as a woman. How is this woman described?

I'm a headstrong boy. I want to paint out every sorrow,
24 to cover the world with colored windows,
let all the eyes accustomed to darkness
be accustomed to light. I want to draw wind,
mountains, each one bigger than the last.
28 I want to draw the dream of the East,
a **fathomless** sea, a joyful voice.

Finally, I'd like to draw myself in one corner—
a panda, huddled in a dark Victorian forest,
32 hunkering in the quiet branches, homeless, lost,
not even a heart left behind me, far away,
only teeming dreams of berries
and great, wide eyes.

From this stanza on, the poem's mood and tone change. What is the change?

36 This pining's pointless.
I haven't any crayons,
any breathless moments.
All I have are fingers and pain.

Pining means grieving, or weeping over something.

40 I think I'll tear the paper to bits
and let them drift away,
hunting for butterflies.

—*Gu Cheng*
Translated by Donald Finkel

fathomless without   **swathe** to wrap
bottom

Nikki-Rosa

Woodlawn is a mainly African-American suburb of Cincinnati, Ohio.

childhood **remembrances** are always a drag
if you're Black
3 you always remember things like living in Woodlawn
with no inside toilet
and if you become famous or something
6 they never talk about how happy you were to have your mother
all to yourself and
how good the water felt when you got your bath from one of those
9 big tubs that folk in chicago **barbecue** in
and somehow when you talk about home
it never gets across how much you
12 understood their feelings
as the whole family attended meetings about Hollydale
and even though you remember
15 your **biographers** never understand
your father's pain as he sells his stock
and another dream goes
18 and though you're poor it isn't poverty that
concerns you
and though they fought a lot
21 it isn't your father's drinking that makes any difference
but only that everybody is together and you
and your sister have happy birthdays and very good christmasses
24 and I really hope no white person ever has cause to write about me
because they never understand Black love is Black wealth and they'll
probably talk about my hard childhood and never understand that
27 all the while I was quite happy

—Nikki Giovanni

The poet says that white people "never understand" that "Black love is Black wealth". What does she mean?

barbecue to grill food outdoors

biographer someone who writes the life story of another person

remembrance a memory

Chicago

Hog Butcher for the World,
Tool Maker, Stacker of Wheat,
Player with Railroads and the Nation's Freight Handler;
4   Stormy, husky, **brawling,**
City of the Big Shoulders:

They tell me you are wicked and I believe them, for I have seen
     your painted women under the gas lamps **luring** the farm boys.
8   And they tell me you are crooked and I answer: Yes, it is true
     I have seen the gunman kill and go free to kill again.
And they tell me you are **brutal** and my reply is: On the faces of
     women and children I have seen the marks of **wanton** hunger.
12   And having answered so I turn once more to those who sneer at
     this my city, and I give them back the sneer and say to them:
Come and show me another city with lifted head singing so proud
     to be alive and coarse and strong and cunning.
16   Flinging magnetic curses **amid** the toil of piling job on job,
     here is a tall bold slugger set vivid against the little soft cities;
Fierce as a dog with tongue lapping for action, cunning as a savage
     pitted against the wilderness,
20   Bareheaded,
       Shoveling,
       Wrecking,
       Planning,
24   Building, breaking, rebuilding,

Under the smoke, dust all over his mouth, laughing with white teeth,
Under the terrible burden of **destiny** laughing as a young man laughs,
Laughing even as an ignorant fighter laughs who has never lost a battle,
28   Bragging and laughing that under his wrist is the pulse, and under
     his ribs the heart of the people,
       Laughing!
Laughing the stormy, husky, brawling laughter of Youth, half-naked, sweating,
     proud to be Hog Butcher, Tool Maker, Stacker of Wheat, Player with
     Railroads and Freight Handler to the Nation.

—Carl Sandburg

amid within; between	**brutal** cruel	**lure** to tempt
brawling fighting	**destiny** fate	**wanton** without mercy

Directions Write the answers to these questions using complete sentences.

Comprehension: Identifying Facts

1. In "The Poet," how is the room where the poet writes described?

2. What is the choice that the poet needs to make in "The Road Not Taken"?

3. To whom does Lucille Clifton dedicate her poem "this morning"?

4. Clifton compares her young self— "myself/coming in"—to three nonhuman things. What are they?

5. How old is the boy in "In a Farmhouse"? How does he make his money?

6. In "My Life Story," what event "left a big scar in the child's head"?

7. How does the speaker in "A Headstrong Boy" want to draw himself?

8. What are some of the positive things the poet in "Nikki-Rosa" remembers about her childhood?

9. What jobs does Carl Sandburg list as part of Chicago's "work"?

10. How does Sandburg compare Chicago to "the little soft cities"?

Comprehension: Understanding Main Ideas

11. What does Jane Hirshfield's poem tell you about the life of a poet?

12. Although Robert Frost describes choosing a path in a wood, what other choices in life might he have been talking about?

13. When Lucille Clifton says "i met myself/coming in," what does she mean?

14. Why are the boy's thoughts in "In a Farmhouse" unusual? Explain.

15. What does the speaker in "My Life Story" mean by saying she "grew up with something missing in her"?

16. What do most of the things the speaker in "A Headstrong Boy" wants to draw have in common?

17. What does Giovanni mean in "Nikki-Rosa" by "Black love is Black wealth"?

18. What does Sandburg like about Chicago? What does he defend?

19. How are "A Headstrong Boy" and "In a Farmhouse" similar? How are they different?

20. List the five poems in this section that tell something about what it means to be young. Briefly describe what each says.

Understanding Literature: Patterns of Rhythm

Every poem has a special rhythm, created by the pattern of stressed and unstressed syllables in the words. When we say a word that has more than one syllable, we stress one syllable more than the others. For example, the word *rhythm* has two syllables. We say "**RHY** - thm," stressing the first syllable.

Two common patterns of rhythm are:

iamb   a pattern of two syllables, the first one unstressed, the second stressed

Example: *And pay no worship to the garish sun*

would be read: *And **PAY** no **WOR** - ship **TO** the **GAR**- ish **SUN***

trochee a pattern of two syllables, the first one stressed, the second unstressed

Example: *Tiger, tiger burning bright*

would be read: ***TI** - ger, **TI** - ger **BURN** - ing **BRIGHT***

21. Which pattern is more like your heartbeat: an iamb or a trochee?

22. Is your first or last name iambic, trochaic, or something else? Write your name using capital letters to show the stressed syllable.

23. How many syllables are there in the first line of "The Road Not Taken"?

24. Is the first line of Frost's poem mostly iambic or mostly trochaic?

25. What rhythm patterns do you hear in the lyrics (words) of your favorite songs? Are any iambic or trochaic?

Critical Thinking

26. How does the message of "The Road Not Taken" apply to your life?

27. If you were a poet like in Hirshfield's poem, where would you write?

28. If you were writing a poem about an event from your childhood, what tone would you use? Explain.

29. What positive and negative qualities would you include in a poem about your home town?

30. Lucille Clifton in "this morning" thinks of herself as a bell ringing "i survive." Describe yourself coming in the door of your school.

Writing on Your Own With traditional Japanese tanka and haiku, one poet wrote a few lines of a poem and challenged another to add to it. Write a few lines of a poem. E-mail it to others and ask them to add to your poem and return it to you.

Skills Lesson

Blank Verse and Iambic Pentameter

One important pattern used in poetry is called blank verse. In blank verse, each line contains ten syllables. Each set of two syllables is iambic. Remember that an iamb is a pattern of two syllables, the first one unstressed, the second stressed. The rhythm of blank verse is called iambic pentameter. *Penta* refers to five. In each line of ten syllables, five are stressed—the second syllables in each pattern.

For example, *today* is an iambic word, because it has the stress, or accent, on the second syllable: to - **DAY**. When you read blank verse, you should hear this pattern: "ta - **DUM**, ta - **DUM**, ta - **DUM**, ta - **DUM**, ta - **DUM**."

William Shakespeare used iambic pentameter in many of his plays. For example, read the following section from *Romeo and Juliet.*

Come, gentle night; come, loving,
   black-browed night;
Give me my Romeo; and, when he shall die,
Take him and cut him out in little stars,
And he will make the face of heaven
   so fine
That all the world will be in love
   with night
And pay no worship to the garish sun.

Juliet tells how much she loves Romeo. "That all the world will be in love with night" contains ten syllables, so it is an example of pentameter. The stress pattern is:

*That **ALL** / the **WORLD** / will **BE** / in **LOVE** / with **NIGHT***

This is an iambic pattern—the second syllables are stressed. Therefore, this part of the play is written in iambic pentameter. It is an example of blank verse.

Review

1. How many syllables are in this line from Juliet's speech: "Take him and cut him out in little stars"?

2. Based on this syllable count, what do we call this rhythm?

3. Which syllables are stressed, or accented, in this line?

4. What do we call this pattern of stressed syllables?

5. Are all the lines in this speech examples of iambic pentameter? Give any examples of lines with a different pattern.

Writing on Your Own Write two lines of poetry in iambic pentameter.

Poetry is different from prose in its form and language. Most poems are written in lines and stanzas. Some poems rhyme, and many have patterns of rhythm. Poets, even more than prose writers, use word "tools" that expand the sounds and add to the meanings of words.

Compared with most prose literature, poems are short. Using few words, poets create word pictures that draw on readers' senses, memories, and personal experiences. Poets use patterns of rhyming words. They use stressed and unstressed syllables to help readers read and understand some poems. Other poems use no rhyme or regular rhythms. This is especially true of poems written more recently. Their meaning comes mainly through word choice and word arrangement.

Like prose literature, poetry is as old as human expression. All cultures have poets and enjoy poetry. The range of subjects, forms, and language possible for poetry is vast.

Selections

■ "Ballads and Songs" includes an eighteenth-century love poem, a cowboy ballad, and a modern ballad about a terrible bombing during the civil rights struggles of the 1960s.

■ The poems in "Rhyme and Rhythm" show different uses of the writer's tools of sound. This section includes a serious limerick, a nonsense poem that makes perfect sense, and a poem that imitates the sounds and creates the mood of bells. Simple rhymes capture the jazzy, sometimes hopeless lives of young people.

■ "Imagery" includes skillful uses of the tools of meaning. Two poems use birds as very different images. Other poems use images featuring colors, sounds, textures, smells, and tastes. Two poems show the power of the Japanese forms tanka and haiku.

■ In "Voices," there are poems from many different groups and a wide range of experiences. Poetry is used to help readers understand people they might never meet in life: unpublished poets, girls at a city high school, a young cotton-picker, a girl growing up in wartorn Vietnam. An experience as simple as choosing one path over another suggests other important choices people must make. Other poems include a happy childhood and a city made almost human by a poet's skillful use of language.

Directions Write the answers to these questions using complete sentences.

Comprehension: Identifying Facts

1. Poets pay attention to two aspects of every word. What are the two?

2. How would you define rhyme?

3. What two characteristics do ballads share with tall tales and legends?

4. Why do poets use imagery?

5. How are alliteration and assonance similar? How are they different?

Comprehension: Understanding Main Ideas

6. In your own words, how would you define poetry?

7. What is the tone of "The Road Not Taken"? Use evidence from the poem to explain your answer.

8. In what ways is poetry like music?

9. Which writer's tool that uses the sound of words do you most like to see used in a poem? Why? Which tool that uses the meaning of words do you like best? Why?

10. Which poem in the unit do you enjoy the most? Explain your reasoning.

Understanding Literature: Form in Poetry

Poets use more than words to communicate. They also use the form of the poem.

Poems are written in lines and stanzas. A line of poetry is not necessarily a complete sentence. It is simply a line of words on the page. To read a poem as the poet intended it to be read, you need to pay attention to punctuation, as you would in prose.

In some poetry, such as "The Road Not Taken," all the lines begin with a capital letter. This does not mean that you are to pause at the end of each line, as if each were a separate sentence. Instead, you need to look for punctuation that tells you to pause: commas, semicolons, periods, exclamation points, colons, dashes. Frost uses all these marks. This punctuation tells you how to read the poem.

Other poems, such as "this morning," have no punctuation. Lucille Clifton does not even use a capital *I* to refer to herself. In a poem like this, you need to look at where the poet ends lines and where she puts space to indicate a new stanza. Stanzas are like the paragraphs of a poem. You can tell by the space between stanzas when one stanza ends and another begins.

Looking at the form of a poem can help you know how it is to be read aloud. The form can also help you find the rhythm in its words.

11. How does punctuation tell you where to pause in a poem?

12. How should you read a poem with no punctuation?

13. Why should you pay attention to lines and stanzas in poems?

14. In the first two lines of Poe's "The Bells," where should you pause?

15. How many stanzas are in Poe's poem?

Critical Thinking

16. If you could spend a few hours with one of the poets (living or dead) in this unit, which one would you choose? Explain your choice.

17. Do you think all poetry should rhyme? Explain your position.

18. Why do you think some writers choose to write poetry, rather than prose?

19. If you were a poet, what kinds of poems would you write? Which subjects would you explore?

20. Which poem in this unit will you remember best? Why?

Speak and Listen

Some poems are meant to be read aloud. Look over Edgar Allen Poe's "The Bells." Pick one stanza and practice reading it aloud with expression and understanding. Make sure the tone of your voice matches the tone of the stanza. When you are satisfied with your work, record the stanza on audiotape.

Beyond Words

Create a work of art (painting, drawing, sculpture) that represents one of the images from a poem in this unit.

Writing on Your Own Write your own poem about a subject that was explored in one of the poems in this unit. Choose any style of poetry you want.

Test-Taking Tip

When a test question asks you to write a paragraph, make a plan first. Jot down the main idea for your paragraph. List the supporting details you can include. Then write the paragraph.

"The essential is to excite the spectators. If that means playing *Hamlet* on a flying trapeze or in an aquarium, you do it."

—Orson Welles, *Les Nouvelles Littéraires*, 1953; quoted in *Citizen Welles*, 1989

"A talent for drama is not a talent for writing, but is an ability to articulate human relationships."

—Gore Vidal, in the *New York Times*, 17 June 1956

Drury Lane Theatre,
Artist Unknown

UNIT 8 *Drama*

Drama is a form of storytelling meant to be performed by actors on a stage. In the Western world, the kinds of drama we see today began in ancient Greece. Then and now, playwrights—writers of plays—tell their stories completely through the words and actions of characters. Plays are often grouped as either tragedies or comedies according to the outcome of their plots.

In this unit, you will read the last act of a classic tragedy of young love, the first scene from a powerful realistic drama about African-American life after World War II, and a short television comedy.

UNIT 8 ■ ABOUT DRAMA

Drama is a special form of literature. Drama is meant to be performed as well as read. The word *drama* comes from the Greek word *dran,* meaning to do, or to act. The ancient Greeks were the first people in the Western world to set the form for the activity that we call drama.

Like other forms of literature in this text, plays are written to tell a story. However, when a play is performed, the story is told completely through the words—called dialogue—and actions of characters. Characters in a play are very similar to the characters in short stories, fables, legends, and tall tales. The play's main character is called the protagonist. There is usually an antagonist who tries to make things difficult for the protagonist. As in all literature, characters in a play can be flat or round, unchanging or changing. Playwrights, or writers of plays, cannot present characters' thoughts, as can writers of fiction. They have to let the characters speak for themselves or be revealed through the words of other characters.

Plays are divided into two groups according to the outcome of their plots: tragedies and comedies. These are shown in the two masks used as symbols of drama. One mask has a smiling face; the other has a sad face. A tragedy is a serious play that ends unhappily, with the suffering or death of the main character. Tragedies usually explore serious subjects, such as the meaning of life and the importance of relationships. Comedies, on the other hand, have happy endings and are written to amuse people. In the comedies of ancient Greece, protagonists accomplished their goals, or got what they wanted. Today, people define comedy more broadly. Today's comedies are expected to make people laugh.

The action of a play is divided into acts and scenes. An act is a major unit of action. Acts are divided into smaller parts, called scenes. Each scene takes place in one setting only. This division into acts and scenes gives a play an order of events and allows settings to change. In Shakespeare's time, the five-act play was standard. Today's plays tend to be in three acts. Many plays have only one act.

Whether or not readers have seen a play on stage, most have seen another form of drama: plays written for television, film, and video. Like all plays, dramas written for these media can be comedies or tragedies. They can tell stories about ordinary people, or about unusual people.

The main difference between plays and other forms of storytelling is that plays are meant to be performed by actors on a stage. The meaning of a play is found not only on the page, but also in the relationship between the play and its audience. Each time a play is performed, it becomes a new experience in some ways for both actors and audience. The dialogue stays the same, as do the costumes and sets. But the way the actors speak the lines and the way they move can change in small, yet important ways. That is why readers of a play need to imagine how lines would be spoken by actors, and how actions would be performed.

In this unit, you will sample three different forms of drama. William Shakespeare's *Romeo and Juliet* is the tragic story of two unlucky young lovers. This tale has gripped audiences around the world for centuries. Lorraine Hansberry's *A Raisin in the Sun* is a realistic modern drama. The play was written forty years ago, and continues to be performed often. "Writer's Realm" is a script written for a television series by Anne Jarrell-France. It shows how today's television writers still use the basics of dramatic form.

Theatre Scene, Edgar Degas

Romeo and Juliet
William Shakespeare

William Shakespeare
1564–1616

About the Author

William Shakespeare, poet and dramatist, is perhaps the best-known **playwright** in the history of western **drama.** People throughout the world have enjoyed his works for centuries. Given this fame, it is surprising that so little is known of the actual man.

We know that Shakespeare was born in 1564 in Stratford-upon-Avon, England. He was the son of a businessman and probably attended the local school, where he would have read the classic plays of ancient Greece and Rome. He married Anne Hathaway in 1582, and they had three children. Little else is known of his life until 1592, when he is mentioned in records of the time as a playwright in London. In 1594, he became an actor and playwright for the Lord Chamberlain's Men, a group that performed in the Globe Theater. Shakespeare retired from the theater and London around 1611, returning to Stratford, where he died in 1616.

Shakespeare wrote tragedies, comedies, and history plays. Most were performed by his theater company, and he acted in several himself. His works are usually divided into three periods. *Romeo and Juliet* is the last play in Shakespeare's first period. It was probably first performed in 1594.

About the Selection

Romeo and Juliet is a **tragedy,** meaning a play that ends with the suffering or death of one or more of the main characters. It tells the story of two young people whom Shakespeare describes as "star-crossed lovers." This means that fate, or chance, is against them. The play takes place in the northern Italian city of Verona. Juliet is part of the Capulet family. Romeo is a Montague. The Capulets and Montagues have been enemies for many years. Romeo and Juliet meet and fall in love before they realize that each is the other's sworn enemy. But their love is very strong, and they secretly marry. Then, in a street fight, Juliet's cousin, Tybalt, threatens Romeo's best friend, Mercutio. Romeo tries to break up the fight, but Tybalt kills Mercutio. In revenge, Romeo kills Tybalt. Angry, the prince of Verona orders Romeo banished from the city. He must go to a nearby town, Mantua.

In the meantime, Juliet's parents have arranged for her to marry another man, Paris. Rather than do this, Juliet seeks the advice of the Catholic brother who performed her secret wedding to Romeo, Friar Lawrence. He gives her a potion which will make it appear as if she has died. The plan is that Friar Lawrence will write to Romeo, tell him what they've done, and have Romeo rescue Juliet from the Capulet family's tomb.

This selection is the fifth, and final, **act** of the play. As Act V begins, Juliet has taken the potion, is believed to be dead, and lies in her tomb. Friar Lawrence has given his letter for Romeo to a messenger. Unfortunately, the messenger is delayed and Balthasar, Romeo's servant, gets to Romeo in Mantua first. Balthasar doesn't know about the plan. He tells Romeo that Juliet is dead. The stage is set for the dramatic **climax** of the play. As is typical in Shakespeare's plays, this act is filled with both **dramatic irony** and **foreshadowing**.

Literary Terms

act a major unit of action in a play

climax the high point of interest or suspense in a story or play

drama a story told through the words and actions of characters, written to be performed as well as read

dramatic irony when the audience or reader knows more than the characters know

foreshadowing clues or hints that a writer gives about something that has not yet happened

playwright a writer of plays

tragedy a play that ends with the suffering or death of one or more of the main characters

Characters in *Romeo and Juliet*, Act V

The Montague Family	Friends of the Montagues	Montague Family Servants	Others
Romeo	Mercutio, *Romeo's friend*	Balthasar, *Romeo's servant*	The Prince of Verona
Montague, *Romeo's father*	*and a relative of the*		Friar Lawrence
Lady Montague, *Romeo's*	*prince of Verona*		Friar John
mother			The apothecary
			Paris's page *(servant)*
The Capulet Family	**Friends of the Capulets**	**Capulet Family Servants**	Chief watchman
Juliet	Paris, *chosen by Juliet's*	Juliet's Nurse	Second watchman
Capulet, *Juliet's father*	*parents to marry her and*		Third watchman
Lady Capulet, *Juliet's*	*a relative of the prince of*		
mother	*Verona*		
Tybalt, *Juliet's cousin*			

Romeo

& Juliet

Act V

Scene I. Mantua. A street.

Enter Romeo.

Romeo If I may trust the **flattering** truth of sleep,
My dreams presage some joyful news at hand.
My bosom's lord sits lightly in his throne,
And all this day an unaccustomed spirit
5 Lifts me above the ground with cheerful thoughts.
I dreamt my lady came and found me dead
(Strange dream that gives a dead man leave to think!)
And breathed such life with kisses in my lips
That I revived and was an emperor.
10 Ah me! How sweet is love itself possessed,
When but love's shadows are so rich in joy!

Enter Romeo's Man [Balthasar, booted].

News from Verona! How now, Balthasar?
Dost thou not bring me letters from the friar?
How doth my lady? Is my father well?
15 How fares my Juliet? That I ask again,
For nothing can be ill if she be well.

Romeo thinks that if he can trust his pleasant dreams, they predict (*presage*) joyful news. His *bosom's lord* is his heart. Romeo's dream is an example both of dramatic irony and of foreshadowing. The audience knows that Juliet lies in her tomb but is not really dead. Romeo doesn't know this. The dream also foreshadows the climax of this final act.

Romeo is happy to see his servant, Balthasar, because he expects that Balthasar has news about Juliet. *The friar* is Friar Lawrence, the priest who secretly married Romeo and Juliet. As the audience knows, but Romeo does not, Friar Lawrence has sent Romeo a letter—unfortunately, Balthasar has arrived before the friar's messenger.

flattering pleasing or soothing to oneself

Capel's monument is
the Capulet family
tomb.

Man Then she is well, and nothing can be ill.
Her body sleeps in Capel's monument,
And her **immortal** part with angels lives.
20 I saw her laid low in her **kindred's** vault
And presently took post to tell it you.
O, pardon me for bringing these ill news,
Since you did leave it for my office, sir.

Office means duty.

Romeo Is it e'en so? Then I defy you, stars!
25 Thou knowest my lodging. Get me ink and paper
And hire post horses. I will hence tonight.

Man I do **beseech** you, sir, have patience.
Your looks are pale and wild and do import
Some misadventure.

Romeo reacts to the
news of Juliet's
supposed death by
announcing that he will
return to Verona that
night. Notice how
Balthasar's words help
us understand Romeo's
feelings. Romeo's *pale*
and *wild* appearance
suggests some
misfortune to come.

Romeo   Tush, thou art deceived.
30 Leave me and do the thing I bid thee do.
Hast thou no letters to me from the friar?

Man No, my good lord.

Romeo   No matter. Get thee gone.
And hire those horses. I'll be with thee straight.

Exit [Balthasar].

Well, Juliet, I will lie with thee tonight.
35 Let's see for means. O mischief, thou art swift
To enter in the thoughts of desperate men!
I do remember an apothecary,
And hereabouts 'a dwells, which late I noted,
In tatt'red weeds, with overwhelming brows,
40 **Culling** of simples. **Meager** were his looks,

Romeo recalls seeing a
druggist *(apothecary)*
nearby, in torn clothing
and with a frowning
expression. The man
was collecting herbs
(simples) used as
medicine.

beseech to beg	**immortal** free from death	**kindred** relatives
cull to collect or sort		**meager** thin

Sharp **misery** had worn him to the bones;
And in his needy shop a tortoise hung,
An alligator stuffed, and other skins
Of ill-shaped fishes; and about his shelves
45 A beggarly account of empty boxes,
Green earthen pots, bladders, and musty seeds,
Remnants of packthread, and old cakes of roses
Were thinly scatterèd, to make up a show.
Noting this **penury**, to myself I said,
50 "And if a man did need a poison now
Whose sale is present death in Mantua,
Here lives a caitiff **wretch** would sell it him."
O, this same thought did but forerun my need,
And this same needy man must sell it me.
55 As I remember, this should be the house.
Being holiday, the beggar's shop is shut.
What, ho! Apothecary!

[Enter Apothecary.]

Apothecary   Who calls so loud?

Romeo Come hither, man. I see that thou art poor.
Hold, there is forty ducats. Let me have
60 A dram of poison, such soon-speeding gear
As will **disperse** itself through all the veins
That the life-weary taker may fall dead,
And that the trunk may be **discharged** of breath
As **violently** as hasty powder fired
65 Doth hurry from the fatal cannon's womb.

Apothecary Such mortal drugs I have; but Mantua's law
Is death to any he that utters them.

> The druggist, Romeo recalls, was very poor and shabby. Such a miserable *(caitiff)* man, he thinks, would sell him poison, which is illegal in Mantua.

> Romeo asks for fast-working *(soon-speeding)* poison. The *trunk* is the body.

> *Mortal* means deadly. *Utters* means sells.

discharge to get rid of

disperse to scatter

misery suffering

penury poverty

remnant a trace

violently extremely; without control

wretch a miserable creature

Romeo Art thou so bare and full of wretchedness
And fearest to die? **Famine** is in thy cheeks,
70 Need and **oppression** starveth in thy eyes,
Contempt and beggary hangs upon thy back:
The world is not thy friend, nor the world's law;
The world affords no law to make thee rich;
Then be not poor, but break it and take this.

75 **Apothecary** My poverty but not my will consents.

Romeo I pay thy poverty and not thy will.

Apothecary Put this in any liquid thing you will
And drink it off, and if you had the strength
Of twenty men, it would **dispatch** you straight.

80 **Romeo** There is thy gold—worse poison to men's souls,
Doing more murder in this **loathsome** world,
Than these poor compounds that thou mayst not sell.
I sell thee poison; thou hast sold me none.
Farewell. Buy food and get thyself in flesh.
85 Come, **cordial** and not poison, go with me
To Juliet's grave; for there must I use thee.

Exeunt.

Romeo persuades the druggist to sell him the poison. He points out how poor and starving the man is. Since "the world's law" hasn't helped him, he need not follow the law. The druggist gives in, but only because he needs the money.

Romeo notes that *gold*—money—has destroyed more people than poison has. For him, the poison is life-giving because it will take him where he thinks Juliet has gone: into death.

contempt scorn	**dispatch** to send	**loathsome** hateful
cordial life-giving liquid	**famine** hunger	**oppression** injustice

Scene II. Friar Lawrence's cell.

Enter Friar John to Friar Lawrence.

John Holy Franciscan friar, brother, ho!

Enter [Friar] Lawrence.

Lawrence This same should be the voice of Friar John.
Welcome from Mantua. What says Romeo?
Or, if his mind be writ, give me his letter.

5 **John** Going to find a barefoot brother out,
One of our order, to **associate** me
Here in this city visiting the sick,
And finding him, the searchers of the town,
Suspecting that we both were in a house
10 Where the **infectious pestilence** did **reign**,
Sealed up the doors, and would not let us forth,
So that my speed to Mantua there was stayed.

Lawrence Who bare my letter, then, to Romeo?

John I could not send it—here it is again—
15 Nor get a messenger to bring it thee,
So fearful were they of infection.

Lawrence Unhappy fortune! By my brotherhood,
The letter was not nice, but full of charge,
Of dear import; and the neglecting it
20 May do much danger. Friar John, go **hence**,
Get me an iron crow and bring it straight
Unto my cell.

Friar Lawrence's *cell* is his small room. Friar John is the messenger who was to have brought the letter to Romeo in Mantua.

Friar John went looking for another religious brother to go with him to Mantua. The other man was visiting sick people. Health officers, thinking that both had been with sick people and might spread disease, wouldn't let either leave. Friar John was unable to go to Mantua.

Friar Lawrence remarks that his letter was urgently important. *Nice* means unimportant.

An *iron crow* is a crowbar, a tool used to pry something open.

associate to accompany	**hence** away	**pestilence** disease
	infectious catching	**reign** to rule

| John | Brother, I'll go and bring it thee. |

Exit.

Lawrence Now must I to the monument alone.
Within this three hours will fair Juliet wake.
25 She will beshrew me much that Romeo
Hath had no notice of these accidents;
But I will write again to Mantua,
And keep her at my cell till Romeo come —
Poor living corse, closed in a dead man's tomb!

Exit.

Friar Lawrence hurries off to the tomb where, in three hours, Juliet will wake up. He plans to write to Romeo again, keeping Juliet with him until Romeo arrives. *Corse* is another word for corpse, or dead body. Juliet is, of course, alive.

Scene III. A churchyard; in it a monument belonging to the Capulets.

Enter Paris and his Page [with flowers and sweet water].

Paris Give me thy torch, boy. Hence, and stand **aloof**.
Yet put it out, for I would not be seen.
Under yond yew trees lay thee all along,
Holding thy ear close to the hollow ground.
5 So shall no foot upon the churchyard tread
(Being loose, unfirm, with digging up of graves)
But thou shalt hear it. Whistle then to me,
As signal that thou hearest something approach.
Give me those flowers. Do as I bid thee, go.

10 Page *[Aside]* I am almost afraid to stand alone
Here in the churchyard; yet I will adventure.

[Retires.]

Paris is the man Juliet's parents chose for her to marry. His young servant is with him.

Lay thee all along means lie flat on the ground. Paris asks the page to listen for the footsteps of anyone coming.

aloof apart

Paris Sweet flower, with flowers thy bridal bed I **strew**
    (O woe! thy canopy is dust and stones)
Which with sweet water nightly I will dew;
15   Or, wanting that, with tears distilled by moans.
The obsequies that I for thee will keep
Nightly shall be to strew thy grave and weep.

Paris has come to Juliet's tomb to scatter flowers and perfume. *Obsequies* are funeral ceremonies.

Whistle Boy.

The boy gives warning something doth approach.
What cursèd foot wanders this way tonight
20 To cross my obsequies and true love's **rite**?
What, with a torch? Muffle me, night, awhile.

[Retires.]

*Enter Romeo, [and Balthasar with a torch,
a mattock, and a crow of iron].*

Romeo Give me that mattock and the wrenching iron.
Hold, take this letter. Early in the morning
See thou deliver it to my lord and father.
25 Give me the light. Upon thy life I charge thee,
Whate'er thou hearest or seest, stand all aloof
And do not interrupt me in my course.
Why I descend into this bed of death
Is partly to behold my lady's face,
30 But chiefly to take thence from her dead finger
A precious ring—a ring that I must use
In dear employment. Therefore hence, be gone.
But if thou, jealous, dost return to **pry**
In what I farther shall intend to do,
35 By heaven, I will tear thee joint by joint

Romeo and Balthasar have a torch (for light), an axe (*mattock*), and a crowbar (also called a *wrenching iron*). The tools are for opening Juliet's tomb.

Romeo plans to take a ring from Juliet's finger and use it for an important purpose (*dear employment*).

---

pry to snoop; to spy   **rite** a ceremony   **strew** to scatter widely

And strew this hungry churchyard with thy limbs
The time and my intents are savage-wild,
More fierce and more **inexorable** far
Than empty tigers or the roaring sea.

40 Balthasar I will be gone, sir, and not trouble ye.

Romeo So shalt thou show me friendship. Take thou that.
Live, and be prosperous; and farewell, good fellow.

Balthasar *[Aside]* For all this same, I'll hide me here-about.
His looks I fear, and his intents I doubt.   *[Retires.]*

Romeo curses the tomb as a *maw*, or stomach, that is stuffed with the *dearest morsel of the earth*—Juliet. He vows to add more food to the tomb—himself.

45 Romeo Thou **detestable** maw, thou womb of death,
Gorged with the dearest **morsel** of the earth,
Thus I enforce thy rotten jaws to open,
And in despite I'll cram thee with more food.

[Romeo opens the tomb.]

Paris This is that banished **haughty** Montague
50 That murd'red my love's cousin—with which grief
It is supposed the fair creature died—
And here is come to do some villainous shame
To the dead bodies. I will **apprehend** him.
Stop thy **unhallowèd** toil, vile Montague!

Paris thinks Romeo, having killed Juliet's cousin, Tybalt, has come to take further revenge on the Capulet family. The family assumes that Juliet died from grief over Tybalt's death.

55 Can **vengeance** be pursued further than death?
Condemnèd villain, I do apprehend thee.
Obey, and go with me; for thou must die.

Romeo I must indeed; and therefore came I hither.
Good gentle youth, tempt not a desp'rate man.
60 Fly hence and leave me. Think upon these gone;
Let them affright thee. I beseech thee, youth,

apprehend to catch; to arrest

detestable hateful

haughty proud; feeling superior to others

inexorable unable to be changed or influenced

morsel a small piece

unhallowed unholy

vengeance force; revenge

Put not another sin upon my head
By urging me to fury. O, be gone!
By heaven, I love thee better than myself,
65 For I come hither armed against myself.
Stay not, be gone. Live, and hereafter say
A madman's mercy bid thee run away.

Romeo begs Paris, whom he does not recognize, not to anger him into more violence.

Paris I do defy thy conjurations.
And apprehend thee for a **felon** here.

Conjurations are appeals. Paris ignores Romeo's plea.

70 Romeo Wilt thou **provoke** me? Then have at thee, boy!

[They fight.]

Page O Lord, they fight! I will go call the watch.

[Exit. Paris falls.]

Paris O, I am slain! If thou be merciful,
Open the tomb, lay me with Juliet.

[Dies.]

Romeo In faith, I will. Let me **peruse** this face.
75 Mercutio's **kinsman**, noble County Paris!
What said my man when my betossèd soul
Did not attend him as we rode? I think
He told me Paris should have married Juliet.
Said he not so, or did I dream it so?
80 Or am I mad, hearing him talk of Juliet,
To think it was so? O, give me thy hand,
One writ with me in sour misfortune's book!
I'll bury thee in a triumphant grave.
A grave? O, no, a lanthorn, slaught'red youth,

Romeo now recognizes Paris, who was a relative of Mercutio, Romeo's best friend. He bitterly regrets having killed him. *County* is a title, like Count. *Betossed* means upset. *To attend* means to pay attention to. *Writ* means wrote or written. *Lanthorn* is a dome with windows; it is also another word for lantern.

---

felon a criminal **peruse** to look at **provoke** to cause someone to take action
kinsman a relative

Juliet's beauty makes the tomb seem like a hall lit for a celebration. *Interred* means buried. The dead man is Paris.

85 For here lies Juliet, and her beauty makes
This vault a feasting presence full of light.
Death, lie thou there, by a dead man interred.

[Lays him in the tomb.]

It used to be thought that people feel happy just before dying. Romeo does not feel this *lightning. Keepers* are jailers.

How oft when men are at the point of death
Have they been merry! Which their keepers call
90 A lightning before death. O, how may I
Call this a lightning? O my love, my wife!
Death, that hath sucked the honey of thy breath,
Hath had no power yet upon thy beauty.
Thou art not conquered. Beauty's ensign yet

Juliet, whom the audience knows is not really dead, has color in her lips and cheeks. An *ensign* is a flag, or banner.

95 Is **crimson** in thy lips and in thy cheeks,
And death's pale flag is not advancèd there.
Tybalt, liest thou there in thy bloody sheet?
O, what more favor can I do thee
Then with that hand that cut thy youth in twain

Romeo, seeing Tybalt's body, promises to kill himself with the same hand—his own—that murdered Tybalt.

100 To sunder his that was thine enemy?
Forgive me, cousin! Ah, dear Juliet,
Why art thou yet so fair? Shall I believe
That **unsubstantial** Death is amorous,
And that the lean **abhorrèd** monster keeps

Since Juliet remains so beautiful, Romeo wonders if Death has fallen in love with her. To protect her from her lover Death, Romeo will stay with her forever in the tomb (by killing himself).

105 Thee here in dark to be his paramour?
For fear of that I still will stay with thee
And never from this pallet of dim night
Depart again. Here, here will I remain
With worms that are thy chambermaids. O, here
110 Will I set up my everlasting rest
And shake the yoke of **inauspicious** stars
From this world-wearied flesh. Eyes, look your last!
Arms, take your last embrace! And lips, O you

abhorred hated   **inauspicious** unlucky   **unsubstantial** not physical; of the spirit

crimson red

The doors of breath, seal with a **righteous** kiss
115 A dateless bargain to **engrossing** death!
Come, bitter conduct; come, **unsavory** guide!
Thou desperate pilot, now at once run on
The dashing rocks thy seasick weary bark!
Here's to my love! *[Drinks.]* O true apothecary!
120 Thy drugs are quick. Thus with a kiss I die.   *[Falls.]*

Enter Friar [Lawrence], with lanthorn, crow, and spade.

Friar Saint Francis be my speed! How oft tonight
Have my old feet stumbled at graves! Who's there?

Balthasar Here's one, a friend, and one that knows you well.

A *conduct* is a guide. The poison is Romeo's *bitter conduct* and *unsavory guide*. The *desperate pilot* is Romeo himself, running his *seasick weary bark* (his body —a *bark* is a boat) onto the rocks—into death.

Stumbling was considered a sign of bad luck to come.

engrossing taking in everything   **righteous** good; right   **unsavory** unpleasant; bad-tasting

Friar Lawrence sees Romeo's light shining from the Capulets' tomb. He remarks that light is wasted on *grubs*—worms—and dead bodies. Since Romeo is now dead, the friar's words are truer than he knows.

Friar **Bliss** be upon you! Tell me, good my friend,
125 What torch is yond that vainly lends his light
To grubs and eyeless skulls? As I **discern**,
It burneth in the Capels' monument.

Balthasar It doth so, holy sir; and there's my master,
One that you love.

Friar Who is it?

Balthasar Romeo.

Friar How long hath he been there?

130 **Balthasar** Full half an hour.

Friar Go with me to the vault.

Balthasar I dare not, sir.
My master knows not but I am gone hence,
And fearfully did menace me with death
If I did stay to look on his intents.

135 **Friar** Stay then; I'll go alone. Fear comes upon me.
O, much I fear some ill unthrifty thing.

Ill means bad; *unthrifty* means unfortunate.

Balthasar As I did sleep under this yew tree here,
I dreamt my master and another fought,
And that my master slew him.

Friar Romeo!
140 Alack, alack, what blood is this which stains
The stony entrance of this sepulcher?
What mean these masterless and gory swords
To lie discolored by this place of peace?

A *sepulcher* is a tomb. The friar sees Romeo's *masterless*—abandoned—and bloody swords. The swords were used to kill Paris.

bliss great happiness	**discern** to recognize; to make out

[Enters the tomb.]

Romeo! O, pale! Who else? What, Paris too?
145 And steeped in blood? Ah, what an unkind hour
Is guilty of this **lamentable** chance!
The lady stirs.

[Juliet rises.]

Juliet O comfortable friar! Where is my lord?
I do remember well where I should be,
150 And there I am. Where is my Romeo?

Friar I hear some noise. Lady, come from that nest
Of death, **contagion**, and unnatural sleep.
A greater power than we can **contradict**
Hath **thwarted** our intents. Come, come away.

Thwarted our intents means ruined our plans.

155 Thy husband in thy **bosom** there lies dead;
And Paris too. Come, I'll dispose of thee
Among a sisterhood of holy **nuns**.
Stay not to question, for the watch is coming.
Come, go, good Juliet. I dare no longer stay.

The friar has heard the watchman coming. Frightened of being discovered, he leaves.

160 Juliet Go, get thee hence, for I will not away.

Exit [Friar].

What's here? A cup, closed in my truelove's hand?
Poison, I see, hath been his timeless end.
O churl! Drunk all, and left no friendly drop
To help me after? I will kiss thy lips.
165 Haply some poison yet doth hang on them
To make me die with a restorative.   *[Kisses him.]*
Thy lips are warm!

A churl is a selfish person. Juliet calls Romeo selfish for leaving no friendly drop of poison for her. A restorative is medicine. She kisses Romeo in hopes of getting some poison from his lips.

bosom a breast; a heart

contagion a spreading disease

contradict to deny

lamentable distressing; sorrowful

nun a member of a Catholic sisterhood

thwart to block or stop

Chief Watchman [*Within*] Lead, boy. Which way?

Happy means convenient.

Juliet Yea, noise? Then I'll be brief. O happy dagger!

[*Snatches Romeo's dagger.*]

This is thy **sheath**; there rust, and let me die.

[*She stabs herself and falls.*]

Enter [Paris'] Boy and Watch.

170 **Boy** This is the place. There, where the torch doth burn.

Chief Watchman The ground is bloody. Search about the churchyard.

Attach means arrest.

Go, some of you; whoe'er you find attach.

sheath a cover or case

[Exeunt some of the Watch.]

Pitiful sight! Here lies the County slain;
And Juliet bleeding, warm, and newly dead,
175 Who here hath lain this two days burièd.
Go, tell the Prince; run to the Capulets;
Raise up the Montagues; some others search.

[Exeunt others of the Watch.]

We see the ground whereon these woes do lie,
But the true ground of all these **piteous** woes
180 We cannot without **circumstance** descry.

Enter [some of the Watch, with] Romeo's Man [Balthasar].

Second Watchman Here's Romeo's man. We found him in the churchyard.

Chief Watchman Hold him in safety till the Prince come hither.

Enter Friar [Lawrence] and another Watchman.

Third Watchman Here is a friar that trembles, sighs, and weeps.
We took this mattock and this spade from him
185 As he was coming from this churchyard's side.

Chief Watchman A great **suspicion**! Stay the friar too.

Enter the Prince [and Attendants].

Prince What misadventure is so early up,
That calls our person from our morning rest?

> The chief watchman says that they cannot understand the cause of these *woes* (misery, sorrows) without knowing the facts.

> *Stay* means keep or hold. They suspect that the friar has had something to do with these deaths.

circumstance a condition; details	**piteous** miserable; sad **pitiful** causing pity	**suspicion** mistrust, doubt

Enter Capulet and his Wife [with others].

Capulet What should it be, that is so shrieked abroad?

190 Lady Capulet O, the people in the street cry "Romeo,"
Some "Juliet," and some "Paris"; and all run
With open outcry toward our monument.

Prince What fear is this which startles in your ears?

Chief Watchman **Sovereign**, here lies the County Paris slain;
195 And Romeo dead; and Juliet, dead before,
Warm and new killed.

Prince Search, seek, and know how this foul murder comes.

Chief Watchman Here is a friar, and slaughtered Romeo's
man,
With instruments upon them fit to open
200 These dead men's tombs.

Capulet O heavens! O wife, look how our daughter bleeds!
This dagger hath mista'en, for, lo, his house
Is empty on the back of Montague,
And it missheathèd in my daughter's bosom!

Juliet's father says that the dagger in Juliet's body has lost its way. It should be in Romeo's back, not in his daughter's breast. His house *is its sheath.*

205 Lady Capulet O me, this sight of death is as a bell
That warns my old age to a sepulcher.

Enter Montague [and others].

Prince Come, Montague; for thou art early up
To see thy son and heir more early down.

sovereign a king

Montague Alas, my liege, my wife is dead tonight!
210 Grief of my son's **exile** hath stopped her breath.
What further woe **conspires** against mine age?

Prince Look, and thou shalt see.

Montague Oh thou untaught! What manners is in this,
To press before thy father to a grave?

215 **Prince** Seal up the mouth of outrage for a while,
Till we can clear these **ambiguities**
And know their spring, their head, their true descent;
And then will I be general of your woes
And lead you even to death. Meantime forbear,
220 And let mischance be slave to patience.
Bring forth the parties of suspicion.

Friar I am the greatest, able to do least,
Yet most suspected, as the time and place
Doth make against me, of this direful murder;
225 And here I stand, both to **impeach** and **purge**
Myself condemnèd and myself excused.

Prince Then say at once what thou dost know in this.

Friar I will be brief, for my short date of breath
Is not so long as is a **tedious** tale.
230 Romeo, there dead, was husband to that Juliet;
And she, there dead, that's Romeo's faithful wife.
I married them; and their stol'n marriage day
Was Tybalt's doomsday, whose **untimely** death
Banished the new-made bridegroom from this city;
235 For whom, and not for Tybalt, Juliet pined.

My liege means my lord. Romeo's father reports that Romeo's mother has died of grief over her son's exile to Mantua.

Seal up the mouth of outrage means to stop the cries of grief. The Prince says that they must find out how these deaths came about. Then he will be *general of your woes*— leader of your grieving. Meanwhile, they must patiently control their reactions to this misfortune.

The friar notes that he himself is the main suspect in this *direful*— terrible—murder. He is prepared both to blame and to excuse himself and others.

Date of breath means term of life. The friar tells them that he secretly married Romeo and Juliet. Their wedding day was also the day that Romeo killed Tybalt. Romeo's banishment to Mantua for that killing was what Juliet grieved about— not Tybalt's death.

ambiguity a mystery	**impeach** to accuse	**untimely** before its proper time
conspire to plot against	**purge** to free from blame	
exile separation from homeland	**tedious** tiring; boring	

You, to remove that **siege** of grief from her,
Betrothed and would have married her perforce
To County Paris. Then comes she to me
And with wild looks bid me **devise** some mean
240 To rid her from this second marriage,
Or in my cell there would she kill herself.
Then gave I her (so tutored by my art)
A sleeping **potion**; which so took effect
As I intended, for it wrought on her
245 The form of death. Meantime I writ to Romeo
That he should hither come as this **dire** night
To help to take her from her borrowed grave,
Being the time the potion's force should cease.
But he which bore my letter, Friar John,
250 Was stayed by accident, and yesternight
Returned my letter back. Then all alone
At the prefixèd hour of her waking
Came I to take her from her kindred's vault;
Meaning to keep her closely at my cell
255 Till I conveniently could send to Romeo.
But when I came, some minute ere the time
Of her awakening, here untimely lay
The noble Paris and true Romeo dead.
She wakes; and I **entreated** her come forth
260 And bear this work of heaven with patience;
But then a noise did scare me from the tomb,
And she, too desperate, would not go with me,
But, as it seems, did violence on herself.
All this I know, and to the marriage
265 Her nurse is privy; and if aught in this
Miscarried by my fault, let my old life

Wrought means brought about. Friar Lawrence had given Juliet a drink that made her look as if she were dead.

The friar had written to Romeo, telling him to come to the tomb on this night, when the drink's effects would wear off.

When Friar John came back with Romeo's letter, undelivered, Friar Lawrence came alone to the tomb at the *prefixed*—set in advance—hour of Juliet's waking up. He planned to hide her in his room until he could contact Romeo. The friar found Romeo and Paris dead. He heard the watchmen, but Juliet would not go away with him. Instead, she *did violence on herself*—killed herself. The friar notes that Juliet's nurse is *privy*—shares the secret—to Juliet's marriage.

betroth to promise in marriage

devise to think up; to invent

dire severe; terrible

entreat to beg

potion a drink with special powers

siege a battle

Be sacrificed some hour before his time
Unto the **rigor** of severest law.

Prince We still have known thee for a holy man.
270 Where's Romeo's man? What can he say to this?

Balthasar I brought my master news of Juliet's death;
And then in post he came from Mantua
To this same place, to this same monument.
This letter he early bid me give his father,
275 And threat'ned me with death, going in the vault,
If I departed not and left him there.

Prince Give me the letter. I will look on it.
Where is the County's page that raised the watch?
Sirrah, what made your master in this place?

280 Boy He came with flowers to strew his lady's grave;
And bid me stand aloof, and so I did.
Anon comes one with light to ope the tomb;
And by and by my master drew on him;
And then I ran away to call the watch.

285 Prince This letter doth make good the friar's words,
Their course of love, the tidings of her death;
And here he writes that he did buy a poison
Of a poor pothecary and therewithal
Came to this vault to die and lie with Juliet.
290 Where be these enemies? Capulet, Montague,
See what a **scourge** is laid upon your hate,
That heaven finds means to kill your joys with love.
And I, for winking at your **discords** too,
Have lost a brace of kinsmen. All are punished.

The friar says that if he was at fault in the deaths, he will turn himself over to the law.

The prince asks Paris's servant what his master was doing in the vault.

The boy recalls that *one with light*—Romeo—came to open the tomb, and that Paris came up to him.

The prince calls both families to see the punishment for their quarreling: their dead children. The prince himself, because he closed his eyes to their quarrels, has lost two relatives—Mercutio and Paris.

discord a quarrel   **rigor** strictness   **scourge** a punishment

295 **Capulet** O brother Montague, give me thy hand.
This is my daughter's jointure, for no more
Can I demand.

Montague   But I can give thee more;
For I will raise her statue in pure gold,
That whiles Verona by that name is known,
300 There shall no figure at such rate be set
As that of true and faithful Juliet.

Capulet As rich shall Romeo's by his lady's lie—
Poor sacrifices of our **enmity**!

Prince A glooming peace this morning with it brings.
305 The sun for sorrow will not show his head.
Go hence, to have more talk of these sad things;
Some shall be pardoned, and some punishèd;
For never was a story of more woe
Than this of Juliet and her Romeo.

[Exeunt omnes.]

FINIS

enmity hatred

Romeo and Juliet
William Shakespeare

Directions Write the answers to these questions using complete sentences.

Comprehension: Identifying Facts

1. What does Romeo say he dreamed the night before this act opens?

2. What does Balthasar, Romeo's servant, tell him about Juliet?

3. What does Romeo ask the apothecary (druggist) to give him?

4. Why was Friar John not able to deliver the letter to Romeo?

5. Who does Romeo meet inside Juliet's tomb?

6. Why has Paris come to Juliet's tomb? Why does Romeo kill Paris?

7. Why does Friar Lawrence leave the tomb without Juliet?

8. What does Juliet do when she realizes that Romeo is dead?

9. Who explains what happened to Romeo and Juliet?

10. What do Romeo's father and Juliet's father do at the end of the play?

Comprehension: Understanding Main Ideas

11. How is Romeo's dream an example both of dramatic irony and of foreshadowing?

12. Why does the apothecary sell Romeo the poison, even when it is illegal?

13. Why is Friar Lawrence upset when he learns that the letter he sent to Romeo hasn't been delivered?

14. What is the setting of each of the act's three scenes?

15. In Scene 3, what does Romeo mean when he says, "Thus I enforce thy rotten jaws to open, and in despite I'll cram thee with more food?"

16. How does Romeo react when he is challenged by Paris?

17. Juliet remains so beautiful in her tomb that Romeo wonders if Death is keeping her as his lover. Why is this another example of dramatic irony?

18. How would this play have been different if Juliet had awakened from her drugged sleep just a few moments earlier?

19. How do both Romeo and Juliet refer to the poison? How is this different from the way most people would think of poison?

20. According to the prince, "all are punished" by the deaths of Romeo, Juliet, Tybalt, Mercutio, and Paris. In what ways is this true?

Review Continued on Next Page

Romeo and Juliet, *Continued*

Understanding Literature: Tragedy

A tragedy is a play with serious themes in which one or more main characters suffers or dies. The Greek philosopher Aristotle said that tragedies make an audience feel both pity and fear. The audience feels pity for the characters' suffering. They feel fear as they watch characters being destroyed. As they become involved in the play's events, however, they are *purged*—washed clean—of these strong emotions.

Shakespeare's tragedies followed the Greek model in some ways, but also showed his own creative genius. *Romeo and Juliet* is Shakespeare's first romantic tragedy. He based it on a story that was already well known. His play made the tale of these tragic young lovers popular for centuries.

21. How might the events of Act V of *Romeo and Juliet* cause the audience to feel pity for the characters?

22. Why might the audience feel fear for the characters?

23. How might the act of forgiveness that Montague and Capulet share in this act affect the pity and fear felt by the audience?

24. Romeo calls himself "fortune's fool." In what ways does Romeo suffer because of chance, fate, or bad luck?

25. How might we say that Romeo suffers because of weaknesses in his character?

Critical Thinking

26. At the end of the play, the prince says, "Some shall be pardoned, and some punished." Who do you think should be punished? Who should be pardoned? Why?

27. How would you describe the character of Friar Lawrence?

28. Do you think Romeo was justified in killing Paris? Why or why not?

29. In your own words, describe Juliet's feelings when she wakes up to find Romeo dead. How would you have felt? What would you have done?

30. How could *Romeo and Juliet* have ended happily? Outline another ending for the play.

Writing on Your Own Write a description of Romeo and Juliet as if they were friends of yours today. Explain why your friends are like the "star-crossed lovers" Shakespeare wrote about over 500 years ago.

A Raisin in the Sun
Lorraine Hansberry

Lorraine Hansberry
1930–1965

Literary Terms

conflict the struggle of the protagonist against himself or herself, another person, or nature

dialogue the conversation between characters in a play

realistic drama plays that tell the stories of ordinary people in a lifelike manner

scene a unit of action in a play that takes place in one setting

stage directions notes by playwrights describing such things as setting, lighting, sound effects, and how the actors are to look, behave, move, and speak

About the Author

Lorraine Hansberry was the first African-American woman to have a play produced on Broadway: *A Raisin in the Sun*, in 1959. Born in Chicago in 1930, she was the child of well-respected parents. Famous African Americans, such as poet Langston Hughes, often came to their home. Her parents also fought against laws that kept African Americans from moving to certain neighborhoods and attending certain schools.

At first, Hansberry planned to be an artist. However, when she moved to New York in 1950, she discovered her true gift, writing. She followed *A Raisin in the Sun* with another play, *The Sign in Sidney Brustein's Window*. This play was less successful. Lorraine Hansberry died of cancer at age 34.

About the Selection

A Raisin in the Sun won the New York Drama Critics Circle Award for Best Play, the first time this prize went to an African American. The play's director was the first African American to direct a play on Broadway since 1907. The play also began the career of noted actor and director Sidney Poitier.

A Raisin in the Sun is a **realistic drama** about an African-American family living in Chicago. The time is "sometime between World War II and the present." (World War II ended in 1945.) Through her **dialogue** and **stage directions**, Hansberry creates an everyday world.

The selection from the play is Act 1, Scene 1. An act is a major unit of action in a play. Each act may contain several **scenes.** Each scene of a play takes place in one setting. Here, readers meet the Younger family and discover the important **conflicts** that will drive the play. The scene takes place in the family's living room, early one morning.

A Raisin in the Sun

What happens to a dream deferred?
Does it dry up
Like a raisin in the sun?
Or fester like a sore—
And then run?
Does it stink like rotten meat
Or crust and sugar over—
Like a syrupy sweet?

Maybe it just sags
Like a heavy load.

Or does it explode?

— Langston Hughes

Act I

Scene One

The YOUNGER *living room would be a comfortable and well-ordered room if it were not for a number of indestructible contradictions to this state of being. Its funishings are typical and undistinguished and their primary feature now is that they have clearly had to accommodate the living of too many people for too many years—and they are tired. Still, we can see that at some time, a time probably no longer remembered by the family (except perhaps for* MAMA*), the furnishings of this room were actually selected with care and love and even hope—and brought to this apartment and arranged with taste and pride.*

That was a long time ago. Now the once loved pattern of the couch upholstery has to fight to show itself from under acres of crocheted doilies and couch covers which have themselves finally come to be more important than the upholstery. And here a table or a chair has been moved to disguise the worn places in the carpet; but the carpet has fought back by showing its weariness, with depressing uniformity, elsewhere on its surface.

Weariness has, in fact, won in this room. Everything has been polished, washed, sat on, used, scrubbed too often. All pretenses but living itself have long since vanished from the very atmosphere of this room.

Moreover, a section of this room, for it is not really a room unto itself, though the landlord's lease would make it seem so, slopes backward to provide a small kitchen area, where the family prepares the meals that are eaten in the living room proper, which must also serve as dining room. The single window that has been provided for these "two" rooms is located in this kitchen area. The sole natural light the family may enjoy in the course of a day is only that which fights its way through this little window.

At left, a door leads to a bedroom which is shared by MAMA *and her daughter,* BENEATHA. *At right, opposite, is a second room (which in the beginning of the life of this apartment was probably a breakfast room) which serves as a bedroom for* WALTER *and his wife,* RUTH.

Time: Sometime between World War II and the present.

Place: Chicago's Southside.

At Rise: It is morning dark in the living room. TRAVIS *is asleep on the make-down bed at center. An alarm clock sounds from within the bedroom at right, and presently* RUTH *enters from that room and closes the door behind her. She crosses sleepily toward the window. As she passes her sleeping son she reaches down and shakes him a little. At the window she raises the shade and a dusky Southside morning light comes in feebly. She fills a pot with water and puts it on to boil. She calls to the boy, between yawns, in a slightly muffled voice.*

RUTH *is about thirty. We can see that she was a pretty girl, even* **exceptionally** *so, but now it is apparent that life has been little that she expected, and disappointment has already begun to hang in her face. In a few years, before thirty-five even, she will be known among her people as a "settled woman."*

She crosses to her son and gives him a good, final, rousing shake.

exceptionally more than usually

Notice all we learn about the setting and about Ruth in these stage directions. Stage directions are usually given in parentheses and printed in italics.

As you read, decide what the most important conflict in this play is.

Ruth Come on now, boy, it's seven thirty! *(Her son sits up at last, in a **stupor** of sleepiness).* I say hurry up, Travis! You ain't the only person in the world got to use a bathroom! *(The child, a sturdy, handsome little boy of ten or eleven, drags himself out of the bed and almost blindly takes his towels and "today's clothes" from drawers and a closet and goes out to the bathroom, which is in an outside hall and which is shared by another family or families on the same floor.* RUTH *crosses to the bedroom door at right and opens it and calls in to her husband)* Walter Lee! . . . It's after seven thirty! Lemme see you do some waking up in there now! *(She waits)* You better get up from there, man! It's after seven thirty I tell you. *(She waits again)* All right, you just go ahead and lay there and next thing you know Travis be finished and Mr. Johnson'll be in there and you'll be fussing and cussing round here like a madman! And be late too! *(She waits, at the end of patience)* Walter Lee—it's time for you to GET UP!

*(She waits another second and then starts to go into the bedroom, but is apparently satisfied that her husband has begun to get up. She stops, pulls the door to, and returns to the kitchen area. She wipes her face with a moist cloth and runs her fingers through her sleep-**disheveled** hair in a vain effort and ties an apron around her housecoat. The bedroom door at right opens and her husband stands in the doorway in his pajamas, which are rumpled and mismated. He is a lean, intense young man in his middle thirties, inclined to quick nervous movements and **erratic** speech habits— and always in his voice there is a quality of **indictment**)*

Walter Is he out yet?

Ruth What you mean *out?* He ain't hardly got in there good yet.

Walter *(Wandering in, still more **oriented** to sleep than to a new day)* Well, what was you doing all that yelling for if I can't even get in there yet? *(Stopping and thinking)* Check coming today?

Ruth They *said* Saturday and this is just Friday and I hopes to God you ain't going to get up here first thing this morning

Notice how the dialogue helps make this play a realistic drama.

disheveled untidy	**indictment** faultfinding	**stupor** a daze
erratic not ordinary; unexpected	**oriented** turned toward	

and start talking to me 'bout no money—'cause I 'bout don't want to hear it.

Walter Something the matter with you this morning?

Ruth No—I'm just sleepy as the devil. What kind of eggs you want?

Walter Not scrambled. (RUTH *starts to scramble eggs*) Paper come? (RUTH *points impatiently to the rolled up* Tribune *on the table, and he gets it and spreads it out and vaguely reads the front page*) Set off another bomb yesterday.

Ruth (**Maximum indifference**) Did they?

Walter (*Looking up*) What's the matter with you?

Ruth Ain't nothing the matter with me. And don't keep asking me that this morning.

Walter Ain't nobody bothering you. (*Reading the news of the day absently again*) Say Colonel McCormick is sick.

Ruth (*Affecting tea-party interest*) Is he now? Poor thing.

Walter (*Sighing and looking at his watch*) Oh, me. (*He waits*) Now what is that boy doing in that bathroom all this time? He just going to have to start getting up earlier. I can't be being late to work on account of him fooling around in there.

Ruth (*Turning on him*) Oh, no he ain't going to be getting up no earlier no such thing! It ain't his fault that he can't get to bed no earlier nights 'cause he got a bunch of crazy good-for-nothing clowns sitting up running their mouths in what is supposed to be his bedroom after ten o'clock at night . . .

Walter That's what you mad about, ain't it? The things I want to talk about with my friends just couldn't be important in your mind, could they?

Travis sleeps on a fold-out couch in the living room.

(*He rises and finds a cigarette in her handbag on the table and crosses to the little window and looks out, smoking and deeply enjoying this first one*)

---

indifference a lack of concern

maximum the most

Ruth (*Almost matter of factly, a complaint too automatic to deserve* **emphasis**) Why you always got to smoke before you eat in the morning?

Walter (*At the window*) Just look at 'em down there . . . Running and racing to work . . . (*He turns and faces his wife and watches her a moment at the stove, and then, suddenly*) You look young this morning, baby.

Ruth (*Indifferently*) Yeah?

Walter Just for a second—stirring them eggs. Just for a second it was—you looked real young again. (*He reaches for her; she crosses away. Then, drily*) It's gone now—you look like yourself again!

Ruth Man, if you don't shut up and leave me alone.

Walter (*Looking out to the street again*) First thing a man ought to learn in life is not to make love to no colored woman first thing in the morning. You all some eeeevil people at eight o'clock in the morning.

(TRAVIS *appears in the hall doorway, almost fully dressed and quite wide awake now, his towels and pajamas across his shoulders. He opens the door and signals for his father to make the bathroom in a hurry*)

Travis (*Watching the bathroom*) Daddy, come on! (WALTER *gets his bathroom utensils and flies out to the bathroom*)

Ruth Sit down and have your breakfast, Travis.

Travis Mama, this is Friday. (*Gleefully*) Check coming tomorrow, huh?

Ruth You get your mind off money and eat your breakfast.

Travis (*Eating*) This is the morning we supposed to bring the fifty cents to school.

Ruth Well, I ain't got no fifty cents this morning.

Travis Teacher say we have to.

Since the Younger family shares the bathroom in the hall with another family, they must hurry to get in first.

emphasis importance

Ruth I don't care what teacher say. I ain't got it. Eat your breakfast, Travis.

Travis I *am* eating.

Ruth Hush up now and just eat!

*(The boy gives her an **exasperated** look for her lack of understanding, and eats **grudgingly**)*

Travis You think Grandmama would have it?

Ruth No! And I want you to stop asking your grandmother for money, you hear me?

Travis *(Outraged)* Gaaaleee! I don't ask her, she just gimme it sometimes!

Ruth Travis Willard Younger—I got too much on me this morning to be—

Travis Maybe Daddy—

Ruth *Travis!*

*(The boy hushes **abruptly**. They are both quiet and tense for several seconds)*

Travis *(Presently)* Could I maybe go carry some groceries in front of the supermarket for a little while after school then?

Ruth Just hush, I said. *(TRAVIS jabs his spoon into his cereal bowl viciously, and rests his head in anger upon his fists)* If you through eating, you can get over there and make up your bed.

(The boy obeys stiffly and crosses the room, almost mechanically, to the bed and more or less folds the bedding into a heap, then angrily gets his books and cap)

Travis *(Sulking and standing apart from her unnaturally)* I'm gone.

Ruth *(Looking up from the stove to inspect him automatically)* Come here. *(He crosses to her and she studies his head)* If you don't take this comb and fix this here head, you better! *(TRAVIS puts down his books with a great sigh of **oppression**, and*

What makes this dialogue sound like real life?

abruptly suddenly, without warning	**exasperated** annoyed or bothered	**grudgingly** unwillingly **oppression** injustice

crosses to the mirror. His mother mutters under her breath about his "slubbornness") 'Bout to march out of here with that head looking just like chickens slept in it! I just don't know where you get your slubborn ways . . . And get your jacket, too. Looks chilly out this morning.

Travis *(With **conspicuously** brushed hair and jacket)* I'm gone.

Ruth Get carfare and milk money—*(Waving one finger)*—and not a single penny for no caps, you hear me?

Travis *(With **sullen** politeness)* Yes'm.

*(He turns in outrage to leave. His mother watches after him as in his **frustration** he approaches the door almost comically. When she speaks to him, her voice has become a very gentle tease)*

Ruth *(Mocking; as she thinks he would say it)* Oh, Mama makes me so mad sometimes, I don't know what to do! *(She waits and continues to his back as he stands stock-still in front of the door)* I wouldn't kiss that woman good-bye for nothing in this world this morning! *(The boy finally turns around and rolls his eyes at her, knowing the mood has changed and he is **vindicated**; he does not, however, move toward her yet)* Not for nothing in this world! *(She finally laughs aloud at him and holds out her arms to him and we see that it is a way between them, very old and practiced. He crosses to her and allows her to **embrace** him warmly but keeps his face fixed with **masculine** rigidity. She holds him back from her presently and looks at him and runs her fingers over the features of his face. With utter gentleness—)* Now— whose little old angry man are you?

Travis *(The masculinity and gruffness start to fade at last)* Aw gaalee—Mama . . .

Ruth *(**Mimicking**)* Aw—gaaaaalleeeee, Mama! *(She pushes him, with rough playfulness and finality, toward the door)* Get on out of here or you going to be late.

conspicuously obviously	**frustration** anger at defeat	**mimicking** imitating
embrace to hug	**masculine** male	**sullen** bad-tempered
		vindicated not guilty

Travis (*In the face of love, new **aggressiveness***) Mama, could I *please* go carry groceries?

Ruth Honey, it's starting to get so cold evenings.

Walter (*Coming in from the bathroom and drawing a make-believe gun from a make-believe holster and shooting at his son*) What is it he wants to do?

Ruth Go carry groceries after school at the supermarket.

Walter Well, let him go . . .

Travis (*Quickly, to the ally*) I *have* to—she won't gimme the fifty cents . . .

Walter (*To his wife only*) Why not?

Ruth (*Simply, and with flavor*) 'Cause we don't have it.

Walter (*To* RUTH *only*) What you tell the boy things like that for? (*Reaching down into his pants with a rather important gesture*) Here, son—

(*He hands the boy the coin, but his eyes are directed to his wife's.* TRAVIS *takes the money happily*)

Travis Thanks, Daddy.

(*He starts out.* RUTH *watches both of them with murder in her eyes.* WALTER *stands and stares back at her with **defiance**, and suddenly reaches into his pocket again on an afterthought*)

Walter (*Without even looking at his son, still staring hard at his wife*) In fact, here's another fifty cents . . . Buy yourself some fruit today— or take a taxicab to school or something!

Travis Whoopee—

(*He leaps up and clasps his father around the middle with his legs, and they face each other in **mutual** appreciation; slowly* WALTER LEE *peeks*

How would you describe Ruth's relationship with her son? With her husband? Between father and son?

---

aggressiveness forceful energy

defiance resistance; opposition

mutual shared

*around the boy to catch the **violent** rays from his wife's eyes and draws his head back as if shot)*

Walter You better get down now—and get to school, man.

Travis *(At the door)* O.K. Good-bye.

(He exits)

Walter *(After him, pointing with pride)* That's *my* boy. *(She looks at him in disgust and turns back to her work)* You know what I was thinking 'bout in the bathroom this morning?

Why is Ruth so short with Walter?

Ruth No.

Walter How come you always try to be so pleasant!

Ruth What is there to be pleasant 'bout!

Walter You want to know what I was thinking 'bout in the bathroom or not!

Ruth I know what you thinking 'bout.

Walter *(Ignoring her)* 'Bout what me and Willy Harris was talking about last night.

Ruth *(Immediately—a **refrain**)* Willy Harris is a good-for-nothing loudmouth.

Walter Anybody who talks to me has got to be a good-for-nothing loudmouth, ain't he? And what you know about who is just a good-for-nothing loudmouth? Charlie Atkins was just a "good-for-nothing loudmouth" too, wasn't he! When he wanted me to go in the dry-cleaning business with him. And now—he's grossing a hundred thousand a year. A hundred thousand dollars a year! You still call *him* a loudmouth!

Ruth *(Bitterly)* Oh, Walter Lee . . .

(She folds her head on her arms over the table)

Walter *(Rising and coming to her and standing over her)* You tired, ain't you? Tired of everything. Me, the boy, the way we live—this beat-up hole—everything. Ain't you? *(She doesn't look up, doesn't answer)* So tired—moaning and groaning all

refrain repeated words   **violent** furious

the time, but you wouldn't do nothing to help, would you? You couldn't be on my side that long for nothing, could you?

Ruth Walter, please leave me alone.

Walter A man needs for a woman to back him up . . .

Ruth Walter—

Walter Mama would listen to you. You know she listen to you more than she do me and Bennie. She think more of you. All you have to do is just sit down with her when you drinking your coffee one morning and talking 'bout things like you do and— *(He sits down beside her and demonstrates **graphically** what he thinks her methods and tone should be)*—you just sip your coffee, see, and say easy like that you been thinking 'bout that deal Walter Lee is so interested in, 'bout the store and all, and sip some more coffee, like what you saying ain't really that important to you— And the next thing you know, she be listening good and asking you questions and when I come home—I can tell her the details. This ain't no fly-by-night **proposition**, baby. I mean we figured it out, me and Willy and Bobo.

Ruth *(With a frown)* Bobo?

Walter Yeah. You see, this little liquor store we got in mind cost seventy-five thousand and we figured the initial **investment** on the place be 'bout thirty thousand, see. That be ten thousand each. Course, there's a couple of hundred you got to pay so's you don't spend your life just waiting for them clowns to let your license get approved—

Ruth You mean **graft**?

Walter *(Frowning impatiently)* Don't call it that. See there, that just goes to show you what women understand about the world. Baby, don't *nothing* happen for you in this world 'less you pay *somebody* off!

Walter wants Ruth's help in getting his mother to lend him money to buy a liquor store with his friends.

graft getting money in a way that is against the law	**graphically** in a visual way	**investment** money put into something, in hopes of a profit
		proposition a plan

Ruth Walter, leave me alone! *(She raises her head and stares at him **vigorously**—then says, more quietly)* Eat your eggs, they gonna be cold.

Walter *(Straightening up from her and looking off)* That's it. There you are. Man say to his woman: I got me a dream. His woman say: Eat your eggs. *(Sadly, but gaining in power)* Man say: I got to take hold of this here world, baby! And a woman will say: Eat your eggs and go to work. **(Passionately** now) Man say: I got to change my life, I'm choking to death, baby! And his woman say—*(In **utter anguish** as he brings his fists down on his thighs)*—Your eggs is getting cold!

Ruth *(Softly)* Walter, that ain't none of our money.

Walter *(Not listening at all or even looking at her)* This morning, I was lookin' in the mirror and thinking about it . . . I'm thirty-five years old; I been married eleven years and I got a boy who sleeps in the living room—*(Very, very quietly)*—and all I got to give him is stories about how rich white people live . . .

Ruth Eat your eggs, Walter.

Walter *(Slams the table and jumps up)*—DAMN MY EGGS— DAMN ALL THE EGGS THAT EVER WAS!

Ruth Then go to work.

Walter *(Looking up at her)* See—I'm trying to talk to you 'bout myself—*(Shaking his head with the **repetition**)*—and all you can say is eat them eggs and go to work.

Ruth *(Wearily)* Honey, you never say nothing new. I listen to you every day, every night and every morning, and you never say nothing new. *(Shrugging)* So you would rather *be* Mr. Arnold than be his **chauffeur**. So—I would *rather* be living in Buckingham Palace.

Walter That is just what is wrong with the colored woman in this world . . . Don't understand about building their men up

With Langston Hughes's poem in mind, notice the dreams of each character. What is Walter's dream? Why is he angry about his wife's reaction to his dream?

---

anguish great pain

chauffeur a hired driver

passionately with great feeling

repetition repeating

utter total; complete

vigorously with energy

and making 'em feel like they somebody. Like they can do something.

Ruth   (*Drily, but to hurt*) There *are* colored men who do things.

Walter   No thanks to the colored woman.

Ruth   Well, being a colored woman, I guess I can't help myself none.

(*She rises and gets the ironing board and sets it up and attacks a huge pile of rough-dried clothes, sprinkling them in preparation for the ironing and then rolling them into tight fat balls*)

Walter   (*Mumbling*) We one group of men tied to a race of women with small minds!

(*His sister* BENEATHA *enters. She is about twenty, as slim and intense as her brother. She is not as pretty as her sister-in-law, but her lean, almost* **intellectual** *face has a handsomeness of its own. She wears a bright-red flannel nightie, and her thick hair stands wildly about her head. Her speech is a mixture of many things; it is different from the rest of the family's insofar as education has* **permeated** *her sense of English—and perhaps the Midwest rather than the South has finally—at last—won out in her* **inflection;** *but not altogether, because over all of it is a soft* **slurring** *and* **transformed** *use of vowels which is the decided influence of the Southside. She passes through the room without looking at either* RUTH *or* WALTER *and goes to the outside door and looks, a little blindly, out to the bathroom. She sees that it has been lost to the Johnsons. She closes the door with a sleepy* **vengeance** *and crosses to the table and sits down a little defeated*)

What do we learn about Beneatha from these stage directions?

Beneatha   I am going to start timing those people.

Walter   You should get up earlier.

Beneatha   (*Her face in her hands. She is still fighting the urge to go back to bed*) Really—would you suggest dawn? Where's the paper?

inflection pronunciation	**permeate** to enter; to soak into	**transformed** greatly changed
intellectual brainy	**slurring** sliding together	**vengeance** force; revenge

Walter *(Pushing the paper across the table to her as he studies her almost **clinically**, as though he has never seen her before)* You a horrible-looking chick at this hour.

Beneatha *(Drily)* Good morning, everybody.

Walter *(senselessly)* How is school coming?

Beneatha *(In the same spirit)* Lovely. Lovely. And you know, **biology** is the greatest. *(Looking up at him)* I **dissected** something that looked just like you yesterday.

Walter I just wondered if you've made up your mind and everything.

Beneatha *(Gaining in sharpness and impatience)* And what did I answer yesterday morning—and the day before that?

Ruth *(From the ironing board, like someone disinterested and old)* Don't be so nasty, Bennie.

Beneatha *(Still to her brother)* And the day before that and the day before that!

Walter *(**Defensively**)* I'm interested in you. Something wrong with that? Ain't many girls who decide—

Walter and Beneatha *(In **unison**)*—"to be a doctor." *(Silence)*

Walter Have we figured out yet just exactly how much medical school is going to cost?

Ruth Walter Lee, why don't you leave that girl alone and get out of here to work?

Beneatha *(Exits to the bathroom and bangs on the door)* Come on out of there, please!

(She comes back into the room)

Walter *(Looking at his sister intently)* You know the check is coming tomorrow.

biology the science of living things	**defensively** protecting oneself	**unison** all together
clinically as a doctor or scientist would	**dissect** to cut up and examine	

Beneatha (*Turning on him with a sharpness all her own*) That money belongs to Mama, Walter, and it's for her to decide how she wants to use it. I don't care if she wants to buy a house or a rocket ship or just nail it up somewhere and look at it. It's hers. Not ours—*hers.*

Walter (*Bitterly*) Now ain't that fine! You just got your mother's interest at heart, ain't you, girl? You such a nice girl—but if Mama got that money she can always take a few thousand and help you through school too—can't she?

Beneatha I have never asked anyone around here to do anything for me!

Walter No! And the line between asking and just accepting when the time comes is big and wide—ain't it!

Beneatha (*With fury*) What do you want from me, Brother—that I quit school or just drop dead, which!

Walter I don't want nothing but for you to stop acting holy 'round here. Me and Ruth done made some sacrifices for you—why can't you do something for the family?

Ruth Walter, don't be dragging me in it.

Walter You are in it—Don't you get up and go work in somebody's kitchen for the last three years to help put clothes on her back?

Ruth Oh, Walter—that's not fair . . .

Walter It ain't that nobody expects you to get on your knees and say thank you, Brother; thank you, Ruth; thank you, Mama—and thank you, Travis, for wearing the same pair of shoes for two semesters—

Beneatha (*Dropping to her knees*) Well—I *do*—all right?— thank everybody! (*Pursuing him on her knees across the floor*) And forgive me for ever wanting to be anything at all! FORGIVE ME, FORGIVE ME, FORGIVE ME!

Ruth Please stop it! Your mama'll hear you.

Why do you think everyone is so interested in Mama's money?

Based on his remarks to his wife and sister, how would you describe Walter's view of women?

Walter Who the hell told you you had to be a doctor? If you so crazy 'bout messing 'round with sick people—then go be a nurse like other women—or just get married and be quiet . . .

Beneatha Well—you finally got it said . . . It took you three years but you finally got it said. Walter, give up; leave me alone—it's Mama's money.

Walter *He was my father, too!*

Beneatha and Walter's mother is expecting a check tomorrow from the life insurance policy of their father, who has died.

Beneatha So what? He was mine, too—and Travis' grandfather—but the **insurance** money belongs to Mama. Picking on me is not going to make her give it to you to **invest** in any **liquor** stores—(*Underbreath, dropping into a chair*)—and I for one say, God bless Mama for that!

Walter *(To* RUTH*)* See—did you hear? Did you hear!

Ruth Honey, please go to work.

Walter Nobody in this house is ever going to understand me.

Beneatha Because you're a nut.

Walter Who's a nut?

Beneatha You—you are a nut. Thee is mad, boy.

Walter *(Looking at his wife and his sister from the door, very sadly)* The world's most backward race of people, and that's a fact.

Beneatha *(Turning slowly in her chair)* And then there are all those **prophets** who would lead us out of the wilderness— (WALTER *slams out of the house*)—into the swamps!

Ruth Bennie, why you always gotta be pickin' on your brother? Can't you be a little sweeter sometimes? *(Door opens.* WALTER *walks in. He fumbles with his cap, starts to speak, clears throat, looks everywhere but at* RUTH. *Finally:)*

Walter *(To* RUTH*)* I need some money for carfare.

---

insurance coverage against loss

invest to put money into something, hoping for a profit

liquor drinks containing alcohol

prophet someone who sees the future

Ruth (*Looks at him, then warms; teasing, but tenderly*) Fifty cents? (*She goes to her bag and gets money*) Here—take a taxi!

(WALTER *exits.* MAMA *enters. She is a woman in her early sixties, full-bodied and strong. She is one of those women of a certain grace and beauty who wear it so unobtrusively that it takes a while to notice. Her dark-brown face is surrounded by the total whiteness of her hair, and, being a woman who has adjusted to many things in life and overcome many more, her face is full of strength. She has, we can see, wit and faith of a kind that keep her eyes lit and full of interest and* **expectancy**. *She is, in a word, a beautiful woman. Her bearing is perhaps most like the noble bearing of the women of the Hereros of Southwest Africa—rather as if she imagines that as she walks she still bears a basket or a vessel upon her head. Her speech, on the other hand, is as careless as her carriage is* **precise**—*she is inclined to slur everything—but her voice is perhaps not so much quiet as simply soft*)

Mama Who that 'round here slamming doors at this hour?

(*She crosses through the room, goes to the window, opens it, and brings in a feeble little plant growing* **doggedly** *in a small pot on the windowsill. She feels the dirt and puts it back out*)

Ruth That was Walter Lee. He and Bennie was at it again.

Mama My children and they tempers. Lord, if this little old plant don't get more sun than it's been getting it ain't never going to see spring again. (*She turns from the window*) What's the matter with you this morning, Ruth? You looks right peaked. You aiming to iron all them things? Leave some for me. I'll get to 'em this afternoon. Bennie honey, it's too drafty for you to be sitting 'round half dressed. Where's your robe?

Beneatha In the cleaners.

Mama Well, go get mine and put it on.

Beneatha I'm not cold, Mama, honest.

Mama I know—but you so thin . . .

What do we learn about Mama from these stage directions?

doggedly stubbornly	**expectancy** expecting or waiting for something	**precise** correct; exact

Beneatha (*Irritably*) Mama, I'm not cold.

Mama (*Seeing the make-down bed as* TRAVIS *has left it*) Lord have mercy, look at that poor bed. Bless his heart—he tries, don't he?

(*She moves to the bed* TRAVIS *has sloppily made up*)

Ruth No—he don't half try at all 'cause he knows you going to come along behind him and fix everything. That's just how come he don't know how to do nothing right now—you done spoiled that boy so.

Mama (*Folding bedding*) Well—he's a little boy. Ain't supposed to know 'bout housekeeping. My baby, that's what he is. What you fix for his breakfast this morning?

Ruth (*Angrily*) I feed my son, Lena!

Mama I ain't meddling—(*Underbreath; busy-bodyish*) I just noticed all last week he had cold cereal, and when it starts getting this chilly in the fall a child ought to have some hot grits or something when he goes out in the cold—

Ruth (*Furious*) I gave him hot oats—is that all right!

Mama I ain't meddling. (*Pause*) Put a lot of nice butter on it? (RUTH *shoots her an angry look and does not reply*) He likes lots of butter.

Ruth (*Exasperated*) Lena—

Mama (*To* BENEATHA. MAMA *is inclined to wander conversationally sometimes*) What was you and your brother fussing 'bout this morning?

Beneatha It's not important, Mama.

(*She gets up and goes to look out at the bathroom which is apparently free, and she picks up her towels and rushes out*)

Mama What was they fighting about?

Ruth Now you know as well as I do.

---

exasperated annoyed or bothered   **irritably** in an annoyed way

Mama *(Shaking her head)* Brother still worrying hisself sick about that money?

Ruth You know he is.

Mama You had breakfast?

Ruth Some coffee.

Mama Girl, you better start eating and looking after yourself better. You almost thin as Travis.

Ruth Lena—

Mama Un-hunh?

Ruth What are you going to do with it?

Mama Now don't you start, child. It's too early in the morning to be talking about money. It ain't Christian.

Ruth It's just that he got his heart set on that store—

Mama You mean that liquor store that Willy Harris want him to invest in?

Ruth Yes—

Mama We ain't no business people, Ruth. We just plain working folks.

Ruth Ain't nobody business people till they go into business. Walter Lee say colored people ain't never going to start getting ahead till they start **gambling** on some different kinds of things in the world—investments and things.

Mama What done got into you, girl? Walter Lee done finally sold you on investing.

Ruth No. Mama, something is happening between Walter and me. I don't know what it is—but he needs something— something I can't give him anymore. He needs this chance, Lena.

Mama *(Frowning deeply)* But liquor, honey—

Notice the way Mama describes Ruth. Apparently, Ruth looks thin and tired. As readers, we wouldn't know this unless a character or the stage directions described Ruth.

Why do you think Ruth has decided to support Walter's plan after all?

gamble to bet money on; to risk

Ruth Well—like Walter say—I spec people going to always be drinking themselves some liquor.

Mama Well—whether they drinks it or not ain't none of my business. But whether I go into business selling it to 'em *is*, and I don't want that on my **ledger** this late in life. *(Stopping suddenly and studying her daughter-in-law)* Ruth Younger, what's the matter with you today? You look like you could fall over right there.

Ruth I'm tired.

Mama Then you better stay home from work today.

Ruth I can't stay home. She'd be calling up the agency and screaming at them, "My girl didn't come in today—send me somebody! My girl didn't come in!" Oh, she just have a fit . . .

Mama Well, let her have it. I'll just call her up and say you got the flu—

Ruth *(Laughing)* Why the flu?

Mama 'Cause it sounds **respectable** to 'em. Something white people get, too. They know 'bout the flu. Otherwise they think you been cut up or something when you tell 'em you sick.

Ruth I got to go in. We need the money.

What does this talk between Ruth and Mama tell you about the family's attitudes toward white people? What does it reveal about the way white people treat the Youngers and other African Americans?

Mama Somebody would of thought my children done all but starved to death the way they talk about money here late. Child, we got a great big old check coming tomorrow.

Ruth *(Sincerely, but also **self-righteously**)* Now that's your money. It ain't got nothing to do with me. We all feel like that—Walter and Bennie and me—even Travis.

ledger an account book	**respectable** decent; proper; fit to be seen	**self-righteously** convinced of one's own goodness

Mama *(Thoughtfully, and suddenly very far away)* Ten thousand dollars—

Ruth Sure is wonderful.

Mama Ten thousand dollars.

Ruth You know what you should do, Miss Lena? You should take yourself a trip somewhere. To Europe or South America or someplace—

Mama *(Throwing up her hands at the thought)* Oh, child!

Ruth I'm serious. Just pack up and leave! Go on away and enjoy yourself some. Forget about the family and have yourself a ball for once in your life—

Mama *(Drily)* You sound like I'm just about ready to die. Who'd go with me? What I look like wandering 'round Europe by myself?

Ruth Shoot—these here rich white women do it all the time. They don't think nothing of packing up they suitcases and piling on one of them big steamships and—swoosh!—they gone, child.

Mama Something always told me I wasn't no rich white woman.

Ruth Well—what are you going to do with it then?

Mama I ain't rightly decided. *(Thinking. She speaks now with **emphasis**)* Some of it got to be put away for Beneatha and her schoolin'—and ain't nothing going to touch that part of it. Nothing. *(She waits several seconds, trying to make up her mind about something, and looks at* RUTH *a little **tentatively** before going on)* Been thinking that we maybe could meet the notes on a little old two-story somewhere, with a yard where Travis could play in the summertime, if we use part of the insurance for a down payment and everybody kind of pitch in. I could maybe take on a little day work again, few days a week—

> What are Mama's plans for the insurance money?

Ruth *(Studying her mother-in-law **furtively** and concentrating on her ironing, anxious to encourage without seeming to)* Well,

---

furtively secretly, as if ashamed   **tentatively** unsurely

Lord knows, we've put enough rent into this here rat trap to pay for four houses by now . . .

Mama *(Looking up at the words "rat trap" and then looking around and leaning back and sighing—in a suddenly reflective mood—)* "Rat trap"—yes, that's all it is. *(Smiling)* I remember just as well the day me and Big Walter moved in here. Hadn't been married but two weeks and wasn't planning on living here no more than a year. *(She shakes her head at the dissolved dream)* We was going to set away, little by little, don't you know, and buy a little place out in Morgan Park. We had even picked out the house. *(Chuckling a little)* Looks right dumpy today. But Lord, child, you should know all the dreams I had 'bout buying that house and fixing it up and making me a little garden in the back—*(She waits and stops smiling)* And didn't none of it happen.

*(Dropping her hands in a **futile** gesture)*

Ruth *(Keeps her head down, ironing)* Yes, life can be a barrel of disappointments, sometimes.

Mama Honey, Big Walter would come in here some nights back then and slump down on that couch there and just look at the rug, and look at me and look at the rug and then back at me—and I'd know he was down then . . . really down. *(After a second very long and thoughtful pause; she is seeing back to times that only she can see)* And then, Lord, when I lost that baby—little Claude—I almost thought I was going to lose Big Walter too. Oh, that man grieved hisself! He was one man to love his children.

Ruth Ain't nothin' can tear at you like losin' your baby.

Mama I guess that's how come that man finally worked hisself to death like he done. Like he was fighting his own war with this here world that took his baby from him.

Ruth He sure was a fine man, all right. I always liked Mr. Younger.

Mama Crazy 'bout his children! God knows there was plenty wrong with Walter Younger—hard-headed, mean, kind of

What were Mama's dreams when she was young?

futile useless

wild with women—plenty wrong with him. But he sure loved his children. Always wanted them to have something—be something. That's where Brother gets all these notions, I reckon. Big Walter used to say, he'd get right wet in the eyes sometimes, lean his head back with the water standing in his eyes and say, "Seem like God didn't see fit to give the black man nothing but dreams—but He did give us children to make them dreams seem worth while." *(She smiles)* He could talk like that, don't you know.

Ruth Yes, he sure could. He was a good man, Mr. Younger.

Mama Yes, a fine man—just couldn't never catch up with his dreams, that's all.

(BENEATHA comes in, brushing her hair and looking up to the ceiling, where the sound of a vacuum cleaner has started up)

Beneatha What could be so dirty on that woman's rugs that she has to vacuum every single day?

Ruth I wish certain young women 'round here who I could name would take **inspiration** about certain rugs in a certain apartment I could also mention.

Beneatha *(Shrugging)* How much cleaning can a house need, for Christ's sakes.

Mama *(Not liking the Lord's name used thus)* Bennie!

Ruth Just listen to her—just listen!

Beneatha Oh, God!

Mama If you use the Lord's name just one more time—

Beneatha *(A bit of a whine)* Oh, Mama—

Ruth Fresh—just fresh as salt, this girl!

Beneatha *(Drily)* Well—if the salt loses its **savor**—

Mama Now that will do. I just ain't going to have you 'round here reciting the **scriptures** in vain—you hear me?

> What do we learn about Walter and Beneatha's father in this dialogue between Ruth and Mama?

---

inspiration encouragement

savor special flavor or smell

scriptures Bible verses

Beneatha How did I manage to get on everybody's wrong side by just walking into a room?

Ruth If you weren't so fresh—

Beneatha Ruth, I'm twenty years old.

Mama What time you be home from school today?

Beneatha Kind of late. *(With enthusiasm)* Madeline is going to start my guitar lessons today.

(MAMA *and* RUTH *look up with the same expression*)

Mama Your *what* kind of lessons?

Beneatha Guitar.

Ruth Oh, Father!

Mama How come you done taken it in your mind to learn to play the guitar?

Beneatha I just want to, that's all.

Why does Mama smile at Beneatha's latest interest?

Mama *(Smiling)* Lord, child, don't you know what to do with yourself? How long it going to be before you get tired of this now—like you got tired of that little play-acting group you joined last year? *(Looking at* RUTH*)* And what was it the year before that?

Ruth The horseback-riding club for which she bought that fifty-five-dollar riding habit that's been hanging in the closet ever since!

Mama *(To* BENEATHA*)* Why you got to flit so from one thing to another, baby?

Beneatha *(Sharply)* I just want to learn to play the guitar. Is there anything wrong with that?

Mama Ain't nobody trying to stop you. I just wonders sometimes why you has to flit so from one thing to another all the time. You ain't never done nothing with all that camera equipment you brought home—

Beneatha I don't flit! I—I experiment with different forms of expression—

Ruth Like riding a horse?

Beneatha —People have to express themselves one way or another.

Mama What is it you want to express?

Beneatha *(Angrily)* Me! (MAMA *and* RUTH *look at each other and burst into* **raucous** *laughter)* Don't worry—I don't expect you to understand.

Mama *(To change the subject)* Who you going out with tomorrow night?

Beneatha *(With displeasure)* George Murchison again.

Mama *(Pleased)* Oh—you getting a little sweet on him?

Ruth You ask me, this child ain't sweet on nobody but herself—*(Underbreath)* Express herself!

(They laugh)

Beneatha Oh—I like George all right, Mama. I mean I like him enough to go out with him and stuff, but—

Ruth *(For devilment)* What does *and stuff* mean?

Beneatha Mind your own business.

Mama Stop picking at her now, Ruth. *(She chuckles—then a suspicious sudden look at her daughter as she turns in her chair for emphasis)* What DOES it mean?

Beneatha *(Wearily)* Oh, I just mean I couldn't ever really be serious about George. He's—he's so shallow.

Ruth Shallow—what do you mean he's shallow? He's *rich!*

Mama Hush, Ruth.

Beneatha I know he's rich. He knows he's rich, too.

Ruth Well—what other qualities a man got to have to satisfy you, little girl?

Beneatha You wouldn't even begin to understand. Anybody who married Walter could not possibly understand.

> How is Beneatha different from Mama and Ruth? What are her dreams?

raucous rough, loud

Mama *(Outraged)* What kind of way is that to talk about your brother?

Beneatha Brother is a flip—let's face it.

Mama *(To* RUTH, *helplessly)* What's a flip?

Ruth *(Glad to add kindling)* She's saying he's crazy.

Beneatha Not crazy. Brother isn't really crazy yet—he—he's an elaborate **neurotic**.

Mama Hush your mouth!

Beneatha As for George. Well. George looks good—he's got a beautiful car and he takes me to nice places and, as my sister-in-law says, he is probably the richest boy I will ever get to know and I even like him sometimes—but if the Youngers are sitting around waiting to see if their little Bennie is going to tie up the family with the Murchisons, they are wasting their time.

Ruth You mean you wouldn't marry George Murchison if he asked you someday? That pretty, rich thing? Honey, I knew you was odd—

Beneatha No I would not marry him if all I felt for him was what I feel now. Besides, George's family wouldn't really like it.

Mama Why not?

Beneatha Oh, Mama—The Murchisons are honest-to-God-real-*live*-rich colored people, and the only people in the world who are more **snobbish** than rich white people are rich colored people. I thought everybody knew that. I've met Mrs. Murchison. She's a scene!

Mama You must not dislike people 'cause they well off, honey.

Beneatha Why not? It makes just as much sense as disliking people 'cause they are poor, and lots of people do that.

Ruth *(A wisdom-of-the-ages manner. To Mama)* Well, she'll get over some of this—

> Notice that the conflicts faced by the Youngers aren't simply between the races. They also struggle against differences of class and income.

---

neurotic a person with disturbed feelings and thoughts

snobbish stuck-up

Beneatha Get over it? What are you talking about, Ruth? Listen, I'm going to be a doctor. I'm not worried about who I'm going to marry yet—if I ever get married.

Mama and Ruth *If!*

Mama Now Bennie—

Beneatha Oh, I probably will . . . but first I'm going to be a doctor, and George, for one, still thinks that's pretty funny. I couldn't be bothered with that. I am going to be a doctor and everybody around here better understand that!

Mama *(Kindly)* 'Course you going to be a doctor, honey, God willing.

Beneatha *(Drily)* God hasn't got a thing to do with it.

Mama Beneatha—that just wasn't necessary.

Beneatha Well—neither is God. I get sick of hearing about God.

Mama Beneatha!

Beneatha I mean it! I'm just tired of hearing about God all the time. What has He got to do with anything? Does he pay **tuition**?

Mama You 'bout to get your fresh little jaw slapped!

Ruth That's just what she needs, all right!

Beneatha Why? Why can't I say what I want to around here, like everybody else?

Mama It don't sound nice for a young girl to say things like that—you wasn't brought up that way. Me and your father went to trouble to get you and Brother to church every Sunday.

Beneatha Mama, you don't understand. It's all a matter of ideas, and God is just one idea I don't accept. It's not important. I am not going out and be immoral or commit crimes because I don't believe in God. I don't even think about it. It's just that I get tired of Him getting credit for all the things the human race achieves through its own stubborn

tuition payment for
education

effort. There simply is no blasted God—there is only man and it is *he* who makes miracles!

(MAMA *absorbs this speech, studies her daughter and rises slowly and crosses to* BENEATHA *and slaps her powerfully across the face. After, there is only silence and the daughter drops her eyes from her mother's face, and* MAMA *is very tall before her*)

Mama Now—you say after me, in my mother's house there is still God. (*There is a long pause and* BENEATHA *stares at the floor wordlessly.* MAMA *repeats the phrase with* **precision** *and cool emotion*) In my mother's house there is still God.

Beneatha In my mother's house there is still God.

(*A long pause*)

Mama (*Walking away from* BENEATHA, *too disturbed for triumphant posture. Stopping and turning back to her daughter*) There are some ideas we ain't going to have in this house. Not long as I am at the head of this family.

Beneatha Yes, Ma'am.

(MAMA *walks out of the room*)

Ruth (*Almost gently, with* **profound** *understanding*) You think you a woman, Bennie—but you still a little girl. What you did was childish—so you got treated like a child.

Beneatha I see. (*Quietly*) I also see that everybody thinks it's all right for Mama to be a tyrant. But all the tyranny in the world will never put a God in the heavens!

(*She picks up her books and goes out. Pause*)

What do we learn about Beneatha and her mother from this episode? How are they different? Why does Mama slap Beneatha?

What is the difference between the way Ruth interprets this episode and the way Beneatha interprets it?

---

precision correctness; definiteness   **profound** deep

Ruth (*Goes to* MAMA'S *door*) She said she was sorry.

Mama (*Coming out, going to her plant*) They frightens me, Ruth. My children.

Ruth You got good children, Lena. They just a little off sometimes—but they're good.

Mama No—there's something come down between me and them that don't let us understand each other and I don't know what it is. One done almost lost his mind thinking 'bout money all the time and the other done commence to talk about things I can't seem to understand in no form or fashion. What is it that's changing, Ruth?

Ruth (*Soothingly, older than her years*) Now . . . you taking it all too seriously. You just got strong-willed children and it takes a strong woman like you to keep 'em in hand.

Mama (*Looking at her plant and sprinkling a little water on it*) They spirited all right, my children. Got to admit they got spirit—Bennie and Walter. Like this little old plant that ain't never had enough sunshine or nothing—and look at it . . .

(*She has her back to* RUTH, *who has had to stop ironing and lean against something and put the back of her hand to her forehead*)

Ruth (*Trying to keep* MAMA *from noticing*) You . . . sure . . . loves that little old thing, don't you? . . .

Mama Well, I always wanted me a garden like I used to see sometimes at the back of the houses down home. This plant is close as I ever got to having one. (*She looks out of the window as she replaces the plant*) Lord, ain't nothing as dreary as the view from this window on a dreary day, is there? Why ain't you singing this morning, Ruth? Sing that "No Ways Tired." That song always lifts me up so—(*She turns at last to see that* RUTH *has slipped quietly to the floor, in a state of semiconsciousness*) Ruth! Ruth honey—what's the matter with you . . . Ruth!

Curtain

Why does Ruth lie to Mama about Beneatha's apology? What does this say about Ruth's role in the family?

Earlier, Ruth said that something had come between her and Walter. Now Mama says the same thing about her and her children. What would you say is happening to this family?

Directions Write the answers to these questions using complete sentences.

Comprehension: Identifying Facts

1. What is the setting (time and place) of this scene?

2. Why does Ruth wake up her son and husband?

3. Why does Ruth say Travis is so tired?

4. What does Travis need for school?

5. What does Walter want Ruth to persuade Mama to do?

6. What is Walter's job? What is Ruth's job?

7. Why does Beneatha need money?

8. Why is Mama expecting a check for ten thousand dollars?

9. What does Mama plan to do with the money?

10. Why does Mama slap Beneatha?

Comprehension: Understanding Main Ideas

11. Why is Ruth angry at Walter when he says Travis will have to start getting up earlier?

12. What is Ruth's relationship with her son, Travis? Support your answer.

13. Why, after Ruth says no, does Walter give Travis the fifty cents he needs, plus another fifty cents?

14. Why does Walter want his mother to lend him money? What is his dream?

15. Why do Walter and his sister, Beneatha, quarrel?

16. Why does Ruth decide to ask Mama for the money Walter wants?

17. Why doesn't Mama want to give Walter money to invest in a liquor store?

18. What were Mama's dreams when she and her husband, Big Walter, were young? What happened?

19. Why does Beneatha say she'll never marry George Murchison? What is the reaction from her mother and sister-in-law?

20. At the end of the scene, Ruth slumps down, nearly unconscious. What clues do you get earlier that she isn't well?

Understanding Literature: Stage Directions

Playwrights write notes about what the stage should look like and what the actors should do. These notes are called stage directions. Stage directions tell actors and directors how the playwright sees the characters and what happens to them.

Some stage directions, such as those for *A Raisin in the Sun*, also give readers important information about characters. For example, the playwright says that "disappointment has already begun to hang in [Ruth's] face."

In real life, the meaning of people's words often comes from the way they are said. For example, the question "So, when are you going to do your homework?" can be asked in different ways. It can be asked with anger, with concern, or simply with interest.

21. How do stage directions help actors? How do they help readers?

22. What do we learn about Beneatha from the stage directions given as she enters the scene?

23. As Ruth reacts to the news Walter reads from the paper, the stage directions say she is to affect (put on, or pretend) "tea-party interest." How does the playwright want the words to be said?

24. Based on the stage directions given, describe the way Walter behaves at the breakfast table.

25. What do we learn about Mama from the stage directions describing her?

Critical Thinking

26. What is different about how Walter and Ruth look at the world? About how they think about the future?

27. What is it about Beneatha that makes her mother angry? Is Mama a "tyrant," as Beneatha says?

28. The little plant struggling to grow on the window sill is mentioned twice in this scene. What does Mama's care of this plant suggest about her character?

29. List three conflicts faced by characters in this scene. Which do you think will turn out to be the most important in the play? Why?

30. Why do you think Lorraine Hansberry called her play "A Raisin in the Sun"?

Writing on Your Own Study the poem by Langston Hughes about a dream "deferred" or delayed. How does it relate to the events in this scene of *A Raisin in the Sun*? Think about the characters' dreams, which dreams have been deferred, and why. Write two paragraphs that explain the connection between the poem and the play.

Writer's Realm
Anne Jarrell-France

Anne Jarrell-France

1948–

Literary Terms

comedy a play with a happy ending, intended to amuse its audience

pun a joke formed by a play on words

script the written text of a play, used in production or performance

About the Author

Anne Jarrell-France has been a television writer, producer, and director. In her scripts, especially the ones she writes for students, she tries to use humor as well as communicate information. One of her projects, "Reading Between the Lines," focuses on learning to be a better reader. Another, "Starfinder," follows the Hubble Space Telescope on its journey. Jarrell-France is now writing and producing videos for the Social Security Administration.

About the Selection

This **script** was written for "Writer's Realm," a series that appeared on public television. (*Realm* means field or specialty in this title.) In it, Anne Jarrell-France imagines that Mary Shelley, author of the science-fiction novel, *Frankenstein,* is discussing her story with her husband, Percy Shelley, and their friend, Lord Byron. Percy Shelley and Lord Byron were both famous English poets in the nineteenth century.

Frankenstein, written in 1816, is about a student of philosophy who discovers a way to create life. He uses the electricity from lightning. With his assistant, Igor, he creates a monster out of parts from dead bodies.

Jarrell-France's script shows how an author might use suggestions from friends to improve her work. "Writer's Realm" presents its ideas using **comedy.** One way the author creates humor is through **puns.** Puns are jokes based on words that have several meanings, or on words that sound alike but have different meanings. For example, in the selection, Mary says that using lightning to bring the monster to life "'sparks' the imagination."

Terms to Know

Angle the way the camera views the actor or scene

Close up (CU) the camera is very close to the person or object

Cut to move quickly from one picture to another

Dissolve (DISS) to move gradually from one picture to another

Long shot (LS) the camera shows the whole scene

MCU medium close up

POV point of view; the camera is the eyes of one of the characters

SFX sound effects; sounds added to create a realistic scene

VO voice over; a character is heard without being seen

Writer's Realm

ANGLE ON HOST.

Notice the two-column format. The left column tells what the audience will see. The right column shows the words the characters will say.

MORGAN
Writers have been using responses from their friends and family for centuries. In fact, they say that's how Mary Shelley wrote her best known story, *Frankenstein*. It's about a Dr. Frankenstein who creates a monster. At least, that's how the *final* draft turned out . . .

Morgan is the host of "Writer's Realm."

TRANSITION TO A **MULTIPLE CANDELABRA** IN AN OLD DARK DREARY ROOM. IT'S THE KIND OF ROOM THAT IS **CONDUCIVE** TO SPOOKY STORIES. THE CAMERA TILTS DOWN AND WE SEE MARY SHELLEY READING A FIRST DRAFT OF HER NEW NOVEL.

MARY
" . . . And, so, the monster that Dr. Quimbly-Smythe created out of plaster and hay was crushed to powder beneath the feet of the townspeople."

As you read, notice how the author creates humor.

SHE LOOKS TO HER AUDIENCE.

Well, what do you think, honestly?

CUT TO PERCY SHELLEY **MUSING.**

PERCY
Mary, I must admit, it gave me quite a shiver.

conducive helpful or useful	**multiple candelabra** a many-branched candlestick	**muse** to think
		transition a change; a shift

Frankenstein,
Universal, 1931

Why does Mary rename the laboratory assistant? Why is "Igor" a better name than "Bertrum"?

CUT TO GEORGE GORDON, LORD BYRON.

GEORGE
Rather! I especially liked the laboratory part. The assistant—what was his name?

ANGLE ON MARY. SHE RISES TO GO OVER TO THE TEA SERVICE AND POURS A CUP OF TEA.

MARY
Bertie?

CUT TO GEORGE. MARY ENTERS THE FRAME AND HANDS HIM A CUP OF TEA.

GEORGE
Yes, that's the one—nasty fellow, what?

TWO SHOT OF MARY AND GEORGE.

MARY
I wanted him to be different.

SHOT OF PERCY.

PERCY
I think you succeeded there. Why the name, Bertie?

MARY.

MARY
Short for Bertrum . . .

PERCY ON CAMERA.

PERCY
Quite. Is he English?

MARY. SHOT WIDENS AS SHE WALKS OVER TO THE TABLE AGAIN.

MARY
No, actually, foreign. Maybe I should give him a more **exotic** name . . . Igor—what about Igor?

SHOT OF GEORGE.

GEORGE
Absolutely—oh, I do like that.

SHOT OF MARY.

MARY
Did I tell you enough about why Dr. Quimbly-Smythe wanted to create the monster out of plaster and hay.

GEORGE.

GEORGE
No, actually, that was to have been my next question.

exotic strange; unusual

SHOT OF MARY SLOWLY
WIDENS.

MARY
Well, you see he thought he
could create life out of dead
things. He'd done quite a bit
of research on the subject,
you know.

GEORGE JOINS MARY AT
THE TABLE.

GEORGE
No, I didn't. That wasn't in
your draft, was it?

Mary has left some
important details out
of her first draft.

MARY IS PREPARING A TRAY
OF COOKIES AS SHE THINKS
ALOUD.

MARY
Not the first, but now I'll put
it in the second. (THINKING
OUT LOUD.) Instead of plaster
and hay, what about him
thinking he can bring the dead
back to life so he uses body
parts to create the monster?

SHE CROSSES TO PERCY
DURING HER SPEECH. SHE
OFFERS A COOKIE TO PERCY.

Ladyfinger . . .?

PERCY.
HE TAKES A COOKIE.

PERCY
How terribly disgusting,
Mary! Must admit, it would
keep the readers' interest a
bit more than plaster and
hay . . . and give a new
meaning to the phrase, "lend
me a hand, will you?"

The use of "ladyfinger"
here is a pun.
Ladyfingers are
cookies—and Mary
has just been talking
about body parts.

Why does Percy think
changing the way the
doctor made his
monster is a good idea?
What is the joke in
"lend me a hand"?

GEORGE SNICKERS.

GEORGE
Why were the townspeople so
upset? You'd think that they
would be proud to have such a
famous scientist in their
midst.

MCU MARY.

MARY
I could elaborate more about
the people being frightened
by the monster. Even have
him escape from the
laboratory once or twice to
terrorize the townspeople.

Here again, Mary
decides to add more
details to her story.

Notice the pun on the word *sparks*.

Why does Percy suggest changing the main character's name? What's wrong with "Quimbly-Smythe"?

MCU PERCY.

PERCY
Good show! What about the lightning being used to bring the monster to life? Don't you think that's a bit overdone?

MARY CU.

MARY
No, actually, I rather like that part. "Sparks" the imagination, what?

LIGHTNING AND THUNDER.

PERCY
Why did you choose the name Quimbly-Smythe?

MARY
A fine family, Percy.

PERCY
Quite, but don't you think another name would be more appropriate . . . something to go along with the Igor character?

MARY AGAIN CROSSES THE ROOM AND SETS THE TRAY DOWN ON THE TABLE.

MARY
I know . . .
I could call him . . .
Frankenstein . . .

GRAND LIGHTNING AND THUNDER DISPLAY, AS MARY WHISPERS.

. . . yes . . .

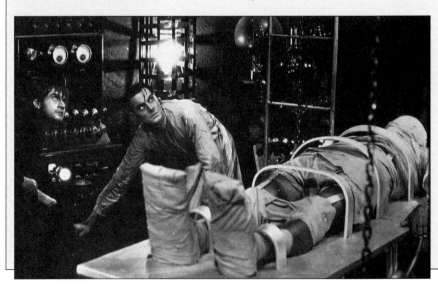

Writer's Realm

Anne Jarrell-France

Directions Write the answers to these questions using complete sentences.

Comprehension: Identifying Facts

1. What name does Mary first use for her scientist? For his assistant?

2. Why does Mary decide to change the assistant's name to Igor?

3. What will Mary have the monster made of in her second draft?

Comprehension: Understanding Main Ideas

4. What is the setting of this script? How does it fit the plot?

5. Where does Mary decide to add more details?

6. Why is Mary serving tea and cookies to her audience—her husband and their friend?

Understanding Literature: Comedy

Comedy has been an important form of drama since the time of ancient Greece. At yearly festivals, playwrights would present their best tragedies. Poets presented satyr plays—comedies that made fun of the gods and their myths. Before long, comedy took a turn. People began to see comedy as a way of looking at their own lives. We still see this kind of comedy on television.

If tragedy causes pity and fear in an audience, comedy brings feelings of safety and relief. Comedies make people laugh. They often feature characters or actions that are exaggerated and outrageous.

7. How would you define comedy? Think about what makes you laugh as a way of finding your own definition.

8. How does this script create humor through its contrast with Mary Shelley's frightening novel?

Critical Thinking

9. How do Mary's changes to her story make it better?

10. How does the author create humor out of characters' names?

Writing on Your Own Use the Internet to look for other teleplays (plays written for television) or screenplays (scripts written for motion pictures). Compare their formats with the two-column format used in "Writer's Realm." Use any format you find to write a short, funny scene about what happens at your house during breakfast.

Drama

Subject and Theme in Drama

Dramas can be written for the stage, the movies, or television. These dramas are similar to other forms of narrative literature, such as short stories, myths, and legends. They follow some of the same rules and patterns. Like a short story, a play tells a story about a main character. There is a plot that explores a certain problem the main character faces. The story takes place in a specific setting.

Drama also has a subject and one or more themes. The subject is its main topic—what the play is about. The theme, or main idea, is what the author says about the topic through the action of the play. For example, the subject of *Romeo and Juliet* is what happens to two unlucky young lovers. Shakespeare includes several themes in the play. One theme is the way people are often pushed around by the conditions of their lives, in spite of trying to do their best. Another theme is the way violence leads to violence, and how people let old quarrels shape their lives. As with most good plays, *Romeo and Juliet* does not announce its themes. The audience gradually realizes what the themes are as they become involved in the drama.

Review

1. What is the difference between the subject of a play and its theme?

2. What is the subject of Act 1, Scene 1, of *A Raisin in the Sun?*

3. What is one theme of Hansberry's play, based on this scene?

4. What is the subject of "Writer's Realm"?

5. What is one theme of *Romeo and Juliet?*

Writing on Your Own Choose a subject you would like to write about. What kinds of themes might come from that subject? Write a two-paragraph description of your subject and themes.

Drama as we know it today dates from ancient Greece. Writers of plays, called playwrights, tell their stories by means of the words—dialogue—and actions of characters. Plays are meant to be performed by actors on a stage. Because of this, plays rely on the special connection formed between the play and its audience.

Drama is often divided into two groups of plays, based on plot. In tragedies, the main character suffers or dies by the end of the play. Tragedies concern serious subjects, such as the meaning of life or the importance of human relationships. Comedies have happy endings and are meant to amuse people. Characters in tragedies tend to be noble, or at least important in their communities. Characters in comedies are usually ordinary people.

Plays are organized into acts. Acts may be divided into scenes, each taking place in one setting. Shakespeare wrote five-act plays; today's plays tend to be in three acts. Many plays are only one act.

Today, plays are written not just for stage performance, but for television and movies. Playwrights write stage directions to help actors, directors, and readers understand such things as setting, lighting, and the way characters speak and move. Writers of television and movie scripts give directions about camera angles and sound effects.

All drama is a form of storytelling that depends on the words and actions of characters. From ancient times to the present, readers and audiences have enjoyed the special power of drama to reveal human character.

Selections

■ *Romeo and Juliet,* Act V, by William Shakespeare, is the tragedy of two young lovers destroyed by family hatreds and their own unlucky fates.

■ *A Raisin in the Sun,* Act I, Scene One, by Lorraine Hansberry, presents the realistic drama of an African-American family in Chicago. They struggle to keep their dreams alive in the face of money problems, social unfairness, and personal conflicts.

■ "Writer's Realm," a script written for television, explores the writing process by imagining Mary Shelley asking her husband and their friend for advice as she writes *Frankenstein.*

Directions Write the answers to these questions using complete sentences.

Comprehension: Identifying Facts

1. In what country did drama as we know it begin?

2. Into what two groups have plays been divided, based on the outcome of their plots?

3. What happens to the main character in a tragedy?

4. What is realistic drama?

5. What are some ways in which comedies can be funny?

Comprehension: Understanding Main Ideas

6. How is drama like other forms of storytelling, such as short stories?

7. How is drama different from other forms of storytelling?

8. How much information do readers get from the stage directions in Shakespeare's *Romeo and Juliet*, compared with the stage directions in Lorraine Hansberry's *A Raisin in the Sun?*

9. Why is *Romeo and Juliet* considered to be a tragedy?

10. What are some of the messages about good writing in "Writer's Realm"?

Understanding Literature: Monologue

A monologue is a speech by one person. *Mono-* means "one." In drama, a monologue is an actor's speech given when he or she is the only person on stage. Monologues usually show a character's thoughts. Playwrights cannot be the all-knowing narrators of short stories or novels. They have to let characters reveal their hearts and minds through their dialogue. By using monologues, playwrights let the audience hear what the characters are thinking.

Shakespeare used monologues in his plays. Many of today's playwrights, however, feel monologues are unnatural. They don't use them.

11. How is monologue different from dialogue?

12. What does a character usually talk about in a monologue?

13. Give an example of a monologue from Act V of *Romeo and Juliet.*

14. How would *A Raisin in the Sun* be different if the characters revealed their thoughts in monologues?

15. Give an example of a monologue you might have seen on television or in a play or film.

Critical Thinking

16. If you could pick the character from this unit you would most like to play on the stage or screen, who would it be? Why?

17. Would you rather see a tragedy or a comedy? Explain your opinion.

18. If you were a theater reviewer for a newspaper, how might you review *A Raisin in the Sun*? What kinds of things would you say about the drama?

19. What kinds of things can you do when you write a television script that you cannot do when you write a stage play?

20. Which play in this unit would you most like to see performed? Explain your choice.

Speak and Listen

Plays are meant to be performed, or acted in front of an audience. Work with other members of your class to perform part of *A Raisin in the Sun*. Practice your dialogue separately, and then together. Present your performance to the class.

Beyond Words

According to the poem that gives *A Raisin in the Sun* its title, a dream deferred—put off—can dry up like a raisin in the sun. Find or create a picture, sculpture, or model that could serve as a symbol for the fate of Romeo and Juliet.

Writing on Your Own Dialogue involves two characters talking together in a play. In a monologue, an actor who is alone on the stage talks about his or her thoughts. Write a monologue for Walter Younger, telling the way he feels and what he is thinking about in Act I, Scene One, of *A Raisin in the Sun*.

Test-Taking Tip

When you read over your written answer to a question, imagine that you are someone reading it for the first time. Ask yourself if the ideas and information make sense. Revise and rewrite to make the answer as clear as you can.

Correcting Common Writing Mistakes

1. Make subjects and verbs agree
- Singular subjects must have singular verbs.
- Plural subjects must have plural verbs.
- Compound subjects must have plural verbs.

2. Make pronouns agree with antecedents
- In gender:
  - Replace the name of a male person with a masculine pronoun.
  - Replace the name of a female person with a feminine pronoun.
  - Replace singular names with *it* or *its*.
  - Replace plural names with *they, them,* or *their.*
- In number:
  - Make the pronoun singular if its antecedent is singular.
  - Make the pronoun plural if its antecedent is plural.

3. Capitalize proper nouns and proper adjectives
- Capitalize proper nouns.
- Capitalize the first word of any sentence or title.
- Capitalize the names of languages.
- Capitalize the pronoun *I*.
- Capitalize all proper adjectives.

4. Use correct verb tenses
- Action verbs tell what someone did.
- State-of-being verbs express the condition of the subject.
- Helping verbs help the main verb express tense, or time.
  - Use one main verb in a verb phrase.
  - Use helping verbs in a verb phrase.
  - Use the main verb last in a verb phrase.
- Make sure the verb tenses are logical.
- Use the same verb tenses if the actions occurred at the same time.
- Use different verb tenses if the actions occurred at different times.

5. Use and spell verb forms correctly
- Form the past tense of a regular verb by adding *-ed* or *-d.*
- Use the past participle to form the past perfect tenses.

6. Use and spell possessives and plurals correctly
- Use a possessive noun to show ownership or a relationship between two things.
- Make a singular noun possessive by adding an apostrophe (') and the letter *s.*
- Make a plural noun possessive by adding only an apostrophe.
- Add both an apostrophe and the letter s if the plural noun does not end in an *s.*

7. Avoid run-on sentences
- Begin sentences with a capital letter.
- End each sentence with a period, question mark, or exclamation point.
- Do not end a sentence or separate two sentences with a comma.
- Use a comma plus a conjunction to connect two complete ideas.

8. Avoid sentence fragments
- Make sure each sentence has a subject and a verb that express a complete idea.
- Use a subject and a predicate.
- Do not capitalize the first word of a phrase that does not begin a new idea.

Paragraphs

The Three Parts of a Paragraph

1. The topic sentence

The topic sentence states the main idea in a paragraph. It is usually the first sentence of a paragraph. It lets the reader know what your paragraph is going to be about. The topic sentence should get the reader's attention. It should make the reader want to read the rest of your paragraph.

Ask yourself these questions to help you write your topic sentence:

- What is the purpose of my paragraph?
- What is the main point I want to make?
- Why am I writing this paragraph?
- What will this paragraph be about?

2. The body

The body of a paragraph is the group of sentences that tell more about your main idea. It supports the point of view of your topic sentence. The body can include:

- Facts
- Details
- Explanations
- Reasons
- Examples
- Illustrations

3. The conclusion or summary

The last sentence of a paragraph is a conclusion or a summary. A conclusion is a judgment. It is based on the facts that you presented in your paragraph. Your conclusion must make sense.

A summary is a statement that briefly repeats the main ideas of your paragraph. It repeats your idea or ideas in slightly different words. It does not add new information.

The Purposes of a Paragraph

Every paragraph has one of five purposes. The five purposes are:

1. To give information or facts

Facts are included in all three parts of a paragraph. You may gather facts by reading, listening, or observing.

2. To explain your ideas

You may use this kind of paragraph to:

- Make something clear
- Help someone understand an idea
- Give the meaning of something
- Give reasons for something

3. To ask for information

In this kind of paragraph, make your questions clear and specific. That way, you get specific answers.

4. To persuade

This kind of paragraph helps you to convince someone to act or believe a certain way. You must be sure of what you are saying. Then you can persuade someone.

5. To tell a story

The story you tell in this kind of paragraph can be imaginary or true. A true story should follow the order in which things happened.

Checklist for Proofreading and Revising

✔ **Use this checklist to proofread and revise your papers.**

Check your paper
- ❑ Do I have a meaningful title?
- ❑ Do I have a conclusion or a summary at the end?

Check your paragraphs
- ❑ Do I start every paragraph on a new line?
- ❑ Is the first line of every paragraph indented?
- ❑ Does my first sentence (topic sentence) in every paragraph explain the main idea of my paragraph? Does it attract my reader's attention well?
- ❑ Do sentences in the middle of my paragraphs support the main idea?
- ❑ Do I include facts, details, explanations, reasons, examples, or illustrations to support my main idea?
- ❑ Do I need to take out any sentences that do not relate to my main idea?

Check your sentences
- ❑ Do I capitalize the first word of every sentence?
- ❑ Do I end every sentence with the correct punctuation mark?
- ❑ Do I express a complete idea in every sentence?
- ❑ Do my pronouns all have clear antecedents?
- ❑ Do I have any run-on sentences that I need to correct?
- ❑ Can I improve my sentences?

- ❑ Can I add adjectives, adverbs, or prepositional phrases?
- ❑ Can I combine short, related ideas into longer, more varied sentences?

Check your verbs
- ❑ Do I have a subject and a verb in every sentence?
- ❑ Do my subject and verb agree in every sentence?
- ❑ Is my verb tense logical in every sentence?
- ❑ Is my verb tense consistent in every sentence?
- ❑ Are my irregular verbs correct?

Check your punctuation and capitalization
- ❑ Did I capitalize all my proper nouns and proper adjectives?
- ❑ Did I capitalize and punctuate all my direct quotations correctly?
- ❑ Did I use a comma to separate words in a series?

Check your spelling
- ❑ Did I choose the correct spelling for each homonym?
- ❑ Did I use an apostrophe only in contractions and possessive nouns?
- ❑ Did I spell every plural noun correctly?
- ❑ Did I spell all words with *ie* or *ei* correctly?
- ❑ Did I drop the silent *e* before adding an ending beginning with a vowel?
- ❑ Did I double the final consonant before adding an ending?

Planning and Writing Reports

Plan the report
- Choose a broad subject you would like to explore.
- Select a topic in that subject area.
- Find out how much information is in the library about your topic.
- Limit your topic so that you have enough information to write a complete report.
- Write a title for your report.
- List your subtopics, or the parts of your larger topic.

Find information
- Go to the library to find information on your topic.
- Look in the library catalog for books that have useful information.
- Check almanacs, encyclopedias, atlases, the Internet, or other sources in the library reference section.
- Check *The Reader's Guide to Periodical Literature* for magazines with information you could use.
- Take notes on the information you find.
- Use index cards.
- Start each card with this information about the source you find facts in:
  –authors' names
  –book or article and magazine title
  –page numbers
  –volume numbers
  –date of publication
- Copy all the information that you may need.
- Copy any quotations exactly as they are printed.
- Use a different card for each source.

Get organized
- Put your note cards in order by topic and subtopic.
- Do not use notes that may not fit anywhere.
- List your main topics.
- Choose an order that seems suitable for your topics.
- Write a final topic outline.

Write your report
- Write your report using note cards and an outline.
- Begin your report with a topic paragraph that states the main idea.
- Use your own words to write the ideas you found in your sources (paraphrase).
- Write an author's exact words if you use direct quotations.
- Name the author or source of any direct quotations you use.
- Repeat your main ideas in a summary paragraph at the end.
- Proofread your report.
- Revise and rewrite it as needed.
- Include a title page at the front of your report.

Prepare a bibliography
- Use the bibliographic information on your note cards.
- Put your cards in alphabetical order.
- Include a blank page after your bibliography.

Handbook of Literary Terms

A

act a major unit of action in a play

action what goes on in a story

alliteration repeating sounds by using words whose beginning sounds are the same

analogy a comparison between two otherwise different objects that share some of the same characteristics

anecdote a short account of an interesting event in someone's life

antagonist the person or force opposing the protagonist

assonance repeating sounds by using words with the same vowel sounds

autobiography the story of a person's life, written by that person

B

ballad a form of poetry that tells a story, passed from person to person, often as a simple song with rhyming words and a refrain

biographical essay an essay about true events in a person's life

biography the story of a person's life, written by someone other than the person

blank verse unrhymed iambic pentameter

C

caricature a character description that is exaggerated to make people laugh

character a person or animal in a story, poem, or play

character development *See* characterization

characterization the way a writer develops characters by revealing personality traits

character trait a character's way of thinking, behaving, or speaking

chronological order a plot that moves forward in order of time

climax the high point of interest or suspense in a story or play

comedy a play with a happy ending, intended to amuse its audience

conflict the struggle of the protagonist against himself or herself, another person, or nature

connotation images or emotions connected to a word

consonance the repetition of consonant sounds usually within the context of several words

creation myth a myth that tells the story of the beginning of the world

Handbook of Literary Terms

D

denouement the resolution to a story

dialect the speech of a particular region of a country, or of a certain group of people

dialogue the conversation between characters in a story or play

diary a daily record of events and feelings

drama a story told through the words and actions of characters, written to be performed as well as read

dramatic irony when the audience or reader knows more than the characters know

E

end rhyme a rhyming pattern in which the ends of lines contain the same sound

epilogue a section coming after the story's end

epiphany the moment in a story when a character recognizes an important truth

essay a short nonfiction work on any subject

exaggeration in literature, making something larger than it is; stretching the truth

excerpt a short passage from a longer piece of writing

F

fable a story that teaches a lesson about life, called a moral, often with animals who act like humans

fantasy imaginative fiction that often has strange settings and characters

fiction literature in which the author creates the events and characters

figurative language language that uses word pictures to compare or describe, and that is not meant to be taken literally

first-person a point of view where the narrator is also a character, using the pronouns *I* and *we*

flashback a look into the past at some point in a story

flat character a character that is based on a single trait or quality and is not well developed

folklore stories, customs, and traditions preserved and passed along by people in a particular area or group

folktale *See* folklore

foreshadowing clues or hints that a writer gives about something that has not yet happened

free verse poetry that does not have a strict rhyming pattern or regular line length and uses actual speech patterns for the rhythms of sound

G

genre a kind of literature

H

haiku a form of Japanese poetry having three lines with five syllables in the first, seven in the second, and five in the third

hero the leading character in a story, novel, play, or film

humor writing intended to amuse

humorist a writer of humor

hyperbole using exaggeration to show that something is important

I

iamb a pattern of two syllables, the first one unstressed and the second one stressed

iambic pentameter five two-beat sounds in a line of poetry where the second syllable is stressed in each pattern

image a picture in the reader's mind created by words

imagery the use of word pictures that appeal to the five senses

internal rhyme rhyme that occurs within one line of a poem

Internet a world-wide network of computers that speak a common language

irony the difference between what is expected to happen in a story and what does happen

J

journal writing that expresses an author's feelings or first impressions about a subject

L

legend a story from folklore that features characters who actually lived, or real events or places

limerick a five-line poem in which the first, second, and fifth lines, and the third and fourth lines, rhyme

M

metaphor a figure of speech that says one thing *is* another

monologue a speech by one person

mood the feeling created by a piece of writing

moral a lesson or message about life told in a story

myth an important story, often part of a culture's religion, that explains how the world came to be or why natural events happen, usually including gods, goddesses, or unusually powerful human beings

N

narrative a story, usually told in chronological order

narrator the teller of a story

nonfiction prose writing about real people and true experiences

novel fiction that is book-length and has more plot and details than a short story

O

onomatopoeia using words that sound like their meaning

oral literature stories that were first told, rather than being written down

P

pamphlet a short printed essay with no cover, or with a paper cover

pen name a false name used for writing

personal account a nonfiction narrative about an experience, told by a person who lived through it

personification giving characters such as animals or objects the characteristics of humans

persuasive meant to influence

playwright a writer of plays

plot the series of events in a story

plot development the way in which the events of a story are told, in chronological order or using flashbacks

poem *See* poetry

poetry literature in verse form that usually has rhythm and paints powerful or beautiful impressions with words

point of view the relationship of the narrator to the story

problem the focus, or main concern, of the plot of a story

prose all writing that is not poetry

protagonist the main character; also called the hero

pun a joke formed by a play on words

purpose a nonfiction writer's main idea or goal

R

realistic drama plays that tell the stories of ordinary people in a lifelike manner

reflective essay a personal essay exploring an author's feelings

refrain repeated words or phrases that create a mood or give importance to something

regionalism a word or phrase that comes from a particular area

repetition using a word, phrase, or image more than once, for emphasis

rhyme words that end with the same or similar sounds

rhyme scheme the pattern created by the ending sounds of the lines of a poem

rhythm a pattern created by the stressed and unstressed syllables in a line of poetry

rising action the events of the plot that add to the conflict

round character a well-developed character possessing a variety of traits

S

satire humorous writing that makes fun of foolishness or evil

scene a unit of action in a play that takes place in one setting

science fiction fiction based on real or imagined facts of science

script the written text of a play, used in production or performance

sequence the order of events

setting a story's time and place

short story a brief work of prose fiction that includes plot, setting, characters, point of view, and theme

simile a figure of speech in which two things are compared using a phrase that includes the words *like* or *as*

stage directions notes by playwrights describing such things as setting, lighting, sound effects, and how the actors are to look, behave, move, and speak

stanza a group of lines that forms a unit in a poem

story-within-a-story a second story told within another story

style an author's way of writing

subject the main topic of a play

subtitle a second, less important title under the first that gives more information about the writing

sudden fiction brief short stories

suspense a quality in a story that makes the reader uncertain or nervous about what will happen next

symbol a person, place, or object that stands for something beyond itself

symbolism the larger meaning of a person, place, or object

T

tall tale a story from folklore that features exaggerated characters who have fantastic adventures

tanka a form of Japanese poetry having five lines with five syllables in the first, seven in the second, five in the third, and seven in the fourth and fifth

theme the main idea of a story or play

third-person a point of view where the narrator is not a character, and refers to characters as *he* or *she*

tone the attitude an author takes toward a subject

tragedy a play that ends with the suffering or death of one or more of the main characters

trochee a pattern of two syllables, the first one stressed and the second one unstressed

turning point *See* climax

U

unreliable narrator a first-person narrator whose views cannot be depended on to be completely true

V

verse word patterns that follow a definite rhythm and rhyme

voice the way a writer expresses ideas through style, form, content, and purpose

W

Web site a collection of linked pages on the Internet, available to the public for information and entertainment

Glossary

A

abhorred hated, 412

abrupt said or done suddenly, without much explanation, 174

abruptly suddenly, without warning, 240, 342, 431

accessible reachable, 74

accommodate to supply someone's needs; to help out, 123

accommodating making up for; making allowance for, 271

accumulate to collect, 272, 316

acknowledge to admit; to recognize, 75

actual true, real, 192

administering managing, directing, 208

admittance entrance, 210

adorned decorated, 339

adviser one who gives advice, 78

aesthetic artistic, 210

affinity attraction, 76

afflicted ailing, ill, 151

aggravated annoyed; upset, 102

aggressiveness forceful energy, 433

aghast shocked, 256

agony great pain, 213

alarum alarm, warning, 367

alcoholic a problem drinker, 269

alcove a small, set in section of a room, 162

algaic coming from algae or water plants such as seaweed, 241

aloft overhead, 67

aloof apart, 408

ambient surrounding on all sides, 337

ambiguity a mystery, 419

ambitious determined, 333

ambush to attack by surprise, 120

amiable friendly, good-natured, 267

amiably kindly, 246, 298

amid within; between, 389

ample sufficient, 297

analyze to study in detail, 309

anguish great pain, 309, 436

anguished distressed, tormented, 214, 236

animate living, conscious, 303

animated made lively, happy, 384

anticipate to look forward to, 171

apathy a lack of concern, 255

apologize to say you are sorry, 36

appalling dreadful, 342

apparatus a device, 235

apparel clothing, 253

apparition a vision or appearance, 81

apprehend to catch; to arrest, 410

apprehension fear, dread, 339

approximately nearly, 337

ardor deep feeling, 209

aroma a fragrance, 307

aspire to hope, 211

assassin a killer, 122

assent agreement, 254

assert to put oneself or one's ideas forward, 206

assess to determine the value of, 318

associate to accompany, 407

assurance promise, 254

atrophy to wither, 273

attribute to credit something to, 252

audible loud enough to be heard, 258

audition a tryout, 329

authentic genuine; of true value, 304

avaricious greedy, 252

avert to turn away, 254

B

ballad a simple song, 33

balmy mild, 366

baptism Christian ceremony for naming and for coming into the faith, 265

barbaric uncivilized, savage, 205

barbecue to grill food outdoors, 388

barnacles small sea animals that attach themselves to rocks or floating objects, 70

barometer an instrument for measuring air pressure, 109

barren without life, 376

barrier something that blocks the way, 278

bated kept low and shallow, 76

beget to breed, 386

beseech to beg, 404

betroth to promise in marriage, 420

bide to wait, 237

Glossary

biographer someone who writes the life story of another person, 388

biology the science of living things, 438

bland dull, unexciting, 205

bleak gloomy, 315

bliss great happiness, 414

blockade to prevent escape, 144

blunt to soften, 377

boisterous noisy, wild, 218

borne carried, 121, 341

bosom a breast; a heart, 368, 415

brawling fighting, 389

brazen made of brass; bold, 366

bristling standing erect, 76

brittle stiff, 176

broach to begin a topic, 254

brutal cruel, 389

brute an animal, 369

buttress part of a mountain that sticks out, 340

C

caldron a large pot, usually used for boiling, 239

cantankerous hard to deal with, 102

captivating charming, 54

cascade a waterfall, 299

caterer someone who supplies food, 319

cavalry soldiers on horseback, 123

champagne a sparkling wine, 319

chariot a two-wheeled cart, 53, 54

chasm a large opening, 54

chaste pure, 386

chauffeur a hired driver, 436

circumstance a condition; details, 147, 417

civic community, 219

clinically as a doctor or scientist would, 438

coffin a box that holds a dead body, 358

coincidence chance, 252

collateral money as protection for payment of a debt, 320

compel to make happen, 368

compensation a payment for damages, 255

compete to be a rival for, 315

competent able to do something, 209

compliance the act of doing what is asked, 143

compressed compact, dense, 337

compromise an agreement that attempts to satisfy both sides, 55

compulsively unable to stop, 340

concussion a blow; a shock, 240

condole to soothe; to sympathize with, 247

conducive helpful or useful, 457

confer to supply, 337

confidant someone to confide in 316

confirm to make certain, 66

confirmation proof, 254

confront to meet face to face, 156, 318

conjecture to guess or suppose, 143

consequence a result or effect, 35, 100, 250

conservative usual, typical, 315

conspicuously obviously, 432

conspire to plot against, 419

consumption tuberculosis, a lung disease easily spread from person to person, 264

contagion a spreading disease, 415

contemplate to study or think about, 79

contemplation study; deep thought, 71

contemporary modern, 304

contempt scorn, 406

contradict to deny, 415

convey to pass along, 255

convict a person in prison, 377

coordinate to move or act smoothly with someone else, 171

cordial life-giving liquid, 406

cosmic the universe, 305

countenance face, appearance, 144

courtship the period before marriage, 272

covet to want, 280, 338

cower to hide, as if in fear, 160

crease a fold; a wrinkle, 273, 304

creation the world, 238, 303

credulity willingness to believe, 251

crimson red, 412

cull to collect or sort, 404

cultural relating to the beliefs and customs of a group, 303

Glossary

D

daft crazy , 234

daunting frightening, 338

decipher to make clear; to explain, 382

decorum proper behavior, 327

defensively protecting oneself, 438

defiance resistance; opposition, 433

defiantly with resistance; with opposition, 227

deliberate carefully saying and meaning every word, 149

deliberately with much thought; knowing exactly what one is doing, 158

deliberation careful thought, 214

delusion a trick; an error, 338

depart to leave, 151

dependence something counted on or necessary, 147

depress to fall, 326

depressing saddening, 251

desirous anxious for, 246

despite in spite of, 266

destiny fate, 389

detachment a separation from, 341

deteriorate getting worse, 129

detestable hateful, 410

devious crooked; sly, 213, 333

devise to think up; to invent, 67, 74, 420

diagnose to determine the medical condition of someone, 193, 269

dicey risky, 343

dignitary someone who holds a high rank or position, 34

dilapidated rundown, in poor condition, 131, 143, 179

dilute to water down; to make weak, 329

dinghy a small boat, 234

dingy dirty, discolored, 157

dire severe, terrible, 207, 420

disapproval objections, 272

disarray confusion, 35

disbelief holding something to be untrue, 178

discard to throw away or cast off, 70, 220

discern to recognize; to make out, 414

discharge to get rid of, 405

disciple a follower, 264

disciplinarian one who punishes, 176

disconsolately impossible to comfort, 81

discord a quarrel, 421

discreet careful, showing good judgment, 173

disengage to pull away from, 223, 338

disheveled untidy, 428

disown to deny one's connection with, 252

dispatch (n.) a message, 121

dispatch (v.) to send, 320, 406

dispensable easily done without, 272

disperse to scatter, 73, 405

disregard to pay no attention to, 67

dissect to cut up and examine, 438

distraught terribly upset, 178

diverge to branch off, 383

doctrine a belief or teaching, 161

doggedly stubbornly, 249, 441

doleful sad, mournful, 207

douse to put out, 267

drastic severe, 108

dubiously with doubt; suspiciously, 250

duct an opening; a tube, 329

dwindle to fade away, 239

E

ebb to flow away; to slow down; to get lower, 81, 368

eerie spooky, 75

elated delighted, thrilled, 316

elation great happiness, 177, 339

eloquence ability to speak with great feeling and expressiveness, 321

emanate to come forth, 206

embarrassment self-consciousness, 332

embed to fix or enclose in something, 53

embrace to hug, 156, 178, 279, 432

emigrate to leave one's native land, 118

emissary someone who is sent on a mission, 40

emotion a feeling, 132

emphasis importance, 430

encircle to circle, 299

encounter to meet or come upon, 199, 304

endeavor attempt; effort, 367

energetic lively, 263

engrossing taking in everything, 413

enmity hatred, 422

ensuing following, 239

enthralled fascinated, 175, 250, 364

entreat to beg, 420

envelop to completely cover, 157

epidemic widespread disease, 304

equilibrium balance, 328

erratic not ordinary; unexpected, 428

erupt to rise up, 159

escalate to get stronger, 340

esteem honor, 307

eternity endless time, 53, 235

euphony a pleasing sound, 366

exasperated annoyed or bothered, 431, 442

exception something that is left out, 122

exceptionally more than usually, 427

exhilarated excited, 318

exhorter one who strongly urges another to do or believe something, 146

exile separation from homeland, 419

exotic strange; unusual, 458

expanse something vast, spread out, 339

expansion growth, 318

expectancy expecting or waiting for something, 441

expectant expecting or waiting for something, 257

expectantly as if looking forward to something, 70

expectation what is expected or looked forward to, 255, 308

expediency practicality, 316

expire to go out; to run out, 257

expostulation objection; complaint, 367

exposure a position with respect to weather or compass points, 107

exquisitely perfectly, 145

external outside, 338

extinguish to put out, 53, 339

extremities limbs of the body; legs, 328

extricate to untangle, 329

exuberant high-spirited, 205

F

fabric material, 272

falter to hesitate, 257

famine hunger, 406

fathomless without bottom, 387

felon a criminal, 411

fervent having strong feelings, 209

fervid burning, passionate, 210

fiendish devilish, evil, 107

flattering pleasing or soothing to oneself, 403

flimsy thin, not strongly made, 129

florid healthy, 205

foretell to tell the future, 366

fractured broken, 191

fragment a small piece, 67

frenzy a state of wild excitement, or disturbance, 29

frivolous playful, 252

froth foam, 235

frustration anger at defeat, 432

furlough a leave of absence, 193

furtive secretive, 159

furtively secretly, as if ashamed, 253, 445

futile useless, 275, 446

futility uselessness, 315

G

gamble to bet money on; to risk, 443

gambler someone who plays games for money, 358

garrulous talkative, 143

gauge a device for measuring, 341

genial friendly, 205

glazed glassy; smooth and shiny, 376

glint to gleam, 377

gloat to delight in, 366

graft getting money in a way that is against the law, 435

graphically in a visual way, 435

grimace an expression of disgust, 248

grotesque hideous, 297

grudgingly unwillingly, 431

guidance direction, instruction, 207

Glossary

H

hallucination a vision that is not real, 132

harmony melody, 366

haste speed, 122, 247

haughty proud; feeling superior to others, 410

heave to lift up and out, 76

heaving moving up and down; panting, 176

hence in the future; away, 383, 407

heritage a birthright; something one inherits, or gets from someone who came before, 166

hierarchy a list in order of importance, 170

hilarious very funny, high-spirited, 208

hindrance something that gets in the way, 107

hospitable welcoming, 247

humanity human beings, 307

humiliate to embarrass deeply, 171

hypnotic causing a dreamlike state, 293

hysterical not able to stop crying, 175

hysterically in wild excitement, 256

I

idealism a belief in the highest standards, 206

illumination a light, 294

illusion an unreal vision; a false impression, 75, 317

illustrate to show; to picture, 309, 332

immaculate very clean, 318

immortal free from death, 53, 404

impart to tell; to make known, 334

impartial fair, 206

impeach to accuse, 419

impel to urge forward, 367

imperious bossy, acting like royalty, 209

imperturbable calm, steady, impossible to upset, 35

implore to beg, 279

impostor one who pretends to be someone else, 34

impresario someone who manages or directs a show, 328

impressive calling one to pay attention or to wonder, 145, 248

inadequate unable to do what is required, 321

inanimate nonliving, unconscious, unmoving, 303

inaudible unheard, 255

inauspicious unlucky, 412

incorruptible honorable, 206

incredible hard to believe, 305

incredibly unbelievably, 297

incredulous not believing, 328

indebted in debt to, 318

indictment faultfinding, 428

indifference a lack of concern, 429

indifferent uncaring, uninterested, unimpressed, 148

inert unmoving, 297

inertia not able to move, 342

inevitable impossible to avoid, 206

inexorable unable to be changed or influenced, 410

infamous well known because of bad or disagreeable things, 143

infatuated foolishly in love, 174

infectious catching, 407

inferior second-rate, 269

infernal tiresome, unpleasant, 143

infirm not solid or stable, 340

inflection pronunciation, 437

infuriated very angry, 299

initiative drive; energy, 342

inquiry a request for information, 144

inquisitive curious, 293

insignificant unimportant, 297

inspiration encouragement, 447

installment one part, 250

institution an important custom, 208

insulated protected from, 338

insurance coverage against loss, 440

intact whole, together, 192

intellectual brainy, 437

intensity strength, 211

intention a plan, 178

intercept to catch, block, or cut off, 247, 267

interminable endless, 145

interminably without end, 221

intermittently off and on, 341

internal inside; unspoken, 309

intersect to meet, 170

Glossary

invest to put money into something, hoping for a profit, 317, 440

investment money put into something, in hopes of a profit, 435

ironically unlike what one would expect, 271, 319

irregular uneven, 155, 293

irreverent not offering the proper respect, 320

irritably in an annoyed way, 442

isolation aloneness, 237

J

jazz popular dance music with strong rhythms, 327, 377

jeer to make fun of, 29

jovial happy, friendly, 219

jubilant joyful, 55

K

kindred relatives, 404

kinky tightly curled, 159

kinsman a relative, 411

knell to ring for a death, funeral, or disaster, 369

L

lament a crying out in grief, 240

lamentable distressing; sorrowful, 415

landmark a marker that shows location, 270, 340

lapse to decline, 221

latter more recent; toward the end, 123

lavish (adj.) abundant, 272

lavish (v.) to provide a great deal of, 52

lease to rent, 270

ledger an account book, 444

lessened made less; taken away, 307

lethal deadly, 80

liability debt, 255

likeness a copy or portrait, 73

lilting musical, 175

limber moving easily, 146

limousine a large, fancy car, 156

linger to be slow in leaving, 174

liquor drinks containing alcohol, 440

literally actually, really, 172

loathsome hateful, 406

lobe a rounded part that sticks out or down, 53

logic reasoning, 178

lottery a drawing of lots—objects used as counters in a game of chance—used to decide something, 218

lullaby a bedtime song, 263

luminous filled with light, 334

lure to tempt, 294, 389

lye a strong solution that can eat away or destroy by chemical action, 159

M

maligned unfairly accused, 250

maneuvering planning a movement to gain you something, 173

marshal to collect, 342

martyr someone who dies for a cause or religious belief, 170

masculine male, 432

material physical, real, 308

maximum the most, 429

maze web; puzzle, 213

meager thin, 404

meander to wander, 340

melancholy sad, 54, 368

mercury a heavy, silver-white metal that is liquid at ordinary temperatures, 107

mere nothing more than, 53

merit to deserve, 207

millionaire a very rich person, 319

mimicking imitating, 432

miraculously magically, 329

miscalculate to misjudge or figure out wrong, 80

misery suffering, 259, 405

moiety half, 210

molest to bother or harm, 121

molten heated until liquid, 366

momentarily for a moment, 236

monotone sameness; on one note, 368

Glossary

monotonous boring, unchanging, 144
monstrosity something that is huge and ugly, 179
morality a system of good conduct, 174
morsel a small piece, 278, 410
multiple candelabra a many-branched candlestick, 457
multitude crowd, 213
muscular strongly built, 176
muse to think, 457
muted quieted, softened, 170
mutilate to tear apart, damage, 257
mutual shared, 433

N

narrative a story, 144
negotiate to manage, 340
neurotic a person with disturbed feelings and thoughts, 450
nocturnal nighttime, 294
nonexistent not there, 326
notorious well known, especially for something bad, 122, 269
nun a member of a Catholic sisterhood, 415
nurture to feed or care for, 303

O

obligation a feeling of gratitude, 144
obscure unclear, 294
obstacle something that gets in the way, 119
occurrence a happening or event, 118
ogre a monster, 65
oppress to wrong someone; to abuse one's power over someone, 160
oppression injustice, 406, 431
oppressive heavy, burdensome, 258
ordeal a terrible experience, 57, 191
oriented turned toward, 428
overcome to win against or get the better of; to make weak or helpless, 119, 307, 317
over-populated overcrowded, 173
overwhelm to take over one's thoughts or feelings, 272
overwhelming extreme, 339

P

pall a coffin, 358
palpitating breathing in and out, 368
pang a sharp pain, 71
paralyzed unable to move, 194
paraphernalia equipment, 219
parasite an animal that depends on another for its life, giving nothing in return, 296
parched dried out, 264
paring peeling, 266
partially partly, 326
participant one who takes part in, 306
passion a strong feeling, 175, 213
passionately with great feeling, 436
penury poverty, 405
perceive to understand, 211
perception an understanding, 211
perfunctory careless; done without much thought, 221
permeate to enter; to soak into, 305, 437
persist to continue, 248
peruse to look at, 411
pestilence disease, 407
petulantly in a grouchy, grumpy way, 224
phenomenal amazing, 319
pigmentation color, 277
piteous miserable; sad, 417
pitiful causing pity, 242, 417
pitifully causing pity, 81
placid calm; peaceful, 299, 334
placidly calmly, 246
plague a disease, 247
poise to hold steady, 246
pomegranate a reddish-yellow fruit with thick skin and many seeds, 54
ponderous heavy, 337
portal a gate, 210
possibility chance, 193
potion a drink with special powers, 420
precede to come before, 208, 220
precise correct; exact, 441
precisely correctly, 225
precision correctness; definiteness, 452
predicament a problem, 328
preoccupied thinking of something else, 253

Glossary

prescribed required, 307
presumptuous overconfident, 248
primeval ancient, 236
privacy desire to be alone, 328
probable likely, 210
procure to get or obtain, 207
profound deep, 170, 452
profoundly strongly, 384
profusely generously; in large amounts, 218
progressiveness the state of being advanced, or accepting of new ideas, 205
projection something that juts out, 239
prolific producing many young, 73
propel to push forward or onward, 271
prophet someone who sees the future, 440
prophetic able to foretell the future, 326
proposition a plan, 435
prosaic everyday, 252
provocative intended to stir up, anger, or excite, 34
provoke to cause someone to take action, 246, 411
prudence wisdom, common sense, 320
pry to snoop; to spy, 409
punctuate to mark at regular intervals, 275
pungent sharp, 308
purge to free from blame, 419
pursue to chase, 122, 250

Q

quaking shaking, trembling, 256
quell to quiet or put down, 120
quest a search for something, 56

R

radiance glowing light, 75
radiant glowing, 211
radical extreme, 246
rampant existing everywhere, 269
rapture great happiness, 367
rapturous extremely happy, 213
rarity something not usually seen, 80
raucous rough, loud, 449
reaction a response, 131, 178
recall to remember, 66

recital a performance of music, 221
recoil to draw back in horror, 342
recollect to remember, 100, 145
reek a terrible smell, 240
refrain repeated words, 171, 434
refreshing giving back strength or life, 75
reign to rule, 407
reinforced made stronger, 242
rejection a refusal to accept or hear, 174
relentless without pity, 209
relentlessly without softening or letting up, 83
reluctantly without wanting to, 55, 219
remembrance a memory, 388
reminiscence remembrance, memory, 143
remnant a trace, 405
repetition repeating, 436
replenish to fill up, 316
repository place for safekeeping, 316
reprimand a scolding, 218
residence a place to live in, 179
resignation acceptance of one's fate, 55
resin a sticky, yellow or brown substance that flows from some trees, 332
resolute determined, 367
respectable decent; proper; fit to be seen, 99, 444
restraint control, 180
retain to keep, 311
retribution revenge; a punishment for crime, 208
reveal to show, 294
reverberate to echo, 259
reverie a daydream; to be lost in thought, 213, 311
rhapsody a joyful song, 206
righteous good; right, 413
rigor strictness, 421
riot a public disturbance, 377
rite a ceremony, 409
ritual a ceremony, 220
rivalry a struggle to win, 293

Glossary

S

sanatorium a hospital for treating certain illnesses, 269

satchel a small suitcase, 321

savor special flavor or smell, 447

scalding burning, 159

scavenge to search for, 280

scour to search thoroughly, 54

scourge a punishment, 421

scriptures Bible verses, 447

security safety, 343

self-righteously convinced of one's own goodness, 444

sensitivity able to be easily hurt, 303

serenely calmly; not at all upset, 145

sheath a cover or case, 416

sheathe to cover with something that protects, 386

shrivel to wither; to dry out, 279

shun to avoid, 365

siege a battle, 420

singe to burn, 263

sinister evil, 254

skirmish a small battle, 120

slur to leave out or substitute sounds, 342

slurring sliding together, 437

smudged smeared, 179

snobbish stuck-up 450

solace comfort, 180

solicitation an invitation, 125

solicitude concern, 328

somber gloomy, 329

sough to sigh or moan, 333

sovereign a king, 418

specification a set of directions, 242

squabble an argument or quarrel, 73

stealthy secretive, 258

steeple a church tower, 368

sternum the breastbone, 327

stimuli agents of change or activity, 338

stipulate to demand as a condition of agreement, 65

strangle to choke, 264

strew to scatter widely, 208, 409

stronghold a protected place, safe from enemies, 65

stupendously amazingly, 337

stupor a daze, 428

subdued muffled, 256

subordinate lower; lying beneath, 207

subterranean beneath the earth, 236

suede leather with a napped, or soft, surface, 186

suffocation not being able to breathe, 341

sullen bad-tempered, 432

sultry sexy, 327

supplemental additional, extra, 341

surge a rush or flow, 339

survive to go on living, 52, 57, 304, 384

suspicion hint, trace; mistrust, doubt, 145, 417

swathe to wrap, 387

swerve to turn sharply, 80

swivel to turn suddenly, 329

symmetry balance, 276

symptom a sign of disease, 193

T

tact skill and grace in dealing with others, 334

tedious tiring; boring, 419

tempest a bad storm, 341

temptation an urge to do something, 158, 172

tenement a city apartment for poorer families that is usually unclean, unsafe, uncomfortable, 170

tentatively unsurely, 445

terse using few words, 269

thresh to strike, or toss about, 239

thwart to block or stop, 415

tiered arranged in rows, one above the other, 374

torrent a flood, 246

tradition a custom, 220

tragedy misfortune, suffering, 304

tragic sad, unfortunate, 306

trance a condition in which one can't seem to move, 180

tranquil untroubled, 144

transcendent far beyond the usual, 145

transformation a major change, 306
transformed greatly changed, 299, 437
transition a change; a shift, 457
transmit to send, 211
tribunal a court of justice, 208
trill two alternating musical notes, 332
tuition payment for education, 451
typhoon a powerful storm, 321

U

unhallowed unholy, 410
unison all together, 438
unpredictability impossible to tell
   in advance, 280
unsavory unpleasant; bad-tasting, 413
unsubstantial not physical; of the spirit, 412
unsurpassed best, highest, 209
untimely before its proper time, 419
untrammeled not bound; free, 205
unwarranted uncalled-for, 337
utter total; complete, 178, 436
uttered said, 280

V

venerable aged; respected, 307
vengeance force; revenge, 410, 437
venison deer meat, 319
verify to prove that something is true,
   234, 319
veritable true, 296
version a form or type, 76, 180
vigilant watchful, 174
vigorously with energy, 436
vindicated not guilty, 432
violent furious, 434
violently extremely; without control,
   176, 405
virago a loud, harsh-sounding woman, 170
virtue goodness, 174, 252
voluminously hugely, 366

W

wane to fade, 309
wanton without mercy, 389
warped curved; out of focus, 179
wary suspicious, 270
waver to back down, 209
wavering quivering, 294
welt a bruise, 306
wend to make one's way, 207
whinny the cry of a horse, 67
wield to hold; to use, 275
wistful sad, 73
wistfully sadly, 254
wretch a miserable creature, 405
writhing wiggling, 56

Y

yoke a wooden bar or frame that joins
   two oxen, 95

Index of Authors and Titles

Index of Authors and Titles

Index of Fine Art

Index

Index

Index

Index

Index

Acknowledgments

Acknowledgment is made for permission to reprint or record the following copyrighted material. Every effort has been made to determine copyright owners. In the case of any omissions, the publisher will be pleased to make suitable acknowledgments in future editions.

Pages 32–36: "The Singing Turtle" from *The Singing Turtle and Other Tales from Haiti* by Philippe Thoby-Marcelin and Pierre Marcelin, translated by Eva Thoby-Marcelin. Translation copyright © 1971 by Farrar, Straus & Giroux, Inc. Reprinted by permission of Farrar, Straus & Giroux, Inc.

Pages 61–62: "The Beginning and the End of the World" from *Indian Legends of the Pacific Northwest* by Ella C. Clark. Copyright © 1953 The Regents of the University of California; © renewed 1981 Ella C. Clark. Reprinted by permission of the Regents of the University of California and the University of California Press.

Pages 65–67: From *The Prose Edda of Snorri Sturluson* translated by Jean I. Young. Copyright © 1954 The Regents of the University of California. Reprinted by permission.

Pages 70–83: "The Moon Spirit and Coyote Woman" (Why coyotes howl at the moon) by Clive Grace. Clive Grace is a British storyteller and writer who lives with his dog, Galen. He is a thoughtful storyteller, like his creation—Tanais the Fox. Reprinted by permission of the author.

Pages 95–103: "Babe the Blue Ox" from *Paul Bunyan*, copyright 1924 and renewed 1952 by Esther Shephard, reprinted and reproduced by permission of Harcourt Brace & Company.

Pages 107–11: "Feboldson, Western Scientist" from *Tall Tale America*, by Walter Blair. Reprinted by permission of The University of Chicago Press.

Pages 129–32: (Print) "The Phantom Hitchhiker" from *The Headless Roommate and Other Tales of Terror* by Daniel Cohen. Copyright © 1980 by Daniel Cohen. Reprinted with permission of the publisher M. Evans and Company, Inc., New York. (Audio) "The Phantom Hitchhiker" taken from *The Headless Roommate and Other Tales of Terror* by Daniel Cohen. Copyright © 1980 by Daniel Cohen; used by permission of the author and Henry Morrison, Inc., his agents.

Pages 155–66: "Everyday Use" from *In Love and Trouble: Stories of Black Women*, copyright © 1973 by Alice Walker, reprinted by permission of Harcourt Brace & Company.

Pages 170–80: "American History" by Judith Ortiz-Cofer from *Iguana Dreams/New Latino Fiction* by Delia Poey and Virgil Suarez, 1972. Reprinted by permission of The University of Georgia Press.

Pages 184–88: (Print) "Thank You, M'am" from *Short Stories* by Langston Hughes. Copyright © 1996 by Ramona Bass and Arnold Rampersad. Reprinted by permission of Hill and Wang, a division of Farrar, Straus & Giroux, Inc. (Audio) Copyright © 1994 by the Estate of Langston Hughes. Reproduced by permission.

Pages 191–94: "Unfinished Message" from *The Chauvinist and Other Stories* by Toshio Mori. Reprinted by permission of UC Regents.

Pages 218–28: "The Lottery" from *The Lottery* by Shirley Jackson. Copyright © 1948, 1949 by Shirley Jackson, and copyright renewed © 1976, 1977 by Laurence Hyman, Barry Hyman, Mrs. Sarah Webster and Mrs. Joanne Schnurer. Reprinted by permission of Farrar, Straus & Giroux, Inc.

Pages 232–42: *The Fog Horn* by Ray Bradbury. Reprinted by permission of Don Congdon Associates, Inc. Copyright © 1951 by the Curtis Publishing Co., renewed 1979 by Ray Bradbury.

Pages 263–80: "Red Moccasins" from *The Grass Dancer* by Susan Power. Copyright © 1994 by Susan Power. Used by permission of G.P. Putnam's Sons, a division of Penguin Putnam, Inc.

Pages 293–99: Reprinted with the permission of Simon & Schuster from *Kon-Tiki* by Thor Heyerdahl, translated by F. H. Lyon. Copyright © 1950, 1960, 1984 by Thor Heyerdahl.

Pages 303–11: From "A Celebration of Grandfathers." Copyright © 1983 by Rudolfo Anaya. First published in *New Mexico Magazine*, March 1983. Reprinted by permission of Susan Bergholz Literary Services, New York. All rights reserved.

Pages 315–22: "Of Dry Goods and Black Bow Ties" by Yoshiko Uchida. Courtesy of the Bancroft Library, University of California, Berkeley.

Pages 326–29: From *Gather Together in My Name* by Maya Angelou. Copyright © 1974 by Maya Angelou. Reprinted by permission of Random House, Inc.

Pages 337–43: From *Into Thin Air* by Jon Krakauer. Copyright © 1996 by Jon Krakauer. Reprinted by permission of Villard Books, a division of Random House, Inc.

Page 359: "Ballad of Birmingham" by Dudley Randall from *Poem Counter Poem*. Reprinted by permission of the author.

Page 364: (Print) "Blesséd Lord, what it is to be young" from *One Day at a Time* by David McCord. Copyright © 1961, 1962 by David McCord. By permission of Little, Brown and Company. (Audio) Manufactured by American Guidance Service under license from Pathways of Sound.

Page 364: "WE REAL COOL" by Gwendolyn Brooks © 1991. From her book *Blacks*, published by Third World Press, Chicago in 1991. Reprinted by permission of the author.

Pages 374–75: "Oranges" from *New and Selected Poems* by Gary Soto. Copyright © 1995. Published by Chronicle Books, San Francisco. Reprinted by permission.

Page 376: "Dreams" from *Collected Poems* by Langston Hughes. Copyright © 1994 by the Estate of Langston Hughes. Reprinted by permission of Alfred A. Knopf Inc.

Page 376: "flock" by Lance Henson as appeared in *American Indian Literature: An Anthology*, edited by Alan R. Velie. Reprinted by permission of the author.

Page 376: "The Red Wheelbarrow" by William Carlos Williams, from *Collected Poems: 1909–1939, Volume I*. Copyright © 1938 by New Directions Publishing Corp. Reprinted by permission of New Directions Publishing Corp.

Page 377: "Haiku" by Etheridge Knight from *Poems from Prison*. Permission granted by Broadside Press.

Page 382: "The Poet" © 1997 Jane Hirshfield, as first published in *The Atlantic Monthly*; also appears in *The Lives of the Heart* by Jane Hirshfield. (HarperCollins, 1997). Reprinted by permission.

Page 384: "In a Farmhouse" by Luis Omar Salinas from *From the Barrio: A Chicano Anthology* by Luis Omar Salinas. Copyright © 1973 by Luis Omar Salinas and Lillian Faderman. Reprinted by permission of HarperCollins Publishers, Inc.

Page 384: LUCILLE CLIFTON: "this morning", copyright © 1987 by Lucille Clifton. Reprinted from *Good Woman: Poems and a Memoir: 1969–1980* with the permission of BOA Editions, Ltd., 260 East Avenue, Rochester, NY 14618.

Page 388: "Nikki-Rosa" from *Black Feeling, Black Talk, Black Judgment* by Nikki Giovanni. Copyright © 1968, 1970 by Nikki Giovanni. By permission of William Morrow & Company, Inc.

Page 389: "Chicago" by Carl Sandburg from *Chicago Poems*. Reprinted by permission of Harcourt Brace & Company.

Page 426: "Dream Deferred" from *Collected Poems* by Langston Hughes. Copyright © 1994 by the Estate of Langston Hughes. Reprinted by permission of Alfred A. Knopf, Inc.

Pages 426–53: From *A Raisin in the Sun* by Lorraine Hansberry. Copyright © 1958 by Robert Nemiroff, as an unpublished work. Copyright © 1959, 1966, 1984 by Robert Nemiroff. Reprinted by permission of Random House, Inc.

Pages 457–60: "Writer's Realm: Frankenstein" by Anne Jarrell-France. Reprinted by permission of the author.

Images Page 8, David Young-Wolff/PhotoEdit; p. 14 (top), Tony Freeman/PhotoEdit; p.14 (bottom), Myrleen Ferguson Cate/PhotoEdit; pp. 16, 26 (top), The Grand Design, Leeds, England/SuperStock; p. 19, Stock Montage/SuperStock; pp. 20, 24, 50–51, 60, 64–65, Judy King; p. 21, Private Collection/C. Pierre/SuperStock; pp. 22, 221, 225, 228 (detail), Diana Ong/SuperStock; pp. 25, 141, 200, 382–83, Christie's Images/SuperStock; p. 26 (bottom), 288 (top right), 291 (right), 353, Kactus Foto, Santiago, Chile/SuperStock; p. 28, *Kitchener-Waterloo Record*, Photographic Negative Library, Dana Porter Library, University of Waterloo, Waterloo, Ontario N2L 3G1; pp. 29, 40, Inese Jansons; p. 31, courtesy of Farrar, Straus & Giroux; pp. 33, 36, 72, 77, 82, George Crespo; pp. 39, 113, 124, 183, 295, 331, 372 (bottom), 380 (middle), 381 (bottom), Brown Brothers; p. 46, Musée d'Orsay, Paris/Lauro Giraudon, Paris/SuperStock; p. 49, Underwood Photo Archives, San Francisco, CA/SuperStock; pp. 53, 56, Scala/Art Resource, NY; p. 55, Tate Gallery, London/Art Resource, NY; pp. 62, 130, 142, 173, 363 (bottom), SuperStock; p. 66, Shana Greger; p. 69, courtesy of Clive Grace; p. 90, Barbara Cesery/SuperStock; pp. 93, 291 (left), 350, Lucia Gallery, New York City/Tsing-Fang Chen/SuperStock; p. 94, San Jose State University, Special Collections; pp. 96, 98–99, 102, Teresa Flavin; p. 106, © Patricia Evans, courtesy University of Chicago; pp. 110–11, Hilber Nelson; p. 115, Mike Benny; pp. 117, 121, 123, 204, 231, 298, 356 (left), 400 (top), Culver Pictures, Inc.; pp. 119, 363 (top), Corbis-Bettmann; p. 128, courtesy Daniel Cohen; p. 138, Anna Belle Lee Washington/SuperStock; pp. 144, 150, 249, 253, 259, Jeff Spackman; pp. 154, 245, 334, 359, 425, UPI/Corbis-Bettmann; pp. 155, 163, America Hurrah Archive, NYC; p. 165, Mary C. Bertoli, SNJM; p. 169, 302, Miriam Berkley Photographer; pp. 176, 327, Underwood Photo Archives, Inc.; p. 187, Joel Iskowitz; p. 190, photo by Steve Mori; pp. 193, 316, 319, National Japanese American Historical Society; p. 203, Private Collection/SuperStock; pp. 207, 212, Kees de Kiefte; p. 217, © Image Photos/Clemens Kalischer; p. 233, Kuroda/Lee/SuperStock; p. 239, Medford Taylor/SuperStock; p. 241, Richard Heinzen/SuperStock; p. 262, photo by Debbie Mulligan, courtesy G. P. Putnam's Sons; pp. 264, 268, 276, 281, 375, Carole Katchen; p. 288 (top left), Christie's Images, London/Bridgeman Art Library, London/SuperStock; p. 288 (bottom left), G. G. Kopilak/SuperStock; p. 288 (bottom right), Elizabeth Barakah Hodges/SuperStock; p. 289, Steidle Art Collection/SuperStock; p. 292, Reuters/Corbis-Bettmann; pp. 306, 310, Pamela Johnson; p. 314, courtesy of the Bancroft Library, University of California, Berkeley; p. 325, © Jim Stratford/Black Star; p. 332, courtesy of the American Federation for the Blind, Helen Keller Archives; p. 336, © 1997 Linda M. Moore/Villard; p. 337, Chigmaroff/Davison/SuperStock; pp. 338, 340, 343, Corbis/Galen Rowell; pp. 339, 358, 362 (bottom), 365, 372 (middle), 373 (middle), The Granger Collection, New York; p. 356 (right), photo by Willie Williams; p. 357, National Portrait Gallery, London/SuperStock; p. 362 (top), courtesy of Little, Brown & Company; p. 364, Lisette LeBon/SuperStock; p. 367, © Richard Hutchings/PhotoEdit; p. 369, © Robert W. Ginn/PhotoEdit; p. 372 (top), photo by Carolyn Soto; p. 373 (top), courtesy: West End Press; p. 373 (bottom), photo by McGuire Studio, courtesy Janice Knight-Matthews; p. 380 (top), © Jerry Bauer, courtesy HarperCollins Publishers; p. 380 (bottom), courtesy of Arte Publico Press, University of Houston; p. 381 (top), courtesy of St. Mary's College of Maryland, St. Mary's City, Maryland; p. 381 (middle), photo by Marion Ettlinger, courtesy William Morrow and Company; p. 384, Yoshi Miyake; p. 385, Jim Ong/SuperStock; p. 386, © Dana White/PhotoEdit; p. 388, © Jonathan Nourok/PhotoEdit; p. 389, Bob Masheris; p. 396, ET Archive, London/SuperStock; p. 399, Private Collections/Bridgeman Art Library, London/SuperStock; p. 400 (middle, bottom), p. 402, © 1981 Paramount Pictures Corporation/Movie Still Archives; p. 413, © 1968 Paramount/Movie Still Archives; p. 416, © 1968 Paramount Pictures/MPTV Archives; pp. 433, 438, 444, 452, © 1960 Columbia Pictures Corporation/Movie Still Archives; p. 456, photo courtesy Ralph France; pp. 458, 460, © 1931 Universal/MPTV Archives.